Egypt's Identities
in Conflict

Egypt's Identities in Conflict

The Political and Religious Landscape of Copts and Muslims

GIRGIS NAIEM

McFarland & Company, Inc., Publishers
Jefferson, North Carolina

LIBRARY OF CONGRESS CATALOGUING-IN-PUBLICATION DATA

Names: Naiem, Girgis, 1963– author.
Title: Egypt's identities in conflict : the political and religious landscape of Copts and Muslims / Girgis Naiem.
Description: Jefferson, North Carolina : McFarland & Company, Inc., 2018 | Includes bibliographical references and index.
Identifiers: LCCN 2017060994 | ISBN 9781476671208 (softcover : acid free paper) ∞
Subjects: LCSH: Copts—History. | Religious minorities—Egypt—Social conditions. | Egypt—Ethnic relations.
Classification: LCC DT72.C7 N35 2018 | DDC 305.6/81720962—dc23
LC record available at https://lccn.loc.gov/2017060994

BRITISH LIBRARY CATALOGUING DATA ARE AVAILABLE

ISBN (print) 978-1-4766-7120-8
ISBN (ebook) 978-1-4766-3057-1

© 2018 Girgis Naiem. All rights reserved

No part of this book may be reproduced or transmitted in any form or by any means, electronic or mechanical, including photocopying or recording, or by any information storage and retrieval system, without permission in writing from the publisher.

Front cover image of Egyptian cross and crescents © 2018 kharps/iStock

Printed in the United States of America

*McFarland & Company, Inc., Publishers
  Box 611, Jefferson, North Carolina 28640
    www.mcfarlandpub.com*

To my family for their support

Table of Contents

Preface — 1

Introduction — 2

One. The Copts and their Influence on Christian Civilization — 11

Two. From Heretic to *Dhimmi*: The Islamization of Egypt — 33

Three. The Islamic Caliphates — 46

Four. The Modern Age: Liberal Egypt — 73

Five. Military Rule: The Re-Islamization of Egypt — 100

Six. Failed Revolution: A Modern Caliph — 138

Seven. Long Live Egypt: A Return to Military Rule — 162

Conclusion: Egypt's Future Identity? — 184

Epilogue — 190

Chapter Notes — 193

Bibliography — 215

Index — 217

Preface

What is Egypt's national identity? This is the question that drives this book. Undoubtedly, the issue of an unclear national identity affects all of Egyptian society, but it weighs most heavily on Egypt's Coptic Christians.

Although religion and politics overlap in Egypt, this book is not a religious work, nor does it intend to scrutinize religious doctrines. It only refers to certain religious elements that form the identity of the Egyptians and shape their behavior as well as their politics. Nor is this book a history book as such, although the historical context is essential to show the evolution of the issue of identity that has impacted Egypt and affected its Coptic Christians. The present work falls into the category of political commentary and analysis of Egypt's past and present, both of which are the basis for Egypt's future. Its purpose is to demonstrate that the inability to define a common national identity and the lack of a shared identity are at the root of most conflicts within Egypt and a cause of repeated political instability. This is evident in the current economic challenges, social unrest and repeated terrorist attacks—on the state as well as the Copts—and in the occurrence of two revolutions in less than three years.

This book differs from other works on the topic of national identity in that it offers a case study of the effect of religion in politics can have on a specific country: Egypt. It describes how politics in religious matters at the fifth century Council of Chalcedon effectively separated the Copts from the rest of the world. As a result, their remarkable contributions to Christian civilization, which have shaped Christian thought for centuries, sank into historical oblivion. This book explores the effect of the process of Islamization and Arabization on Egypt and its impact on the Egyptians since the seventh century Arab conquest. It explains how and why the rise of fundamentalism in recent times is shaping Egypt and is affecting the Christian community, and even moderate Muslims, although to a much lesser degree. By linking the modern day behavior of radicals to their historical practice, this text shows that their actions are neither unique to, nor a product of, present-day political circumstances.

Introduction

The Question of Identity

Is Egypt's identity Islamic, Arab or Egyptian? Are they separate, intertwined or contradictory? The monotheistic religion adopted by the Pharaohs made it easy for their direct descendants, the Copts, to adopt Christianity, and like their forefathers, they formed a great civilization. Egypt, the land of Akhenaten, a pioneer of monotheism, became the birthplace of Orthodox Christianity. In the 7th century, Arab Muslims came to Egypt and Islam became dominant. Now Egypt is home to al-Azhar, the most prestigious mosque and university in the Sunni Islam world, located in Cairo. In recent times Egypt has gone through periods of political turmoil; the country's political instability was part of what came to be known as the Arab Spring, and it had a great impact on its Coptic Christian community. The ransacking and destruction of seventy-three churches by radical Islamists on August 14, 2013, was the most salient, though similar incidents have occurred regularly since. There are a number of causes behind these incidents, but the most important is the absence of a well-defined identity for Egypt as a nation.

The Copts can only identify themselves as Egyptians; the term Copt *means* Egyptian. But, not all Muslims identify themselves the same way. Secular, liberal, and leftist Muslims also identify themselves as Egyptians; however, some see themselves as both Egyptian and Arab. In general, they share a common ground with the Copts based on their Egyptian identity—but fundamentalist Islamists and the masses they control identify themselves by their religion, not their nationality. Although the different Muslim groups disagree ideologically, there is still a strong common ground among them due to their shared religion. The fundamentalists share no common ground with the Copts, and the most radical are hostile to them as well. Even though the Copts speak Arabic and share some of the same common culture, the fundamentalists don't accept the Copts, believing that Islamism and Arabism are synonymous and only Muslims can bear both. For the fundamentalists, embracing an Egyptian identity means a retreat from Arab-Islamic unity.[1]

The famous liberal Muslim intellectual Taha Hussein came out in support of Egyptian identity. In the last century he declared that Egypt didn't share much with its Arab neighbors, and that Islam and Arabic alone couldn't be sufficient for unity between Egypt and other Arab states.[2] Despite the historic inability of Egypt to unify with other Arab states, fundamentalists continue to call for Arab-Islamic unity in order re-establish an Islamic caliphate, and promote the Islamic identity of which they see themselves as guardians.

Historically, Islam, its culture and traditions, has been the ideology of the state. This fact reduces the Coptic Christians to a subordinate position called *dhimmi* or "protected people." It is an Islamic term that refers to people of the Scripture—Christians and Jews who did not accept Islam. For Copts to be treated as *dhimmi* means that they will never enjoy equality. Because Islam has been the ideology of the state and because its Coptic citizens are not Muslims, they are not considered to be full citizens, as they lack the Islamic identity.[3]

In Islamic identity, the political bond of culture, society and state are based on the Islamic religion; this automatically excludes Christians. This exclusion is manifested in forbidding Christians from assuming top offices such as president or governor. In an Islamic state these roles have a religious aspect, such as applying Islamic *sharia* law, leading prayers and going on *jihad*. The fundamentalists would interpret this to mean a total absence of Christians in any state or government position. To them Christians should be treated as the historical *dhimmis*, allowed to run their own businesses and forced to pay the Islamic poll-tax, or *jizyah*, tolerated as long as they show respect to Muslims and accept the sovereignty of Islam.[4]

The fundamentalists still preach the *dhimma* status for the Copts. *Dhimmis* are humiliated, subjugated and limited in their rights to public expression of their religion. They aren't allowed to proselytize and it is inappropriate for them to compete with Muslims in the economic, social and political sphere. When Copts seek positions of prestige and power it is perceived as a threat of Christian domination over Muslims. Wealthy Copts and those who have made it to senior positions attract jealousy against the whole Christian community because they are seen as not accepting the dominance of Islam. Asking for Coptic rights is considered an aggressive claim for control, separatism and even revenge which raises suspicions and fears. Although these claims are baseless given the twelve-century-long history of Islamic caliphates in Egypt, they demonstrate that fundamentalists leave no room or leeway for basic rights for the Copts. Fundamentalist Islamists accuse Copts who ask for their rights of *istikbar* (arrogance) while radical Islamists see violence as a justified response to such requests. To clarify, they think of *dhimmis* the same way they think of women: segregated, weak, having a lesser function in the society, required to show modesty and humility and legally unequal. Just as a traditional man protects his women from breach of honor, they are required to protect their *dhimmis* from intruders because *dhimmis* are not allowed to defend themselves. Moderate Muslims, who constitute the majority, don't accept this rhetoric, but a large part of the populace, mostly illiterate, still relies upon the interpretation of fundamentalists.[5]

The fundamentalists also believe that all Muslims are equal regardless of their race, culture or nationality: a non–Egyptian Muslim would have more rights in Egypt than an Egyptian Christian.[6] A Supreme Guide of the Muslim Brotherhood, Muhammad Mahdi Akef, said a Copt can't be the president of Egypt. He clarified his point by adding that he would support any Muslim for the position even if he is "from Malaysia" rather than an Egyptian Christian.[7]

The Copts are seen as traitors, exploiters, betrayers and a handy scapegoat for all the ills of life. The fundamentalists have become xenophobic and they accept any baseless accusation against the Copts without question. These accusations, however false, become real to the masses and the anti–Copt conspiracy theory of the Middle Ages is once again revived. Copts are accused of collaborating with foreign powers and secretly attempting to control Egypt. The fundamentalists see the world as two camps: Muslims and the "others." In their eyes Egypt's Copts come under the camp of the "others," a part of the crusading West, their co-religionists, who are targeting Muslims to weaken and devastate the Muslim community.[8]

Therefore, they are suspicious of local Christians being pawns of western interference, which they see as Christian neocolonialism. Another Muslim Brotherhood Supreme Guide, al-Hidibi, said the Copts should be expelled from the military and any posts attached to national defense. He said that Copts could be "the agents of our enemy."[9] This concept of being agents for the enemy goes back to the Crusader campaigns in the Middle East, centuries ago; the Copts were treated with mistrust due only to the fact that they were Christians, like the invaders.

Fundamentalists suspect that the Copts could be manipulated not only by foreign powers, but by local enemies as well. The Copts are seen as being manipulated by the leftist, liberals and secularists, all of whom they consider foes of Islam. It is an "us" against "them" ideology. Based on this ideology, Coptic Christians have to accept being ruled by Islamic *sharia*. When Copts refuse the application of *sharia*, they are accused of practicing the tyranny of the minority. The fundamentalists can't accept this refusal because in their minds *sharia* is the ultimate of Islamic Arab civilization and Copts should be subject to it. Therefore, they believe Copts should join them in calling for *sharia* because it is the desire of the majority. Islam is presented to the masses as the solution to all of their problems.[10]

The Arab nationalist identity started to develop toward the end of the Ottoman Empire, as a reaction to injustice on the part of the ruling Ottomans. This vision was predicated on culture and language as the basis of the political identity of the state and society. On the surface Arab nationalism is based on secular ideology; therefore, any native speaker of Arabic, holder of Arabic culture and those who see themselves as Arabs would be complete members of the Arab nation. Thus, they would enjoy, in theory, full rights regardless of their religion.[11]

President Nasser, in the 1960s, was the champion of Arab nationalism, but his ideology threatened and alienated the Copts. Although they are native speakers of Arabic, Copts have never been believed to be Arabs nor do they see themselves as possessors of Bedouin culture. All Arab states have a Muslim majority and they don't separate Islam from politics. So, when Nasser championed the idea of pan–Arabism, Copts criticized it because they realized that pan–Arabism and Islamism were intertwined. This eventually led to their alienation from the political scene. So, while Copts are excluded in the Islamic identity by religion, in the case of Arab nationalism they are excluded more or less by culture.

Copts identify with the Egyptian identity, and they've been described as the direct descendants of the Pharaohs. Ethnically, Copts aren't Semitic or Hamitic but are Mediterranean, and they take pride in being genuine descendants of the ancient Egyptians.[12] The Copts find their pride in defining themselves as the heirs of a venerable land and culture that far predates the coming of the Arabs to Egypt. Therefore, they believe they shouldn't be treated as second-class citizens in their own homeland. Key to the Coptic perception of self is the profound connection to their land and history.[13] This feeling of being rooted in the land of Egypt is a view that it is not shared by the fundamentalists, who believe in one nation of Islam that doesn't acknowledge borders or sovereignty, and that could claim Egypt as one of its provinces. Muhammad Mahdi Akef publically announced this ideology in his statement "Tuz fi Masr" (To hell with Egypt). According to him, "nationality is Islam."[14]

This sentiment is not shared by secular and liberal Muslims. There was a time between the end of the nineteenth century until the end of 1920s when a consensus of Egyptians formed a secular and liberal Egyptian identity. Egyptians were fighting one common enemy and the Copts and Muslims needed to unite against the British occupation.[15]

During the colonial British period, Egyptians began addressing the issue of identity. The first constitution in 1923 had a secular leaning which based Egyptian citizenship on birthright regardless of religion, race, or creed. Still, it did have an article stipulating that "Islam is the state religion." Such an article was understood in the context that the head of the state has to be a Muslim and Islamic *sharia* law would be a source of legislation, but not the only source. At this time in Egypt's liberal experience, the government avoided making a clear distinction between secularism and religion in forming its political and cultural identity. So, Egypt could be seen as "secular–Islamic." The succeeding regimes made their own systems, forging the two together. They might emphasize one dimension but not totally ignore the other.[16] Although the Egyptian identity is secular, it was never fully secular, or it was not what most people consider secularism.

However, the consensus that formed the Egyptian identity was demolished by the rise of the Islamic movement of the Muslim Brotherhood (MB) in 1928. It has suffered even more after the resurgence of fanaticism since the 1970s.[17] The steady ascendance of the Islamic movement culminated in the rise of the MB to the presidency in June 2012.

The fear of the MB regime and the panic about restrictions they would enforce were not only intimidating to the Copts; the moderate Muslim majority was also fearful of the limitations the MB would impose on Egyptian society. Just as Egyptians formed a secular national identity in order to unite against the British, the same secular Egyptian identity has been revived to unite the Copts and moderate Muslims against fundamentalism. After removing the MB President Morsi on July 3, 2013, President el-Sisi has become a staunch supporter of Egyptian nationalism in his attempt to combat radicalism. Egyptian identity had already been championed by the secular Egyptian youth who initiated the January 25, 2011, Revolution against the Mubarak regime. But many Egyptians believe that their revolution was hijacked by the MB, who excluded the "others." In fact, the June 30, 2013, Revolution that led to the removal of President Morsi was a struggle over Egypt's identity.

Yet, just as the 1923 constitution had an article stipulating that "Islam is the state religion," the 2014 constitution states the same, with the addition of "the principles of Islamic *sharia* are the principle source of legislation," making the Islamic *sharia* law the only source of legislation. Again, despite championing a secular Egyptian identity, the state is avoiding making a clear distinction between secularism and religion in forming its political and cultural identity.

Throughout Egypt's history, religion has been a part of politics. The relationship between Islamic identity and the position of the Copts is an inverse one—the less the imposition of Islamic identity, the better the position of the Copts and, for that matter, moderate Muslims. It was only during the liberal era and under el-Sisi that the influence of Islamic identity in Egyptian society was minimized, allowing Copts to be integrated into society, giving them room for political participation and permitting them to enjoy a respite from radicalism and mob aggression. The history of the Copts is marked by cycles of aggression with periods of respite, and they are experiencing another such period under el-Sisi. But, leading up to this the Copts paid a price.

History Repeats Itself

With the threat of fundamentalism looming over them, the Copts came out en masse on Sunday, June 30, 2013, to protest against the MB regime. The fear of the MB regime was echoed on that day by the largest turnout of Copts in their written history. They poured out into the streets of Egypt as one cohesive body joining their moderate Muslim countrymen. But, the MB capitalized on the conspicuousness of the Coptic presence to accuse the Copts of being the real power behind Morsi's removal. The feasibility of a Christian minority as the principle actor in removing an Islamist president in a Muslim majority country was not questioned by their followers.

In reaction to Morsi's removal, the MB leaders mobilized tens of thousands of their followers to take to the streets to demand Morsi's return to power. They had already arranged a sit-in next to the famous mosque of Rabaa al-Adawia in Cairo from which they used their propaganda against the government and the Copts. Shortly after the breakup of the MB sit-in by the security forces on Wednesday August 14, 2013, the MB and their supporters attacked seventy-three churches in thirteen different municipalities of Egypt's total twenty seven.[18] Sixty-four of these churches were stormed within a twelve-hour span after the dismantling of the MB sit-in. Of this number, twenty-seven churches were torched and the rest were either destroyed or looted. In addition, two monasteries, a convent, four Christian schools, two Christian NGOs, an orphanage, a YMCA,[19] thirty-nine houses, seventy-five shops, seventeen pharmacies, forty-eight cars and twenty two buildings, all owned by Copts or the Coptic Church, were either burned, destroyed or looted by radical mobs hurling stones and Molotov cocktails.[20] One of the outcomes of these attacks was the death of fifteen Copts.[21] In some villages, radicals put a black X on Christian stores to identify them to assaulters. Some of the churches they attacked were converted into mosques and prayers were chanted in them. Two security guards working on a Christian-owned tour boat were burned alive. They burned a Christian school and then paraded the nuns through the streets as if they were war hostages.[22]

The Copts expected retaliation but never the mass church burnings and simultaneously large-scale attacks. The Coptic community was under siege and Wednesday, August 14, now known as "Black Wednesday," marked a day of sorrow in their recent history. Despite the shock of intensity and severity of this crisis, it was not the first one of its kind. Another significant mass church attack like it occurred in the 14th century.

In 1320, during the time of the Mamluk Sultan al-Nasser Muhammad ibn Qalawun, mobs attacked al-Zahri Church. According to al-Maqrizi, the renowned medieval Muslim historian (1364–1442), they identified and killed Copts, looted the church's valuables, and left the church a pile of rubble as they shouted, "*Allah Akbar!*" or "God is great." They also attacked the Mar Mina Church, a well-endowed church nearby. They scaled the walls, opened the doors, stole money and precious fabrics and then proceeded to two other churches to continue their rampage. They robbed and burned the churches and the Coptic houses around them. At the Church of the Girls, so named because it housed nuns, more than sixty nuns were disrobed and taken as slaves. The streets were full of looters carrying the valuables of the churches and houses that were attacked. There was so much smoke and dust everywhere that people thought it was "the day of judgment." Attacks were also carried out on four churches in the northern Mediterranean city of Alexandria, two in Buhayrah in Lower Egypt and six churches in the area of Qus in Upper Egypt. Other reports of destroyed churches came from the cities of Damietta, Gharbia, Sharqia, Damanhur, Minia, Manfalout and Aswan.[23]

The mass attacks on churches in the 14th century left more than sixty churches destroyed, pillaged, and burned and could not have been carried out all over Egypt at the same time after the Friday prayer without careful preplanning. It was the first demonstration of the existence of a largely organized radical community in Egypt and their strong influence on the populace who carried out their plans. This event also showed the political power of the populace and their impact on the social and cultural structure of Egypt which has endured throughout history until today. The historical significance of this event is important in revealing the deep rooted history of radicalism. And, while in other crises the Copts became the main target and their personal rights and positions were compromised, here the churches, the symbol of their identity, became the targets.[24]

In contemporary time, the MB aimed to deliver a similar message on Black Wednesday. In this way they lobbied the masses in an attempt to restore their lost political gains through violence in the hope that it would destabilize the new government forcing it to make political concessions. The similarity between the two incidents is not coincidental, even down to the targeting of nuns in both crises.

However, destroying churches did not start in the 14th century. The Fatimid caliph al-Hakim systematically destroyed an even larger number of edifices at the beginning of the 11th century. In this case, the populace acted based on the decree of the caliph.[25]

These large-scale attacks on the Copts centuries ago are engraved in the history of both Copts and Muslims. It is for this history that Copts joined moderate Muslims to protest against the MB regime in the 21st century. They were concerned that history might repeat itself, and their fears were fulfilled in August 2013.

The Copts have been able to survive by clinging to their Coptic identity. Their Coptic Church is one of the oldest and has been one of the most influential churches. It claimed its position through the ever-famous School of Alexandria, prestigious theologians, renowned monks and the thousands of Copts who died for their faith, all of which have influenced the Christian world. And, all of which have given the Copts a deep sense of identity that has allowed them to survive. This begs the question: Who are the Copts?

One

The Copts and Their Influence on Christian Civilization

The two words Copt and Egyptian are identical in meaning, and both come from the Greek word *aigyptos*. This in turn was a phonetic corruption of the Old Egyptian *Hak-ka-Ptah*, which means the temple of Ptah. Ptah was one of the most revered deities in Egyptian mythology: the god of all creation. With the manipulation of the prefix and suffix of the Greek word, the word *gypt* was left to give us the word "Egypt" in European languages and the word *Qibt* or *Gybt in* Arabic. This word was used to identify the people living in the land. Early Arabs called Egypt *dar al-Qibt* (home of the Copts). Because the indigenous people of the land were Christians, the word Coptic and Christian became synonymous.[1]

The exact number of Copts in Egypt is unknown. It is said they constitute approximately 10 to 15 percent of the population. The unofficial population of Egypt in 2015 was 90 million, which makes them between 9 and 13 million. The Copts constitute the biggest Christian minority in the Middle East and in any Islamic country.

The Coptic Orthodox Church shares the same theology with the Syrian, Armenian, Ethiopian, Eritrean and Indian Churches collectively known as the Oriental Orthodox Churches. While the Coptic Church differs theologically with the Eastern Orthodox Churches—Greek, Russian and Eastern European—it shares a lot of Christian culture and tradition. But, Coptic Christianity differs in tradition and theology with the Catholics and Protestants with respect to beliefs and practices.[2] The Coptic Church is centered in Egypt and has its own Pope, and it has branches on five continents. The See of Alexandria was one of the four original apostolic sees of early Christianity, along with the sees of Jerusalem, Antioch and Rome.

Saint Mark the Evangelist

The Copts are proud to trace their national church's history back to its founder St. Mark, one of the four Evangelists and the author of the oldest Gospel used by St. Matthew and St. Luke, and probably by St. John as well. St. Mark is considered by the Coptic hierarchy to be the first in an uninterrupted chain of 118 patriarchs.[3] The exact date of the arrival of St. Mark to Alexandria is debated. It varies between AD 43 and AD 61, but this is how early Christianity was introduced to the Egyptians making Egypt's Coptic Orthodox Church as old as Christianity itself.[4]

It was easy for Copts to accept Christianity. Their ancestors acknowledged the concept of the triad; the famous Osiris, Isis and Horus triad is an example. Also, Ancient Egyptians believed in one powerful being, such as Akhenaten. This made it easy for the Copts to accept the Christian Trinity and the One God, and as their forefathers were concerned with the afterlife and resurrection, when the Copts converted to Christianity, they were enthralled with the second coming of Christ. The Ankh, which was in the hand of the Pharaoh or a god, symbolized eternal life, and looked like a cross but with a rounded tip. Thus, the Copts identified it with the cross.[5]

The new faith penetrated into the most remote areas of Egypt. This is supported by the discovery of the oldest Biblical papyri written in the Coptic language, found buried in Upper Egypt. Most of these are dated earlier than the oldest authoritative Greek versions of the Bible, written in both the fourth and fifth centuries, including the *Codex Sinaiticus*, the *Codex Alexandrinus*, the *Vaticans* and the *Codex Ephraemi Syri Rescriptus*. Remnants of these papyri going back to the second century are to be found in many manuscript repositories in the world. The most famous collection is the Chester Beatty Papyri, now in Dublin, Ireland. Another amazing papyri collection, mostly Gnostic or apocryphal and written in the Sahidic and the sub–Akhmimic Coptic language, was discovered under the sand in the remote area of Nag Hammadi, Upper Egypt, in 1930. This proves, without any doubt, the thorough influence of this new religion, Christianity, among Copts.[6] These Coptic papyri and others not mentioned here are considered the source of today's tests of the Bible,[7] and they are only one example among many others of the prominent position the Coptic Church in Christianity. In Coptic Egypt, one has the impression of being in the starting place of Christian civilization.[8]

As St. Mark introduced Christianity to Egypt, he introduced martyrdom as well. He was arrested in AD 68 by pagans who put a strong rope around his neck and dragged him through the streets of Alexandria until his body was torn and his blood covered the streets.[9] St. Mark baptized the Coptic Church with his martyrdom, and he set an example for them to follow. As he was their first Pope, he was also the first of a multitude of Egyptian saints and martyrs. The persecution of the Copts has continued for centuries, reaching its peak in the time of Diocletian, which is known in the Coptic history as the "age of persecution."

Age of Persecution and Coptic Calendar

The spread of Christianity in the third century was sporadically slowed by persecution. The first wave of persecution occurred as a result of an edict of Septimius Severus in 202. Pagan assaults on Christians in Alexandria in 249 and a new edict by Decius in 250 renewed the assault.[10] However, the time of Diocletian (284–305) was the time of greatest sadness for the Copts. Under his reign the Coptic Church suffered one of the most decimating waves of persecution in Christian history; it was the most violent and longest of them all. Torture and executions of Copts occurred daily with no respite throughout the country. Tertullian, a priest from Carthage who lived at the same time as these events declared, "If the martyrs throughout the world were to be put on one side of the scales and the Coptic martyrs alone were to be put on the other, the later would outweigh the former." Eight hundred thousand Copts were killed by Diocletian.[11]

There was such widespread persecution that Christian cities and villages were entirely wiped out in one incident. The intensity of persecution of Diocletian forced Egyptians to pray in catacombs, homes and in monasteries in the inner desert because he demolished all the churches. There are many old churches in Egypt, but even the oldest only dates back to the end of the fourth century as the older churches were victims of Diocletian's anger.[12]

The bloodshed and martyrdom during the time of Diocletian is an integral part of the Coptic heritage and became a powerful engine enabling Copts to endure subsequent persecution. Due to the magnitude of martyrs during the time of Diocletian, the Church came to be called the Church of Martyrs. The Coptic Church created its own calendar, the Coptic Calendar or the Calendar of Martyrs, to retain the memory of their forefathers who lost their lives for the sake of Christ and remember how much is owed to them for preserving the Christian faith.[13] Copts chose the year Diocletian was enthroned in 284 to be the beginning of their calendar and the days following are abbreviated with AM (*anno martyrum*), or "after the martyrs."[14] It records and arranges the stories of those who died for their Christian faith. Each day contains the martyr's name, means of death and a brief biography. The priest reads the stories of the martyred to the congregation as part of the church service. By reading these stories, the Church is instructing the people and giving them a model to follow. Eighteen centuries later the Copts are still killed for their faith by violent radical Islamists. By reading these stories the church is strengthening its people to withstand attacks as their forefathers did.

The Copts have not stopped providing martyrs to the calendar since the time of Diocletian. The last martyrs added to the Coptic Calendar were in 2015 when the Islamic State in Iraq and Syria (ISIS) beheaded 21 Copts in Libya. "Oh Lord Jesus Christ!" were the last words of one martyr heard on the video aired by ISIS; these last words attest to the strong faith of the martyrs. The Coptic victims were beheaded solely based on their Christian identity. It is this same Coptic identity, developed throughout the ages, which allowed them to hold steadfast to their faith. Pope Tawadros, the 118th Pope of the Coptic Church, called them "martyrs of the faith," while Pope Francis referred to them as "our brother Copts, whose throats were slit for the sole reason of being Christian, that the Lord welcome them as martyrs."[15] Pope Tawadros announced that they would be commemorated in the Coptic Calendar on the 8th of the Coptic month of Amshir, which is February 15, a procedure similar to canonization in the Latin Church.[16] Indeed, persecution and martyrdom have been significant parts in the formation of the Coptic identity. Yet they are not the sole elements.

The Catechetical School of Alexandria

It is in the great city of Alexandria, then the cultural capital of the world, rich in interracial culture, Greek philosophy, Hebraic teachings and Oriental doctrine that Christianity was introduced. When Egyptians became Christians they realized the need for a school to preserve and spread the new religion. They believed that if they wanted to persuade and win deeply educated men to the new faith they had to be as educated and more erudite than their targeted audience. To help them obtain this erudition, St. Mark opened the Catechetical School of Alexandria. Although many catechetical schools were opened in many different parts of the world where Christianity was introduced, their impact was limited to giving basic catechism to pagans and newcomers. But, in Alexandria it was totally a different matter. Its school became the epicenter of robust intellectual life. The teachers of the school were scholars who were well vested in Hellenistic literature, philosophy and holy books left to the Church by the Synagogue.[17]

Ancient Egyptians reconciled their scientific background with their religious beliefs, as evidenced in the building of the great Pyramids. They didn't see science as an enemy to religion but, to the contrary, saw that science benefits religion. Thus, the School of Alexandria was opened to philosophers and scholars believing that science and philosophy could serve Christianity.[18]

The School became the first prestigious seat of Christian teaching in the world. When it came to Egypt, Christianity was based on the life, wisdom and teaching of Christ, it was an amorphous faith without formal dogma. It is in this institution of scholarship, the School of Alexandria, that Christianity and the Scripture came under critical study that led to the first system of theology and exegesis of the Bible. Additionally, the greatest teachers and theologians of that time were associated with the School and kept it going, even under the persecution of the Romans. The influence of these scholars had a great impact on world thinkers, has shaped Christian thought and contributed to Christian civilization for centuries, even until today.[19] Clement (d. 211–215) is one of the deans of the School that the Christian world will always remember with gratitude. He wrote several treatises and books, but he is well known for his trilogy: *Protrepticus*, *Paidagogos* and *Stromata* (*The Exhortation*, *The Educator* and *Miscellaneous Studies*). His works were aimed at converting the pagans and correcting the false doctrine of heretical leaders. His approach was to gently persuade rather than to argue. He was genuine in his desire to bring salvation to all people no matter their class, education, or culture.[20]

Clement's most remarkable work for the Coptic Church, however, was the creation of the Coptic script, which put in writing the native tongue of Egypt. According to tradition, it was Clement, in cooperation with Pantaenus, a previous dean of the School, who undertook the task. Their work resulted in a written form of the Coptic language, which was previously the Pharaonic language, using the Greek alphabet. They added an extra seven letters for the sounds that didn't exist in Greek. At that time Greek was the common language of the world. It was not possible for the Gospel to be written with the hieroglyphic pictograph nor with the demotic script, the script preceding Coptic. Not only had they given Egyptians a precious gift of a simplified method of reading and writing, but they translated both the Old and New Testament into the Coptic language.[21]

Clement's teachings and writings had a great impact on his contemporaries and the successive ages. Clement was an incredible representative of an incredible age: an age where people could believe in God despite persecution of emperors, hatred of pagans and raillery of philosophers.[22]

But Clement was not the only master of his age. His student and successor, Origen (d. 254) was the most distinguished exegetical scholar of all times.[23] Astonishingly, he became the dean of the School of Alexandria at the age of eighteen. Origen was the son of a Coptic martyr, so he encouraged students to witness for their faith. His students who gave up their blood for their belief are countless. He visited them in their prisons, went with them to their tribunals and walked with them to the last spot before they were martyred. As Origen got older his reputation and wisdom became widespread. Very well-known bishops from churches around the world sought out his teachings, among them Alexander of Jerusalem and Theostite of Caesarea,

Palestine. Firmillion, Bishop of Caesarea Cappadocia, was proud to be his life-long student. Origen even corrected reputable theologians; Berylle, Bishop of Bostra, admitted his mistakes after he spoke with Origen.[24]

Origen's works are considered to be some of the most important in Christian thought. One of his greatest works was the *Hexapla*, a milestone in Biblical scholarship. It is an edition of the Old Testament arranged in six parallel columns comparing the Hebrew text of the Old Testament, the Greek translation of Hebrew and the Greek versions of Aquila, Symmachus, Theodotian and the *Septuagint*. Nothing like this attempt had ever happened in Biblical study before. It is the first remarkable achievement of Christian erudition.[25] Another of his significant works was *De Principiis*, in which he organized the whole Christian faith into four books. In a treatise entitled *Contra Celsus* he defended Christian faith from Celsus, the pagan philosopher. During the time of persecution of Emperor Maximinus he wrote *The Exhortation to Martyrdom*. Another remarkable work was *On Prayer*, which had a tremendous impact on early believers. His renowned exegetical commentaries *Scholia* were translated into Latin by Rufinus, the church historian.[26] Origen's productivity was amazing. Bishop Epiphanius of Salamis in Cyprus said Origen wrote six thousand books. Jerome claimed that no one can read all of Origen's books because they are so many. He was the teacher of bishops, and two of his students were ordained popes of the Coptic Church.[27]

Clement and Origen are emphasized to give but two examples of the prominent work and influence of the scholars of the School of Alexandria on Christianity. Its deans were held in high esteem, thus, many of them were ordained as popes of the Coptic Church. Also, great bishops and scholars from different parts of the world were affiliated with it, among them St. Gregory Nazianzus, St. Basil, St. Jerome and Rufinus.[28] Indeed, the Catechetical School of Alexandria is the earliest and most important institution of theological studies in Christian antiquity. The work of its scholars still constitutes the basis of any kind of study of Christian theology.[29]

Perhaps because of the significance of the School of Alexandria in Coptic history, the Copts highly value education. The percentage of Copts in different levels of education is disproportionate to their numbers, which is regarded an impressive achievement when one considers that the illiteracy rate in Egypt is among the highest in the world; about 26 percent of the population is illiterate.

The School of Alexandria laid the theological groundwork to defend Christianity against heresies and heretics. Through its extensive study and understanding of Greek philosophy, science, and Christian theology, it produced pillars in the faith who led the world in Christian thought, and it shaped dogma. Thus, the Coptic Church, also known as the Church of Alexandria, became a leader of the ecumenical councils leading the Christian world.

During the early persecutions, converts to Christianity were attracted to the new faith unanimously with no time to think of expansive doctrines. But with the conversion of Emperor Constantine (306–337) to Christianity, the external persecution declined, leading to the rise of theological discussions of differences and doctrines. The result of this was the emergence of heresies, which are the digressions away from the orthodox teaching of the Church upheld by church leadership. Church history has witnessed numerous heresies, but in Egypt two major ones gained a lot of attention. They are Gnosticism, which had its roots on the second century, and Arianism, which was a daunting and pervasive threat in Egypt and throughout the whole Roman Empire in the fourth century.[30]

A lot of what we know about Gnosticism came through the famous Coptic papyrus manuscripts discovered in the Nag Hammadi area in Upper Egypt, which contain *The Secret Books of the Egyptian Gnostics*. Gnosticism, which means knowledge, was a religious order based on many pre–Christian and pagan beliefs which were galvanized in a Christian setting by putting Gnostic principals into the language of the Holy Scripture. They explained their beliefs using the terms, symbolism and concepts of Christianity. The concept of the redemption of human beings was the Greek gnosis or the revealed knowledge of God which He kept for the elite. They believed in a Supreme Being or God of unknowable character that is hard for human beings to understand. For Gnostics, Christ had a false human body with no flesh or tangibility. So, when he was crucified they believe that he was either saved through a miracle or He was substituted with Judas Iscariot or Simon of Cyrene. This is similar to another less famous and older first to second century heresy, Docetism.[31]

Gnosticism was condemned by the Church and in the end was publicly superseded by another more threatening heresy that involved emperors, patriarchs and the different hierarchies of the Church, and lasted for more than fifty years. It was the greatest battle of the fourth century. The issue was Christological, meaning the Trinitarian unity and the relationship of the Father to the Son and to the Holy Spirit.[32] This was the heresy of Arius (250–336), who denied the divinity of Christ and conceived of the Holy Spirit as not God, but rather a lesser god to the Logos.[33] Arius's doctrine was strongly combated by the Coptic Church, most especially by Athanasius (296–373) at the Council of Nicaea in 325.

Athanasius and the Council of Nicaea

The debate over the issue of the divinity of Christ threatened to bring the Roman Empire to civil war. To bring unity back to the Church Emperor Constantine had to call for the Council of Nicaea in 325.[34] This was the first time in the history of Christendom that bishops from all over the world, at that time numbering three hundred and eighteen, convened to settle an issue.[35]

Athanasius, who was educated in the School of Alexandria in his native city[36] and was still a deacon, stood between the world's bishops to defend Orthodoxy. Athanasius was able to crush the Arian heresy by the power of his faith and logic. It is easy to understand why the illustrious Athanasius became the Coptic Church's 20th Patriarch in 328.[37]

The outcome of the Council was the Nicene Creed, the first of its kind in the history of Christianity. It was a great victory for Coptic theology and remains so to this day. This is the Creed that all church denominations still confess where the divinity of the Son was affirmed and became the basis for the Christian faith for all ages.[38] Athanasius is the author of the Nicene Creed, the confession of faith used by all Christians worldwide.[39]

One would think that after the Council of Nicaea Arianism would have totally vanished, but history proves otherwise. Athanasius spent forty-six years of his life as the Pope of Alexandria, seventeen of them were in exile. He was banished five times due to his rigorous defense against the spread of Arianism, which continued to regain the support of various emperors.[40] In some instances during his battle against this heresy, emperors replaced Athanasius with other bishops, but the Copts did not accept these intruders. Thus, the Coptic Church went through periods of persecution aimed at forcing the Egyptians to give up their belief in the divinity of Christ and their support for Athanasius.[41]

With all these years of exile it is hard to imagine that Athanasius would find time to write, but he did. Among numerous treatises, exegesis and books, *On the Incarnation of the Divine Word* and *Life of Anthony* are possibly the most significant. The latter is a biography of the world famous Coptic monk, St. Anthony. During his exiles, Athanasius spent a lot of time with the Coptic monks in the dessert. A remarkable impact Athanasius had on the Catholic Church was his introduction of Egyptian monasticism to the Church of Rome during his years of exile in that city.[42]

Athanasius was fearless and when he was told, "The whole world is against you," he replied with the perennial phrase, "Then I'm against the world" (*Athanasius contra mundum, et mundum contra Athanasius*). Because of his extensive work and contribution in defending Christianity, the Church Universal granted him the titles "Defender of the Upright Faith" and "Athanasius the Apostolic," because he upheld the correct faith of the Apostles.[43]

On a side note, the influence of the Coptic Church in the Council of Nicaea can also be seen in two separate matters. After settling the major issue of Arius, the representatives of the Council discussed, among other things, a specific date for Easter. Because they had heard of the Epact cycle that was calculated by the Copts during the time of the 12th Coptic Pope

Demetrius (191–230), the Council adopted it and asked the Coptic Pope to write an annual Paschal letter to the rest of his brother bishops, including that of Rome, telling them the date for Easter each year. On the issue of rebaptism, bishops at the Council upheld the 14th Coptic Patriarch Dionysius's (248–264) decision that baptism can only be done once and those who renounce Christianity can be accepted if they are sincere without being baptized again.[44]

Millions of Christians worldwide, regardless of their denomination, can only be indebted to the works of the Coptic Pope Athanasius. Although the cinders of Arianism had not yet been put out when he died in 373, Athanasius had done everything in his power to prepare the ground for its total defeat at the next Ecumenical Council of Constantinople, in 381. It was only at that time that the Nicene Creed that he had so carefully worded was secured for all ages of Christianity.[45]

Timothy and the Council of Constantinople

The second ecumenical Council was held in Constantinople in 381, on the invitation of Emperor Theodosius the Great, to try the heretic Macedonius and others, including Apollinaris and Sabellius. The Council was attended by one hundred and fifty bishops. Presiding over the Council in succession was the 22th Coptic Pope Timothy (378–384), Meletius of Antioch, Gregory Nazianzus and Nectarius of Constantinople.[46] Apollinaris denied the humanity rather than divinity of Christ. Sabillius considered Father, Son and the Holy Spirit as only one hypostasis and did not differentiate between the three. Macedonius denied the divinity of the Holy Spirit.[47] The outcome of the Council was the condemnation of all three and the expansion of the Nicene Creed to include a clause regarding the Holy Spirit, thus putting it in the form still upheld today.[48]

At the council, brethren bishops asked Timothy to clarify certain issues regarding the Christian faith. His answers became church canons for the Christian world. Church law books, especially those of the Greek Orthodox Church, documented Timothy's answers as church canons. These books say that when Timothy was asked the first question he answered with canon one, when asked the second question he answered with canon two, and so on.[49]

It is at the Council of Constantinople that politics began to interfere with religion, which would have an irreversible impact on the Copts in the future Council of Chalcedon. Constantinople, the eastern capital of the Empire, began to be looked at as "New Rome." At this Council, the See of Rome was raised in position to be first, followed by Constantinople, then Alexandria and then Antioch. This raised the status of Rome and Constantinople as the two capitals of the Empire above the other Sees, based on political status rather than theology. Timothy didn't approve of this step, but there wasn't much he could do about it.[50]

Despite this, the Council of Constantinople was a victory for the Nicene Creed and Athanasius' teaching of the Trinity. Unfortunately, it didn't achieve the desired unity of the Church for very long. A new problem regarding the Christology would appear and necessitate another ecumenical council in Ephesus in 431 where the Coptic theology would yet again play an important role in settling a new debate.

Cyril and the Council of Ephesus

The 24th Coptic Pope, Cyril "the Great" (412–444), is well-known for his conflict with the obstinate heretic Nestorius over another level of Christology.[51] Nestorius, the Patriarch of Constantinople (428–431), believed that Christ was separated into two individuals. One is divine, and therefore perfect, while the other is human and, consequently exposed to human frailty. For Cyril there was no separation, but rather a union which is full and complete without mixing, fusion or change. This union can't be separated or divided and represents the two natures of the Son of God. Another argument made by Nestorius was related to the Virgin Mary. The Orthodox revere her by giving her the title *Theotokos*, which means "mother of God." Nestorius was against that title because he considered Mary to be only the mother of Christ, not of God. Cyril condemned Nestorius and Nestorianism in twelve anathemas known in the Christian world as the twelve anathemas of St. Cyril.[52]

The imperial family was not happy with this dispute in the Church and decided to convene the third Ecumenical Council at Ephesus in 431 to maintain order and settle the dispute. The two hundred bishops at the council adopted the title *Theotokos* for Mary. They unanimously condemned Nestorius and he was exiled. After the Council of Ephesus and until the death of Cyril, the Coptic Church enjoyed unquestionable leadership in the Christian world.[53] Wherever the believers in the Incarnate Word are, they allocate first place to Athanasius and second to Cyril among the protectors of the Christian faith.[54] After Cyril the Great died, the Copts elected Dioscorus (444–451) to be their 25th Pope. His time witnessed the greatest schism in the history of Christendom.

Dioscorus and the Council of Chalcedon

Eutyches, an archimandrite at Constantinople (380–456), so totally opposed Nestorius' teachings of separation of the two natures of Christ that he fell into a heresy himself and contradicted the Orthodox faith already established by the previous three ecumenical councils. He was so intent on showing the unity of the two natures of Christ that he said that the human nature was swallowed up and disappeared in the divine nature, thus denying the human nature of Christ. Such teaching was condemned by the Coptic Pope Dioscorus, and he excommunicated Eutyches. Eutyches feigned Orthodoxy, so Dioscorus readmitted him to the Church, but then Eutyches went back to his heresy. Thus, the Council of Chalcedon was convened in 451 to try Eutyches. The Council, as well as the Coptic Church, excommunicated him. But, while the Council excommunicated Eutyches, they also deposed Pope Dioscorus.[55]

The Council decision was based on the *Tome* of Pope Leo I of Rome confirming two distinct natures in Christ, or *dyophysites*. Copts have never denied the two natures of Christ, but believe in their unity. The two natures are united and inseparable without mixture, nor mingling, nor confusion.[56] Because of this unity the Copts came to be known as *monophysites* and the Council of Chalcedon exiled Dioscorus to Gangra, in Asia Minor, accompanied by imperial guards. He stayed there for about five years until his death.

Many church history books refer to the problem of Chalcedon as the desire of Pope Leo of Rome, the first See and capital of the Roman Empire, to have control over the rest of the Churches. The Constantinople See, the second capital of the Roman Empire, was not theologically strong and many of its Patriarchs and leaders were subject to condemnations. We have seen evidence of this in Macedonius, Nestorius and Eutyches. Being prominent at the time, the Church of Alexandria and its popes, who were beyond any doubt leaders, confronted their heresies. It seems that their ability to do so attracted some ill feelings against the Coptic Church. This ill will set the Church up for an unfortunate fate.

Leo had the support of the Emperor Marcianus and his wife Pulcheria. Although it was a religious council of bishops, the two political leaders attended the council and granted their support to Leo. Pulcheria had already sent Leo a letter affirming their faith to him: "I myself and my husband the strong king, diligently believe according to your faith." Pulcheria had given up her vow of virginity as a nun in order to marry Marcianus, and Leo was the one who validated her marriage as the rest of the bishops were not quite comfortable doing so because she had disregarded her sacred vow. Additionally, Pulcheria deplored Alexandrine leadership over church matters.[57]

The role of political power in religious matters emerged through Leo, the Emperor, and his wife in the council of Chalcedon. Although Dioscorus himself was the first to excommunicate Eutyches for his teachings, influenced by Leo, the Council deposed Dioscorus. Eutychianism is still rejected to this day by the Coptic Church just as much as Nestorianism and Arianism. Egyptians believe that behind the actions in Chalcedon lie a great deal of politics and personal interest. By humiliating Dioscorus, the Constantinople See usurped Alexandria and took second place to Rome. The Alexandrines, with their thorough understanding of the doctrine of the nature of Christ, were not going to be controlled by the Council. Egyptians were in full support of their Pope Dioscorus and national feelings started to rise; thus, the national church of Egypt was started.[58]

The result of the Council of Chalcedon in 451 was the first schism of the Church Universal since its conception. The churches that refused Chalcedon came to be known as Non-Chalcedonians and they include the Coptic, Syrian, Armenian, Ethiopian, Eritrean and Indian Orthodox Churches. Other churches that accepted the Council are called Chalcedonians and they include the Catholic Church, the Greek Orthodox, and later, the Protestant churches.[59]

The theological differences between the *monophysites* in Alexandria and the *dyophysites* in Rome and Constantinople have been overestimated as the main reason for the rupture between the two ancient brethren in the Eastern and Western churches. The Copts have never acknowledged the western identification of Alexandrine Christianity with the Eutychianism that started in Constantinople and which they consider a clear heresy. Copts don't call themselves *monophysites*. It is an incorrect term that can only describe Eutychians, and it was invented by the Romans and the Greeks to insult the Copts and their followers.[60]

The issue in Chalcedon was more linguistic than real and the term *monophysite* has been misunderstood throughout history, causing the Coptic Church to face severe persecution.[61] After the Coptic Church rejected the Christological formula of Chalcedon, it became separated from the rest of the Christian world. A minority in Egypt stayed in unity with Constantinople and Rome the heart of Chalcedonian faith; they were known as the Melkite Church. Today they are known as the Greek Orthodox Church, which has its own patriarch in Alexandria with a few thousand followers.[62]

The decision taken at Chalcedon caused an irreparable schism. And, since Copts had never been subject to Rome but rather parallel, the word "schismatic" that Catholic historians used to refer to the sister Coptic Church was deemed an unacceptable allegation. The Copts considered the apostolic Sees of Alexandria, Antioch, and Rome on equal status, thus, they lived in harmony with mutual respect for each other even when Alexandria was, beyond any doubt, prominent.[63]

The immediate result of Chalcedon was severely felt in Egypt. Byzantine Emperors thought the best way to keep stability in their empire was to keep the Church united—to force the Copts to accept Chalcedon. They did everything in their power to impose that unity through vicious attacks on the

Copts. Copts went into another phase of persecution but this time it was from their fellow Christians and Byzantine Emperors, all in an attempt to obliterate any remnants of separation in Egypt. Civil, military, and church authority were combined and given to Apollinaris by the Emperor. Apollinaris was the governor, military general, and Patriarch of Alexandria and held undivided power in his hand to force the Chalcedonian doctrine on stubborn, unyielding Copts. The Copts resisted the military rule of the Church and the intruder patriarch and followed their own national popes, who are elected to the See of St. Mark in Alexandria. For many years successive Egyptian Popes of Alexandria had to live in hiding, running from one monastery to another as they were sought by the troops of the Melkite Patriarch. Between the period of Chalcedon in 451 and the Arab conquest of Egypt in 641, Egyptians were unbearably taxed, severely tortured and persecuted.[64]

Pope Dioscorus himself was tortured, his hair was pulled out and his teeth were broken. The Melkites refused to distribute wheat to the Copts in order to starve them into conceding and accepting Chalcedon. They attacked Coptic churches, closed them, put the Imperial seal on the doors and posted guards to keep worshipers from entering. Copts went for a whole year without churches, communion or baptism. They also suffered attacks on Coptic monasteries and the monks; St. Samuel lost one of his eyes as a result of the violence. He is always portrayed without an eye in icons as yet another visual reminder for devout Copts to emulate. In the process of attacking the churches and monasteries the Melkites took many church valuables, Coptic icons and relics of saints.[65]

The 26th Coptic Pope, Timothy, along with his brother Anatolius, was exiled to Gangra for seven years. The 27th Coptic Pope, Peter, was exiled and replaced by the Melkite patriarchs, Timothy, Antony and John, but the Copts refused them. The 33rd Coptic Pope, Theodosius, was exiled from his see for 28 years. Coptic popes, unable to openly enter the great city of Alexandria, disguised themselves in costume so they could enter and strengthen the Coptic congregation in their faith. When Islam came to Egypt in the seventh century, Benjamin, the 38th Coptic Patriarch, had been in exile for 13 years. Forms of persecution included torture, attacks on churches, forced exile and death. In one day the number of Copts who were killed for believing in the one nature doctrine reached 30,000, and the Church celebrates their martyrdom on the 23 of the Coptic month of Mesra (approximately August 30th). This era was characterized not only by the heroism of the patriarchs but also of the Coptic people themselves, who neither yielded to nor accepted the intruder patriarchs, thus forming a strong Coptic identity.[66]

After the tragedy of Chalcedon, the Coptic Christians sank into oblivion as far as the rest of the world was concerned. Some European medieval and early modern travelers were aware of them, but Western Christianity forgot about them until the Presbyterian Christian mission ironically came to convert them to Christianity in the 1860s. When the Presbyterian missionaries came, the Coptic Bishop of the province of Assiut asked them a rhetorical question: "We have been living with Christ for more than 1800 years. How long have you been living with Him?"[67]

Monasticism

Despite the loss of their leadership role in the fifth century, going back in time we find a more enduring Coptic contribution to the Christian civilization. At the time of the Catechetical School of Alexandria and the ecumenical councils, a new, formidable institution arose: monasticism, which is a purely Coptic gift to Christendom. It is the most salient and far reaching contribution of Coptic Christians to the Christian world. Monasticism was developed through Coptic piety and in the image of Christ and his Apostles. It developed into a way of life that, when it was introduced to Europe, became the only custodian of Christian civilization in the Dark Ages. Coptic monasticism has gone through different stages since its beginning.[68]

When we talk about monasticism, the first person to come to mind is St. Paul. He is considered to be the first hermit in the whole world. His biography was written by Jerome in AD 374. St. Paul was born in Alexandria in AD 235 and lived as a hermit for eighty-six years. He died in AD 347 at the age of one hundred and thirteen.[69] St. Paul lived alone worshipping God for about eight decades without seeing a human face.[70]

Yet, St. Paul is not considered the establisher of monasticism as he lived in absolute solitude and didn't establish a monastic order for other monks to follow. It was St. Anthony who is historically the founder of Christian monasticism. He was born in Coma (modern Qiman al-Arus) in AD 251, a village about seventy-five kilometers south of Cairo.[71] When St. Anthony went into the desert he was twenty years old and he spent eighty five years in austerity and asceticism. The Coptic Patriarch Athanasius spent two years with him and wrote his biography.[72]

The *Life of Anthony* by Athanasius is the most remarkable work in the ever-widening field of Christian biography. The *Vita Antonii*, which was written in Coptic, has been translated into numerous languages and has contributed more than any other work to the spread of monasticism.[73]

In the church, St. Anthony heard the Gospel of Mark 19:21: "If thou wilt be perfect, go and sell that thou hast and give it to the poor and thou shalt have treasure in heaven; and come and follow Me." The wealthy St. Anthony took this as a divine sign and literally gave away all his riches. He left his home and started an ascetic life right outside his village. He spent his nights in prayer without much sleep. He only ate once a day after sunset and at times went without food for two to four days. His diet consisted of bread, salt and water. He slept on a mat for a bed and sometimes he slept on the bare ground. St. Anthony lived as a solitary ascetic at Pispir for about twenty years and did not leave his cell. Monks began to fill the desert around him, in this way the first monastic community was established at Pispir.[74] St. Anthony's fame reached the imperial palace and Constantine corresponded with him, asking for his blessings.[75]

St. Anthony's biography is the first hagiography dedicated to someone outside the popular center of the Church. Not only did he dramatize the Biblical call for absolute obedience, but he also redefined Christian identity. The man on the fringe of church life became the center for many and symbolized the true style of a monk.[76] The life of St. Anthony and the hardships he voluntarily undertook for his faith, engaged the minds of the western world. Yet, St. Anthony didn't organize the monastic life the way it is known to us now. The organization within monasticism came with the renowned monk St. Pachom.

St. Pachom established a community of his own in AD 323 in the village of Tabennesi, close to Akhmim, about 80 kilometers south of Assiut. There, coenobitic monasticism developed in contrast to Antonian style monasticism, thus marking an evolution in the monastic order.[77] In the Pachomian order, the monastery consisted of many buildings surrounded by one enclosing wall. Within this wall existed the cells of the monks, a church, a meeting hall, a refectory, a kitchen, a library, a hospital, a guest house, a house for the gate keeper and workshops.[78] In addition to prayer, an important goal of the monastery was to be self-supporting, hence, there was a great emphasis on work such as cultivating the land, animal husbandry and producing handiwork and crafts for sale. It is important to note that the monks of the Pachomian style of monasticism were among the Patriarch Athanasius's strongest supporters.[79]

The Coptic coenobitic order became the wonder of the ancient Christian world. Monasticism was spread to the rest of the world by holy men of medieval times. As mentioned previously, Athanasius introduced monasticism to Rome during his exile there. However, there were other apostles of the Coptic coenobitic system, the holy men who stayed for years in the Pachomian establishments and traveled also to the monasteries of Kellia, Scetis and Nitria in the western desert. There are many prominent names but we have to start with St. Jerome (342–420), who translated the *Regula Sancti Pachomii* into Latin. This was the version used by St. Benedict of Nursia (480–550) in forming his famous monastic rule. Other names include St. John Chrysostom (347–407); Rufinus (345–410), the famous church historian who wrote *Historia Monachorum*; St. Basil (330–379), the author of the

Eastern Liturgy used to this day and the founder of a Byzantine monastic system on the model of St. Pachom; St. John Cassian (360–435), the father of monasticism in Gaul who spent seven years in Egyptian monasteries and wrote the *Institute* and the *Conferences* about monastic life; Palladius (365–425) Bishop of Helenopolis in Bithynia, who gathered information about the lives of the monks in *The Lausiac History* or the *Paradise of the Fathers*; St. Eugenius, the father of Syrian monasticism; and many more from Europe, Ethiopia, Nubia and North Africa.[80]

The Pachomian style was also influential beyond medieval times. St. Benedict failed to adapt the Pachomian system of uniting convents into clans with yearly meetings for mutual inspections of their activities. Hence, the Benedictine houses became independent and wealthy. The Benedictine monks gave up hard work for the hired labor of villagers and chose to have a luxurious life, losing the good value of the Pachomian style of surveillance by other monks. Only the Cluniac reform in the tenth century was able to cure the situation by going back to the spirit of the Pachomian system. Consequently, in the eleventh and twelfth centuries, the Carthusians, the Cistercians, Franciscans and the Dominicans were established on the basis of unity of their convents under the supervision of a central authority. In the sixteenth century, the Jesuits unwittingly followed the Pachomian style. It is very clear that the contributions of Copts in the area of monasticism have maintained their impact all the way to the modern period.[81]

St. Macarius the Great (300–390) was another important contributor to monastic order. He founded a monastic rule in Nitria Valley (Wadi al-Natrun) in the western desert that was a blend between the orders of St. Anthony and St. Pachom. In this respect monasteries would have monks within the walls and solitaries would be outside the walls, in the desert.[82] These settlements attracted ascetics from the whole world of Christianity. The holy men who visited and resided in the Pachomian establishments also sojourned to the monasteries of the western desert and wrote about them for their own communities. The instructions and stories of the monks were documented in the *Sayings of the Desert Fathers* and were translated into many different languages having a great impact on Western Christian civilization.[83]

St. Shenoute of Atrip (350–465) is another renowned Coptic monk, but unlike St. Pachom, his influence was mainly national. He is known as the father of Coptic literature and he greatly contributed in the formation of the Coptic identity after Chalcedon. St. Shenoute accompanied St. Cyril on his trip to Ephesus in 431, and after the tragedy of Chalcedon, St. Shenoute's sense of nationalism was intensified, so he started a relentless movement to eliminate anything Greek from Coptic literature.[84] St. Shenoute used Sahidic, the Coptic dialect spoken in Upper Egypt, for his writings, and he made it the literary language of the Church for the next seven centuries.[85]

Monasteries have become Christian cultural centers. Wall paintings, manuscript production and translation have thrived there. Before print, monks recopied old texts and produced new translations and compositions.[86] They safeguarded manuscripts in the monasteries' libraries for western and eastern scholars to study and compare. Thus, monasteries played a significant role in preserving Christian heritage.

Coptic Missionaries

A byproduct of historic importance to the Coptic monastic movement was their missionary endeavors. All of the great names mentioned above were the best ambassadors and missionaries of Coptic Christianity. But Copts themselves spread Christianity and their impact exceeded the borders of Egypt. To the west in Cyrenaica, modern day Libya, Christianity was introduced in the early days when St. Mark traveled there from Alexandria; he must have been accompanied by Alexandrines. People of Cyrene were educated in Alexandria: Cynesius of Cyrene (370–414), bishop of Ptolemais, received his education at the School of Alexandria and was ordained by the Coptic Pope of Alexandria, Theophilus. After the Council of Nicaea in AD 325, based on the Nicene Fathers' decision, Cyrenaica was regarded as an ecclesiastical province of the See of Alexandria. This is still the case until today and Cyrenaica is part of the title of the Coptic Pope as an area of his jurisdiction.[87]

The impact of the Coptic Christian missions was much more influential in the upper side of the Nile Valley in Nubia. This is due to two facts. The first was the persecution the Copts felt in the north, which made them fly to the south, away from their persecutors. The second one was the rise of monasticism that expanded all over Egypt and all the way to the far south. This penetration of the south led to the ordination of Bishop Longinus to promote the Egyptian doctrine in Napata, the capital of the Nubia. Monasticism spread among Nubians, who established many monasteries and churches.[88]

The conversion of the Nubian Kingdom to Christianity wasn't the last station of Coptic influence. It reached farther south to Abyssinia, present day Ethiopia. Christianity was originally brought there from Alexandria by Frumentius. Pope Athanasius ordained him a bishop under the name *Abba Salama*, meaning "the father of peace." After the Council of Chalcedon, Ethiopia was a strong supporter of the Egyptian doctrine.[89]

Copts also spread Christianity into the East, but on a limited scale. The Egyptians went to Palestine, Syria, Cappadocia, Caesarea and some parts of Arabia. Origen, the great theologian, went to Bostra to discuss theological issues. Mar Augin of Clysma, Suez, founded monasticism in Mesopotamia and Persia and had a great impact on the Syrian and Assyrian Christians. In the second century, Pantaenus, the dean of the School of Alexandria, introduced the Gospel into India and Arabia Felix, or Yemen. In Europe the influence of Copts started with the two exiles of Athanasius the Apostle. The first started in Constantinople and ended in Trier, where he spent part of AD 336 and AD 337; it would be hard to believe that Athanasius didn't preach during that time. Athanasius spent most of his second exile in Rome (339–346) as a guest of Julius I in the Roman curia. Not only did he establish a good relationship between Alexandria and Rome, but most importantly he introduced Coptic religious life and monasticism to the Romans.[90]

The influence of the Copts also reached Switzerland, as is evident from the story of the Copt St. Maurice and his 6,600 soldiers, commonly known as the "Theban Legion," who were martyred in the name of Christ at the hand of Emperor Maximian (286–305).[91] A town is named after him: St. Moritz in Switzerland. Fellow members of the Legion, Felix, his sister Regula and Exuperantius reached the lake of Zurich, where they baptized converts until they were beheaded by Decius, the Roman governor of the area. One of Zurich's greatest cathedrals, Grossmünster, is built on the spot where they are buried, while the Wasserkirche is built where they were martyred. Across the Limmat River from Grossmünster is the Fraumünster cloister where there are eight ancient frescos telling the stages of their martyrdom. The icon of the three saints carrying their heads on their hands is the subject of the coat of arms of Zurich. A similar story, with some changes, has been told about the town of Solothrun where St. Victor, in Coptic *Boktor*, is revered as the patron saint of the town.[92]

St. Verena was a Coptic nurse who accompanied the legion to Europe to help care for them during battles. After their massacre she didn't return to Egypt, but stayed there to preach. She died in Switzerland and a church was built over her body. Her picture is portrayed holding a comb in one hand and a pitcher of water on the other because as a nurse she took care of the sick and taught them cleanliness.[93]

Coptic influence also reached the British Isles far before St. Augustine of Canterbury did, in AD 597. Irish Christianity, the influential civilizing agent between northern nations in the Middle Ages, was the child of the Coptic church. Seven monks from Egypt are buried in Ireland and there are many ceremonies and elements of architecture in Ireland at that early time reminding us of earlier Egyptian Christian remains.[94] In September of 2010, Irish scientists found fragments of Egyptian papyrus in the leather cover of an ancient book of psalms that was unearthed from a peat bog, according to Ireland's National Museum in Dublin. About 1,200 years old, this manuscript "potentially represents the first tangible connection between early Irish Christianity and the Middle Eastern Coptic Church," according to the Museum.[95]

Coptic Music, Art and Architecture

Another area of Coptic influence is Coptic music. Coptic tunes are Ancient Egyptian music that made its way into the Church hymns. In the first century, Philo, a Jewish philosopher from Alexandria said that the Early Christians took the Ancient Egyptian tunes and added Christian texts to them. The Coptic "Golgotha" hymn that Copts sing on Good Friday to commemorate Jesus' death on the cross is taken from Ancient Egyptians, who sang it during mummification. Another example is the Coptic hymn "Pek Ethronos." Its first half was full of sadness for the death of Pharaoh, while the second half was full of joy to celebrate his trip to the god Ra in the sun boat to eternity. Clement of Alexandria and Athanasius were influenced by such heritage and this is clear in their compositions. Clement composed the Praise of the Lord the Savior and Athanasius composed the "Monogenis."[96] It is conceivable that masters like these as well as the Coptic missionaries who crossed to Europe taught Coptic chanting. There is a theory that suggests an interaction between Coptic and Gregorian chanting.[97] Hilary from Poitier (386), the first Latin hymn composer, and Ambrosius, the prince of Latin hymns, are also among those who were deeply impacted by Egyptian music.[98]

The chanting of the three well-known church liturgies of St. Gregory, St. Cyril and St. Basil are mainly Coptic. Although St. Basil and St. Gregory had foreign texts, their music is purely Egyptian, with the exception of the last part of the liturgy of St. Basil, which is influenced by the Byzantine style. The St. Cyril liturgy was written by St. Mark, the Gospel writer, to be given to Egyptians, but the Coptic Pope Cyril reorganized parts of it in AD 430, and thus it got its name from him. It was the only liturgy prayed in all churches until the 6th century. Thus, the St. Cyril liturgy became the base for the other two liturgies, and when they adopted it, they adopted its pure Egyptian style, part of the artistic and cultural heritage of Egyptian music.[99]

The eminent Coptic musicologist and scholar Ragheb Moftah and the scholar Ernest Newlandsmith of London Royal Music Academy wrote down the Coptic chanting which, before 1927, was handed down only orally through church cantors, thus keeping the heritage of the Church from being lost.[100] In 1927, after listening to Coptic chants and reducing the tunes to notations, Newlandsmith said, "Western music has its origin in ancient Egypt." If we accept this scholar's assessment, then we should accept that Coptic music is a link between the music of ancient Egypt and Western music.[101]

Pictures on Egyptian temples record commonly used instruments that were adopted by the Church such as the harp, cymbals, and the triangle. The last two are still used today. In the early centuries of Christianity, the Egyptian harp appeared in Europe, in Ireland, and in Italy. Eventually it became the national symbol of Ireland and among the most popular instruments on the continent.[102] Whether through music or musical instruments, the Copts linked their ancestor's heritage with the Western world, and they extended their Christian influence as well.

Close to music is the field of Coptic arts. It is hard to find a major museum in the world without a section dedicated to Coptic art. In its authenticity and vigor, Coptic art became unique in the Christian world. The motifs of Coptic art can be seen in stonework, painting, woodwork, ivories, terracotta, and above all it is seen in the materials produced by Coptic looms.[103]

Coptic textile and loom weaving, techniques inherited from the Pharaohs, have been the most superb of Coptic arts. They can be found in wall hangings, sheets, curtains, and cloth trimmings. The tunic the clergy used was woven in both silk and linen so fine that it looked like embroidery. Christian designs and motifs were seen in the form of a fish, grapes, and some biblical scenes such as Mary carrying baby Jesus on the donkey on their trip to Egypt. The images were lively and stylistic, and Coptic textiles became so popular that they had a great market all over the Roman Empire in the early days of Christianity.[104] Coptic textile and fabrics were also influential on the style of modern day master artists, a source of inspiration for Picasso, Matisse and Derain.[105]

A good example of Coptic terracotta art is St. Mena flasks, or pilgrim flasks, found in several major museums, including the Louvre. St. Mena was an Egyptian soldier in the Roman army who was martyred because he refused to give up his Christian religion. The flasks were bought by pilgrims during their visits to St. Mena, near Alexandria. The bottles were filled with holy water or oil from the shrine of the saint and were carried as a souvenir from the pilgrimage. A typical bottle has an oval shape and a short neck with two handles, one on either side. Both sides of the bottle are identical, showing St. Mena wearing a tunic and cloak flanked by two camels. His name is written in Greek letters (O AGIOS MENAS). Some flasks go back as far as between the fourth and the seventh century and have been discovered in many different parts of the world, such as Heidelberg, Germany; Milan, Italy; Dalmatia, Yugoslavia; Marseille, France; Dengela, Sudan; and Jerusalem.[106]

In architecture, we can assume that the basilica style in the world of Christianity can be traced to the Ancient Egyptians, with Coptic craftsmanship being the bridge between the Pharaonic temple and the modern cathedral. At first, Copts routinely transformed old temples into churches. Later on, when they began to build their own churches, they copied the style of their ancestors, the Egyptian master builders of antiquity.[107]

Old Pharaonic temples consist of three main parts. First, is the outer gate with two pylons, leading to a spacious court lined by two rows of columns, with a narrow roof made out of stone; this area is designed for general worshippers. Beyond that section is the hypostyle, which is designed with lots of columns in close rows to support a huge stone roof and is kept for the royal family and aristocrats. The third part is at the end of the temple, a dimly lit room engulfed with mystery. This inner shrine is called *sanctum sanctorum* or "holy of the holies" and it is the place of the deity, which was restricted to the Pharaoh or the high priest.[108]

Coptic churches have kept these three sections. The inner room is the sanctuary and is covered with the iconostasis and only accessible to priests and deacons to perform the mystery of the sacraments. In front of the sanctuary is the middle section of the church which was reserved for baptized worshippers. The third part at the entrance is open and left for the unbaptized catechumens. However, the last division doesn't exist anymore, as unbaptized catechumens were eliminated with the spread of Christianity. Thus, there was no need to keep three transverse sections and they were replaced with three perpendicular sections of the nave and aisles. In this way, the basilica style started in Coptic architecture as is evident by the St. Mena Cathedral (395–408) west of Alexandria, and the White and Red monasteries of St. Shenoute at Sohag. This change in architecture was progressively embraced by the rest of the Christian world.[109]

Lost in History

The contribution of the Copts to Christian civilization is apparent. The School of Alexandria, the renowned Coptic theologians and the Coptic monks have shaped Christian thought and left their impact until today. The Copts have produced incredible literature and exegetic works and their era was characterized by research, scholarship and erudition. Yet, despite the incredible achievements of the Coptic period, it is shocking how few people of the West know or have even heard about this era. They are unaware of Coptic Christians, their history and the challenges facing them today. Even those who know give it little thought.[110] It is equally shocking how little most Egyptians know about this period as well, though it is understandable. Coptic history and civilization is ignored by the Egyptian government and it is not part of Egypt's "official" history.

The Council of Chalcedon marked the end of the Coptic period and the beginning of a period of severe persecution of Copts by their Christian brothers. Since then they have been largely forgotten; they have lived in oblivion. Although Egyptian Christians were well known to European mediaeval and early modern travelers, Western Christendom lost sight of them until the advent of Christian missionaries in the nineteenth century who came, ironically, to convert them.[111]

In the West people know only Catholicism and Protestantism, yet the

Coptic Church played a significant role in forming the root of both. The Catholic and the Protestant Churches acknowledge the theology of Athanasius and Cyril, who defended Christianity against Arianism and Nestorianism, yet, as a result of Chalcedon, the two churches refer to them as early church fathers, not mentioning that they were Copts.

But this most ancient church survived. Such a phenomenon is attributed to the strong spirituality of the Copts. It was developed and watered by the blood of their martyrs and reinforced by a consciousness that they are sons of their forefathers: the founders of the early Christian Church. Inside this fortress of faith, they kept their purity against intermarriage with continuous waves of invaders. The Church was the cementing ingredient among those descendants of Pharaonic Egypt. The way of worship developed to be a way of life and a symbol of an old culture and tradition for the isolated Coptic Christians in their ancient land.[112]

The fact that God blessed the Copts in Isaiah 19:25, "Blessed be Egypt my people" gives them a sense of fortitude. Copts remember with pride that Christ was a refugee in their land, running away from Herod's persecution: "Out of Egypt I called my son" (Matthew 2:15). The Copts' history of persecution gives them a taste of affinity with Christ. Indeed the history of the blood the Copts have shed for their faith and the teachings of their forefathers formed a strong Coptic identity.

This identity did not allow their spirit to break and they were able to keep their faith while keeping a deep hatred of the Byzantine persecutors and anything Byzantine. Their natural expression of such hatred was seen in their adherence to the inaccurate term *monophysitism*, Coptic language, and in their Coptic literature and art. It is at this point in the history that the Arab conquest of Egypt occurred. The Copts were bystanders who observed the fight between an enemy and an invader on their soil. It was a point in history where a new page was turned in their record of suffering and fortitude.[113]

The Greeks lost to the Arabs. Cyrus, the last Chalcedonian patriarch-prefect to Egypt, surrendered on Good Friday April, 6, 641. Thus, a new chapter for the Copts started under Arab rule, ending the relationship between the Christians of the East and the West for more than a millennium.[114]

Two

From Heretic to *Dhimmi*
The Islamization of Egypt

Egypt, the granary of the world, was very well known to Arabs for its richness in pre–Islamic days. Amr ibn al-As, the first Arab conqueror of Egypt, had visited Alexandria when he led Arab trade caravans to Egypt. It was the untold wealth of Egypt and his familiarity with its roads and fortification that encouraged Amr to make a case to Caliph Umar, the second Rightly Guided Caliph, for conquest.[1] In addition to the economic value of Egypt, the rise of the Arab Muslims was aided by two major factors. Christians in the Byzantine Empire were bitterly divided in their argument over the nature of Christ, and the Byzantine and Persian Empires were exhausted by their constant mutual wars. These two factors created a power vacuum and consequently paved the way for the Arab conquest not only of Egypt, but of other countries once under the rule of both empires.[2] Thus, after the Arab conquest, Egypt's wheat and tax money went to Medina in Arabia instead of Constantinople.[3]

After, the Arabs besieged the strategic Babylon at the apex of the Nile Delta, Amr negotiated surrender with the self-seeking Cyrus, the Chalcedonian Patriarch-Prefect to Egypt, whom Amr mistook for a Copt.[4] Cyrus was given the usual three choices: (1) adoption of Islam; (2) unconditional surrender and payment of tribute for protection; or (3) the sword. Cyrus negotiated secretly with the Arabs against the will of his people; his soldiers wanted to continue fighting. He accepted Amr's assurance that the Christians would be respected and their possessions, rights of inheritance, churches and the practice of their religion would be untouched.[5]

Cyrus was motivated by his desire to obtain certain privileges and retain his domination of the Coptic Church under the protection of the Arabs. After the fall of Babylon, the Arab troops proceeded to Alexandria. Alexandria was also besieged and negotiations with Cyrus were reopened. The predicament of the Alexandrians was not only the surrender of the city in September 642, but also Cyrus's approval to make Christians pay a tax of two gold dinars per head. Cyrus was obsessed with keeping his control over the Copts.[6] Because of this obsession, the port city of Alexandria fell without any naval intervention; Arabs came with neither naval support nor equipment. Arabs accredited their success to Allah's intervention on their behalf.[7] On the other hand, Cyrus's Emperor Heraclius blamed Cyrus, calling him an "abject coward and a heathen."[8] Thus, the Copts became subject to Arab rule.

In all, Cyrus's persecution of the Copts lasted for ten years and was intense until the end. The Coptic Patriarch, Benjamin, was on the run in the desert for the entirety of Cyrus's rule. Patriarch Benjamin's brother, Mena, was tortured. His skin was burned with torches until his body fat melted. When he still refused to accept Chalcedon, they put him in a sack full of sand and drowned him.[9] During the Arab siege, the Copts of Babylon were imprisoned, and, on Easter Sunday, the Roman soldiers cut off their hands on what is known as the day of vengeance.[10]

Before Amr conquered Egypt, the prophet of Islam, Muhammad, sent one of his messengers to invite Cyrus to convert to Islam, around AD 628. Cyrus didn't accept Muhammad's invitation, but he didn't want to send Muhammad's envoy home empty handed. So, he sent Muhammad gifts including two concubines. Muhammad kept one for himself, Mariyah al-Qibtiyah or Mary the Copt, who bore his son, Ibrahim. However, just as Cyrus was mistaken by Amr as a Copt, so, too, was Mary, who was probably of Roman descent.[11]

Many Arab history books teach that the Arabs came to Egypt in order to liberate the Copts from the torture of the Byzantines, and that Copts welcomed the Arabs as liberators. Elsewhere, history records that the Copts were neutral between oppressors and invaders.[12] It is true that the Coptic Patriarch Benjamin was revered by Amr and was able to come back and run the Church in peace. But, this doesn't mean that the Arabs favored the Copts. The Arabs didn't know or understand the sectarian differences between *monophysites* and *dyophysites*, which in itself was a great relief to the Copts. The Copts who had been living under the religious terrorization of the Melkites now found themselves on an equal footing with them.[13] At this early stage of the Islamic conquest of Egypt, the Copts were a great asset to the Arabs in running the new government.

The Arabs did not possess any tradition or training in governance, nor did they have any system which they could substitute for the ancient and well-organized civil service of Egypt. Moreover, there were a large number of vacancies within the government apparatus after the departure of the Greeks, who refused to be Arab subjects. Thus, the Copts were needed to fill this void. Leaving their country was not an option for Copts.[14] Amr became aware of the political value of the Copts after the departure of the Greeks.

Their value pragmatically superseded the religious ban on their employment. The teaching that non–Muslims can't have authority over Muslims was forgotten in matters of economic and political survival.[15] Copts were vital to the new state, as they helped in building the new bureaucracy; they were the experts in administration, finances and taxes. They also transferred their expertise in agriculture, industry and artifacts to the new state. They were running the country at the beginning of the era of Arab rule.[16]

Now that Egypt was under the rule of the Arab Muslims, it was to be governed by the Islamic *sharia* law. Whereas Copts had no place in society under the Byzantines, Arabs allowed a place—although inferior and unequal—for the Copts. This was considered a reprieve.[17] The Copts were no longer treated as heretics, but they were not treated as equals either. The new inferior status they were allowed in the Islamic state would be called *dhimmi* or "protected people." The cost of such protection would be hard to pay.[18]

The price of being a *dhimmi* would become more onerous than the price of being a heretic, and the effects would last much longer. Some Copts even fled to Byzantine ruled lands to escape the hardships they faced.[19] *Dhimma* status would become a legal status similar to the heretic status under the Byzantines. *Dhimma* would be credited for the process of the Islamization and Arabization of Egypt and the steady diminishing of Coptic culture and, sometimes, people. It lasted for one thousand two hundred years, from the Arab conquest of Egypt until the rule of Muhammad Ali's family and the period of European colonization in the 19th century.[20] *Dhimma* is a product of *jihad*, and fundamentalists believe that both are at the core of Islamic identity, a belief that has greatly influenced the treatment of the Coptic Christians.

Jihad *and* Dhimma

In the previous chapter we talked about the different theological debates of Christology that engaged all the Christians of the world at that time and how the outcome affected Copts in Egypt. It will be equally important to highlight a few Islamic doctrines that have affected Christians in general. Radical Islamists interpret these doctrines in a way that justifies their treatment of the Copts. They praise God and shout *Allah Akbar* when they burn Coptic churches and homes and kill the Copts, believing that attacking Copts is a form of *jihad*. This is in stark contrast to moderate Muslims' interpretation of the same doctrines.

Jihad, or holy war, is one of the tenets of Islam. As the Arabs grew more powerful, their wars crossed the borders of Arabia. The *jihad* became a war of conquest, subject to legislation, with the main aim of converting non-Muslims. Jews and Christians, known in Islam as "People of the Scripture" or "People of the Book," were given the option of keeping their religion under the *dhimma* status. That is because they are believed to have acquired part of the truth and because Jesus and the Jewish prophets are mentioned in the Quran.[21] Islam is seen as a continuation of monotheistic religions that came to finalize and conclude all previous contributions. It is believed to be the only true religion and Muhammad is the last messenger coming from Allah. Islam came to correct and complete both Christianity and Judaism. The tool to achieve this goal is *jihad*.

Jihad also includes the treatment of the conquered peoples and the financial system applied to the conquered lands such as *jizyah*, *kharaj*—land tax—and other forms of taxation. The main purpose of *jihad* is to bring all non-Muslims under the law of Islamic *sharia*. Human beings are divided into two camps: Muslims and others. Muslims form the Islamic community, or *umma*, who possess the territories of *dar al-Islam*, or "the house of Islam," and are governed by *sharia*. Others are called *harbis*, dwelling in the *dar al-harb*, or "the house of war," so called because they are destined to be under Islamic authority and *sharia* either by war or conversion to Islam. *Jihad* is a permanent state of struggle and is the Islamic right of conquest. It allows temporary truces according to the political situation known as *muhadana*. These truces can be revoked by the Muslim leader or imam. *Jihad* is a duty for all Muslims. Each Muslim contributes to it based on his ability: in person through military participation, or through material contribution. *Jihad* can be launched through proselytism, propaganda and other means to win over hearts, or *ta'lif al-qulub*. Jihadists are rewarded in this life with the spoils of war and in the afterlife by going to paradise.[22]

A dweller of *dar al-harb* is an enemy who can't go to the *dar al-Islam*. However, the safety of such a person can be guaranteed through *aman* or "temporary protection." Once the Muslims win the holy war, the inhabitants of *dar al-harb* become prisoners of war. Depending on the religious political leader and the situation of the conflict, they can be killed, exiled, taken as slaves or come under the protection of *dhimma* status.[23]

Many Muslims believe that Jews and Christians have falsified their holy books by omitting parts that predict the coming of Muhammad. Therefore, they persist in error, and, subsequently, they should be humiliated and segregated from the Muslim community. Some scholars, jurists and caliphs outlined the prohibitions on *dhimmis*. They were banned from certain towns because their presence would profane them. Jews and Christians were banned from talking in a group in the streets and had to walk with their eyes lowered on the left side of any Muslim.[24] They couldn't ride a horse; they were only allowed to ride donkeys, but they had to dismount when they passed a Muslim assembly.[25]

For a *dhimmi* to be distinguished from Muslims they had to wear different clothing. In this way it was easy for Muslims to find and humiliate them. They weren't allowed to dress in silk garments or fine clothes. Even their shoes had to be different, made of coarse material and of an unpleasant color.[26] It was banned to greet a *dhimmi* first. If a *dhimmi* greeted a Muslim, then he could reply by saying "and upon you." Muslims didn't go to meet a *dhimmi* and he was not allowed to sit among Muslims. They couldn't call a *dhimmi* brother or wish him success, as was the tradition among Muslims. They couldn't give him charity or take him as a witness. Muslims weren't allowed to call a *dhimmi* sir or master. A Christian would be called, "You there, Christian" or "You there, O cross." A Jew would be called, "You there, Jew." On the other hand, a *dhimmi* was required to show utmost respect to Muslims. He must not deceive them, be rude to them, raise his voice to them or go in to their presence without permission. To allow a *dhimmi* to break these regulations was akin to allowing them to show their lack of the true religion, lifting them up from lowliness and inferiority.[27] In today's Egypt, fundamentalist Islamists still exhort Muslims publically in mosques, in social media, and on television to abstain from wishing Copts "Merry Christmas."

Christian churches were banned from sounding their bells except very softly in the heart of the church: such a sound was a sign of infidelity. Malik ibn Anas, also known as Imam Malik, a highly respected scholar (711–795), said, "When bells are sounded, the anger of the Compassionate is aroused, whereupon angels descend to the four corners of the Earth and sing, Say He is One until the anger of the Lord is appeased." The sound of bells is to be replaced by the call to prayers.[28] Today, church bells in Egypt have mainly been silenced.

The *dhimma* status is not only about humiliation, but it has a legal basis in *sharia*. Any and all legal cases were based on *sharia* law. A *dhimmi* couldn't give evidence against a Muslim. His oath was not acceptable in Islamic court, which made it extremely difficult for his Muslim opponent to be condemned. In order for a *dhimmi* to defend himself, he could only buy Muslim witnesses. A Muslim couldn't be sentenced to death on account of a crime against an infidel. Not accepting *dhimmi* testimony was serious when a Muslim accused a *dhimmi* of speaking ill of Muhammad or Islam. In such accusations, which were punishable by death, there was no way for a *dhimmi* to oppose the testimony of a Muslim in the Islamic court, and the only way out of death was conversion to Islam.[29] That testimony wasn't accepted marked the refusal of free, open speech: a refusal to listen, to make contact, to exchange ideas and to share points of view. Suppression of speech alienated and silenced *dhimmis*, as individuals and a community.[30]

A consequent result of *dhimma* status is *jizyah*. It is an Arabic word that means penalty. The *jizyah* is a tax paid in return for the protection of *dhimmis*, and it symbolizes the humiliation and submission of *dhimmis*. *Dhimmis* are not considered full citizens of the Islamic state even though, as in case of the Copts, they are the native people of Egypt. As a result, Copts were treated like second-class citizens in their homeland. They became alienated and weren't an important part of the community. Ibn Qayyim al-Jawziyya, a renowned Jurist (1292–1350), said this about the *jizyah:* that it is "to spare the blood (of the Zimmis) [*dhimmis*], to be a symbol of humiliation of the infidels as an insult and punishment to them, and as the Shafi'tes indicate, the *jizyah* is offered in exchange for residing in an Islamic country."[31]

The Muslim authority obliged everybody to pay the *jizyah* in person; it was not permitted to send a third party to pay it on another person's behalf. No one could escape humiliation and everybody was vilified.[32] According to some jurists, the *jizyah* was to be paid by individuals at a humiliating public ceremony where the *dhimmi* was to be hit on the head or on the nape of the neck while paying it. Proof of paying *jizyah* was a piece of parchment to be worn around the neck or in the form of a seal worn on the wrist or the chest. This allowed a *dhimmi* to move from a place to another. The absence of such a receipt resulted in the imprisonment of the *dhimmi*. The seal the *dhimmi* wore became a symbol of dishonor.[33] Another element of this humiliation dictated that the *dhimmi* had to stand while the Muslim receiving the *jizyah* sat, and after paying the *jizyah*, the *dhimmi* would present his beard and the Muslim official would hit it while saying, "Pay the dues of Allah, O enemy of Allah, O infidel."[34] Hitting the *dhimmi* symbolized the escape of the sword through the insult. The payment of *jizyah* was done in the lowest and dirtiest public place, such as the *suq*, or marketplace.[35]

Inequality also came from the manner in which people were classified. Among early Muslims in Egypt there were two groups: Sunni and Shiite. Sunni Muslims, the majority, were above the Shiite, and Arab Muslims above non–Arab Muslims. New non–Arab converts to Islam were called *Mualli*. They were considered people without roots and had to be connected to an Arab to gain imaginary relations.[36] *Mualli*, which means "client of the Arabs," enjoyed a higher degree of social standing than a *dhimmi*, but they still were of a lower class than Arab Muslims. They weren't treated the same way as Arabs, as they were considered inferiors.[37] In this classification, the Copts came at the bottom of the scale because they are not only non–Muslim but non–Arab as well.

Between *jihad* and *dhimma* there exists a self-perpetuating cycle. The *dhimmis* became a precious source of support for the conquerors. They formed the entire economic infrastructure, were in possession of valuable skills and were adept at professions unfamiliar to the Arabs. They upheld the military apparatus through their taxes in money and kind, thus, allowing Arabs to pursue their *jihad* without financial obstacle. Pursuing *jihad* produced more *dhimmi* conditions that favored expansion of Arab rule and domination.[38] When Copts protested against the rulers' abuse of the *dhimma* status, some were killed and others were banished.

The *dhimma* status and its restrictions have affected Copts through the centuries. It has resulted in the decline of a unique civilization. The application of *dhimma* facilitated the transition of a conquering minority into a ruling majority and transformed a majority into a second class minority. It dictated that the Copts teach their Arab rulers the skills of organization, management of finance, the administration of towns and villages and the system of taxation. In addition, they taught them the arts of architecture and engineering.[39]

Moderate Muslims look at *dhimma* and *jihad* as historical concepts and not applicable in today's world; radicals see them as timeless concepts and a means to re-establish the Islamic caliphate. Radicals are guided by the interpretation of certain Islamic scholars and certain *hadith* (sayings of Muhammad). Moderate Muslims reject the interpretation of these same scholars, and moderate sheikhs have deemed these same *hadith* weak. Muslim scholars from the prestigious al-Azhar say Islam is tolerant of other religions. Hence, they describe radical Islamist attacks perpetrated on Copts as isolated cases. They add that these acts of violence are not compatible with the teachings of Islam; therefore, those who commit them don't represent the real Islam.

On the other hand, radical Islamists, who claim they are pious and strong adherents to the Quran and the *hadith*, say al Azhar, including the Grand Sheikh and the Mufti, doesn't represent real Islam. Because these two highest positions have to be ratified by presidential decree and al-Azhar has long issued *fatwas* (Muslim religious edicts) in support of state policy, radicals consider them "state employees" and a "mouthpiece for the state." Therefore, the radicals believe that al-Azhar clergy are not at liberty to preach true Islam because that might contradict state policy. They claim that the state dictates to al-Azhar clergy when to speak and what to say to the public. Because radicals believe attacking Copts is a form of *jihad*, when al-Azhar scholars condemn the radicals' attacks on Christians, not only do the radicals believe they are politically motivated to do so, but they believe that al-Azhar scholars are condemning *jihad* itself.

Some radical Islamists are also scholars and some are educated in al-Azhar itself. Umar Abdel Rahman, who served a life sentence in the U.S. on charges of trying to explode the World Trade Center in the 1990s, was an al-Azhar professor. He was the spiritual mentor of the radical Islamic Group that justified killing Coptic jewelers and taking their money in their *jihad* to establish an Islamic state. This happened quite frequently in the 1980s, especially in Upper Egypt.[40] Additionally, the imprisoned mufti of the Muslim

Brotherhood (MB), which the state declared a terrorist organization, Sheikh Abdel Rahman al-Barr, was also an al-Azhar professor.

Moderate scholars state that the Quran speaks favorably of Christians. It describes them as non-arrogant and being the nearest to the Muslims: "and you will find the nearest of them in affection to the believers those who say, 'We are Christians.' That is because among them are priests and monks and because they are not arrogant" (Quran 5:82). In other verses Christians are assured of their salvation (2:62, 3:55). The Quran permits Muslims the food of Christians and allows Muslim men to marry Christian women (5:5). The Quran also talks of Jesus' miracles (3:49). These are a few of the many verses to which moderate Muslims refer.

These verses, however, don't hold much weight among radicals. They refer to other verses that moderate Muslims believe are taken out of their historical context. They emphasize verses such as, "Fight those who do not believe in Allah or in the Last Day and who do not consider unlawful what Allah and His Messenger have made unlawful and who do not adopt the religion of truth from those who were given the Scripture-[fight] until they give the jizyah willingly while they are humbled" (9:29). They focus on verses that suggest that Christians are guilty of *kufr* "unbelief" and *shirk* "polytheism" (Quran 5:72). The most quoted verse is: "O People of the Scripture, do not commit excess in your religion or say about Allah except the truth. The Messiah, Jesus, the son of Mary, was but a messenger of Allah and His word which He directed to Mary and a soul [created at a command] from Him. So believe in Allah and His messengers. And do not say, 'Three'; desist—it is better for you. Indeed, Allah is but one God. Exalted is He above having a son. To Him belongs whatever is in the heavens and whatever is on the earth. And sufficient is Allah as Disposer of affairs" (4:171). They frequently quote Quran 3:71 which suggests that the Scriptures are not intact and are corrupt, *tahrif*.

They refer to a verse that Jesus professed the coming of Muhammad (Quran 61:6). The most impacting verse they use stipulates that Jesus wasn't crucified, but rather he was lifted up to God out of the hands of the Jews (Quran 4:157–8).

All Christians' concept of salvation is anchored on Christ's crucifixion. Moderate Muslims acknowledge differences in religions, and they accept co-existence: "For you is your religion, and for me is my religion" (Quran 109:6). But, radical Islamists attack the Copts, the followers of a "polytheistic and corrupt" religion. Thus, if Christians show any manifestation of their beliefs it incites them and is seen as an invitation to apostasy, which is the worst abomination.[41]

In addition to the Quran, the radicals are also guided by some *hadiths*. In *Sahih Al-Bukhari*, the most authentic book after the Quran, Allah's Apostle

(Muhammad) said, "By Him in Whose Hands my soul is, son of Mary (Jesus) will shortly descend amongst you people (Muslims) as a just ruler and will break the cross and kill the pig and abolish the *jizyah*. Then there will be abundance of money and nobody will accept charitable gifts."⁴²

ISIS referred to this *hadith* when they beheaded the Copts in Libya. In a five-minute video entitled "A message signed with blood to the nation of the cross, the people of the cross, the followers of the hostile Egyptian church" and beginning with the Islamic phrase "In the name of Allah, the compassionate, the merciful," they show in detail the beheading of twenty one Coptic Christian hostages on February 15, 2015. The onscreen narrator says,

> All praises due to Allah the strong and mighty. And may blessings and peace be upon the one [Muhammad] sent by the sword as a mercy to all the worlds ... oh crusaders safety for you will be only wishes especially when you are fighting us all together, therefore, we will fight you all together until the war lays down its burdens and Jesus, peace be upon him, will descend breaking the cross, killing the swine and abolishing jizyah.

The next image shows all twenty-one Copts pushed to lie flat on their stomachs; they were all slain simultaneously, and their heads were placed on their backs. ISIS's rational for this massacre is that it was in retaliation for the Egyptian Church's protection of two Coptic priests' wives who radicals claim wanted to convert to Islam.

According to survivors, ISIS members were knocking on doors looking for Copts, who could be identified by the cross tattoos they traditionally put on their wrists.⁴³ The Fatimid caliph al-Hakim (996–1020) tried to abolish the Coptic practice of tattooing the cross on the wrist, but he was unsuccessful. More than a thousand years later, the Copts are targeted because they identify themselves with the symbol of the cross. The victims were beheaded based on their Coptic identity. There have been Coptic martyrs since the early centuries, but for many Egyptians, Christians and Muslims alike, it was hard to believe that this crime could occur in 2015 in the manner that it did. People read the stories of the martyrs of the early centuries and imagine what happened. ISIS showed it in real time.

Given that the Quran speaks favorably of Christians—the argument of moderate Muslims—how, then, could ISIS justify their crime against the Copts in Libya? How do radical Islamists justify killing the Copts in Egypt? The radicals don't share the moderate Muslims' views regarding Christians, because they apply the doctrine of *al-Nasikh wal-Mansoukh*, or the "abrogator and the abrogated."

The Arabic etymology of the word *nasikh* is a legal term in *sharia* that means to annul previous verses. The doctrine of abrogation allows the annulment of verses from the Quran without deleting them from the text. So, when verses are in conflict with one another, the earlier verse is overridden by the later one. The abrogated verse is still part of the Quran, but it is cancelled by the abrogating verse.

Some scholars state that the verses revealed in Medina abrogated the earlier ones revealed in Mecca. Therefore, the Quran is divided into two sets of verses: ones in Mecca and ones in Medina. The ones in Mecca are the ones that were lenient in their treatment of the People of the Book written at the beginning when the community of Muslims were just developing. When they migrated to Medina, they became powerful enough to confront their opponents; therefore, the verses of Medina were more stringent.[44]

According to a scholar of Islam, al-Suyuti (1445–1505), every verse about peace and forgiveness was abrogated by the following verse: "And when the sacred months have passed, then kill the polytheists wherever you find them and capture them and besiege them and sit in wait for them at every place of ambush. But if they should repent, establish prayer, and give zakah, let them [go] on their way. Indeed, Allah is Forgiving and Merciful" (9:5). Some Islamic theologians call this verse "the verse of the sword," others call it the "Ultimatum." These scholars state that this is one of the last verses revealed. Al-Dahhak ibn Muzahim, an authentic transmitter of *hadith*, said that this verse abrogated all previous peace agreements in order to lift up any restraint on Muslims to fight pagans, including those agreements reached by Muhammad with the pagans in Arabia. The Shafi'i school of jurisprudence took this verse as a justification to fight Christians and Jews who don't pay the *jizyah* imposed on them. Al-Suyuti said that one hundred and twenty-four verses in the Quran were abrogated by this verse. Thus, radical Islamists interpret this verse to justify violence towards the *mushrikeen*, the polytheists. It is used to justify violence toward Christians, whom they see as believing in more than one God: God the Father, the Son, and the Holy Spirit.[45] In contrast, moderate Muslims don't accept violence against Christians, referring to "There shall be no compulsion in [acceptance of] the religion" (Quran 2:256).

Islamization of Egypt

Arab history books state that religious freedom for the Copts was secured under the Islamic caliphates. How then were the Copts reduced to being a minority in their own country? The process of the Islamization of Egypt is credited for the change in demography in which Muslims became the majority. This process, however, occurred over several centuries and throughout many Islamic dynasties.

The realty of the concept granting and upholding the promise of religious freedom for the Copts was illustrated by the English historian, Alfred Butler (1850–1936):

> and, although religious freedom was in theory secured for the Copts under the capitulation, it soon proved in fact to be shadowy and illusory. For a religious freedom which became identified with social and financial bondage could have neither substance nor vitality. As Islam spread, the social pressure upon the Copts became enormous, while the financial pressure, at least, seemed harder to resist as the number of Christians or Jews who were liable for the poll tax diminished year by year, and their isolation became more conspicuous.

As their numbers decreased the pressure against them increased; hence, large numbers converted but many did not and held steadfast to their faith despite overwhelming pressure.[46]

The financial pressure on the Copts was extremely difficult to escape. Amr was able to collect twelve million gold dinars. Abd-Allah ibn Sa'ad, his successor, raised that amount by two million more. This was met by a number of rebellions that were inevitably put down. The revenue from taxation of the *dhimmi* kept decreasing in the Umayyad and Abbasid dynasties until it was stable at three million in the ninth century. This decline was mainly due to Copts converting to Islam to escape excessive taxes and the humiliation imposed on them. Conversion was so steady that Arab rulers, at one point, tried to discourage it in order to keep the flow of revenue to the state.[47]

With the exemption of converts from the *jizyah*, revenue was severely impacted. In order to make up the difference, some caliphs doubled the *jizyah* on the remaining Copts. Caliph Umar ben Abd al-Aziz (718–720) transferred the burden of paying the *jizyah* of a Copt who died to the Coptic community. It was even said that Copts paid the *jizyah* of converts to Islam.[48] Neither death nor conversion lifted the burden of the *jizyah*. It was a legacy passed from one generation to the next.

The symbolism of *jizyah* rather than the tax itself was the origin of a deep feeling of alienation because the *dhimmis* had to pay the victor for the right to live in their own homeland. Saved from death, a *dhimmi* continuously paid money to buy his life and performed acts of submission to temporarily keep his death sentence on hold. The result of the labor of the *dhimmi* was not only for the state, but funded Arab expansion and strengthened Arab acquisitions. Therefore, the *dhimmi* worked for the benefit of the power of his conqueror and the community that excluded and humiliated him.[49]

A contemporary example of how the historical *dhimmi* still works for the benefit of a community that excludes him is the funding of al-Azhar University. Taxes on the public, including Copts, support the university, yet Copts are banned from studying at its civil branch which offers degrees in empirical and social sciences. As the main function of al-Azhar University is to provide religious education, the curriculum dictates the teaching of the *dhimma* status.

When Amr made his deal with Cyrus, it was the protection tax, *jizyah*, that was negotiated. Later on trade tax, *mekos*, was imposed. There were many other forms of taxation which were applied to manufacturing, fishing and grazing.[50] *Kharaj*, land tax, on Coptic farmers increased despite the fact that it was shared by a decreasing number of farmers. This led to Coptic peasants leaving their lands and villages in search of a life where the tax burden was manageable.[51]

The taxes imposed on Copts led to numerous revolts in many different parts of Egypt between 725 and 832. These revolts were put down by the different governors. A scholar in Middle Eastern Studies, said, "Coptic resistance to taxation by force of arms was broken. The despair which followed these crushing defeats seems finally to have set in train the movement of mass conversions to Islam.... We may say that the defeat of the rebellion broke the backbone of mass Coptic allegiance to Christianity."[52]

There was a different form of taxation that came under the *Covenant of Umar* which was not on the table when Amr made his deal for the surrender of Egypt. The *Covenant of Umar* is a document that placed social, economic, political and legal restrictions and above all humiliation on the Christians. It defines the circumstances they would face for keeping their religion and it played a major role in the process of Islamization.[53] The text for this covenant was believed to be written by the Christians of Syria to seek their security from Caliph Umar and it became significant in regulating the relations between the Arabs and the *dhimmi* subjects. It states:

> When you came to us we asked of you safety for our lives, our families and property, and the people of our religion on these conditions: to pay tribute out of hand and be humiliated; not to hinder any Muslim from stopping in our churches by night or day, to entertain him there three days and give him food there and open to him their doors; to beat the gong [used in eastern churches in lieu of a bell] only gently in them and not to raise our voices in chanting; not to shelter there, nor in any of our houses, a spy of your enemies; not to build a church, convent, hermitage, or cell, nor repair those that are dilapidated, nor assemble in any that is in a Muslim quarter, nor in their presence; not to display idolatry nor invite to it, nor show a cross on our churches, nor in any of the roads or markets of the Muslim; not to learn the Quran nor teach it to our children; not to prevent any of our relatives from turning Muslim if he wish it; to cut our hair in the front; to tie the *zunnar* [a special belt] round our waists; to keep to our religion; not to resemble the Muslims in dress, appearance, saddles, the engraving on our seals [i.e. not to engrave them in Arabic]; not to use their *kunyas* [titles]; to honor and respect them, to stand up for them when we meet together; to guide them in their ways and goings; not to make our houses higher than theirs; not to keep weapons or swords, nor wear them in a town or on a journey in Muslim lands; not to sell wine or display it; not to light fires with our dead at a road where Muslims dwell, nor to raise our voices at their [?our]

funerals, nor bring them near Muslims; not to strike a Muslim; not to keep slaves who have been the property of Muslims. We impose these terms on ourselves and our co-religionists; he who rejects them has no protection.[54]

Reading these restrictions on the Copts and their churches in this covenant, one understands why churches are violable. They have been pillaged, demolished, and most commonly torched. In 2013, under Egypt's Islamist President Morsi, the radical mobs attacked St. Mark's Coptic Orthodox Cathedral in a political gesture to show that even the Christian headquarters was not immune from their wrath. After Morsi's deposal, there were incidents of arson all over Egypt to burn and sabotage churches. Any behavior of a Copt, if seen as undesirable, could be interpreted as exceeding his rights put forth for him as a *dhimmi*. This could result in reprisal against him and his whole community. When Copts practice their political rights, it is also interpreted this way. When they joined their moderate Muslim counterparts in protest against President Morsi, their political participation resulted in mass church burning.

It is said that Caliph Umar ordered the destruction of any church that was built after the Hijrah (Muhammad's emigration to Medina in 622) and allowed only the ones that already existed before that time to remain. Erwa ben Muhammad was Caliph Umar's representative to Egypt to enforce his ruling.[55] Sheikh Damanhuri (1689–1764), a grand sheikh of al-Azhar, wrote an essay in 1739 entitled "The presentation of the clear proof for the obligatory destruction of the churches of Old and New Cairo." In this essay he stated that Muhammad said, "No emasculation and no church in Islam." As emasculation is prohibited, then constructing churches would be equally prohibited.[56]

The process of Islamization turned the Copts into a minority. The protected status given to *dhimmis* in their own land in return for submission created, for centuries, a protection that was only conditional and dependent on the character of the ruler. This insecurity was further aggravated by the fact that *dhimmis* were totally dependent on the occupier for their security.[57] They surrendered to a passive existence and developed a sense of helplessness and vulnerability as a result of permanent insecurity and submission. The physical and psychological debasement they faced led to an inferior existence.[58]

In light of the *dhimma*, how did the Copts survive? How, despite all economic, social, political and legal privileges of joining Islam, did they prefer to stay committed to their faith? A short answer is that they developed a deep sense of a Coptic identity rooted in a church that withstood centuries of hardship. This identity would allow them to survive successive Islamic dynasties that would last for centuries. This gives rise to two more questions. How did different Islamic caliphate dynasties go about treating the Copts? And, how did the process of Islamization impact Egypt and its Copts over the different dynasties?

Three

The Islamic Caliphates

The Umayyad Dynasty, 661–750

Fundamentalists say Islam is *deen wa dawla* or "a religion and a state." Its political system is governed by God's law, sharia, so political decisions in the Islamic state can be looked upon as sanctified. History reveals a series of politically motivated assassinations among the caliphs, starting as early as Muhammad's companions, the earliest Muslim caliphs also known as *al-Khulafa al-Rashidun* or "The Rightly Guided Caliphs." Believed to be one of the best caliphs, the second Rightly Guided Caliph, Umar, was stabbed to death by an opponent in 644 while he was praying. He was followed by another Rightly Guided Caliph, Othman, who was a member of the strong Umayyad tribe. Othman was murdered in 655 by a group of five hundred angry soldiers who surrounded his house killing him in retaliation for his removal of Amr from Egypt. The fourth and final Rightly Guided Caliph, Muhammad's cousin Ali, was also stabbed and murdered by an opponent in 661. Ali's followers chose his oldest son Hasan to be his successor, but Hasan relinquished his caliphate to Mu'awiya in exchange for a subsidy. Thus the Rightly Guided Caliphs came to an end and Mu'awiya became the caliph and the establisher of the Umayyad dynasty.[1]

The Rightly Guided Caliphs not only were Muhammad's companions, the conduits of his *hadith* and the most pious of Muslims, but were family as well. Caliph Umar's daughter Hefsa was one of Muhammad's wives. Caliph Othman was married to two of Muhammad's daughters, Ruqayya and Umm Kulthum. Caliph Ali was married to Muhammad's daughter Fatima. It is notable that neither family ties nor friendship with Muhammad provided them any protection against political assassinations. Despite being Muhammad's closest allies and the guardians of the religion, three of the four Rightly Guided Caliphs were murdered. Yet, fundamentalists still believe that the caliphate is the optimal political system and they strive to re-establish it.

When Mu'awiya assumed the caliphate, some Muslims saw the Umayyads as usurpers, believing that the caliphate should belong to the descendants of Ali. Mu'awiya asked his son Yazid to be his successor before he died. But upon his death, followers of Ali (the Shiite) tried to make Ali's younger son and Muhammad's grandson, Hussein, the caliph. Some of Yazid's people murdered Hussein by cutting off his head, and they sent it to Yazid in Damascus.[2] The fact that Muhammad's grandson Hussein was beheaded indicates that no one was immune from political murder.

When Mu'awiya became the caliph he killed all of Ali's relatives, so he would have no rivals. Amr, who had conquered Egypt under the second caliph, Umar, supported Mu'awiya's struggle for power. With his caliphate based in Damascus, Mu'awiya asked Amr, who Othman had already withdrawn from Egypt, to reinvade it under his name and dynasty. Amr proceeded to Egypt with six thousand soldiers and demanded that Egypt's Governor, Muhammad ibn Abu Bakr, surrender. Ibn Abu Bakr was also the son of the first caliph, Abu Bakr, and he was Muhammad's brother-in-law. Ibn Abu Bakr refused to give up Egypt. In the end Amr was able to seize control, and one of his followers murdered Ibn Abu Bakr. He encased him in a donkey skin and set him on fire. Amr again became the governor of Egypt and remained so until he died.[3]

The Umayyad dynasty was difficult for Egypt's Copts. Pressure was exerted on the Copts in order to extract as much money from them as possible.[4] It was a time of political power struggle, and the need for money to fund it was great. Compared to his first term, Amr's attitude toward Egypt had changed.

When he returned to Egypt, Amr demanded that the Copts give him their valuables. If they concealed or did not voluntarily surrender any portion of them, they would be killed. In a story told by Ibn Abd al-Hakam, an early Muslim historian, a Christian named Peter was rumored to have some valuables concealed from Amr. He denied any concealment and was put in prison. Peter's cellmates revealed that he had mentioned the name of a monk from Mount Sinai. Peter's signet ring was confiscated and Amr used it to forge a letter to the monk telling him to send Peter's possessions to him. When retrieved, the riches hidden beneath the stone slabs of a cistern amounted to 32 bushels of gold coins. Amr confiscated the money and beheaded Peter in front of his mosque.[5]

The ruler, Abd al-Aziz ben Marwan (685–705), imposed a dinar *jizyah* on each monk even though monks were originally excluded from paying the tax. Coptic bishops were no exception, and he imposed a yearly 2000 dinar *jizyah* on them. Some Copts had taken refuge in the monasteries to escape the *jizyah*, but now the monasteries no longer provided a safe haven. To ensure the flow of revenue, ben Marwan ordered a census to count the monks all over Egypt.[6] Since monks and bishops were being taxed, they had to work harder to get money or sell some of the riches of the church. Their spiritual lives and development may have suffered due to the need to pursue hard labor to pay their taxes. Less study, less scholarship, and less care were given to the spiritual lives of their congregations. Steadily decreasing assets negatively affected the Coptic community in more than just financial ways.

Moreover, taxation on monasteries and monks increased to the point that the church leadership attempted to bypass it by paying bribes. This practice of paying extortion money created and perpetuated a financial burden on the Church.[7] Abd al-Aziz ben Marwan tried to extort a large sum of money from the Coptic Patriarch John by putting him in prison. After the ransom sum was reduced, thus making it possible for the Coptic community to raise the money, the patriarch was released.[8]

In addition to the financial burden, monks as well as bishops were also mistreated. When Bishop Gamoul of Oseem could not pay a thousand dinar tax imposed on him by Obeidallah ben al-Hajab, responsible for the *kharaj* under caliph Hisham ben Abd al-Malik (724–743), the Bishop was hung by his arms naked and whipped in front of the people until he bled. Monks had to wear a steel ring on their left hands for identification; not abiding by this rule would be punished with amputation of a body part. Many monks were mutilated, had their eyes gouged out, were whipped or killed. In one incident, all the monks of the Nitria Valley monasteries were castrated.[9] Wearing a ring that bore the name of the monk and his monastery was a proof that the monk had paid the *jizyah*. The absence of a ring meant that he hadn't paid the poll-tax and could be punished.[10]

Abd al-Aziz ben Marwan decreed that all the crosses in the land of Egypt be broken and he wrote banners that read, "Muhammad is the prophet of God" ordering them to be put on the churches.[11] He also added banners that said, "Isa (Jesus) is a prophet and God did not have a son," and banned church services.[12]

The following ruler, Abd Allah ben Abd al-Malik (705–709), emulated Abd al-Aziz. When the Coptic patriarch went to greet him upon his arrival to Egypt, Abd Allah ben Abd al-Malik arrested him and held him until he paid three thousand dinars in ransom. He released him three days later when a church deacon convinced the ruler to take the patriarch on a tour to different towns in order to collect the large sum. Al-Kindi, an early Muslim philosopher, accused the ruler of encouraging bribery and filling his pockets with the *jizyah* money.[13]

In 706, Abd Allah ben Abd al-Malik decreed that the Arabic language be the official language of the bureaucracy; Arabs were suspicious of Copts because they didn't speak their language. As a result of this measure, many Copts were compelled to leave their jobs to be replaced by Arabs or by those who spoke Arabic, and they were forced to study Arabic if they wanted to go back to their jobs. Abd Allah ben Abd al-Malik's decree severely affected the use of the Coptic language and was significant in the process of Arabization of Egypt. Increasing the pressure on Copts, the Caliph Umar ben Abd al-Aziz (718–720) required that Muslims replace Christians in the bureaucracy. If Copts wanted to keep their jobs they had to convert to Islam; many Copts were forced to convert. The caliph's decree was also instrumental in the process of the Islamization of Egypt. He also invoked the *Covenant of Umar* with its restrictions destroying crosses and banning Christians and Jews from wearing normal clothes. Not only were crosses destroyed, the following caliph, Yazid ben Abd al-Malik (720–724), ordered the demolition of icons and statues from churches as well. Some Pharaonic heritage also fell victim to their anger.[14] Destroying such a heritage meant destroying the civilization and culture of the Egyptians.

Radical Islamists react violently to statues even if they are considered priceless or pieces of shared human history. ISIS illustrated this on February 26, 2015, in a museum in Mosul, Iraq by destroying irreplaceable ancient statues from the Assyrian era that dated back to the 7th century BC. "The Prophet ordered us to get rid of statues and relics, and his companions did the same when they conquered countries after him," an unidentified man said in the video showing ISIS men smashing the statues with sledgehammers and pushing them to the ground. The Afghan Taliban dynamited ancient Buddhas, which also had immeasurable cultural and historical value, in 2001.[15] In the present day, the Egyptian Salafists, ultra-conservative Islamists, advocate for the destruction of statues in Egypt. They label Egyptian civilization "rotten," publically calling for the destruction of the Sphinx and the Pyramids.[16]

After the surrender of Babylon, Arab behavior changed dramatically, and consequently, many Copts converted to Islam, to escape the *jizyah* and having suffered decades of daily humiliation and financial hardship.[17] With so many Copts converting and markedly decreasing the revenue of the state, the rulers began to tax monks, bishops and patriarchs. They also imposed taxes on animals and travel.[18] Copts tried to move from one area to another to avoid the hardship of severe taxation. To curtail movement, a new tax was imposed, forcing people to pay ten dinars for permission to move, to use the Nile or even to leave the country. Those not abiding by the rule would be crucified or have their hands or legs cut off. Due to the travel restrictions, people waited for over two months to get travel permits, which aggravated the economic situation of the Copts.[19] A widow was forced to pay her transportation tax twice when her son, who was carrying the permit, was attacked and killed by a crocodile.[20] During the time of Hefs ben Abd al-Waleed (742–745), some 24,000 Copts converted to Islam to escape the *jizyah*.[21]

The treatment of Copts led to political turmoil and protests in Lower Egypt, but they did not result in any major changes. To pacify the public, the caliph would change the ruler of an area and limit the taxation for a time to the *jizyah* only. In this way Copts would enjoy a brief respite until a new ruler came and imposed more taxation.[22]

Caliph Mu'awiya's own words regarding the Copts summarizes their treatment during the Umayyad dynasty. He said that he found three types of people in Egypt: One-third is human, one-third is quasi-human and one-third is not human. The first third refers to the Arab Muslims. The second third are the converts who support the Arabs. The final third refers to the Copts.[23] However, economic and internal problems led to the downfall of the Umayyad dynasty. Abbas, a descendant of an uncle of Muhammad, became the new caliph. The Abbasids defeated the Umayyad caliph Marwan II, but he was able to escape to Egypt.[24]

The Abbasid Dynasty, 750–868

The Abbasid army arrived in Egypt with the aim of taking Egypt from Marwan. Marwan flew to Upper Egypt in the hope of reorganizing and forming a stronger army to fight the Abbasids. Still seeking money at this critical time, Marwan and his soldiers robbed and destroyed Christian houses on their way. The Copts rebelled and refused to pay him the *kharaj*, so he destroyed some of their churches. In one incident, he demanded that the Copts give him 3,000 dinars, but they were only able to collect 2,000. So, Marwan turned one third of a church into a mosque for the unpaid thousand dinars. In the end, he was able to form an army and to come back to Cairo to fight the Abbasids.[25] But the Umayyads were defeated and the Abbasids beheaded Caliph Marwan and sent his head to Abbas.[26] Now Egypt would be ruled by the Abbasids, who transferred the capital of the caliphate from Damascus to Baghdad.

Initially, the Abbasids had good intentions for the Copts and promised them security once they had consolidated themselves. The Abbasids released the Coptic Patriarch Kha'il, who Marwan had imprisoned for his unsuccessful attempt to quell a Coptic uprising against the Umayyads. They also mitigated the tax and treated the Copts better than the Umayyads had.[27] But all too soon, history repeated itself. The Abbasids reneged on their promises and doubled taxes on the Copts.

The Abbasids were greatly concerned with strengthening their grip on their new dynasty and became very harsh in dealing with their opponents and in eliminating the Umayyads. They grew ungrateful towards those who had helped them in their fight to assume power, and executed them to eliminate a future threat to their dynasty. Even their general, Abu Moslem, who was credited for their success in their wars, was perceived as a threat and was murdered.²⁸ In an attempt to strengthen their power, the Abbasids frequently assigned and replaced governors to inhibit one governor from becoming too strong. This was detrimental to the Copts because the governors knew that they would be replaced soon; they took advantage, in order to enrich themselves before they were removed from office, by doubling the taxes on the Copts. They also mistreated them in the same manner as had the Umayyads.²⁹ This resulted in several revolts in the land.

The Copts revolted against Egypt's governor Yazid ibn Hatem (762–769) who harshly mistreated them and their Patriarch Mina.³⁰ Another revolt occurred during the reign of the governor Allaith ibn al-Fadl (799–803); the people of al-Hoof revolted because the ruler misrepresented the measurements when surveying the land. They marched to al-Fustat, where Allaith killed many of them. He arrested eighty of their leaders and then cut off their heads. He exhibited the heads to the people of al-Fustat in order to deter any further revolt.³¹

The major revolt that had a significant impact on the Copts and changed the demography of Egypt happened in Bashmur, in Lower Egypt. It was a real threat to the Abbasids, to the extent that in 831, Caliph Ma'mun came all the way from Baghdad to suppress it himself.³² Patriarch Yousab entreated the desperate people of Bashmur to abandon their plans of protest, knowing that they would be defeated by the caliph's army, which greatly outnumbered them.³³ Patriarch Dionysius of Antioch predicted the same outcome for the confrontation, and he, too, attempted to stop the revolt, to no avail.³⁴

The people of Bashmur did not listen to the advice of their Pope; the Abbasids had mistreated them to such a degree that Copts were interchangeable with cattle, chained to mill stones and whipped like animals, forced to move the heavy stones used to mill the wheat. They were so overburdened with taxes that some Copts sold their children to pay the *jizyah*. They felt that geography would aid them in their fight, believing the Abbasids would not be able to navigate the maze-like swamps to reach them, so they decided not to pay the *jizyah* and declared their revolt.³⁵

The result of the confrontation was lethal for the Copts; they had no military experience whatsoever and were routed. Ma'mun's army killed the men, took the women and children as slaves, took their money and destroyed their churches.³⁶ After crushing the revolt, Ma'mun ordered the departure of 3,000 Copts, who were sent to Baghdad. They were loaded on ships and most of them died en route. He also sent 500 Copts to Damascus to be sold as slaves. Al-Maqrizi said the Copts were totally humiliated and broken to the point that they could no longer revolt.³⁷

The revolt of Bashmur was the last Coptic revolt, and it was followed by a massive Coptic conversion to Islam. This has always been the case: after each Coptic revolt was crushed, many Copts converted to Islam.³⁸ For the first time, as a result of this great conversion, Coptic Christians were reduced to a minority in their own homeland.[39]

During the Bashmur revolt, mobs robbed Christians all over Egypt. They kidnapped a large number of Christians and sold them into slavery. Poor Copts accepted Islam to escape the deprivation they faced, and the number of Copts continued to diminish.[40] The ninth century saw a trend toward conversion as a result of economic hardship, social disability, legal inferiority, the lack of security and being faced with constant hostility.[41]

During the reign of Caliph al-Mutawakkil (847–861) the Copts suffered even more social disability. Caliph al-Mutawakkil decreed that *dhimmi*:

> be required to wear honey-colored hoods (taylasdn) and girdles (zunnar); to ride on saddles with wooden stirrups and with two balls attached to the rear; to attach two buttons to the conical caps (qalansuwa) of those who wear them and to wear caps of a different color from those worn by the Muslims; to attach two patches to their slaves' clothing, of a different color from that of the garment to which they are attached, one in front on the chest, the other at the back, each patch four fingers in length, and both of them honey-colored. Those of them who wear turbans were to wear honey-colored turbans. If their women went out and appeared in public, they were only to appear with honey-colored head scarves. He gave orders that their slaves were to wear girdles, and he forbade them to wear belts (mintaqa). He gave orders to destroy their churches which were newly built and to take the tenth part of their houses. If the place was large enough, it was to be made into a mosque; if it was not suitable for a mosque, it was to be made an open space. He ordered that wooden images of devils should be nailed to the doors of their houses to distinguish them from the houses of the Muslims. He forbade their employment in government offices and on official business where they would have authority over the Muslims. He forbade that their children attend Muslim schools or that any Muslim should teach them. He forbade the display of crosses on their Palm Sundays and Jewish rites in the streets. He ordered that their graves be made level with the ground so that they should not resemble the graves of the Muslims.[42]

Al-Mutawakkil's decree leveling the graves of *dhimmis* with the ground was to strip even dead *dhimmis* of any ostensible sign indicating honor or respect. *Dhimmis'* cemeteries were considered a part of the realm of hell; therefore, they were not respected and were open to acts of profanity and destruction.[43]

As a result of al-Mutawakkil's decree, the Abbasids made good use of the valuables taken from the churches that were destroyed. Marble pillars and stones taken from the churches that they destroyed were sent to Baghdad to be used in the palaces of the caliphs.[44] Whereas, in 785, Egypt's ruler Ali ibn Soliman had accepted fifty thousand dinars from Copts to entice him to change his plan of demolishing some churches in Egypt, al-Mutawakkil as a caliph, would not.[45]

Social disability combined with the firing of Copts from the bureaucracy during al-Mutawakkil's reign led to another wave of conversion. The Copts could no longer hold up their heads and bear the humiliation heaped on them. Those who did not convert to Islam were unable to raise their voices in prayer, lest they be heard and attacked. Once again, more conversion meant more pressure on the remaining Copts, as the burden of taxation became greater to compensate for the diminishing funds. However, respite came with the murder of al-Mutawakkil at the hands of his son Muntasir, who assumed power for one year.

When al-Musta'in (862–866) became caliph he gave the Copts back some of their churches and allowed them to renovate them. So, the Copts began, once again, to worship publically.[46] Periodically, one caliph acknowledged the injustices of another and tried to restore some of the property destroyed, but he could not restore the people who were lost by their conversion. These people with their culture and heritage were irretrievably lost. Once they converted to Islam, they could not go back to Christianity, as this is punishable by death, according to *sharia*.

This period of respite was interrupted by the appointment of Ahmad ibn al-Mudabbir in 866, when he took charge of the taxes in Egypt. He doubled the *jizyah* on the Copts. When the Coptic patriarch was unable to pay the money, he was whipped two hundred lashes in front of his church and people, similar to the incident of Bishop Gamoul of Oseem during the Umayyads' rule. Some Copts travelled to Baghdad to complain to Caliph Mu'taz (866–869) who agreed to lift up the *jizyah* from the monks and to lower it for the rest of the Copts in accordance with Amr's treaty.[47] He also ordered that lands, churches, monasteries and stolen artifacts should be returned to the Copts.[48] With this, the Copts won another period of respite.

However, the power of the Abbasids had begun to wane during the time of Caliph Mu'tasim (833–842). He had appointed Turkish slaves to work as personal bodyguards and eventually they were put in command. Within a short period of time, these Turkish guards became so strong that they were able to appoint and depose caliphs as they wished.[49] Their influence and power led to the emergence of the short-lived Tulunid dynasty in Egypt.

The Tulunid Dynasty, 868–905

Egypt's governors had dreamed of ruling Egypt independently, away from the central authority, but only Ahmad Ibn Tulun was successful in achieving this dream of separating Egypt from the Abbasid rule.[50] Thus, for the first time since the Arab conquest, Egypt became autonomous. Ibn Tulun established a short-lived dynasty that ruled Egypt from within.[51]

In his strategy to combat the animosity of the caliph, Ibn Tulun strived to gain the support of the whole population, including the Copts. Thus, under the Tulunids, Christians were not generally mistreated.[52] Ibn Tulun granted the Copts freedom to practice all their religious ceremonies, build churches and monasteries, and undertake commercial businesses without restriction.[53] Most importantly, he reduced the *kharaj* and hired Copts to positions in the bureaucracy overseeing agricultural activities, their area of expertise, such as irrigation, canals, and bridges to facilitate the life of farmers. During his time Egypt witnessed great economic prosperity.[54]

Ibn Tulun's use of the Copts' expertise is evident in one of the most outstanding Islamic monuments in Egypt: the mosque of Ibn Tulun, which was designed by a Coptic engineer, Ibn Katib al-Firghani. Ibn Tulun was very pleased with the engineer's work and rewarded him with 10, 000 dinars. The Ibn Tulun mosque is one of the oldest and most famous existing mosques in Egypt.[55] This Coptic engineer devised the use of the pointed arch about 200 years before similar techniques appeared in Gothic architecture in Europe. He also built the nilometer—used to gauge the level of the annual flood of the Nile—at the south end of Rhoda Island in Cairo; it still stands to this day.[56]

Despite the fact that he was tolerant of Copts and did not impose new taxes on them, Ibn Tulun still extracted as much money as he could from their patriarch. Acting on a rumor that the Coptic Patriarch Kha'il had riches and treasures hidden away, Ibn Tulun ordered the Patriarch to surrender these treasures to him. Despite the Patriarch's protests that these treasures did not exist, Ibn Tulun imprisoned him for a full year. The Patriarch was released only after he agreed to pay a ransom of 20,000 dinars in two installments. He was able to gather the first installment through donations from the Coptic congregation and by selling some churches in Alexandria and Cairo. But, because he could not pay the second installment, he was put back in prison and stayed there until Ibn Tulun died.[57] One of the churches the Patriarch sold was to the Jewish community and was turned into a synagogue, and still exists in the Coptic Cairo area, close to the famous Hanging Church.[58]

Ibn Tulun considered the Coptic Patriarch a dangerous enemy. Thus, he wanted to keep him poor by extracting money from him at any opportunity. The fact that the Coptic Patriarch was hesitant in his endorsement of Ibn Tulun's rule in the beginning contributed to this animosity. The Coptic Patriarch was late to support Ibn Tulun because he knew that the Abbasid's caliph didn't accept Ibn Tulun as the legitimate governor of Egypt; the Patriarch didn't want to get caught in the struggle between them. Another reason for the Patriarch's reticence could be attributed to the favoritism Ibn Tulun showed for the Melkites over the Copts. In a Coptic manuscript from this time, it states that Ibn Tulun favored the Turks over the Arabs and preferred the Melkites over the Copts. He habitually stayed at a Melkite monastery known as Dair al-Quaseer. He used one of the cells there for contemplation. This strengthened his ties with the monks and, when they complained of the taxes, he lessened their burden and gave them special privileges.[59] Ibn Tulun's tolerance was reflected in the fact that churches were not destroyed during his tenure, yet the Copts lost some of their churches when Patriarch Kha'il sold them to pay for his ransom.

Ibn Tulun died in 884 and his son Khumarawayh succeeded him, ruling until 895.[60] Khumarawayh released Patriarch Kha'il from prison, and he waived his financial obligation. Like his father, he maintained a good relationship with the monks of the Dair al-Quaseer monastery. He visited it periodically and stayed in a special room he built for himself.[61] And, because of the favoritism shown by Ibn Tulun and Khumarawayh to the Melkite church, the Chalcedonians were able to appoint a Melkite Patriarch in Alexandria, after 200 years of absence.[62]

Khumarawayh was assassinated through a *harem* (women's quarters) conspiracy in Baghdad during a visit in 895.[63] Khumarawayh's successor was a young boy unable to stand up to the Abbasids, who wanted to retake Egypt. they succeeded in doing so in 905. With the downfall of the Tulinids, Egypt became, once again, a subject province of the Abbasids. In 935, Muhammad ibn Tughj, the son of Ibn Tulun's Turkish lieutenant, became the governor of Egypt. The caliph gave him the title "Ikhshid," and he was given autonomy in Egypt, resulting in a new dynasty called the Ikhshidid.[64]

The Ikhshidid Dynasty, 935–969

Like the Tulinids, the Ikhshidids were tolerant of the Copts, and they did not invoke the laws that restricted the *dhimmis*. Muhammad al-Ikhshidi officially celebrated Epiphany with Christians, an unprecedented occurrence for a ruler. Epiphany was the most festive night in all of Egypt: the streets remained open, people celebrated with food and music and swam in the Nile to gain healing and protection from disease. But, Muhammad al-Ikhshidi extracted a great quantity of money from the Copts to meet the payroll for his soldiers. This forced the Copts to sell even more of their church property.[65]

Some incidents of intolerance occurred under the Ikhshidids, but they came from the populace rather than from the leadership. The populace objected to the renovation of churches, and when the Byzantines celebrated a victory against the Muslims at the Syrian borders, the populace found this a pretext to attack and vandalize churches in Egypt. They associated Copts, as Christians, with the Christian Byzantines.[66]

Egypt's governor, Cafour the Ikhshidid, was also tolerant of the Copts, and one of his viziers was a Copt. Cafour allowed Copts to have religious services on the decks of boats in the shipyards, where Christians constituted the majority of the workers.[67] This period of respite, however, was disturbed by a famine, which resulted in great hardship and death. Many poor Copts died, further decreasing their already diminishing numbers.[68]

The son of Cafour, who assumed power after his father's death, was only eleven years old. This, and the fact that the Abbasids were so weakened, gave the Fatimids the opportunity to conquer Egypt in the year 969.[69] Thus, another dynasty would begin in Egypt.

The Fatimid Dynasty, 969–1171

The Fatimids were the descendants of Abu Muhammad Obeidallah, the grandson of the Prophet Muhammad's daughter Fatima. In 909, Obeidallah proclaimed himself to be the *Mahdi*, or Messiah. He was denounced by the caliph in Baghdad but was able to become the caliph in Tunis, where he became the head of the Isma'ili sect, a Shiite rival to Sunni Islam in Baghdad. He was able to establish a caliphate from Morocco in the West to Egypt in the East, and, in 969, Egypt was conquered by the Fatimids.[70]

The Fatimid Caliph al-Mu'izz came to reside in Egypt in 973. The Fatimids wanted Cairo to be a center of culture, like Baghdad was for the Abbasids, so they established al-Azhar mosque and made it the center of Shiite culture.[71] With the construction of al-Azhar the Copts encountered one of their earliest problems with the Fatimids, as many of the mosque's columns were taken from Coptic churches.[72]

The policy of the Fatimids towards the Copts fluctuated between tolerance and persecution. They allowed them to flourish, yet they persecuted them. At the beginning, the Fatimids, as Shiite Muslims, were unable to get the full support of the Sunni Muslim community in Egypt. Hence, al-Mu'izz treated the *dhimmis* well in order to garner their support.[73] A practical reason for the better treatment was that the Copts were efficient in financial matters, so al-Mu'izz hired them in the bureaucracy. Whether for political or practical reasons, the better treatment caused problems to erupt among the populace when they noticed that he had set aside religious prejudice by hiring Copts in the government.[74]

To appease and gain the support of the populace, al-Mu'izz began to demonstrate animosity toward the Christians. He started by annulling the Ikhshidids' tradition of attending Christian ceremonies. He banned Christians from riding boats in the Nile during Epiphany and banned them from any appearance of religious festivities.[75] Yet, one of his main aides was a Christian, Quzman ibn Mina, surnamed abu al-Yumn.[76] This reveals a pattern prevalent throughout the years: In daily life Copts were demeaned and disenfranchised, but when they served a purpose, their skills were utilized.

Coptic history reveals that al-Mu'izz's life changed remarkably after experiencing an incredible incident. His contemporary Sawirus (Severus) ibn al-Muqaffa, Bishop of al-Ashmunin, relates this incident in the widely known *The History of the Patriarchs*. In 978, one of al-Mu'izz's aides, Ya'qub ben Killis, a Jewish convert to Islam, told al-Mu'izz that the Christians believed that those who have faith could move a mountain, referring to the verse of the Gospel of Matthew (17:20): "If you have faith as a mustard seed, you will say to this mountain, Move from here to there, and it will move; and nothing will be impossible for you." Seeking a justification for further persecution, ben Killis suggested that this belief be put to the test. So, al Mu'izz summoned Patriarch Abraham and demanded to see this miracle or, he threatened, the Copts would be killed. With trepidation the Patriarch asked the Copts to fast for three days. The Virgin Mary interceded and revealed that a poor devout shoemaker named Simon would the lead the Copts in prayer. The miracle was performed on Moqattam Mountain in Cairo. Al-Mu'izz was so affected by the miracle that he praised God and declared the Christian faith to be a true faith.[77]

The account goes on to say that after witnessing the miracle, al-Mu'izz told the Patriarch that he would grant him any request. So, the Patriarch asked that the Church of St. Macarius and the Hanging Church be rebuilt. When the news of the rebuilding of the two churches spread, a significant portion of the populace strongly objected to the decision. A sheikh came and threw himself into the hole being dug for the foundation of the St. Macarius Church, proclaiming that they would only build the church over his dead body. Al-Mu'izz ordered workers to proceed with the work, but Patriarch Abraham interceded, asking al-Mu'izz to spare the sheikh's life.[78] Another incident demonstrating al-Mu'izz's change in his attitude toward the Christians is his decision to allow Christians who were forced converts to Islam to return to Christianity and his willingness not to punish a Muslim who converted to Christianity.[79]

Some people would call the story of the miracle a fantasy, others believe it is possible; Muslims don't have any reference to it, while Copts believe it happened. Whether people interpret the verse of Matthew (17:20) literally is not the question, nor is it relevant whether or not people believe in miracles; the story is mentioned because it is an important part of Coptic history and identity.

Al-Mu'izz's heir and son al-Aziz (976–996) was also very tolerant of Christians. Al-Aziz was sympathetic toward Christians and allowed churches to be built and rebuilt in exchange for gifts of money. He tried to demolish the social differences between Muslims and *dhimmis* and he called for equality between both of them. He married a Malekite Christian and had a daughter who was sympathetic to the Christians.[80] In his reign he appointed two of his wife's brothers as Malekite Patriarchs. The first was Aristis, who became a Patriarch over Jerusalem and the other, Arsenius, was appointed Patriarch over Cairo.[81]

Additionally, al-Aziz hired a lot of Christians in the bureaucracy and, as happened before, this antagonized the populace. Al-Aziz had to fire some of the Coptic employees in order to pacify the angry people; however, he was compelled to rehire them for their expertise. This decision was strengthened by requests he received from his wife and daughter to reinstate them. During the time of al-Aziz, Patriarch Abraham, who al-Aziz greatly respected, moved the See of the Coptic Patriarch from Alexandria to Cairo, the new capital. Al-Aziz also allowed the Patriarch to fix destroyed churches without first obtaining his permission.[82] More than a thousand years after al-Aziz's reign, churches still could not be fixed without obtaining permission from the Egyptian authorities. Something as minor as fixing a leaking toilet required permission from the government. In this respect al-Aziz was even more sympathetic than any of Egypt's leaders of the 21st century, excluding President el-Sisi, who approved a law to regulate the building of churches.

The Copts enjoyed a period of respite under al-Aziz, but his son al-Hakim (996–1020) is known to be one of the most severe caliphs in his persecution of the Copts and in his imposition of restrictions on their liberties. He killed thousands of people, beginning with his own aides and viziers.[83] In 997, al-Hakim beheaded his Christian vizier, Isa ibn Nasturus, who had begun his service under al-Aziz. Nasturus's position was assumed by another Christian, Fahd Ibn Ibrahim, who was also killed by al-Hakim. Soon after Ibrahim's brother, Abu al-Ghalib, who was a head of a *diwan*, faced the same fate. In 1018, another of ibn Nasturus's sons, Said, was fired from his vizier position and later executed. Even al-Hakim's uncle, Patriarch Arsenius, became one of his victims, and he incarcerated Aristis, his other uncle.[84] Al-Hakim was contradictory in that he would hire Copts for highly responsible positions, yet he would then kill them at some point in their tenure.

In one of the stories, al-Hakim asked ten Coptic scribes to convert to Islam. One, Abu Najah al-Kabir, refused to convert, so he was condemned to be whipped, and given one thousand lashes. He was dead well before the lashes were completed, but al-Hakim insisted that the punishment be carried out in full even on his dead body. Some of the rest of the ten scribes died as a result of torture while others, unable to bear the pain, converted.[85]

Al-Hakim enforced dress restrictions on the Copts and ordered the removal of cross tattoos from their hands. He ordered Christians to wear heavy crosses around their necks of a cubit and a half in length and killed all the swine in Egypt.[86] He imprisoned Patriarch Zacharias because of a slanderous rumor that he had a lot of money, and the Patriarch was given the choice to convert to Islam, be burned, or thrown to the lions. A man called Madi went to al-Hakim to petition the release of a Christian friend imprisoned with the Patriarch. The friend asked Madi to intercede with al-Hakim to release the Patriarch as well. To ensure the Patriarch's release, Madi asked al-Hakim to release everybody in the prison.[87] The Patriarch sought refuge in the monasteries of Wadi al-Natrun for nine years and churches were shut for three years during that period.[88]

When al-Hakim learned that Christians held processions around the Church of the Holy Sepulcher in Jerusalem on Palm Sunday and Easter, he ordered that the church be leveled to the ground. The news of this destruction of the holy site was received with great sadness not only in the East but also in the Western world. This act is said to be one of the reasons for the Crusades.[89]

In 1009, al-Hakim issued an order to cancel all Christian celebrations in Egypt and seized Church endowments to benefit the treasury. In 1013, he ordered that all churches and monasteries be destroyed, and leveled to the ground throughout Egypt. The populace implemented his ruling and went as far as desecrating Coptic graves and using the bones for fuel to heat the water in the baths.[90] This practice of destroying graves was brought to the world's attention in January 2016 when ISIS leveled and desecrated 2,000 graves in areas under their control.[91]

Al-Maqrizi said that after al-Hakim razed the churches, he allowed people to pilfer their assets and build mosques on the same sites. Al-Hakim also allowed the Muslim call to prayer at the Church of Abba Shenouda in Old Cairo.[92] Executing the call to prayer from a church, as occurred during al-Hakim's rule, has happened recently after the January Revolution, on March 5, 2011. After the mobs in the village of Sul in Itfeh, Giza province, burned down al-Shahidain (Two Martyrs) Coptic Church, they initiated a call to the prayer from the site of the church.[93] The significance of issuing the call to prayer from a church is that the building has been claimed as a mosque and, henceforth, can be used as such. The act of issuing the call to prayer converts the church into a mosque.

While burning the Church of al-Shahidain, the mobs shouted, "*Allah Akbar*" and claimed that the church would only be rebuilt over their dead bodies.[94] This is similar to what happened during the time of al-Mu'izz when the sheikh threw himself into the foundation of the St. Macarius Church, claiming it would be built over his dead body.

Al-Hakim was unpredictable in his persecution: a Jewish street would be closed and blocked until all its people were killed. He entombed women alive in public baths.[95] Al-Hakim's order to ban the use of the Coptic language in houses and public places almost killed the Coptic language and culture.

The punishment was severe: a person violating this ban would have his tongue cut off. The extremity of this measure can be understood when we realize that a mother could no longer communicate with her children in her first language. Not only did this act severely impact the Copts during the reign of al-Hakim, but he set a precedent that following rulers upheld.[96] By the fourteenth century the Coptic language had died out as a literary language. A few centuries later it disappeared as a spoken language; however, part of it is still used today, with Arabic, in the church liturgy, as a symbol of identity and a remnant of the old culture.[97]

During al-Hakim's tenure, many Copts converted to Islam, especially when faced with his ultimatum: death or renunciation of their Christian faith. Many others immigrated to Byzantine-controlled areas.[98] Freedom of worship promised by Amr when he conquered Egypt was ignored by al-Hakim and his successors—so much so that, over the centuries, some Copts fled to the lands of the Chalcedonians, their first persecutors, to escape the extreme persecution they faced in Egypt.

How did the Coptic Church survive? When al-Hakim annulled church services the Copts bribed the provincial rulers to have religious services and take communion inside their houses.[99] They concealed their faith and worshiped in secret in private places during his reign.[100] This was an old practice as the Copts used to worship secretly in catacombs during the early centuries of persecution.

Another factor in the survival of the Coptic Church was, ironically, al-Hakim himself. Puzzlingly, after years of persecution against the Copts, at the end of his days, al-Hakim decided to reverse his stance on the Christian people. He wrote a letter to grant them permission to resume worship and to begin rebuilding their once-destroyed churches and monasteries.[101] Upon learning that al-Hakim had changed in his outlook, a monk called Poemen, who with other Christians had been forced to convert to Islam, asked al-Hakim to allow them to go back to their Christian faith. Although it was hard to believe, they were allowed to do so. Al-Hakim befriended this monk and allowed him to build a monastery, which still exists in Cairo until this day; it is called Barsoum al-Erian, and is located in Helwan, south of Cairo. Most surprisingly is that al-Hakim became a frequent visitor to the monastery and even ate with the monks there. When they asked him to allow their patriarch to meet with him he agreed to their request and decreed that the patriarch be permitted to return to his See, after nine years of absence.[102]

So, what happened to cause al-Hakim to become tolerant of Christians? Following the Ismailite doctrine, he pronounced himself the incarnated Allah and asked his followers to worship him. His followers believe he survived in divine form and they are waiting for his return. The death of al-Hakim was an event shrouded in ambiguity and mystery. He suddenly vanished in 1021.[103]

Before he disappeared, he habitually went out to the Moqattam Mountain, where he claimed God spoke to him the same way He spoke to Moses.[104] Al-Hakim had followers who became his disciples, and considered him the Christ.[105]

Al-Hakim was succeeded by his son Caliph al-Zahir (1021–1035), who was sympathetic to the Copts and allowed them to rebuild destroyed churches and worship. He also permitted Copts who were forcibly converted to Islam to return to Christianity and pledged to rebuild the Church of the Holy Sepulcher in Jerusalem. And, the Copts enjoyed another temporary period of respite.[106]

However, Egypt passed through a difficult time during the reign of Caliph al-Mustansir (1035–1094). A civil war erupted between al-Mustansir's Sudanese troops, which were favored by his Sudanese mother, and troops from Turkey, supported by the Berbers from Northwest Africa. The Berbers terrorized the Coptic monasteries and churches. Between 1066 and 1067, they killed 63 monks in the area of al-Ashmunin in Upper Egypt.[107] In this time of turmoil, al-Mustansir sought the help of the commander in chief of Acre and the governor of Damascus, Badr al-Jamali, to help him quell the rebels. Badr al-Jamali was an Armenian Christian convert to Islam and his time marked the rise of Christians into high positions in the government. Badr came to Egypt in 1073 with an army of thousands of Armenian Christians and their families. With such an army, he was able to be the de facto ruler of Egypt. They formed such a great community that the Armenian patriarch came to Egypt and was well received by Badr. Badr went as far as forming a synod to settle differences between Christians of Egypt, Nubia and Abyssinia. He appointed Christian officials and built churches.[108]

But with the rule of al-Emir (1101–1130), Christians were fired from the bureaucracy and humiliated again under the *dhimma* status. The fate of Abu Najah is indicative of this shift. He was the chief tax collector and counselor to the caliph, but he was resented by populace to the extent that al-Emir allowed the governor of al-Fustat to execute him in 1129. He was nailed to a post, thrown into the Nile, and stones and garbage were hurled at him.[109] When Copts such as Abu Najah advanced themselves and were in the favor of the caliph, they earned the jealousy and resentment of the populace. To keep peace the caliph always conceded to the demands of the mob,[110] and thus the cycle of abuse was perpetuated.

The situation changed after the death of al-Emir. Al-Hafiz became the caliph (1130–1149) and hired an Armenian Christian, Bahram, as a vizier. Bahram was a military commander who was originally summoned by the caliph's son Hasan to help him strengthen his position during his fight with his brother. Bahram arrived only to find that the caliph had poisoned Hasan. Bahram promoted the interests of the Armenians and Christians in general.

He called some thirty thousand Armenians to immigrate to Egypt, built churches, and hired a lot of Christians in the bureaucracy—all of which caused the populace to see Bahram as a great threat to the community.[111]

Considering the outsized influence of Bahram, the reaction of the community was not slow in coming. The biggest threat came from Ridwan b. al-Walakhshi, a militant angry at the increasing influence of Christians. With support from the community, Ridwan formed an army of Bedouins and other troops and declared war against Bahram. Ridwan forced Bahram to flee to Qus, in Upper Egypt, where his brother was residing. Ridwan followed him, and an agreement was reached whereby Bahram would retire to a monastery close to Akhmim, in Upper Egypt, and most of his troops would return to their homeland. Once Bahram left Cairo, Caliph al-Hafiz made Ridwan his new vizier.[112]

The first thing Ridwan did was to purge the Christians from the bureaucracy. For this purpose he created *diwan al-jihad*, a type of inquisition office which investigated all ministries. He also reverted back to the dress restrictions on Christians and Jews and doubled their poll-tax. However, the caliph became alarmed at Ridwan's increasing power and imprisoned him.[113]

Al-Hafiz died and was followed by his son al-Zafir (1149–1154). Al-Zafir's vizier, Ibn al-Sallar, also imposed dress restrictions on Christians and extracted even more money from them. Ibn al-Sallar was assassinated in 1153 and a few months later the caliph himself was murdered. From that time until the end of the Fatimid era in 1171, Egypt was ruled by two child caliphs: al-Fa'iz and al-Adid.[114] Caliph al-Adid's vizier Shawar burned the old city of al-Fustat in 1168, fearing that the Crusader King Amalric of Jerusalem would use it as a military base. The fire lasted for fifty-four days and was disastrous for the Copts, since they constituted the majority of the city's population. This is but one example of the problems the Copts faced as a byproduct of the Crusades.[115]

In general, the Fatimid rule after al-Hakim was marked by two major characteristics. There was an undying popular hostility toward the Copts from the lower classes, who didn't like the power the Christians had gained in finance and tax issues. The second, was the state's continuous need for money. When the caliphs couldn't stop hostile sentiments, they would pacify the public by firing Copts from the bureaucracy. But once again they would rehire them because they realized their government couldn't run efficiently without the unpopular Copts. On the other hand, the personal tolerance of the Fatimid caliphs didn't mean that they decreased their demands for money from their Coptic subjects. They increased taxes on them during the war of the Franks in Syria because they needed more funds. The whole nation had to pay the extra burden, and the Copts were the first to pay. After the death of Pope Macarius II in 1128, the Copts didn't have a patriarch for more than two years because they were too poor to afford the 3,000 to 6,000 dinars needed for the state to issue a decree to nominate the new patriarch.[116]

The Fatimid dynasty began to weaken during the rule of caliph al-Adid: there was much instability in Egypt. There were many moves and countermoves to keep control of the land, including one deal between Amalric and Shawar to fend off Shirguh, the uncle of the famous Salah al-Din, Saladin. The result of these struggles was the downfall of the Fatimid dynasty in Egypt, and the rise of the Ayyubid dynasty, with Saladin victorious.[117]

The Ayyubid Dynasty, 1171–1250

Two major developments occurred under the Ayyubid dynasty, increasing militancy, undermining the Coptic community and putting the Copts under increasing pressure: the intensification in the establishment of *madrasas* (religious institutions) and the Crusades.

The *madrasas* were designed to teach Sunni Islam and to combat the Fatimid Shiites. Al-Azhar mosque, originally established as a university for the study of Shiite Islam, was turned into a Sunni university. A large number of *madrasas* were created, allowing them to play a significant role in the social, religious and political development of Egypt.[118] The results of the *madrasas* were quickly felt as Shiism rapidly faded, and it became very difficult to find Shiite Muslims outside noble families. The Shiites became the smallest minority in Egypt, far smaller than the Christian minority. The Ayyubids succeeded in eradicating Shiism from Egypt and in returning Egypt to the Sunni fold. But, the impact of madrasas wasn't only felt by the Shiites. As they rapidly decreased, the attention of these *madrasas* was no longer directed at heterodoxy, but rather at the larger Christian community, whose influence attracted the resentment and concern of the populace. The *madrasas* trained a cadre of officials who found their way into the most influential positions in the bureaucracy. These officials would secure their interests not just against Shiite Muslims, but against Christians, as well. The *madrasas* trained a large number of students who competed with Copts for a limited number of jobs in the bureaucracy. It became easier for the elite to dismiss Copts, which again put a lot of pressure on them to convert to Islam in order to keep their jobs. The existence of *madrasa* graduates in the government also made the government more stringent, at the expense of Copts in general. The *madrasas* raised the consciousness of its graduates and the community and were also credited with playing a major role in the Islamization of Egypt.[119]

In addition to their competition with Copts in government posts, the graduates of *madrasas* filled positions within the Muslim religious community.

They were *katib* (clerks), *imam* (prayer leaders), *mufti* (granters of legal opinion), *qadi* (judges), *na'ib qadi* (substitute judges), *qadi al-qudat* (chief judges) and *nazir waqf* (overseers of endowment). The general term used to refer to such graduates is *ulama* and they have played an important role in the community and in influencing the public against the Copts, especially those serving in the government. By the end of the Ayyubid dynasty, there were more than fifty *madrasas*, and one would surmise that there were few Muslim officials who hadn't attended one.[120]

Another significant function of the *madrasa* was that political leaders in Egypt used them to gain power. The first of such leaders was Ridwan, who acknowledged the political importance of the *madrasas* and, thus, established one within a year of assuming the post of vizier. In this manner he increased his patronage over the community, and the students who studied at his *madrasa* were obliged to him for their education, becoming potentially loyal candidates for jobs in his government. Through this process he could replace the Christians in the bureaucracy and easily govern the country. Ibn al-Sallar, who followed, pursued the same strategy and established his own *madrasa*. Saladin gained support in his struggle against Shawar from Ridwan's *madrasa*, where he was a student with his son. Then, Saladin (1138-1193) himself created two *madrasas* in al-Fustat. When Saladin seized Jerusalem from the Franks in 1187, he ordered the construction of a *madrasa* in the Church of St. Anne, which stood on the site where the Virgin Mary was born.[121]

The second major development that occurred under the Ayyubid dynasty was the Crusades. During that time Coptic Christians were treated with suspicion because they shared the same religion as the enemy. Did the rulers know of *monophysitism* and *dyophysitism*? To them both fell into the same category of the "other": Christians. The Crusaders came under the banner of the cross, which made the populace antagonistic towards Coptic Christians, whom they already called "worshipers of the cross." Thus, a new chapter of suffering started for the Copts. One must also remember that the Western Christians saw Eastern Christians as schismatic heretics.[122] Hence, the Copts had friends in no quarter—the Muslims wrongly allied them with the Crusaders and the Crusaders wrongly accused them of being heretical.

The rulers carefully watched the Christians, and the governors increased the taxes on them yet again. Initially, Saladin's behavior was not much different than his predecessors: he fired Christians from the bureaucracy, imposed dress restrictions, and banned them from riding horses. Additionally, he imposed such excessive fines on them that they had to sell their assets to be able to pay them. Such measures resulted in more conversions of Copts to Islam. The Ayyubids razed the Cathedral of St. Mark on the shore of Alexandria, fearing that it was a potential fort for the Crusaders in the war.

The Copts tried to pay two thousand dinars to stop the destruction, but to no avail. Moreover, Saladin sent troops to Nubian Upper Egypt to weaken the strong elements of Coptic Christianity there. His troops destroyed the monastery of St. Simon near Aswan in 1173 and arrested the Coptic bishop along with a large number of Copts. They were all put into prison and later were sold as slaves.[123]

However, Saladin's treatment of the Copts didn't last for very long and he rescinded his anti–Christian policies, changing the situation of the Copts remarkably. The Copts attributed this better treatment to the prayers of the Coptic Pope Mark and their own prayers. But the worldly explanation was that Saladin realized he needed the expertise of the Copts in his bureaucracy during the wars. And, most importantly, he realized that the Copts did not support the Crusaders.[124] On the other side of the equation, the Crusaders' hostility towards the Copts was evident in the act of banning of them from their yearly pilgrimage to the Holy Sepulcher.[125] And, the Crusaders expelled the Eastern Christians from their church in Jerusalem when they gained control of it.[126]

In 1187, Saladin's final victory over the Crusaders in Jerusalem shifted the Ayyubid sentiment towards Copts. As a result, Saladin gave the Copts a monastery adjacent to the Church of the Holy Sepulcher known as *Dier al-Sultan,* or monastery of the Sultan (Saladin), to reward their non-cooperation with the Crusaders. Copts who had been fired were returned to the bureaucracy and he hired a Copt, Safie al-Dawla, as his private secretary.[127] It is worth mentioning that the Saladin Citadel in Cairo was built by two Coptic engineers, Abu Mansour and Abu Mashkour.[128]

After the death of Saladin, Egypt faced two more Crusader campaigns. The arrival of Louis IX, King of France, to surround the city of Damietta raised popular suspicions again, resulting in acts of violence against, and widespread murders of, Copts. From its side, the government extracted additional taxes from the Copts in order to support a wartime economy.[129]

The relationship between the Copts and the Ayyubids was generally shaped by the wars of the Crusades. When al-Malik al-Kamil (1218–1238) realized that the Copts didn't support the Crusaders he treated them with decency.[130] He visited St. Macarius monastery, and was generous and sympathetic with the monks. When the monks complained of not having a Pope, al-Kamil offered them the needed permission to elect one with no fee.[131]

Towards the end of the Ayyubid dynasty, the Mamluks, or slaves who were brought to Egypt by Sultan Nedjmeddin, did well in the war against the Crusaders.[132] They originally constituted about twelve thousand Caucasian slaves; some of them were Circassian and others were Turkish.[133] Their number and fierce fighting allowed them to gain enough power to end the Ayyubid dynasty and start their own.

The Mamluk Dynasty, 1250–1517

The Mamluk period was characterized by conspiracies and turmoil, which led to a sense of diminishing security resulting in failure in the economic sphere.[134] In this atmosphere, the Copts suffered greatly. Coptic suffering under the Mamluks was especially felt through the restrictions on their employment in the bureaucracy and excessive violence against them from the populace.[135]

Coptic expertise in finance and taxes was the only thing that the Mamluks valued in the Copts and it allowed them to retain important positions in the bureaucracy. But the populace could not accept Christians exercising power over Muslims and they expressed their anger violently.[136] In response to public pressure, the Mamluks fired the Copts from their positions in the bureaucracy. But these terminations didn't last long, though the rehiring of Copts was not out of respect or appreciation but rather out of necessity.[137] Hence, a part of the explanation for how the Copts survived was that they found a niche in society, however shaky and insecure, and they made themselves valuable. Despite the ebb and flow of discrimination, they clung to the flimsy handhold they had found and did not succumb completely to the waves of oppression.

The Copts enjoyed a status, albeit limited, in the bureaucracy of the Mamluk government from 1293 to 1354. This status, however, did not stop massive forced conversions to Islam. This wasn't so much because the Mamluks were advocating conversion, but rather due to violent attacks by the populace. These attacks disturbed the social and the political balance of Egypt, so to regain stability, the Mamluks invoked the *Covenant of Umar* and restricted the employment of Copts in the bureaucracy. The accumulated pressure resulted in such a widespread conversion of Copts that, by the middle of the fourteenth century, they had become a very small minority in Egypt.[138]

Pressure on Copts also came from the continued anti–Christian sentiment that resulted from the Crusades. The Mamluks forced the Coptic Christians to pay the price of fighting the Crusades, as had previous rulers. They squeezed money out of them without fear of protest, as Copts were now far fewer in number.[139] The Crusades only helped to strengthen the Mamluks' hatred of the indispensable Copts because each time the Mamluks fired them, they were faced with the complete paralysis of the state apparatus. They had no choice but to resort to rehiring the only segment of Egyptian community capable of fixing the deteriorating situation, which fostered further resentment.[140] When Sultan Aybak (1250–1257) found his treasury empty due to the wars he had waged, he did not hesitate to hire Sharaf al-Din Abu Said, a Coptic Christian, to allocate more money for his treasury.[141] Yet when the

Mamluks hired Copts, they invariably faced pressure from the populace to fire them. It was an endless cycle.

Al-Maqrizi's story of Ain al-Ghazal, during the time of Sultan al-Ashraf Khalil, in 1290, is illustrative. Al-Ghazal attempted to collect a debt owed to his employer, an *emir*. When the debtor refused, al-Ghazal became adamant. Bystanders didn't appreciate a Copt having authority over a Muslim, even to collect a debt owed to another Muslim. They pulled him off his donkey to force him to free the debtor. Al-Ghazal sent for and received aid from his employer, who sent men to subdue the crowd. This enraged the mob, which then petitioned the Sultan. Sultan al-Ashraf decreed that no Christian or Jew could work for *emirs* and that the *emirs* must demand that their Coptic employees convert or be beheaded. The public's response to the Sultan's order was to pillage and loot, kidnap women, and kill men in the Coptic and Jewish quarters. Fearing further chaos, the Sultan banned Copts from working in the state bureaucracy. He arrested the Coptic employees; those who converted could keep their jobs, those who wouldn't faced beheading. All the Copts converted.[142]

A similar incident happened in 1301 when a Moroccan vizier visited Egypt. He saw a Copt riding a horse and wearing a white turban, being followed by some poor people begging. The Moroccan vizier was upset to see Christians in Egypt riding horses, wearing fine clothing and working in government positions. He convened with Sultan al-Nasser Muhammad ibn Qalawun, telling him that Christians in Morocco had no such rights or authority over Muslims. Influenced by this complaint, the Sultan ordered that Christians could not work for the bureaucracy and invoked the *Covenant of Umar*, forcing the Christians and Jews to suffer a return to their past, diminished status.[143]

The start of the fourteenth century saw yet another layer of pressure placed on Copts in response to stories of how Muslims were treated in parts of Spain under the Christians, as well as rumors of a Mongol-Christian agreement in the East, which was perceived as a threat to the Islamic caliphate. These stories brought about retaliation in Egypt in the form of anti–Christian sermons and writings and several peaks in the violence against Copts.[144] The most destructive movement against Christian churches occurred in 1320. As mentioned in the introduction, more than sixty churches were destroyed in one event during the reign of the Sultan al-Nasser Muhammad ibn Qalawun. This incident comes second in intensity only to the more contemporary events after President Morsi's deposal in 2013, which led to the burning and destruction of seventy-three churches.

Violence against Copts and the cycle of firing and hiring them continued into the fifteenth century. During the time of Sultan Malik Mu'ayyad Abu Nasr, in 1419, the chief of police Sheikh Sadr ad-Din Ahmad b. al-Ajami was summoned and rebuked because Christians disobeyed the law regarding their distinctive clothing. After much deliberation, the decision was made that *dhimmi*s would not be allowed to work for the bureaucracy and that clothing restrictions would be enforced upon them, as a form of humiliation. Then the sultan summoned Al-Akram Fada'il, his Christian scribe, who was beaten, unclothed and shamefully paraded in the streets of Cairo accompanied by the chief of police who said, "This is the reward for Christians employed in government offices." He was then imprisoned.[145]

The cycle of hiring and firing and the intensity of the attacks from the populace led to still another period of intense conversion to Islam, but Coptic converts were not well received nor fully accepted by the public. Coptic conversion was mainly motivated by the discrimination and humiliation they faced and was also driven by the need to maintain employment. The public understood this insincerity of conversion and the converts to Islam were hated by their new co-religionists. The jealousy the populace once had for the Copts working within the bureaucracy was augmented with contempt for Coptic converts.

Consequently, some of the Coptic converts preferred death to this miserable life. They reached such a level of despair that they committed acts that could only lead to their deaths. Al-Maqrizi mentioned that, in 1388, some Coptic converts publically renounced Islam and expressed their desire to become Christians again. They were all beheaded. In 1392, four monks publically challenged Islamic jurists and spoke against Islam. They were burned alive.[146]

ISIS documented this practice in a 22-minute video they released to the world. On February 3, 2015, Jordanian pilot Moaz al-Kasasbeh was captured by ISIS, imprisoned in a steel cage and burned alive. The pilot was a Muslim but his crime was similar to that of the monks. The monks spoke against Islam, while the pilot fought against Islam by raiding ISIS strongholds. It is said that the first Rightly Guided Caliph Abu Bakr was the first caliph to burn someone, al-Fogaa, alive.[147] The Caliph's son, Muhammad ibn Abu Bakr, was burned in a donkey skin when Amr returned to Egypt. And, as mentioned earlier, being burned alive was the punishment Egyptian radicals inflicted on two men guarding a Christian-owned tour boat in August 2013.

Coptic conversion to Islam was treated with skepticism because it was understood that conversions were a matter of convenience, not convention. A large number of Coptic functionaries converted to Islam in order to keep their jobs, but after their conversion they maintained their beliefs and their loyalty to Christianity and their fellow Copts. Al-Maqrizi said that the Copts "outwitted the Muslims by professing Islam and then proceeding to do as much harm as they could with no one left to stop them, since they professed Islam outwardly, they played an active role in affairs, their orders were carried out, and their words, obeyed."[148]

Such was the case of Taqiy al-Din, who was forced to convert to Islam by his Mamluk employer. He made his way to a high position in the bureaucracy. Because of his position as *nazir al-nuzzar* (chief supervisor of financial bureaus), Taqiy al-Din was in charge of the cadastral survey of 1315. He came up with certain measures in favor of his previous co-religionists, enabling them to avoid the communal tax by changing their village of residence. Such an act was regarded by some contemporary historians as motivated by his forced conversion to Islam. Although he converted to Islam and was obliged by his new religion's ordinances, his affiliation and concerns were with Christians. A legal notary at the time said that Copts' communal tax dramatically dropped based on Taqiy al-Din's measures and he stated that if Taqiy al-Din had ruled the land, he could have not treated Copts any better.[149]

A more instructive story of insincere conversion is al-Nashw, a wealthy convert from Christianity. After his death, people found many jars of wine and some pork meat, in addition to a gold cross and a jeweled hand of Virgin Mary in his possessions. Because of this, they didn't bury him with the Muslims; he was buried in a Jewish graveyard. Al-Nashw's brother Rizq Allah was pushed to convert by Sultan al-Nasir Muhammad. Another Copt, Taj al-Riyasah, was beaten by an emir until he conceded to become a Muslim. Yet another, Karim al-Din al-Kabir, was forced to become Muslim in his middle age at the hands of a Mamluk emir who pursued him relentlessly until he converted.[150]

During the time of al-Malik al-Salih, in 1352, al-Maqrizi mentioned that in one day, in the village of Qalyoub, in the Delta, 450 Copts converted to Islam and a great deal of land endowed to the Church was taken and given to emirs.[151] Because many Copts were forced to convert to Islam, and due to the large waves of conversion, converts often came before inquisitorial courts that questioned their fidelity and loyalty to Islam.[152] As converts to Islam often were not sincere, the public put pressure on Coptic converts by making them go to the mosque regularly and banning them from bequeathing their assets to their Coptic family members. This created pressure on the other members of the families to convert in order to keep the possessions and wealth within the family; otherwise their inheritances would be confiscated.[153]

The discrimination against Copts continued throughout the reign of the Mamluks. In 1385, Sultan Barquq banned Christians from celebrating the Coptic New Year, and those who were caught celebrating got their hands cut off. In 1400 Emir Yalbogha destroyed a church, and in 1419 Christians were banned from riding mules in Cairo. Outside of Cairo, Christians were allowed to ride mules, but men were required to ride side-saddle, like women. In 1445 and 1446, churches were destroyed and their valuable contents were sent to the authorities. For the year 1448, the annalist al-Sakhawi recorded that there was not a single church in Egypt that had not been damaged.[154] The two renowned Coptic monasteries of St. Paul and St. Anthony were raided by the Bedouins in 1484; they killed the monks and destroyed two great libraries by burning the precious volumes within. The two monasteries were in ruins for eighty years.[155]

It was argued that the Mamluks "gave the coup de grace to Christianity in Egypt." Coptic Christianity as a cultural force faded from Egypt's social life: "Conversions to Islam, always a steady trickle, now became a flood, and even regions like Upper Egypt ... became in majority Muslim."[156] Before the advent of the Arabs, the Coptic Church consisted of about 100 dioceses. By the fourteenth century the number had shrunk to only 40,[157] and Copts were reduced to only 7 percent of the population of Egypt.[158]

The fading of Coptic culture from Egyptian society was accompanied by the loss of the language. The process of Arabization that led to the disappearance of the Coptic language took many different forms, and occurred over several centuries; with the loss of the Coptic language, a great portion of the Coptic culture was lost as well.

Arabization

In 727, during the time of the caliph Hisham (724–743), a major attempt was made to settle Arabs in Egypt. A few thousand people from the tribe of Qays, in the Arabian Peninsula, were transferred to Egypt.[159] The newcomers settled in the Eastern part of the Delta, where they worked in agriculture, and they thus came into close contact with Copts. This was the beginning of Arab Muslims working and mingling with the Copts in daily life, and it marked the beginning of the Arabization process.[160] The early Arabs did not mingle with Copts because Caliph Umar banned them from working in agriculture or owning lands, in order that they might focus on *jihad*. With the assurance that the occupation would be permanent, these restrictions were lifted and Muslims started to become land owners.[161]

More Arab tribes came. The timing of these Arab immigrations coincided with Coptic revolts. It might be that the caliph wanted the Arabs to come to Egypt to work in agriculture so they could support the Arabs against the Copts. Or, perhaps he encouraged their immigration to replace the Copts who had died or had escaped during the revolts, to take their lands and keep agricultural production going. Then Arab tribes started to flow to Egypt.[162] Egypt's wealth was known to be remarkable, so this, too, may have drawn many Arabs to come to Egypt and settle.[163]

Additionally, the tradition of *irtiba*, or "transhumance," by which soldiers went to relax in different parts of the country in the spring, also helped the Arabization process. During *irtiba*, soldiers from various tribes were assigned to vacation in different areas for about three months. They would eat, hunt, and fatten their horses, all the while coming in close contact with the Coptic peasants who were forced to host them.[164]

Another important custom was *al-ribat*, which is to dispatch soldiers to coastal towns, mainly in and around Alexandria but also to al-Arish, Rashid, Damietta and al-Burullus, in order to give rest to the soldiers stationed there. After Amr established himself, he planned for a contingent from Medina to come and stay in Alexandria every year. The soldiers changed twice a year and they didn't live in camps as they did in al-Fustat, but rather, during their *al-ribat*, they lived in regular houses.[165] They, too, came into close contact with the Copts.

The Arabization process also occurred at the military camp, al-Fustat. It was established very close to the city of Babylon and gradually the camp turned into a town. Because of its proximity to Babylon, interaction with the professional Copts who were hired to manage the city started.[166] Additionally, Arab rulers who arrived with their Arabic armies and their families aided the process. In a short period of time, the number of soldiers in Egypt during the time of Umayyad caliph Mu'awiya reached forty thousand.[167]

But the spread of Arabic either through *irtiba, al-ribat*, or immigration would not have been successful without the *Covenant of Umar* where Copts were forced to show respect and honor, to entertain and give food to Arabs, and host them for three days.[168] Thus, the Arabs came into closer contact with the Copts and the Arabic language started to encroach on the everyday activities. The conqueror had no motivation or need to learn Coptic. Arabs were very proud of their language as it is the language of the Quran. Therefore, Copts were obliged to learn Arabic in order to deal with the conquerors of their lands, homes, and material goods.

The Coptic language received a significant blow in 706 when Abd Allah ben Abd al-Malik decreed the Arabic language to be the official language of the bureaucracy. Copts feared losing their jobs, so they worked hard to learn Arabic. Gradually the Arabic language also became the language of culture and politics.[169] But, it wasn't until the twelfth century, after the end of the Fatimid dynasty, that Arabic was spoken throughout the majority of Egypt.[170]

This crossover from Coptic to Arabic was far from smooth or easy. History is full of examples, small and great, of hardships faced by those who did not learn Arabic fast enough. Because Patriarch Michael (728–752) did not understand Arabic, he had to elicit the help of a translator to communicate with Abd Allah ben Marwan. The resulting communique was written in both Coptic and Arabic.[171] Moussa, the Bishop of Oseem, suffered physical abuse for his lack of Arabic knowledge. When he was travelling to meet the Caliph Marwan in 750, he was met by soldiers who knocked him down and started to beat him in order to extort money from him. Yohanna, a deacon who was accompanying him, had to translate the soldiers' demands.¹⁷² But, the most serious impact on the Coptic language was the Fatimid Caliph al-Hakim's ban on the use of Coptic in streets, houses and public places and the penalty of cutting off the tongue of a person who was heard speaking it. The usage of Coptic was restricted to within the walls of the monasteries and the churches. At one point, priests in the church put curtains on the altars during the service lest the rulers know that the Coptic language was being used, lest the church be attacked. Arabs viewed the Coptic language with suspicion, and al-Isbaugh ibn Abdel Aziz ibn Marwan even ordered the translation of certain Christian religious books into Arabic, so that Arabs would be able to detect any anti–Islamic material within.¹⁷³

It was during the time of Patriarch Gabriel ibn Turaik (1131–1146) that the Bible and liturgies began to be read in Arabic after being first read in Coptic. In the thirteenth century, the Arabic language became dominant and Coptic scholars such as Awlad al-Assal and Ibn al-Makin wrote their books in Arabic. The first to find it necessary to write in Arabic was Sawirus (Severus) ibn al-Muqaffa. One of his major works was the translation of *The History of the Patriarchs,* which he undertook because a large portion of the Coptic community were unable to read Coptic.¹⁷⁴ The masses of Copts who rushed to learn Arabic to keep their jobs, and the increasing number of Coptic converts to Islam who had to study the Quran in Arabic, were major factors in the process of Arabization. Another factor was the decreasing number of clergymen who were the guardians of the Coptic traditions and language. Monasteries started to go empty due to the steady decrease in the number of Copts and the pressure on those remaining to convert. Priests started to learn Arabic so they could communicate with their congregations who now spoke Arabic.¹⁷⁵

However, al-Maqrizi mentions that monks and some women and children in the isolated parts of Upper Egypt in the area of Assiut continued using Coptic until the 15th century. And, in 1798 when the French emperor Napoleon occupied Egypt and wanted to hear the Coptic language spoken, a Coptic man was brought from Upper Egypt to demonstrate it for him.¹⁷⁶ Now, the Coptic language is used only during the liturgy, as a symbol of identity.

In 1453, the great Christian city Constantinople was in the hands of the Muslim Ottomans. It was re-named Istanbul and became the capital city of the Islamic caliphate. In 1517, the Ottomans attacked the Mamluks in Egypt, and Egypt became part of the Ottoman caliphate.¹⁷⁷ A new page of painful survival in the history of the Copts was turned. Although they were reduced to a small minority, their Coptic identity was strong enough to carry them through hardship under yet another caliphate.

Four

The Modern Age
Liberal Egypt

The Ottoman Empire, 1517–1798

In 1517, the Ottomans, under Sultan Selim I, defeated the Mamluk army led by Sultan Tumanbay. With the Ottomans' victory, they killed Tumanbay and displayed his head on the Bab Zuwayla city gate in Cairo.[1] This set the stage for Egypt to be governed by yet another foreign ruler. The Copts had endured for eight and a half centuries before the coming of the Ottoman Turks. The Coptic language had already been displaced by Arabic, and they had gone from being a majority to being the minority in their own homeland.

Under Ottoman rule different faiths were divided into millets, or religious groups, each one represented by a leader. It was a semi-autonomous system where Christians and Jews were ruled by their own laws and religious authority, and the ecclesiastical authority dealt with the government as a representative of its own people.[2] Still, this system didn't alleviate the pressures on Christians.

Pressure came from another governing system established by the Ottomans. Selim I wanted to achieve two main goals: to ban any potential threat of separating Egypt from the Ottomans and to get as much tax money as he possibly could. To achieve his goals and keep the balance of power in his hands, Selim I divided the administration between three competing authorities. The first authority was the ruler, or pasha, who was assigned the collection of tribute. He only had a three-year term in office, so he could not gain too much power. Second was the army garrison, whose main job was to defend Egypt. And finally were the Mamluks, who were assigned the local government because they were familiar with its administration. This system served Selim I very well, but it brought Egypt into political and financial crisis. Egypt ended up being subject to three different agencies of taxation instead of one.³ In addition to sending the tax money to Istanbul, the governors were also concerned with filling their own coffers with additional taxes and the Copts were easy targets.⁴ They already existed in a state of oppression, and their suffering was further aggravated by poverty and plagues.⁵ The Ottomans were an improvement compared to the severity of the Mamluks, but by no means did their rule mark an end to discrimination.

Some examples of this discrimination included forcing *dhimmis* to wear bells around their necks when attending public baths and banning them from riding animals in town in front of the houses of Ottoman notables; sometimes Christians were banned from riding at all.⁶ The Ottomans also banned Christians from eating during the fasting period of Ramadan, when Muslims refrain from food.⁷ Five centuries later, in June 2016, Egypt's highest religious authority in charge of *fatwas* stated on its Facebook page that eating in public during Ramadan fasting hours is "a sin as it is in violation of etiquette in Muslim countries." Police even shut down some cafes for openly serving food during the fasting period. Due to public outcry from Egyptian liberals, who considered it an infringement on personal freedom, the *fatwa* was removed.⁸

Discrimination against the Christians under the Ottomans was best captured by a Danish traveler in 1761. He reported that in Cairo no Christian or Jew could be seen on horseback. They only rode donkeys and had to dismount when they saw even the lowest level Muslim lord. These lords were always on horseback, accompanied by an insolent servant with a big baton who preceded his master and warned others to show due respect, all the while shouting "*Enzil*" or "Get off." If a man refused, he would be beaten until he complied. A French merchant was lashed on an occasion such as this. In another incident, a physician was also insulted because he was tardy in dismounting from his donkey. Because of these incidents, no European dared to walk in the streets without having a person who knew these lords and could give a warning before the lords reached him. Christians and Jews were even forced to dismount when they were in front of the gate of the janissaries, the house of the chief *qadi*, mosques, and the Muslim cemetery. They had to go out of their way to avoid such places as even the land they were standing on was considered holy and they would be accused of profaning it. Due to these restrictions, European merchants lived in one single contained place and kept to themselves, with rare outside communication.⁹ Al-Gabarti, a well-known Muslim chronicler (1753–1825), said that when Copts were forced to wear *dhimmi* clothes, they were followed and harassed by the populace. Should they be caught not wearing the discriminatory attire, they would be stoned and have dust thrown in their eyes. Copts were even forced to change their names. In 1785, Hasan Pasha forced Copts who were named after prophets mentioned in Islam such as Abraham or Moses to change their names. Thus, Christian employees had two names: one for work and one at home.[10]

The English merchant Edward Brown, who visited Egypt in 1673 and 1674, gave another account of the Copts, describing them as "among the most dejected and distressed nation in the universe," seen as infidels by the Turks, heretics by the Catholics, and looked down upon by the West for their poverty. But he commented them on their good qualities: "They have very just notions of the causes and consequences of Christ's coming." Additionally, the monks were charitable and helped the Arabs in the desert. He adds that "they are wonderfully sincere in all their acts of devotion." He commented on their work ethic calling them, "industrious mechanics, laborious peasants or stewards to Turkish lords who make choice of them for their remarkable fidelity...."[11] Over a century earlier, Selim I chose Coptic craftsmen and engineers to go with him to Istanbul. A Coptic financial expert, Mu'allem Barakat, who served under Tumanbay, was also taken to Istanbul to work at the *diwan* of the sultan.[12]

In addition to the physical and social restrictions on them, the Copts faced another set of rules regarding the restoration of churches. For example, permission to restore a dilapidated church could be granted only if the building materials from the original church were used. If the Copts broke the rules, their neighbors would notify the religious authorities, who would demand that the Ottoman government take action. This might take the form of a fine, which would be resented by the religious authority and perceived as a bribe. Alternative rulings could be to close down or demolish the church.[13]

The role given to the neighbors to watch changes or developments in churches was conspicuous during President Mubarak's tenure. All churches were guarded by police personnel due to continuous threats. Quite often the guards fell victim to radical Islamist assaults when churches were attacked. In addition to guarding the churches against attacks, a second part of their job was to watch for any building activity, or building materials going in and out of the churches. Because they were usually not well-educated, many of the policemen weren't able to read a permit if the need arose, and it was the Islamist neighbors who really did the job of watching the churches. They informed the authorities with suspicions of building activities and took matters into their own hands. Despite it being illegal, they fearlessly demanded that church officials show them permits. In many cases they attacked a church without verifying that the requisite permits had been obtained. This attitude dates back to the time of the Ottomans.

Permits were also required for Copts to be able to perform their pilgrimage to Jerusalem under the Ottomans. But obtaining the right permit did not necessarily mean safety from violence. The Copts had to pay a large sum of money, 1,000 dinars, in order to obtain a permit to be able to perform their pilgrimage trip. Al-Gabarti reported, " They [Christians] departed with great pomp, with immense baggage and provisions, with litters in which their women and children were carried and with drums and pipes.... They employed Bedouins to march with them as guards and they gave them money, clothes and other gifts. This display became known throughout the city and the people disapproved of it." Al-Garbarti illustrates the animosity felt by some by explaining that, at one point, a man accused the head mufti of taking a bribe and establishing a precedent in allowing Christians the permit for pilgrimage. The man told the head Mufti that the Christian pilgrimage to Jerusalem would compete with the Muslim pilgrimage to Mecca: "It will become a custom, guilt for which will lie upon you until the Day of the Resurrection." The head mufti reacted and, according to al-Gabarti,

> left in a rage and permitted the common people to attack the Christians and plunder their possessions. Also among those who went out was a group of students from al-Azhar who banded together against the Christians, stoned them, beat them with sticks and clubs, plundered their possessions and humiliated them.... The Christians' fortunes suffered a great reversal in the incidences; everything they had spent was lost and scattered.[14]

The Copts had to bow to the expectations of their neighbors; otherwise, they could face intolerance and violence. When Copts neglected their usual caution, they became targets of retaliation. Because of their suffering during the time of the Ottomans, Copts had a tendency to live together in specific areas of the cities.[15] In the villages, Coptic houses were built directly adjacent to each other, in one section. Sometimes these clusters of houses would only have one gate, or *bawaba*, leading to the whole compound and it was closed every night. This custom still exists to some degree in old parts of certain villages in Upper Egypt.

However, despite hatred and animosity, the Coptic community managed to survive. The Copts' talents and qualities continued to make a long line of governments dependent on their expertise during the Ottoman period. Therefore, the Ottomans had no provocation to treat the Copts any worse than previous rules had.[16] They were very astute in their bookkeeping accounts which they kept in Coptic characters that only they could decipher. This ensured a level of job security for them as they became of value to the state. The Copts who were able to keep their positions as bureaucrats in the state apparatus helped their fellow Copts by establishing philanthropic organizations, and they were even able to convince the authorities to restore some of the churches.[17]

During different financial crises before the French campaign, the Coptic professionals were in a position to endure. When taxes were low, profits from trade and agriculture could be saved. When taxes increased, especially after 1775, as they collected the taxes they were, of course, in a position to benefit from the revenue. The Coptic community benefitted from these Coptic professionals in a myriad of ways: restoration and painting of churches and monasteries and, in rare cases, building of new churches.[18] When there was a famine in 1739–1740 and an uprising two years later, poor Christians who failed to pay their taxes were sold into slavery, but some rich laity in the Church were able to redeem them.[19] In these ways more well to do Copts assisted their community, helping it to survive.

History recorded some Coptic professionals who reached a level of prominence, such as Mu'allem Rizq, who became a senior financial advisor to the Mamluk, Ali Bey al-Kabir. Other prominent Copts include the two al-Gauhari brothers, Ibrahim and Girgis, who were highly successful. Ibrahim (d. 1797) successfully obtained a *firman* (a decree), from Istanbul to build a Coptic cathedral; it still exists in Ezbekieh, Cairo, today. After the death of Ibrahim, his brother Girgis (d. 1810) became the head of the *diwan* of the last two Mamluks. He also lived through the French campaign and later on became Muhammad Ali's financial secretary. He was lenient in taxation, which made Egyptians like him, but angered Muhammad Ali, who exiled him—only to bring him back after four years because of his indispensable financial expertise.[20]

But the efforts of more prosperous Copts could not lessen the effects of *dhimmitude*. Under the Ottomans the Coptic population continued to dwindle through reoccurring discrimination and conversion to Islam through pressure from the ruling authority. Their number around the end of 18th century shrank to only 150,000 out of 3 million, or 5 percent of the total population. Another indicator of the decreasing Coptic population was the notable decrease in tithes given to the Church. After the Arab conquest in the 7th century, 600,000 people were on record as tithing; by the end of the 18th century, the number had dropped to only 15,000. Based on accounts of European travelers visiting Egypt in the 17th century, the number of bishops had fallen to twelve in 1671, compared to the seventy that existed in the 7th century. Coptic monks, who once could have been found across all of Egypt, were restricted to only four monasteries.[21]

Towards the end of the 18th century, the ineffectual rule of the Ottomans, combined with the interests of foreign powers in Egypt's strategic location, led to the rise and fall of the short-lived French campaign of Napoleon Bonaparte in Egypt.[22]

The French Campaign, 1798–1801

The French Campaign was the first time since the Arab conquest that Egypt was ruled by a so-called Christian nation, even though Napoleon was very keen to portray himself as a Muslim and a protector of Islam. He appeared wearing oriental clothing, and he attended the mosque to share in the celebration of Muhammad's birthday. Additionally, he banned proselytizing during his campaign in Egypt; still, this approach did not deceive the Muslim community in Egypt, which was suspicious of his sincerity and perceived him as an infidel.[23]

The fact that the French were perceived as Christians had its own repercussions for the Coptic Christians. When the French arrived the populace attacked Christians, based on previous assumptions that they would support their co-religionists. Some *ulama* of al-Azhar mobilized the populace against Copts in Cairo, and the Mamluks who fled to Upper Egypt beleaguered the Copts there as well.[24] The Ottoman sultan sent an army under the leadership of Nasif Pasha to fight the French, but Nasif Pasha, who was unable to achieve victory, diverted attention from his failure by using Christians as scapegoats. He ordered their killing in Cairo, something the mobs willingly participated in. A great number of Copts were murdered, but the killing was stopped by Othman Bey, a military officer, who convinced Nasif Pasha to rescind his decree.[25]

In 1798, after the French gained control of Egypt, Girgis al-Gauhari wrote an appeal to Napoleon, "the true son of the French Revolution and the exponent of the principles of liberty, equality and fraternity," to abrogate the restrictions imposed on the Copts and grant them equality with other Egyptians.[26] Napoleon wanted to treat all Egyptians equally, but he did not want to give the Copts their freedom all at once. That would be politically dangerous as he would be confronted with great resistance from the rest of the population, most specifically regarding the Copts' freedom of worship. Napoleon, however, did overturn some of the *dhimma* status laws by allowing the Copts to ride horses and mules, dress with no restrictions, and bear arms.[27]

These were improvements to the status of the Copts; for the first time since the Arab conquest, some of their basic rights were restored to them. They were not favored by the French "co-religionists"; they were just not oppressed by them.[28] On many occasions, Napoleon corresponded with his commanders, telling them to show preference to Muslims over Copts. But, like previous rulers, Napoleon sought the help of the Copts in financial and tax issues.[29]

Even though Napoleon was preoccupied with befriending the Muslims, they continued to believe he was an infidel, never accepting him as a true believer. And, some persisted in believing that his presence in Egypt was supportive of the Copts. Time spent trying to minimize the animosity on his behalf angered his soldiers. Perhaps such resentment allowed his General, Kleber, to show some sympathy for the Copts. When Napoleon transferred power to Kleber upon his return to Paris, Kleber allowed the Copts to form a Coptic legion.[30]

Eventually, General Kleber was assassinated by a student from al-Azhar and was succeeded by General Menou in 1800. Menou, unlike Kleber, was very suspicious of the Copts.[31] He fired them from the bureaucracy.[32] Menou converted to Islam, called himself Abd Allah, and married a Muslim, but this did not earn him Muslim trust either. He, too, was suspect just as his commander Napoleon was before him.[33]

While they differed in their perception of the Copts, both Kleber and Menou agreed on Mu'allem Ya'qub (1745–1801), a Copt who was a financial commissioner, then a military leader. Ya'qub later became a controversial historic character: Was he a collaborator in the French occupation, or a leader of national independence? Although al-Gabarti was a member in the *diwan* that collaborated with the French campaign, he portrayed Ya'qub as a vengeful defender of the Copts and a collaborator with the French. This view is perpetuated by fundamentalist Islamists, but it stands in stark contrast with another renowned Muslim Egyptian historian, Muhammad Shafiq Ghurbal (1894–1961), who thought that Ya'qub had a precocious political sense and could see the objective foundations of possible independence before anyone else had conceived of it.[34]

Mu'allem Ya'qub accompanied the French General Desaix in his wars against the Mamluks in Upper Egypt. He did very well and, after achieving victory, Desaix granted him a sword of honor. Kleber gave him the title colonel and Menou promoted him to the rank of a general. On his request, Mu'allem Ya'qub attained approval to form a Coptic legion; thus, he was the first Copt to form a Coptic military unit since the Arab conquest. When the Mamluks and mobs attacked Christian neighborhoods in Ezbekieh, Cairo, Ya'qub came to their defense.[35]

However, Ya'qub left Egypt with the French when they withdrew. The reason for his travel would only be made public more than a century later: he left in order to return and reclaim Egypt for its people through the creation of an Egyptian army.[36] Ya'qub's detailed plan, the 1801 project for the independence of Egypt, was brought to light in 1924 from documents found in the British Foreign Office. Ya'qub and his men showed an early expression of national Egyptian identity, a desire that the national Egyptian movement accomplished in the Revolution of 1919. But, Ya'qub's independence project died with Ya'qub's unexpected death at sea on August 17, 1801, and he was buried in Marseille, France.[37]

No thoughts of national Egyptian identity were formulated by Egyptians before Ya'qub's plan for the independence of Egypt. The fundamentalists' and secularists' diverging views of Ya'qub underline Egypt's identity issue. Both the Ottomans and French were occupiers, but fundamentalists could only see the French as such because the Ottomans were representing the Islamic caliphate. For them the Islamic nation has no boundaries and it includes every Muslim regardless of their language or nationality. Ya'qub's independence project would separate Egypt from the caliphate which could undermine its Islamic outlook. In the fundamentalist Islamist ideology, the secular Egyptian identity is subjugated by the trans–border Islamic identity. Perhaps it is for this reason Egyptians did not govern their own county for centuries and were content to be ruled by foreign Muslim rulers, be they Abbasids, Fatimids, or Ottomans.

Yet, in the long chain of foreign occupiers, the French had a strong impact on Egypt despite the fact that they stayed the shortest period. They made a contribution not only to Egypt, but to human civilization, by discovering the Rosetta Stone, which allowed Champollion to decipher ancient Egyptian hieroglyphics. They also recorded a comprehensive description of ancient and modern Egypt in *Descrioption de l'Egypte* or *Description of Egypt*. By facilitating Egyptians to re-discover their ancient Egyptian history, the French aided the Egyptians in forming their own Egyptian identity. This identity would be the common unifying ground between Copts and liberal Muslims in their fight against the British a few decades down the road.

In any case, the British saw the French as a threat to their route to India and wanted to expel them from Egypt. They supported the Mamluk beys and helped to push the French out of Egypt. On the other side, the Ottomans were adamant in their desire to regain Egypt. The French left in 1801, after staying in Egypt for only three years, and control passed to the Sultan of Turkey. After the departure of the French there was a power vacuum, which led to internal fighting among different groups in Egypt—the Mamluk beys, the *ulama*, the notables, and the generals.[38] This environment of conflicting power struggle dominated the period up until 1805 which marked the beginning of the era of Muhammad Ali. The conflicting factions treated the Copts with suspicion, in part due to Ya'qub's stance, but also because they were Christians like the French. Some Copts who had assumed prominent positions under the French were murdered after their departure. Malaty, a Copt who headed a *diwan*, was arrested and beheaded at Bab Zuwayla in Cairo. Antoon Abu Taqyyah, Ibrahim Zidan, and Abd Allah Barakat were among other prominent Copts who were killed, without due process of law, during this period.[39]

Obviously, the characteristics that have allowed Copts to survive and find some modicum of success throughout history did not save them from vulnerability, prejudice, discrimination, exploitation or even murder. The Copts in Egypt were and still are despised by fundamentalists. Their hard work, perseverance, and faith have earned them this hatred.[40]

Muhammad Ali and His Family, 1805–1882

In 1801 Muhammad Ali arrived in Egypt as a junior commander in the Albanian forces that were sent by the Ottoman sultan to drive the French out of Egypt. After securing the support of the notables and *ulama*, Muhammad Ali succeeded in establishing himself as the ruler of Egypt, in 1805, and the Ottoman sultan acknowledged his position.[41]

Muhammad Ali had a vision for Egypt, but the major obstacles to his ambitions were the Mamluks, who had grown very powerful and influential. They continuously increased their number by importing more slaves from Turkey, converting them to Islam and training them as soldiers.[42] In 1811, Muhammad Ali realized their increasing threat to his rule and decided to get rid of them in what is known as "the massacre of the citadel." He hosted a banquet at the citadel in honor of his son Toson, who would be leading the army to fight the Wahhabis in Arabia. Muhammad Ali invited the Mamluk leaders, and in one fell swoop he murdered them all, except for one who escaped on horseback. He followed this intrigue by ordering a general massacre of the Mamluks throughout Egypt.[43]

After the massacre, Muhammad Ali became the uncontested leader of Egypt and was ready to achieve his vision. He turned Egypt into an autonomous entity, developed its resources, and modernized it. In his process of making Egypt a modern state, Muhammad Ali relied heavily on French experts, as he saw France as an ideal state to be emulated. With the help of these experts, he built a strong Egyptian military, ammunition factories, arsenals and military schools. Despite these advances in the military, Copts did not benefit as they were not allowed to join the military.[44]

In his attempt to develop education, Ali established different specialized schools in engineering, medicine, pharmacology, and languages. He sent nine scholarship missions to study in Europe, a total of 319 students, including one Copt.[45] French influence on Muhammad Ali was quite apparent in education, whether through the student missions he sent to France or through the role of the French in developing modern education in Egypt. He allowed the French to build their own missionary schools where Catholic monks and nuns were the teachers. Moreover, he granted the French the necessary property for their schools. This was especially true after he realized that the aim of these missionaries was to convert the Orthodox Copts—not Muslims—to Catholicism. A few decades later, when the British occupied Egypt, their missionaries intended to convert the Copts to Protestantism and they, too, established their own schools.[46]

Missionary work in Egypt was a double-edged sword. Converting one kind of Christian to another by missionaries not only indicated a sense of superiority from their side, but also divided the already suffering Coptic

Church. The Coptic Church was caught in a difficult position trying to survive, caught between the hardships it had been facing for centuries and the new threat of Catholic and Protestant missionaries, who were progressively succeeding in converting Copts. On the other hand, the missionary schools provided Copts with a good education and allowed them to learn foreign languages, which helped them to advance economically. The Coptic Church felt the need to reform and provide its people with modern education.

Indeed, education was the most important vehicle that led Egypt to modernity, a fact Muhammad Ali was well aware of. When he tried to modernize Egypt he went around its traditional institutions and created a modern parallel system to challenge the old one.[47] By relying on French educational expertise, he made the government educational system rise above the old traditional institutions. Traditional Muslims had to choose between the old-fashioned *madrasas*, and schools that prepared their children to compete in the now modern society. Muhammad Ali's approach had an immediate impact on the society, as it helped moderate the fundamentalist elements by exposing Egyptians to different ideas and thoughts.[48]

In addition to education, Muhammad Ali also relied heavily on agriculture in his process of modernization. He expanded the land under cultivation and planted strategic crops for the purpose of export, such as long-staple cotton, rice and sugarcane.[49] He enhanced agricultural production through land reform. He gave his family members the largest tracts and gave lands diminishing in size to his top assistants, military leaders, senior state officials, Bedouin leaders, middle state employees and local notables. Control of land was pretty much control of the socio-political discourse of the country.[50] Most important in his agricultural reform was that tax farming was discouraged and private investment was encouraged, which had a positive socio-economic effect on the country. This provided the Copts with the opportunity to advance through the new system of land ownership.[51]

To support his agriculture policy, Muhammad Ali dug new tunnels and built bridges, roads and barrages. He also built different kinds of factories, especially for textiles and sugar refining. As a result of Muhammad Ali's social, economic and industrial revolution a Coptic elite emerged as land owners and investors. They were the descendants of merchants, administrators, and consultants who had served in the bureaucracy for centuries. A famous example is Girgis al-Gauhari, who was Muhammad Ali's financial secretary.[52]

Muhammad Ali was reconciliatory with the Copts and he was tolerant of other religions. In 1831, he exempted Copts who worked for the Alexandria arsenal from paying the *jizyah*. He did not enforce the rules dictating the wearing of humiliating attire by *dhimmis*, and he annulled restrictions on Coptic religious ceremonies. Under his rule, Copts were allowed to visit the holy land in Jerusalem on a yearly basis. During drought, when he asked people to pray for the Nile to overflow, Christians joined in the prayers and went to the Nile riding horses. He granted the senior Coptic officials the title "Bey" for the first time.[53] He even hired Copts as rulers in local municipalities.[54] Al-Gabarti recorded that Muhammad Ali provided the Copts with weapons to join him in his fight against both the Turks and the British.[55] The Copts experienced a degree of freedom that had not been granted to them by any previous rulers and they were given the chance to participate in building the Egyptian modern state.

During Muhammad Ali's rule there was no general policy to humiliate or discriminate against the Copts. However, as had happened before, when the ruler was tolerant, the humiliation of the Copts came from an angry populace. There were several notable incidents, but the one that involved Sedhom Bishay of Damietta, in 1844, was the most significant. Bishay was a bureaucrat who was wrongfully accused of insulting Islam by the populace. He came before a *sharia* judge, and based on this serious accusation, he was given the choice to either convert to Islam or be killed. Bishay refused to convert. He was whipped, and paraded throughout the city riding backward on a water buffalo to humiliate him.[56] Sedhom Bishay died as a result of severe torture and the Coptic Church celebrates his martyrdom, which occurred on the 17th of the Coptic month of Baramhat 1565, or March 25th, 1844.

Severely humiliated, the Copts complained to Muhammad Ali who ordered an investigation to be opened. When he realized that Sedhom Bishay was innocent, he exiled the judge who had charged him. In order to show respect to the Copts, Muhammad Ali ordered that Sedhom Bishay be revered in Damietta, and he granted him an official funeral. The procession of priests and deacons, robed in their church garments, raised crosses and banners and moved through the city under the protection of soldiers. This was unprecedented, as Copts were not allowed to show Christian signs in public. From this incident, Copts gained the right to raise their crosses publically in their funerals.[57]

Muhammad Ali's tolerance was also evident in his relationship with the Coptic Patriarch Peter, whom he granted the needed permits to build and renew churches.[58] Coptic history mentions that the prayer of the Patriarch was considered a decisive element in their relationship and it also mentions that the daughter of Muhammad Ali was healed by the prayer of a Coptic bishop. But the worldly reason for the good relationship between Muhammad Ali and the Church was the nationalist stance of the Patriarch. The Czar of Russia had offered the Patriarch the protection of the Russian Orthodox Church. The Pope responded to the offer with a famous quote, stating simply, "while the Russians live under a czar who would die, the Copts live under a King who is immortal." Muhammad Ali was impressed by the Pope's stance and visited him to thank him for his nationalist position.[59]

Coptic survival during this period was greatly aided by the character of Muhammad Ali. He distanced himself from religious ideology, and, in this way, he tolerated the Copts and he modernized Egypt. Unlike today's fundamentalist Islamists, who are threatened by the "Christian West," Muhammad Ali was not intimidated; rather, he sought their help. He relied on the Europeans, "the Crusaders," and cooperated with "the infidels" in the modernization process to develop Egypt. He realized that the *madrasa* did not have the potential for the development he was envisioning, nor for the technological advancement to which he aspired. He went around it to develop the educational system—the most important element in advancing a nation. When he sent al-Azhar students to study in Europe, he was acknowledging their shortcomings and exposing them to new ideas which they could emulate and implement upon their return to Egypt.

When Muhammad Ali adopted modern European systems in science and education he began a renaissance, turning Egypt into a significant regional power. He established a new order, which became the principle framework for Egypt's path to modernity for the next century.[60] Consequently, Muhammad Ali is considered the founder of modern Egypt.

Muhammad Ali died and his son Ibrahim Pasha took over in March of 1848, but seven months later he, too, died. Abbas Helmy al-Awal, Muhammad Ali's grandson, took over in November 1848, and attempted to reverse Muhammad Ali's policy of modernization. He dismissed foreign advisors and shut down secular schools.[61] Abbas Helmy hated the Copts; he fired them from their positions in the bureaucracy and contemplated the idea of transferring them *en masse* to the Sudan, thus making Egypt fully Muslim. But, he was murdered in his palace before this plan could be carried out.[62]

Another son of Muhammad Ali, Said Pasha (1854–1863), succeeded Abbas and reversed Abbas's anti–European policy. Like his father, he was reform-minded and tolerant. He initiated agricultural reforms; built railways, telegraphs, and harbors; and most importantly, he initiated the digging of the Suez Canal. He abrogated celebratory processions of Coptic converts to Islam that used to be performed throughout the city. Such processions were demeaning not only to the Copts but to Christian foreign residents as well. He appointed a Christian as a governor in Sudan.[63] But what made Said's term in office remarkably significant in the history of the Copts is that it witnessed the emancipation of the *dhimmi*s in Egypt.

The emancipation of the *dhimmis* came as a result of the European concept of protection, which was ideologically influenced by the Declaration of the Rights of Man. The emancipation of *dhimmis* could only occur with principle changes in values, in which human rights were observed in full, as opposed to the previous doctrine of toleration. The toleration of the Christians was a relationship between a superior and inferior, a relationship which created and sustained inequality. Rights mean safety and human dignity; toleration means the absence of dignity. The European powers based their military and technological assistance on the condition of religious equality in the Ottoman Empire. This caused conflict between the Ottoman authority and the religious communities across the empire.[64]

Despite great resistance from the *ulama* and the common people to the Ottoman reforms, a proclamation of the Hatt-i-Sherif of Gulhane, in 1839, promised equal rights to all subjects of the Ottoman Empire. This proclamation was the result of European insistence and, in 1856, when military and technological assistance became crucial to the survival of the Ottoman Empire, France, Britain and Austria were able to force the Ottoman sultan to issue the proclamation of the Hamayoni Line, or Hamayoni Decree, acknowledging the legal equality of all of his subjects before law. The European powers demanded that the rights of *dhimmis* to dignity, equality and security for themselves, their families and properties must be acknowledged; a European working for the sultan couldn't see a Christian *dhimmi* being so humiliated without feeling his own prestige being incredibly impacted.[65]

The foreign Western powers' pressure on the Ottomans regarding the issues of human rights, equality, and justice resulted in the emancipation of the *dhimmi*s. Thus, the abandonment of the *jizyah* was established, allowing *dhimmis* to serve in the military. After the *jizyah* was lifted, a Christian would only pay tax if he wished not to serve in the military. Therefore, the *jizyah* became a legitimate and legal reason upon which to base release from military service, and no longer was payment of *jizyah* based on religion.[66] With the significant developments of the abolishment of *dhimma* status and the implementation of the Hamayoni Decree, the question arises: Did discrimination against Copts stop?

The purpose of the Hamayoni Decree was to eliminate discrimination against *dhimmis*. Some of the important articles of the decree were the reestablishment of previous laws concerning Christians, especially personal status laws; formation of a Lay Council; submission of permits to build a church by the Coptic pope to the authority; a ban on forced conversion; equality between Muslims and Christians in employment; mandatory conscription regardless of religion; a ban on discriminatory terms based on religion from the *diwans*; and prohibition from offending people based on religion. The Hamayoni Decree was meant to facilitate Copts to build churches. Yet, the required permits proved to be a major source of abuse by the authorities. In 1934 al-Ezabi Pasha, deputy minister of interior at the time, issued a ministerial decree placing 10 conditions on getting permits.[67]

These conditions were: (1) Is the land on which the church is to be built empty or agricultural land, and does it belong to the person presenting the request? (2) What is the distance between the proposed church and surrounding mosques? (3) If the land is vacant, is it near to Christian or Muslim settlements? (4) If it is close to Muslims, do they have any objection? (5) Is there another church belonging to this denomination in the same town or village? (6) What is the distance between the nearest church belonging to this denomination and the town in which the requested church is to be built? (7) What is the number of Christians in the area? (8) If the land on which the church is to be built is close to the Nile, or bridges or public utilities belonging to the ministry of irrigation, an approval should be sought from the ministry itself. Also, if it is near to railway lines the railway authorities should also give their approval. (9) An official report should be made on all of the above points, and it should indicate the surrounding buildings near the requested spot on which the church is to be built, including the nearest shops, and the distance between these shops and the church. (10) The person making the request should have all these papers signed by the head of the denomination and the engineer who is responsible for that area and present all the requested papers for approval.[68] So, al-Ezabi's conditions made it extremely difficult to get any permits, if only for condition (4) that gave the locals veto power over building churches; thus, making permission based on the good will of the ruler and the social and political situation at the time of the request.[69]

The al-Ezabi ministerial decree stated that churches can't be built or repaired without a decree from Egypt's king. When the monarchy was abolished in 1953, the word "president" was substituted for the word "king."[70] When Egypt got its independence, it abolished foreign decrees, but the Hamayoni Decree from Ottoman times was the only one to be retained in the sovereign and independent Egypt. It lasted for 160 years, until the parliament passed a law, in August 2016, regulating the building of churches.

Through government and fundamentalist Islamists' practices, the Hamayoni Decree was emptied of its intention of eliminating discrimination against Christians. Unlike mosques, which are built with no restrictions, churches must have an approved building permit. Abrogating the *dhimma* status after twelve hundred years was remarkable, yet the Copts did not enjoy equality. The lifting of the *dhimma* status marked a new era, in which the Copts were transformed from *dhimmis* to second-class citizens.

This was evident during the rule of Said Pasha, when Copts started to serve in the military; senior military officials pushed them to convert to Islam, making conversion a condition for promotion. Coptic Pope Kyrillos the Fourth (1854–1861) complained of this treatment to the European councils, who demanded Said either exempt the Copts from military service or treat them justly.[71]

The Pope's complaint to foreign councils greatly angered Said and may have led to the pontiff's death by poisoning.[72] Some of Said's anger could be attributed to the character of the Pope himself. The Pope was well known for being on good terms with all Christian denominations. Said may have been intimidated by the Pope's potential as a leader who could possibly be offered foreign protection, as his predecessor Peter was offered by Russia. In any event, Pope Kyrillos' death followed shortly after Said's summons. The Pope was only 46 years old.[73]

After the death of Said Pasha, Egypt's rule went to Ismail Pasha (ruled 1863–1878), a grandson of Muhammad Ali. Like his grandfather, Ismail was a modernizer: he dug more tunnels, established more factories to refine textiles and sugar, expanded railways, and built hospitals, barrages, palaces and other projects. He sent more students to Europe to study, and he is credited with establishing the first cabinet and Parliament in Egypt. Ismail was educated in Vienna and Paris, and he was influenced by the European Enlightenment to the extent that he wanted to make Egypt an extension of Europe.[74]

To this end, Ismail built the first opera house in Egypt and asked the famous Verdi to write the renowned opera *Aida*, to be performed at the opening of the Suez Canal. He built the Egyptian Museum and encouraged many different magazines to be published during his time. Egyptians witnessed a social transformation in their dress and food.[75] Ismail opened Egypt to thousands of expatriates and Cairo became a cosmopolitan city. He took the opportunity with the opening of the Suez Canal to build new neighborhoods in Cairo based on the European style with parks, big streets, streetlights, and more modern palaces.[76] The time of Ismail was a real renaissance for Egypt, and the Copts benefited from his achievements and tolerance, with some of them gaining the title of Pasha.[77]

Many see the time of Ismail as the "golden age" for the Copts. During his rule, they participated in the political life of Egypt; Ismail made it possible for them to run for the parliament after he established it in 1866. At this first parliament there were three Copts out of seventy-five members. He appointed Copts to senior positions in the bureaucracy, as governors and even judges. The head of his *diwan* was a Copt. He included more Copts in the awards of government scholarships to study in Europe. He encouraged Coptic schools and he donated 1,500 feddans of agricultural lands to generate income for these schools.[78]

The Coptic schools quickly developed a reputation for excellence. Copts have always valued education, and in the generations following Ismail Pasha, a large number of Coptic schools were established. At one point, they constituted 4 percent of all the schools in Egypt and 16 percent of the secondary schools. More than 25 percent of all students in all secondary schools were Copts—in girl's schools the percentage was even greater. Of this 25 percent, a little less than half were pupils in Coptic schools. A majority of the rest were pupils in foreign schools, in particular schools run by missionaries.[79]

Coptic schools became revered for their academic and moral standards; in fact, three Prime ministers were graduates of Harit al-Saqaien Coptic School.[80]

The Coptic Church's educational reform movement was led by Pope Kyrillos the Fourth (noted earlier as having been mysteriously poisoned after a meeting with Said Pasha). He is known in Arabic as "Abu al-Islah" or "the father of reform." He established many prestigious schools and not only were they free, they were also open to Muslim students. He established schools for Coptic girls, which enrolled Muslim girls as well. He imported the first privately owned printing press from Europe to print books.[81]

Before it was introduced by the missionary and Coptic schools, teaching girls was almost unheard of. Educating Muslim girls with Christian girls in these schools greatly helped in forming a moderate community. Missionary schools produced a new class of Muslims who were Europeanized and were influenced by the French values of egalitarianism and democracy. Without liberalizing the society, it would have been impossible for the Copts to advance economically and to play an important political role in Egyptian politics with the advent of the 1919 Revolution against the British Occupation. The educational opportunities the Copts enjoyed in this era became an asset to Egypt's national movement.

However, Ismail had a lavish lifestyle and built up more foreign debt on top of the already high foreign debt accrued by Said. Said's policy concerning the Suez Canal was remarkably generous to the concessionaries and it did not serve Egypt's interests in the transit trade.[82] Because Egypt accumulated tremendous debts with European governments and banks, the Europeans were given the opportunity to intervene in Egypt's affairs, and, ultimately, Ismail was deposed. His successor and son Tawfiq followed him, but there was a popular revolt led by Egyptian officers and, soon after, the British occupation of Egypt started, in 1882.[83]

The British Occupation and the Nationalist Movement, 1882–1952

To secure its control over the Suez Canal, the British occupied Egypt and turned it into a British protectorate. The Suez Canal that had such potential benefit for Egypt caused it to lose the autonomy that Muhammad Ali had strived so hard to achieve. His family members continued to rule Egypt and retained their honorary titles of pasha, khedive, sultan and king, but the real power lay on the hands of the British.[84]

The British rule was characterized by a sense of superiority and the fact that a portion of the Egyptian population, the Copts, shared their religion was insignificant to them. Like the Crusaders, the British saw Coptic Orthodox Christians as missing the true, spiritual part of Christianity, hence, not on par with European Christianity. The main advocates of this view were the British Christian missionaries. They were unsuccessful in converting Muslims because they were impeded by the serious legal repercussions they faced, including death. So, they realized it was much safer to shift their focus towards the "heretic" Copts, finding some success, especially in Upper Egypt.[85]

Also, like the French ahead of them, the British concluded that it would be more beneficial for them to associate themselves with the Muslim majority rather than the Coptic minority. They decided to rely on other non–Egyptian Christians, mainly the Syrians and Armenians, to substitute for the Copts in the bureaucracy. Lord Crommer, the British High Commissioner, did not think highly of the Copts. He did not trust them and considered them to be opportunists. He appreciated Syrian Christians and found them more advanced and closer to the European mentality. For him, the Syrian and Armenian Christians were the elite of the Orient. Therefore, the initial attitude of the British towards the Copts was negative.[86]

On the other hand, Lord Crommer did not think highly of Muslims either. He thought of them as anti-female and intolerant. But, he realized it was important that Islamic traditions and culture be honored. He made Friday, the Muslim holy day, a governmental day off and the Quran the single religious book to be officially recognized. Also, he proclaimed Muslim sheikhs to be the only religious teachers allowed in government schools. By the end of 1911, an English historian said, "To exalt the Muhammadan and to tread down the Christian, to license the majority and to curb the minority, is the policy which our government has not avowed but practiced."[87]

Gradually, the British worked on limiting the presence of the Copts in the bureaucracy. The less wealthy, yet educated Copts saw clear injustice in their lack of representation in favor of the Syrians, Armenians and British. The discriminatory policy was a good enough reason for the Copts to turn against the British. They realized that they were losing their traditional hold on the bureaucracy and losing their security.[88] As a result of the British restrictive policy, Copts moved towards private business. One of the most successful for them was journalism.

An unintended consequence of their move to journalism was that the Coptic press played an early role in the national movement and shaped people's views. The Coptic press, *al-Watan* or "the Homeland" (founded in 1877) and *Masr* or "Egypt" (founded in 1895) are only two examples of nationalistic papers that influenced political thought.[89] Another unintended consequence came from Crommer's economic policies, which benefited the Copts, especially the wealthy. In keeping with common imperialistic practices of the time, import taxes were low, to discourage industrial competition with British products, and a variety of technological and organizational improvements in agriculture for export were encouraged. The improvements in agriculture were a boon to wealthy Copts.[90]

The Copts accrued wealth under the British, especially before World War I. In 1907, the Copts constituted 7 percent of the population but had acquired 16 percent of cultivated land and buildings. They paid about 19 percent of the total land taxes collected. They owned about one fourth of the country's wealth and controlled about 60 percent of Egyptian trade. They were represented in professions such as crafts, farming and the bureaucracy though to a lesser degree than before. It could be said that, at that time, Coptic Christians were leading Egypt into the future.[91]

The fundamentalists objected to the newfound opportunities and prosperity of the Copts. The anti–Coptic sentiment flared with the British appointment of Boutros Ghali Pasha, a Copt, to head the Court of Dinshaway. In 1906, that court charged Egyptian villagers with the murder of a British soldier. The punishments ranged from flogging to execution and caused widespread unrest, which Mustafa Kamil and his a pro–Islam National Party used to rally Egyptians against the British. Other nationalists joined in the campaign.[92] Anger worsened when Boutros Ghali was appointed as Egypt's prime minster (1908-1910). This was the most senior executive political position a Copt had ever assumed.[93] Boutros Ghali's assumption of the premiership was based on his competency and his experience as a Cabinet minister. It was his skill that secured the appointment, even though the British thought that his religion would be an obstacle. It also helped that he had a good relationship with Egypt's Khedive. Boutros Ghali's personality and appointment angered many, and al-Wardani, who was associated with a Mustafa Kamil's pro–Islam National Party, assassinated him. Afterwards, al-Wardani was celebrated as a Muslim national hero who had killed an arrogant Christian. People paraded through the streets of Cairo chanting anti–Christian slogans and "*al-Wardani qatal al-nosrani*" or "al-Wardani killed the Nazarene [Christian]."[94] Al-Wardani's action was supported by a strong press campaign that argued Ghali was properly removed.[95]

Fearing pan–Islamic tendencies, a Coptic conference was held in Assiut in March 1911 to respond to the prevalent anti–Christian sentiment. The purpose of the conference was to establish "The Rights of the Minority," a document that would outline and safeguard minority rights.[96] The conference lamented the fragile tolerance demonstrated by the short-lived Coptic premiership. It called for the reform of the bureaucracy, petitioned for Sunday as a holiday, and for Christian instruction in government school. These last two requests paralleled the rights of Muslims to take Friday off and to receive Islamic instruction in school.[97] The conference also requested that Copts be represented in councils and in the judiciary.[98] No longer *dhimmis*, the Copts were searching for the rights of citizenship.

Public opinion was against the Coptic conference. Within weeks an Islamic conference, although it was called the Egyptian conference, was held in Heliopolis, Cairo, to counter the Coptic conference and to address the Coptic demands. The British High Commissioner, Eldon Gorst, had already criticized the Coptic conference, while the Islamic conference was supported by Egypt's Khedive Abbas II and Egypt's Prime Minister Mustafa Riyad.[99] The outcome of the Heliopolis conference was a total refusal of the Coptic demands.[100] In the congress, Lutfi al-Sayyid, a prominent Muslim intellectual, said

> that a state should have more than one religion is perfectly unthinkable and it would be absurd to admit that religious minorities can exist animated by political ambitions towards the exercising of public rights other than those of an essentially religious nature that are guaranteed by freedom of worship. The religion of the Egyptian people is Islam. For Islam is both the religion of the government and of the majority.[101]

In addition to being a prominent political figure, Lutfi al-Sayyid was a lawyer who defended the villagers in Dinshaway.[102]

Eventually, the British occupation of Egypt led to a movement for independence. The notion of Egyptian nationalism started to emerge and the Copts integrated themselves with their moderate Muslim counterparts to fight for Egypt's independence from the British. The wealth that Coptic notables, land owners and businessmen had gained was transformed into a degree of power. The Copts' new position in society was greatly aided by the educational level they had acquired. The combination of wealth and education became great assets for Egypt's independence movement in the 1920s. The Copts became an integral part of the national movement that brought Egypt from being ruled by Britain to a measure of self-rule under a "liberal experiment." It was a short-lived experiment, but Egypt witnessed democracy for the first time, and this allowed the Copts to achieve some significance.[103]

After World War I came to an end and the Ottomans were defeated, Saad Zaghlul, an Egyptian nationalist, formed a delegation to seek independence from Britain, in 1918. The delegation, or al-Wafd, became the name of the political party he would later establish. Intimidated by his actions, the British arrested Zaghlul and his compatriots and exiled them to Malta in March 1919. This action instigated the 1919 Revolution. In response, the British released them and allowed them, under the leadership of Zaghlul, to travel to the Paris Peace Conference to discuss Egypt's political future and its independence. Egyptian demands were denied and Zaghlul and his colleagues were exiled again, this time to the Seychelles. When he returned from his exile, Zaghlul became Egypt's uncontested leader. In 1922, Britain abolished its protectorate on Egypt, and the Egyptians were able to write their first constitution in 1923. Zaghlul became Egypt's Prime Minister in 1924.

The importance of the 1919 Revolution to the Copts is that they were accepted by Zaghlul's national movement. It was a secular, liberal movement that based nationalism on the Egyptian identity, separate from pan–Islamism.[104] The impact of the French and their education on liberal Egyptians made the notion of basing nationalism in secularism and separating it from religion an easy, logical choice. This generation had been deeply impacted by the European model of a separation of state and religion. Saad Zaghlul and the secular movement incorporated the Copts under the motto of the unity of the Muslims and Christians: "the unity of the crescent and the cross...."[105] While Saad Zaghlul was in exile, a Coptic priest, Sergius, was invited to stand in an al-Azhar pulpit to preach to the people against the British. The opposite was also true; when the British closed the mosque down, nationalists and Muslim sheikhs were invited to speak at the church.[106] Another illustration of this unity was apparent when Yousef Wahba, another Copt, accepted the British nomination to be Egypt's Prime Minister during the difficult period of 1919. The Coptic community rejected the nomination and criticized it as a British intrigue to divide and rule.[107] For the Copts, his appointment only drove a wedge between them and the Muslim community. He finally resigned.

In this period the unity between Copts and Muslims was unprecedented. Having one common enemy was a great unifying factor, and people rallied under the slogan, "Religion Is for God and the Homeland Is for All." The 1919 Revolution united Egyptians by putting aside religious differences, and al-Wafd ensured that Coptic participation in politics was not only tolerated but was supported.[108] The Copts participated heavily in the 1919 Revolution and helped in the formation of al-Wafd. Their role in the revolution was highly visible on various levels, including demonstrations, strikes and decision-making. At the Paris Peace Conference, five Copts participated in discussions of Egypt's political future. The participation of the Copts and a written endorsement of Egyptian Jews made it quite obvious that al-Wafd had obtained the support of Egypt's minorities. After the 1919 Revolution, with the clear contribution the Copts had made to its success, in addition to their support to al-Wafd, people acknowledged Coptic loyalty; up to this point, Coptic participation had been met with suspicion.[109]

This loyalty was well-earned. When Saad Zaghlul was exiled some Copts were exiled with him. When the British arrested the revolution leaders, the Copts were among them, and when they opened fire on protesters, Copts were among those killed.[110] The degree of trust the Copts gained allowed them political advancement. Under the British, the Legislative Assembly had allowed the Copts four seats out of seventeen reserved for ethnic minorities and professional groups. This reflects the British view that Egypt was made up of distinct groups, without a unifying national identity. Zaghlul and most Copts refused the proportional representation. Interestingly enough, in the first parliamentary elections after the revolution, the number of Copts exceeded what the special status would have permitted.[111]

Trust in the Copts also came from the nationalist Coptic stance on difficult issues. When Britain gave Egypt its independence, it made stipulations in the 1922 independence treaty that gave them the right to intervene in Egypt's affairs in order to protect minorities. Being part of the national movement, the Copts strongly spoke out against the divisive British proposal. It would create the image that the Copts were affiliated with foreign interests and seeking foreign protection.[112] The British idea of protecting the Christians was meant to inhibit hostility against them, but in reality it would encourage it.[113]

The trust the Copts gained convinced a lot of Muslims of their ability to fulfill their new positions. The popular support they acquired, in turn, attracted more members from the Coptic community to the al-Wafd party.[114] The Copts continued to progress in al-Wafd, and the first Egyptian cabinet, after independence and under the leadership of Saad Zaghlul, included two Copts and a Jew. The Speaker of the House, Wissa Wassef, was also a Copt.[115] This was the only time in Egypt's history that a Copt would reach that most senior legislative position. In 1927, the Copt Makram Ebeid reached the position of General Secretary of al-Wafd, and by 1933 Copts constituted about 40 percent of its executive committee.[116]

Only because Egypt's national movement was secular and liberal in nature did the Copts excel and thrive, but they were not the only group that benefited. Egyptian women, who were ignored and put down by fundamentalism, were emancipated. Egypt's feminist movement started with the 1919 Revolution. Hoda Sha'rawi established the Egyptian Feminist Union and numerous feminist societies. She was the head of the Women's Central al-Wafd Committee, which organized large protests against the British during the 1919 Revolution, bringing Egyptian women out into the streets. She and two other feminists, Nabawiya Moussa and Ceza Nabarawi, made up the Egyptian delegation to the 9th International Feminist Conference in Rome, in May 1923. This conference put Egyptian women on the world scene for the first time. But most significant was that the three women took off their veils, returning to Egypt without them, and they never wore them again. Thus, they started the process of modernization of Egyptian women and set an example for so many others to unveil.[117]

The emancipation of Egyptian women was an important factor in Egypt's development in this era. They became singers, actresses, journalists, lawyers, and teachers to name but a few of the professions now open to them. In addition to their professional contributions in the workforce, they greatly helped in moderating Egyptian society. Saad Zaghlul's wife Safia Zaghlul was able to play a significant role after her husband was exiled. She became a central figure of al-Wafd, and her house became a center for the party. In this era, Egyptians had no problem with her being a woman; rather, they esteemed her and called her *Umm al-Masriyyin* (The Mother of the Egyptians), and her house in Cairo was called *Bayt al-Umma* (the House of the Nation). Liberating Egyptian women was only conceivable by liberal Egyptians in the cultural context of Egyptian identity, in which women at one point in history were queens and goddesses.

Contrary to most trends in history, Egyptian women of the liberal era who championed Egyptian identity enjoyed far more freedom than their compatriots today. The fundamentalist Islamists who have radicalized the Egyptian society are increasingly threatened by women as a source of *fitna* or "temptation"; therefore, they feel women have to be fully covered, and they must be segregated. They preach that conservatism is protection for women. But despite the fact that most Egyptian Muslim women today are veiled, according to a 2013 United Nations study ninety-nine percent of women in Egypt are still harassed. It has become such a widespread phenomenon that the Egyptian government, for the first time, criminalized the harassment of women, in 2014.[118]

During Egypt's liberal era, the emphasis on the secular Egyptian identity broke through to the awareness of the all Egyptians. Liberal Egypt was able to introduce the Arab world's most famous female singer: the iconic Umm Kulthum. Around the same time, Egypt's most famous sculptor, Mahmoud Mukhtar, connected Egypt's future to women's emancipation. His statue of *Nahdit Masr* ("Awakening of Egypt"), which stands in front of Cairo University, emphasizes Egypt's Pharaonic character, thus embracing the Egyptian identity. It depicts the Sphinx and an Egyptian peasant woman lifting up her veil, symbolizing the adoption of Egypt's glorious past and the freedom to move towards the future. Also during this secular era, Egypt produced the only Arab Nobel Prize winner of literature: Naguib Mahfouz.

Umm Kulthum, Mukhtar and Mahfouz are only examples in a very long list of prominent Egyptians who played significant roles in Egypt's culture and soft power. They turned Egypt into a tolerant society and made it the Middle East's cultural center, from which it led the Arab world. This position and sphere of influence has been severely shaken by the steady increase of fundamentalism after the liberal era. Female singing has dwindled, as fundamentalists believe that a woman's voice is a "blemish" and music is against *sharia*. Sculpting has become a symbol of idolism and fundamentalists continuously call for the destruction of statues. Studying sculpting is now a rare endeavor in a land of statues. Literature has also been in decline, as creativity is challenged and freedom of expression is stifled by the fundamentalists.

Naguib Mahfouz was stabbed in the neck in 1994 by a radical Islamist, based on a *fatwa* issued by al-Azhar to ban his book, *Awlad Haritna* (*Sons of Gabalawy*), which they perceived as insulting to Islam.

The arts, creativity, cinema, theatre, literature, the translation movement, modern languages, diversity and modernization were all components of the liberal era that produced an atmosphere of moderation and tolerance. The emancipation of women created a less radicalized society that benefited not only women, but Copts as well; the Copts witnessed the most peaceful period in their history.

Another important fruit of the 1919 Revolution was that Egyptians wrote their first constitution. The Constitution of 1923 established the concept of a secular state and introduced the principals of citizenship and equality for all Egyptians, regardless of their religion.[119] However, it included an article which stipulated that "Islam is the state religion." This article provided a precedent, and it has been a part of Egypt's constitutional amendments and new constitutions ever since. This article eliminated the concept of separation between religion and state. While it is true that a number of European constitutions record a state religion, the interplay between religion and government in these countries is very different than in the Middle East, where politics and religion are intertwined. There was popular support to have Islam as the official religion of the Egyptian state, and al-Wafd, though popular, could not risk opposing popular demand. Such an article did not make Egypt a theocracy, but it allowed the state to apply the principals of Islamic *sharia* law, build mosques, teach Islam, train sheikhs and celebrate Muslim holidays at the expense of the state. For example, taxes collected from both Muslims and Copts are spent on Muslim institutions but no funds are given to Christian institutions. At one point, in 1946, up to 90 percent of the budget for al-Azhar came from government coffers.[120]

In this liberal era discrimination against Copts was at its lowest, but by no means had it ended. Sometimes the attitude of the government towards Copts was discriminatory and it was difficult for Christians to obtain jobs in the bureaucracy.[121] The 1937 census showed a decline of Coptic representation in government jobs from 35 percent to 9.1 percent. There is no law on the government books that accounts for this decline; however, it can be attributed to unwritten policy. The government believed that a Coptic minority which was disproportionally represented in the bureaucracy would make it lose its credibility. Several Coptic press articles recorded the results of this tacit admission. They recorded examples of demotions, unfair transfers, the promotion of Muslims over more qualified Copts and a reticence in the hiring of Copts.[122]

Another form of discrimination during the liberal era came from the Egyptian education system. Education in the government schools became problematic for the Copts because of the incorporation of religious instruction. In government schools Islamic religious teaching constituted a large part of the curriculum, especially in the elementary grades. The Copts feared that their children would be exposed to the temptation of conversion as younger students are more naïve and don't often question what they are being taught. The Coptic community was not only upset that their children were being exposed to Islamic religious instruction but also with the government's inability to give equal Christian religious instruction. In 1921, the state agreed to offer Christian education in primary schools. In 1933, the state passed a law that made religious education compulsory for Muslims, but it excluded non-Muslims who were required to make their own arrangement for instruction during the time Islamic instruction took place.[123] At that time the Copts were well equipped to fill the void. This government law came just as the Sunday School Movement conceived by the Coptic reformer Habib Guirguis was beginning to reap rewards in religious education within the Church.

Guirguis (1876–1951) established the Sunday School Movement in 1918. Through the Sunday schools, Guirguis was able to compensate for the shortcomings of Christian religious education in government schools, and he wrote a Christian religion curriculum for them. The effect of the Sunday School Movement became far-reaching, as it became the backbone of the Church's renaissance in the 20th and 21st centuries. By 1935, Sunday school branches in Egypt had reached eighty-two, with thirty in Sudan. He also helped establish Sunday schools in Ethiopia. Guirguis's objective was to revive Christian education in order to encourage the Christian spirit and Coptic identity in the children who, in turn, would be future leaders.[124]

In this period of history, Habib Guirguis also played an important role in educating the clergy in order to revive the Church and to stop the proselytizing process of the foreign missions. The lack of education and the negligence of the clergy had made the work of the foreign missionaries very easy among the Copts. Also, lack of funding left poor Copts without help; the patriarchate was even unable to pay the salaries of its employees.[125] When Guriguis became the dean of the Coptic theological school, he went on a tour all over Egypt to collect money, and he was able to raise enough to fund new buildings for the school, including a dormitory and a new library. He introduced the study of philosophy, psychology, history and languages. He also requested that bishops limit ordination of the clergy to seminary graduates to guarantee a certain level of education. The active Guirguis established Coptic societies for preaching, education, and children, and as a prolific writer, he issued about 47 publications.[126] Habib Guirguis instigated a real transformation of the Church through his establishment of the Sunday School Movement and the Coptic societies. Like the deans of the School of

Alexandria, he was a teacher of future bishops and popes. In his revival of the Church, Guirguis made Copts more aware of their Coptic identity.

Generally during the liberal era, al-Wafd wanted to separate religion from nationalism in its desire to build a secular state where all Egyptians, regardless of religion, would have equal rights and responsibilities. But another nationalistic movement did not adopt Western European ideologies: the pan–Islamism movement that was championed by the political leader Mustafa Kamil and Egypt's King Fouad. They envisioned Egypt as an Islamic state worthy to inherit the Caliphate from the Ottomans after their defeat in World War I.[127] Their platform was based on an Islamic identity for both politics and society and was represented by numerous Islamic organizations. Already in 1927, there were the Society of Young Muslims, the Society for the Benevolence of Islamic Morals, the Good Islamic Way, the Society for the Preaching of Islamic Virtues, the Society for the Revival of Religious Law, the Salafiya Society and Young Egypt. These societies started a progressive process of re–Islamization of national life. In 1928, the sheikh of al-Azhar declared that nationality is religion.[128]

The most salient and far-reaching Islamic society was the Muslim Brotherhood (MB), which was established by Imam Hasan al-Banna in 1928. The organization's motto summarizes their stance: "Allah is our objective. The Prophet is our leader. The Quran is our constitution. *Jihad* is our way. Dying in the way of Allah is our highest hope." Al-Banna refused the Western model of secular and democratic government because it went against the principals of the Islamic *sharia*. With the creation of the MB, the modern political Islam movement was born in Egypt. The MB became a mass movement and turned out to be the largest Islamic society, with branches in Arab, Islamic and Western states. The MB offered an alternative to the powerful secular nationalist movement and was able to secure the support of Egypt's king, Farouk.[129] In 1937, King Farouk, with the assistance of his former tutor, Mustafa al-Maraghi, sheikh of al-Azhar, tried to abolish the constitutional democracy and transform Egypt into a theocracy, but they were unable to do so because of the power of al-Wafd. Al-Maraghi revived religious sentiment by accusing al-Wafd of being manipulated by the Copts, whom he described as "foxes" in a radio program in February 1938. Friendship between Copts and Muslims is against *sharia* law, he declared, while advocating for the application of *sharia*.[130]

Since their establishment, the MB has been anti–Copt. They thought the Copts possessed far more power than they had a right to and they disapproved of their authority, which they deemed against *sharia*.[131] The MB blamed al-Wafd for the position of authority the Copts enjoyed and accused it of bias towards Copts. They preached that Copts wanted to isolate Muslims through their heavy support of al-Wafd. They initiated a wide-scale propaganda campaign against al-Wafd through sermons, speeches and articles.[132] The dissemination of their propaganda was aided by the organizational skills of the MB, who possessed printing presses, bookshops, youth clubs, clinics, and schools.[133]

The MB's power kept increasing while al-Wafd's power was decreasing. Al-Wafd eventually lost power, and when it returned in 1950, it was so weak that it sought the support of the MB. This caused the Copts to begin to lose faith in al-Wafd, whose press had already spoken positively of the MB's principles. There were anti–Coptic demonstrations in Cairo where people chanted, "Christianity is finished in Egypt," "One faith in Egypt—Islam," "Today the English, tomorrow the Christians." The MB painted crosses on the houses of the Christians to single them out. Prior to the demonstrations, they had already called for the boycotting of services and products produced by the Copts. In March 1947, when tempers flared in Zagazig in the Delta, a Coptic Church was burned. In 1949, a church was pillaged and crosses were removed from the domes of other churches. In January 1952, a Coptic church, school and social service building were destroyed and three Copts were killed in the Suez. These events reinforced the message that the al-Wafd government had abandoned the Copts, who had seen al-Wafd as their only hope.[134]

The rise of MB indicated the decay of al-Wafd. There was a breach between the two leaders of al-Wafd, the Muslim Nahas Pasha, and the Christian Makram Ebeid Pasha. This breach caused the majority of Copts, who supported Makram Ebeid, to withdraw from al-Wafd, further weakening the party at a time when pan–Islamic nationalism was growing, especially among the proletariat class.[135] Social and economic problems became challenging to the liberal government of al-Wafd. There was increasing criticism of the openness toward the West, which led intellectuals to revert back to Islam for inspiration.[136] Additionally, Egypt's king funded the MB to counter al-Wafd and, at one point, the British also collaborated with the MB to maintain their power in the country.[137] There was a fierce fight between the king and the British to reduce the influence of al-Wafd and to manipulate power. The dream of liberalization was interrupted due to this power struggle.[138]

With the rise of the MB, the general mood of Egypt became conservative. The MB spread anti–Western and anti–Coptic sentiment, which impacted every sphere of life, be it social, political, economic, educational or cultural. The MB also created a military wing in the 1940s that committed violent attacks, including bombings and political assassinations. Threatened by this dangerous aspect, the state dissolved the MB in December 1948. In response, the MB assassinated Egypt's Prime Minister Mahmoud Fahmi al-Nuqrashi.[139] But dissolving the MB did not mean its end, by any means. It continued to play a political role from underground where it was divided into cells and it formed its own secret organization.[140]

In this power struggle the situation was ripe for Nasser and the Free Officers to launch their coup in July 1952 establishing a military regime in Egypt. Egypt's European communities left and the Egyptian society started to become decreasingly diverse and increasingly closed. The imminent result of the military regime was that Egypt's liberal democracy experiment became a part of Egypt's history, and it marked the end of Coptic political power. The military rule would last for sixty years, until the rise of the MB to power in 2012.

Five

Military Rule
The Re-Islamization of Egypt

Nasser, 1956–1970

On July 23, 1952, Gamal Abdel Nasser and 89 other Free Officers launched a military coup d'état, later called a revolution, ousting King Farouk, who was exiled to Europe. Egypt was taken over by a Revolutionary Command Council of 11 officers who were led and controlled by the powerful Nasser, with Major General Muhammad Naguib as the figurehead President. Consequently, Naguib was ousted and put under a house arrest, and Nasser became Egypt's President (1956–1970).[1] By deposing King Farouk, the last member of Muhammad Ali's family, Nasser broke a historical trend of thousands of years of foreign rule. So now, what would the situation of the Copts be under the rule of a fellow Egyptian?

The military regime started with a declaration of faith in the Egyptian identity. To cement this declaration with actions, the statue of Ramses II was moved from Memphis to downtown Cairo (Ramses Square), and an obelisk from Tanis was erected in a public garden on the banks of the Nile in al-Gezerah, Cairo. However, Arabism or Arab nationalism would very soon surface to challenge this identity and would come to characterize Egypt. It would replace the Egyptian identity that had been championed by liberal Egyptians during the short-lived democratic, liberal experiment. This new orientation towards Arab nationalism was due to several factors. Partly it was a result of the Arab awakening and partly it resulted from the shortcomings of the liberal and democratic era. The newly established Jewish state of Israel as a western outpost in the middle of the Arab world was another factor.[2] Nasser's character was yet another reason for the rise of Arab nationalism and he used it as a platform from which he could lead the Arab world. In 1954, Nasser wrote *Philosophy of the Revolution*, in which he talked of the "heroic and glorious roles which never found heroes to perform them." In this book he outlined his ambition to be the leader of the 55 million Arabs, then of the 224 million Africans, and finally of the 420 million Muslims.[3] Nasser was hoping to unite Arabs based on their shared culture and history.

In his endeavors to promote his ideology, Nasser exaggerated the Arab character of Egypt to the degree that it alone formed the basis for the Egyptian cultural heritage, and this character became the foundation of the Egyptian national spirit. The Egyptian identity of Egypt was dissolved by Arabism to the point that Nasser removed the name of Egypt from the title of the country: Egypt became the United Arab Republic.[4] Nasser's regime turned Cairo into the political capital of the Arab world. Unlike the members of Muhammad Ali's family who looked towards Europe, Nasser looked towards the Arabs. He brought thousands of Arabs to Egypt—artists, reporters, students and political activists—to make Cairo an appealing destination.[5]

The Copts were threatened by Nasser's Arab nationalism and ideology. Nasser's ambition to unite Arabs based on their shared culture and history excluded the Copts. The Copts kept their own unique culture and identity, evident in their Coptic traditions, music, art, and, to some extent, Coptic language, which is distinct from the Arabs' Bedouin culture. Their history precedes the Arab conquest of Egypt, and the portion of history they share with the Arabs after the conquest is marked by humiliation and repression as *dhimmis*. So, whereas previously the Copts were excluded from the Islamic identity by religion, now they were excluded from the Arab identity by culture.

But Arab nationalism was not the only alarm from Nasser's regime sounding for the Copts. The fact that the Free Officers Movement did not include any Copts was another alarm. Despite their prominent political role in the independence of Egypt, the Copts were ignored by the Free Officers, a fact which indicated to them that there was no role for them to play in the future of their country. The Copts were also threatened by the fact that the Free Officers Movement collaborated with the MB. The movement included some members of the MB: Nasser himself was one. In the early years of his political career, Nasser was in close contact with the MB founder Hasan al-Banna and became a member of the MB's "secret cell" within the Egyptian military in 1942.[6]

Although Nasser joined the MB, he was not really an Islamist but rather a nationalist with his own separate vision. He pragmatically joined and sought the assistance of the MB, who were a strong power on the ground. He needed their help to seize power, but once the monarchy was ended, it was inevitable that disagreements between Nasser and the MB would arise over the direction and the orientation of Egypt. Consequently, the MB withdrew their support for Nasser when they realized he was shifting away from their Islamic ideology. They criticized his secular stance and abstention from implementing *sharia*. The confrontation reached a peak in October 1954 with an assassination attempt by the MB on Nasser. Nasser's reaction was not long to come. He outlawed the MB organization, dismantled its infrastructure and conducted a wide-scale crackdown on their leaders. He detained them and brought them before revolutionary tribunals, where some received life sentences in prison, while others faced death penalties. Some leaders were able to escape to the neighboring Arab states while others went underground within Egypt.

Nasser's character and his presidency were complex and controversial. He joined the MB, yet they suffered during his tenure. He pushed aside the Islamic identity of Egypt and championed the secular stance, yet much of the re–Islamization of Egypt started during his term. Although he was secular, he did not believe in the separation of state and religion. In his endeavors to achieve his ideology, Nasser made good use of religion in public life. During the Suez War of 1956 (tripartite aggression of Britain, France and Israel), Nasser went to al-Azhar mosque to deliver a passionate speech, telling the people that fighting was not only a nationalistic duty but also an Islamic one, all the while quoting verses from the Quran. The influence of al-Azhar and, by default, religion, was on the rise during his term. He transformed al-Azhar from a purely Islamic institution into a major modern university with branches all over Egypt. He allowed al-Azhar to build its own educational system through a vast network of primary and secondary schools all over the country.[7]

In 1957, Nasser decreed religion would be a basic subject in schools that students had to pass to move to the next year.[8] He established numerous Islamic bodies and organizations. In 1954, he established the Islamic Congress, and in 1960, he established the Supreme Council for Islamic Affairs. In 1963, Nasser established The Quran Channel, the region's first religious radio station. In addition to reciting the Quran, its programs preach that Islam is the solution to the ills of society.[9] In 1964, he established the House of Quran. And notably, the largest number of government mosques were built during the tenure of Nasser.[10] In contrast, the Coptic community was far from Nasser's attention.

Even when Nasser introduced "Arab socialism" as the optimum political system, he referred to religion to gain legitimacy for this ideology, which is known for its vilification of religion as the opium of the masses.[11] Nasser said, "Islam in its early days was the first socialist nation, the nation that Muhammad established was the first socialist nation. He was the first to implement the policy of nationalization (*ta'mim*)."[12]

Nasser applied a policy of nationalization in 1961 which was preceded by agrarian reform in 1952. He wanted to redistribute wealth in Egypt, a policy that would affect different segments of the Egyptian society but would be a major economic blow to the Coptic community. In Nasser's agrarian reform, individual ownership of land could not exceed 200 acres. The Copts had already acquired substantial plots of cultivated land and they invested their wealth into buying more land as a source of security and power. Hence, Nasser's land reform hit Copts very hard, as he stripped them of their wealth and power.[13]

Nasser's nationalization of industry and business further hurt the Copts who owned large businesses. The new revolutionary regime appropriated their businesses, which led to the loss of another form of revenue for the Copts, as well as economic and political influence.[14] The business nationalization policy harmed the Copts more than Muslims because it annulled numerous skilled jobs in which Copts composed the majority of the skilled workers. As a result of Nasser's policy, the Copts lost about seventy-five percent of their properties and jobs.[15] His policy impacted poor Copts and the Church as well. The rich Copts had always helped them through charity and an internal net of support. But with the nationalization policy, the flow of funds was interrupted. Moreover, Nasser confiscated Coptic *waqf* (endowment) lands. It is true that Nasser's land reform and nationalization policies hit all rich Egyptians, but they hit the Copts the hardest as, disproportionately, they owned large pieces of land and businesses.

Nasser's nationalization policy also reached Coptic schools. In 1958, Nasser imposed a new curriculum aimed at Arabizing the students through history and Arabic language lessons. Through this curriculum Arab identity was made superior to Egyptian identity, and by 1961, he nationalized Coptic schools altogether. The independence and excellence the Coptic schools enjoyed in the liberal era was lost as a consequence. The Copts lost the freedom to teach their history and culture, as now they were forced to abide by the government curriculum.[16]

Today, students study a truncated form of Egyptian history that starts at the seventh century, which is the advent of the Arabs to Egypt. The Coptic period is cut out, not considered a part of Egypt's history. Due to Nasser's ideology, students today can study English, French, and other languages, but Coptic is not permitted because it was seen as contradictory to the process of Arabization. Great emphasis is given to the Arabic language with its poems and literature. As Arabic is the language of the Quran and in accordance with government curriculum, Coptic students are required to learn and memorize parts of the Quran if they want to pass to the next year, even if the sections of the Quran they study talk about *dhimmis* or go against Christian belief.

Nasser's nationalization policies covered all aspects of life. The privately owned banks, insurance, transportation, export, import, and financial companies, in addition to many other businesses, all came under the control of the government. Nasser didn't only want to control the economy but also to limit the creation of any viable independent economic establishments of any kind. Within ten years of Nasser's regime, the Egyptian land and business owners who had politically and socially formed the liberal era society were totally eliminated from the political scene. In one decade, Nasser eliminated a whole class that had taken a century to be established.[17] While eliminating this class of Egyptians, Nasser not only ended the liberal era but also the democratic values it represented, and the Copts were among the first victims.

Democracy was replaced by Nasser's one party regime: the Arab Socialist Union. Nasser annulled political parties in 1954, eliminating al-Wafd, in which Copts were salient members. This led to the disappearance of major Coptic leadership on the political scene.[18] With the dissolution of political parties, Copts were unable to nominate themselves and their representation in the parliament fluctuated between zero and 3 percent. In the general election of 1957, no Copt won. Nasser implemented a new constitutional principal which allowed him to appoint ten members to the parliament. To combat the lack of Coptic representation, most of his appointees were Copts.[19]

This tradition of appointing Copts to the Parliament became a custom for successive presidents, and it was the only way to achieve Coptic representation. However, it is only cosmetic, meant to give the appearance of balance to the Parliament, as these appointees have never been real representatives of the Coptic community. They are carefully chosen to be the most loyal to the government and its voice. Many believe that appointed representatives are worse than no representatives. Nasser's regime alienated the Copts even when it tried to accommodate them. With the dissolution of al-Wafd and the decrease in Coptic presence in the government, the political role of the Copts was fragmented.[20]

Alienation of the Copts under Nasser's regime led to a new phenomenon of Coptic exodus, which started in the mid–1950s. A large number of Copts immigrated to the U.S., Canada and Australia. The Coptic immigrants were well educated, and while they were welcomed and respected by their adoptive homelands, their exodus was a "brain drain" to Egypt. After Nasser's nationalization laws were issued, wealthy Copts fled the country with a portion of their money to start new lives in western countries.[21] Waves of Coptic immigration during Nasser's rule would be followed by other waves, most recently after the January 25th Revolution in 2011.

The remaining Copts were unable to express their political and social concerns not only because of the annulment of political parties and the fact that their vibrant press was nationalized and shut down, but also for fear of upsetting Nasser, who turned Egypt into a police state where telephones and media were tapped and censored. Freedom of expression became a fleeting dream from the "good old days."

Fear of Nasser was felt all the way up to the leadership level of the Church. Pope Kyrillos the 6th was challenged with a lack of money to build a cathedral for the growing number of Copts, as Nasser's policy curtailed the revenue coming into church. Pope Kyrillos was reluctant to address the need to build a cathedral with Nasser, so he sought the mediation of an influential journalist who was one of Nasser's top advisors.[22] The Pope was anxious about bringing his legitimate concerns to Nasser for fear that he might cause a rupture between the Church and the regime, not to mention between the Church and the greater population.

In the end, Nasser agreed to give the Church half a million Egyptian pounds, half of it in cash and half of it in assistance offered by various government construction companies. While Nasser understood the rationale behind building a cathedral, he was also influenced by the emerging role of the World Council of Churches and the impact they could have on the situation of the Copts in Egypt. At this time in history, there was a great western interest in churches worldwide in order to combat communism. This concern resulted in the establishment of the World Council of Churches in 1948, and initially the organization had substantial economic and ideological support from the West.[23]

In an unprecedented move Nasser attended the opening ceremony of St. Mark's Coptic Orthodox Cathedral, in 1968, accompanied by the Ethiopian Emperor Haile Selassie and representatives from the world's churches. Nasser was on good terms with the discreet Pope Kyrillos and he promised him that the Church would be allowed to build 25 churches a year.[24] But the reality was that this number could not even be reached after a decade. The total number of churches build between 1962 and 1972 was 22.[25]

Some of Nasser's policies profited the Copts. Poor Coptic farmers benefitted slightly from Nasser's land reform when they received small parcels of land. However, a government with no Christian representatives did not treat Copts justly nor redistribute land fairly.[26] There were also unintended benefits for the Copts. Nasser's refusal of the fundamentalist ideology put him in confrontation with the MB, especially after they tried to assassinate him. A byproduct of Nasser's repression of the MB was that Copts enjoyed one of their most peaceful periods as they were not a main target of the now weakened Brotherhood. Another unintended result of Nasser's policy was that the Coptic Church started to spread internationally. When the Copts immigrated to new countries, not only did they take their professional experience, but they took their religious beliefs as well. Consequently, the Church started to have new congregations in these countries while still under the leadership of the mother Coptic Church in Egypt. The number of churches overseas would grow remarkably in the coming years, and the Coptic community abroad would be among the strongest supporters of the Church.

In general, Arab unity proved to be an unachievable goal and Nasser's ideology and endeavors were miscalculated adventures. He unified Egypt with Syria as the United Arab Republic in 1958, only to see the union to collapse three years later. He sent the Egyptian army to intervene in the Yemeni civil war (1962–1967) which caused major harm to Egypt economically and politically. Nasser triggered the Six Day War of 1967, the outcome of which was devastating for the Arab countries involved. The Egyptians lost all of the Sinai while the Syrians lost the Golan Heights to Israel, which also annexed East Jerusalem and the West Bank. With the exception of Egypt, the land that came under Israel's control during that conflict is still within Israel's possession until today. Both the Israelis and the Arabs attributed the outcome of the Six Day War to God. For many Jews, only a miracle would allow a newly created, small country surrounded by Arab states to achieve such a sudden undreamed-of victory. For many Arabs, the defeat was interpreted as God's punishment for their departure from Islam and God's *sharia* law. The humiliation of this war, referred to as *naksa* or "setback," was very hard to overcome. An immediate outcome of this defeat was that the MB found fertile ground not only from which to lobby people against Nasser's policies but also to promote their values and ideology. This time, without Nasser's interference, the re-Islamization process was much stronger. Egypt's resources were already depleted by the war in Yemen and the Suez War had further burdened the economy. With the *naksa*, Egypt went through a period of war economy in which more repression and poverty prevailed, thus, bringing people closer to religion. This was the situation until Nasser died, on September 28, 1970.

Nasser was a true Egyptian leader after thousands of years of foreign rule, yet he did not champion the Egyptian identity, and his ideology hurt Egypt politically and economically. He was not anti–Copt, but his policies irrevocably ended their political and economic power. Nasser's Arab nationalism did not serve Egypt's interests at any level, as history has revealed. Suffice it to say it dissolved the Egyptian identity, the only bond that can tie Copts and Muslims together.

Sadat, 1970–1981

After Nasser died, Anwar al-Sadat succeeded him as Egypt's President, in October 1970. Sadat was a prominent member of the Free Officers Movement and vice president when Nasser died, yet he abandoned Nasser's ideology and policies. He allowed the formation of political parties and sacrificed Nasser's socialism in favor of *infitah* or "open-door policy" for private and foreign investments. He revisited Nasser's pro–Soviet position, found it lacking, and allied himself, instead, with the U.S. Unlike Nasser's "what was taken by force, can only be restored by force" approach, he initiated peace with Israel, and through the Egypt-Israel peace treaty, the Sinai returned to Egypt. For this Sadat won the Nobel Peace Prize and emerged in the international community as a man of peace. But did Sadat bring peace to Egypt and its Coptic community?

Sadat inherited several serious problems from Nasser; most pressing were a fully occupied Sinai and a moribund economy. Sadat also faced a lack of legitimacy. The Arab world and the majority of Egyptians gave Sadat's succession a lukewarm reception. The unexpected death of the charismatic Nasser would make it difficult for any other successor to replace him.[27] Nasser's followers predicted that Sadat would not last for very long and that it was only a matter of time for a political maneuvering to bring Nasser's real successor into the forefront.[28] But Sadat had time on his side.

Within seven months of assumption of power on May 15, 1971, Sadat took a dramatic step to consolidate power against his opponents. He arrested the most important Nasserite figures—those who were in control of the most important offices: the Minister of Defense, the Head of Intelligence, the Speaker of the House, the Minister of Information and the leadership of the Arab Socialist Union. After arresting them, he charged them with conspiracy to overthrow his regime.[29] Sadat was a good reader of history; in emulation of Muhammad Ali's "massacre of the citadel," he was able to get rid of any potential opposition in one single strike. But, because Sadat killed his opponents politically, he called his massacre a "corrective revolution." It worked, and Sadat would keep this in mind for the future.

Nasser was not the only charismatic leader whose influence Sadat had to deal with. One year after Sadat's ascendance to presidency, another charismatic leader emerged in Egypt, though not a political one. After the death of Pope Kyrillos the 6th, Pope Shenouda III was ordained the new Pope of the Coptic Church in November 1971. Pope Shenouda was a true son of Coptic stock and an impressive man. Like his spiritual great grandfathers, he became a monk at a young age. A sign of his fortitude is the fact that he lived in solitude in Egypt's Western desert for six consecutive years in a life of prayer and meditation, in a cave he carved out himself.[30] The humble monk's sand-spotted black garment could not, however, conceal the qualities of a leader. This life of unity with God he chose was interrupted when Pope Kyrillos ordained him the Bishop of Education.

Pope Shenouda turned out to be a philosopher, poet and talented preacher. Every week more than seven thousand people attended his Wednesday sermons. He became a prolific author with a hundred and one books to his name, over half of which were translated into foreign languages. He was editor-in-chief of *al-Kiraza* magazine, the Coptic Church's official publication.

He was the Dean of the Coptic Theological Seminary, a reminder to the Copts of the glorious days when the Popes were chosen from among the deans of the School of Alexandria.[31] The Copts raised him to the level of the early fathers, calling him "Athanasius of the 20th century" while moderate Arab Muslims called him the "Pope of the Arabs" due to his stance in the Arab-Israeli conflict. The popular Pope became a distinguished religious leader and the Arab World's most influential Christian. His popularity, however, made Sadat's antagonism towards him inevitable. Sadat's confrontations with the Pope would characterize his tenure and his relationship with his Coptic citizens.

With the lack of political participation and the near absence of a Coptic elite in this period of uncertainty, the Copts turned to the Church as the only outlet from which they could voice their concerns and demands. When they were denied equal opportunities and were treated like second-class citizens by the state, the Copts went to the Church for protection. Pope Shenouda was obliged to meet the needs of his people since they could not rely on the state. He represented them in church matters and gave voice to their concerns, mainly against discriminatory legislation and laws. Thus, a pedagogue was posed to face a politician.

The first interaction between the Pope and Sadat was quick to come with the incident of al-Khanka in November 1972. The catalyst was the never-ending issue of building and repairing churches, which seemed to threaten the state and the fundamentalist Islamists alike. Some residents of al-Khanka neighborhood set a Bible Society building ablaze because the Copts were using it as a church before obtaining the proper permit for it. The Coptic clergy and men went to pray at the burnt site, an act that was seen as a challenge to the radical Islamists of al-Khanka and which led to more violence.[32] The significance of the incident of al-Khanka is that Sadat held the Pope responsible for the violence. Sadat blamed the Pope because the Coptic clergy, who went to pray at the burnt site, marched their way to the site as if in protest, which not only provoked the radicals of al-Khanka but challenged Sadat's authority as well. The Pope denied the allegations, stating that in an attempt to discourage clergy and lay Copts from going to the site the police stopped their busses from reaching their destination, forcing them to go on foot. They prayed under the protection of the police and left in peace before violence broke out.[33]

Sadat took the incident as a pretext to confront the Pope and he transferred the issue to the Parliament, asking them to form a fact-finding committee. The committee was formed and headed by Gamal al-Utayfi, the Deputy Speaker of Parliament, and the results of the investigation were published in a document called al-Utayfi's report. According to the report, on November 6, 1972, the first day of the Muslim holiday Eid al-Fitr, some

Five. Military Rule 109

Muslims set the Bible Society ablaze because "The use of the premises as an unlicensed church angered some residents of al-Khanka." Six days later Coptic priests and citizens went to pray at the burnt site in the morning. In the evening, after they returned from their work and universities, some Muslim youth were told of the prayer service that occurred in the morning. They regarded this as "a challenge and provocation to their feelings." They gathered at a nearby mosque where the imam led the march towards the police station to complain all the while chanting, *"Allah Akbar."* On their way back, they set fire to some Coptic homes and shops. Importantly, the report documented an increase of attacks on Copts in the previous two years. There had been eleven incidents between June 1970 and November 1972, ten of which had occurred since Sadat assumed power. The report said these attacks reflected tension augmented by "a strong religious current."[34]

Sadat saw the use of the unlicensed church as a challenge to state authority and a test for him; for this reason, he blamed the Pope for the violence. Yet, al-Utayfi, who was believed to be close to Sadat, held the state responsible in numerous issues behind the violence against the Copts, and he voiced recommendations that Sadat neither liked nor accepted.[35] Successive presidents did not accept al-Utayfi's report either, but for the Copts, the report was vindicating. It stated that one of the problems leading to violence against the Copts was the harsh legal conditions of the Hamayoni Decree and al-Ezabi's ten conditions: the fact that building a church is limited by its proximity to a mosque and needs the consent of the Muslim neighbors not to mention a presidential decree, all make it impossible to build a church. Al-Utayfi's report identified the problem as:

> one of the most important reasons leading to friction and the arousal of divisions is the non-formulation of any easy process for the regulation of such licensing without there being a need for the issuing of a presidential decree in each case. This is because acquiring such a decree requires much time during which it often happens that the features of the site slated for the establishment of the church have changed, such as the establishment of a mosque nearby, which would prevent compliance with the ten conditions. Owing to the slowness of the procedures, many Coptic societies often resort to establishing such churches without a license. In some cases the administrative party tolerates that, and in other cases an investigation is held with the person responsible in the society. This is a situation that appears to create a contradiction, between respect for the rule of law on the one hand, and respect for the freedom of practicing religious rites on the other, a principle guaranteed in the constitution in its forty-sixth article....[36]

Prior to the incident of al-Khanka, rumors had circulated of a report alleging that Pope Shenouda had held a meeting in March 1972 at which he outlined a plan to increase the number of Copts to equal that of Muslims, to impoverish the Muslims, and to enrich the Copts, so they could regain Egypt from the hands of the Muslim occupiers in the same manner Spain went back to Christianity after eight centuries of Arab occupation. Al-Utayfi's report stated, "This report was formulated, and was distributed in a manner suggesting it was a genuine official report." Al-Utayfi's report added that even though the effect of this pamphlet was dangerous, the authorities did not take any measures to warn people it was a fabrication. Although the report was unfounded, the fundamentalist Islamists used it to incite the populace against the Copts, and the first fruit of the report came two months before al-Khanka, September 1972, with an assault on the Orthodox Renaissance Association at Sanhur, Buhayrah. The following month, the fundamentalists printed and distributed one hundred copies of the alleged report and in November 1972 the al-Khanka incident occurred.[37]

The ideas in this pamphlet are preposterous. How long would it take the Copts who represent around ten percent of the population to match the Muslim population in number? While it is conceivable that the fundamentalists would use the pamphlet to lobby the populace against the Copts, it is surprising that Sadat himself, according to some officials, was convinced of the contents of it. Sadat perceived Pope Shenouda as a potential threat, fearing he was attempting to assume political leadership among the Copts.[38] Much like Said Pasha, who felt threatened by Pope Kyrillos the Fourth, Sadat felt threatened by Pope Shenouda. The forged pamphlet created a myth about Pope Shenouda and the Coptic community. In fact, it introduced the new Pope to the society as a conspirator and set the stage for Sadat to further accuse him. This myth has never died; it is sustained by fundamentalists who recall it whenever it serves their cause.

To ease the tension after al-Khanka and to promote the need for unity in this difficult time of Egypt's history, Sadat paid a visit to al-Azhar and the Church. In the meeting with the Pope, Sadat stated that Copts build illegal churches that "provoke Muslims," so to solve the issue, he promised the Pope 50 permits a year.[39] The number was double what Nasser offered Pope Kyrillos, but he, too, did not fulfill his promise. Sadat's meeting with the Pope, however, may have cleared the air for a short time, which was what Sadat needed as he was facing other internal issues.

The main issue he faced was his delay in meeting the Egyptians' concern to overcome the humiliation of the 1967 defeat and to liberate Sinai. Sadat had already promised that 1971 would be the "year of decision" in his fight for liberation. The year came and went and nothing happened. His public image was steadily deteriorating. Nasserites and leftists increased activity on the ground, causing unrest, especially among students on the university campuses. Sadat's reaction to these street politics was to release thousands of MB detainees from Nasser's time to counter the Nasserites and leftists and to support him.[40]

Sadat's approach to the MB was a natural choice. Sadat himself was believed to be religious. He was the Secretary General of the Islamic Congress in 1954 and, like Nasser, he was in close contact with the MB founder Hasan al-Banna. Sadat was indebted to Hasan al-Banna because he gave Sadat's first wife a monthly stipend while Sadat was in prison in the early stage of his political career.[41]

After Sadat released the MB from prison, he supported them politically and financially so they would help him strengthen his shaky regime. "I want to raise Muslim youth and finance them to be our outpost at the university." Sadat said to Mahmoud Gamea a very close friend and aide he chose to be in charge of implementing his plan in Lower Egypt. This is how the MB came back to the scene after Nasser had crushed them. Their cadres who escaped to other countries returned to Egypt and the wealth they had acquired gave economic power to the group. They reissued their mouthpiece, *al-Da'wa*, after two decades of being shut down, and the group started to reorganize its constituency all over Egypt.[42] In this manner, the MB was given free rein to spread its teachings, especially in institutions of higher learning, throughout Egypt. So, it was Sadat himself who created the "strong religious current" al-Utayfi's report mentioned as being responsible for the radical Islamist attack on the Copts in al-Khanka.

Sadat, who was in dire need of this "religious current," could not blame the radicals for the incident of al-Khanka, so he instead held the Pope responsible for the violence. By blaming the Pope and taking the issue to the Parliament, Sadat wanted to portray himself as a decisive leader. And by manipulating the Copts, "the historical scapegoat," Sadat would secure the support of the fundamentalist Islamists.[43] Sadat did not want internal problems to hinder his next dramatic move: the initiation of the 6th of October 1973 War against Israel.

In a move that astonished the world, Egyptian troops crossed the Suez Canal and destroyed the "impregnable" Bar Lev Line in order to regain the Sinai. After the war, the Egyptians overcame the humiliation of the *naksa*, and Sadat emerged as Egypt's undisputed leader, with the needed legitimacy he had been lacking. The self-confident Sadat had free rein to carry out his vision for Egypt. He implemented limited political liberalization in which he allowed the formation of political parties to end the one-party regime. He also implemented an economic and diplomatic open-door policy to the West. Through this, Sadat would rely on a new business class internally and the United States externally. His regime remained authoritarian, yet with a higher degree of tolerance for political pluralism compared to Nasser's. In this atmosphere there was even more freedom for the MB to act.[44]

Sadat allowed al-Wafd to come back to the political scene in 1977, but his authoritarian regime would not allow it to become a viable opposition party. Al-Wafd was caught between authoritarianism and Islamism and was unable to play its political role, which discouraged Copts from rejoining the party. The secular stance of the newly returning al-Wafd was very weak and they were unable to counteract the powerful role Sadat gave religion in politics. And, the Copts continued to be left out with no political channels to express their concerns.

The role of religion in Sadat's politics became clear when he attempted to make *sharia* the basis of legislation. Sadat added a phrase to Article Two of the 1971 constitution which already stipulated that Islam was the state religion. The new addition read, "principles of Islamic law are a main source of legislation." Sadat wanted to Islamize the law in Egypt. Based on Sadat's instructions, the Speaker of the House declared that *sharia* would be the basis for all legislation. The head of the appellate court was instructed to form a committee to review all laws to ensure their compatibility with *sharia* and to make the necessary changes to align them. Some of the proposed laws were harsh, such as cutting off the hand of a thief for stealing and whipping anyone caught with alcohol. In this spirit, a judge applied *sharia* without waiting for the actual laws to be issued by the legislation. He sentenced a man accused of drinking alcohol to be whipped 80 lashes as prescribed by *sharia*. In his verdict he said a judge should apply the law of God and not wait for the law to be legislated. Among the proposed legislation was the apostasy law. According to this law, anyone changing his religion from Islam to another is first given the chance to repent or recant his decision. If he does not, he would face the death penalty. Two witnesses are all that is needed to charge a person with apostasy.[45]

According to the proposed law, if a Christian converted to Islam and wanted to go back to Christianity he would be killed. If someone converted to Islam, but was advised to go back to Christianity by a family member or a priest, the advisor would also be killed as an instigator to apostasy. This would open the door to abuse as all it would take would be two people falsely witnessing against a Copt claiming that he had converted to Islam but denied it for him to be killed. This also would provide an easy way to confiscate the money of a rich Copt as his Christian heirs would lose their inheritance; Christians cannot inherit from Muslims. The only way to keep both his life and his wealth was to convert, much as in the times of the caliphates.

The Church felt threatened and called for a Christian conference, the second in their history. On January 17, 1977, the conference took place in Alexandria to voice their disagreement against the application of *sharia*. Were this proposal to be passed, it would take them back to the *dhimma* status. Although their previous conference in Assiut in 1911 achieved nothing, at least they would voice their concerns.[46] Several recommendations for the state were developed which outlined Coptic concerns, but the authorities banned this communiqué from being published. Among other things the communiqué recommended the freedom of practice of religion, equality and the representation of Copts in the local councils. They requested the annulment of the Ottoman laws which restrict the building of churches and the prohibition of discrimination against the Copts in appointments at all different levels in the government. They also asked for freedom to write and publish literature about Coptic heritage. Most importantly, they petitioned the authorities to annul the bill of apostasy and not to apply laws based on *sharia* to non–Muslims. To support their claims and peacefully protest, the conference decided that the Coptic community would fast and pray for three days (January 31–February 2, 1977) seeking God's guidance and help. Being part of the Coptic community, the Coptic diaspora sent letters of condemnation to the Egyptian Parliament regarding the projected laws. By this time the Coptic Church had spread in the United States, Canada and Australia.[47]

As had happened with the 1911 conference, an Islamic conference was held to counter the Christian conference. The grand sheikh of al-Azhar, Abdel Halim Mahmoud, convened the conference in July 1977. In addition to denying the Coptic demands, the conference decided that any law not compatible with Islam is null and void and resisting the laws not compatible with *sharia* is the duty of all Muslims. It was also decided that Islamic law and its application is not contingent on the Parliament's decision, it is holy law whether Parliament accepts it or not: No man can discuss the law of God.[48] The state supported the Islamic conference and, contrary to its stance of banning the Christian conference communique, it allowed the Islamic conference communique to be published in the largest Egyptian newspaper: *al-Ahram*.[49] Although the conference conclusions were only recommendations, the suggestion that the resistance to laws not compatible with *sharia* is a duty of all Muslims was threatening to the Coptic community.

The demands of Christian conference were similar to those of the conference in 1911, which sought basic rights. The difference was that the recent conference was in large part managed by the Church, as the Coptic elite were almost nonexistent and Coptic representation had disappeared. The Copts had no body or political party to represent or advocate for them other than the Church. So, the Church was pushed to be the de facto political representative of the Copts. In the liberal era, the Coptic conference demands were rejected, even when *sharia* was not on the table. Under Sadat, the Islamic conference outspokenly asked for the application of *sharia*—a reflection of a new tide to reassert Egypt's Islamic identity.

On August 30, 1977, Pope Shenouda convened with the Holy Synod and wrote a memorandum to the state, declaring their objection to the application of *sharia* law. Once again the Coptic community fasted and prayed, seeking God's support. In light of this, Sadat decided to meet with Pope Shenouda and the Synod on September 21. A few days before, on September 12, Egypt's Prime Minister visited the Pope to assure him that *sharia* would not be applied, and eventually it was withdrawn.[50]

During the meeting with the Pope and the Synod, the unresolved issue of building churches arose once again. To demonstrate the difficulties the Church faces, the Pope related the story of the "14-mosque church" in Giza, where each time building of the church began a mosque was built close to it. According to the ten conditions of al-Ezabi this would annul the building of a church. Fourteen attempts to build the church failed because the neighbors built fourteen mosques. The Pope explained that, as Copts did not want to trouble them to build the fifteenth mosque, the Bishop of Giza bought a house and knocked down the inside walls to create a big space for people to pray. What could he do, the Pope asked, if he needed to pray and couldn't? Thus, he illustrated the rationale behind the illegal church. Sadat did not comment on the illegality of the church, as he understood the harsh situation leading to its formation.[51]

Yet, praying in a house doesn't satisfy the radical Islamists, as they attacked the house on the pretext that it was being used as an unlicensed church. Both Sadat and al–Utayfi's report mentioned "Muslim provocation" that resulted from the building of illegal churches. There is a long list of unlicensed mosques; small mosques in businesses, public parks, on the side of the roads and empty spaces are common occurrences. Building mosques is based on will and is allowed at any place and in any number. Why does a church need a permit if a mosque doesn't? This is a question asked by many Copts, though, understandably, the Coptic diaspora are more vocal.

Prior to meeting with Pope Shenouda and the Synod, Sadat had visited the United States, where he was met with protests from the American Coptic community. Sadat complained of the protesters in his meeting, but the Pope reminded him of the help they had given during the October War when they sent thousands of blood transfusion sets and hundreds of thousands of blankets for Egyptian soldiers. This showed how much the expats loved and wanted to serve their country, he explained. Sadat accepted the Pope's explanation.[52] But, this was not the end of the Coptic diaspora issue. It would resurface and, once again, be a sore spot for Sadat.

Although Sadat shared his anger at the American Copts, he concealed another source of anger at the meeting. In April 1977, Pope Shenouda was invited to visit the United States to meet with President Carter at the White House. It was the first official visit of the Pope of Alexandria to the U.S. and was enthusiastically celebrated by the Coptic community there. The Pope invited Egypt's ambassador to the U.S. to be part of the meeting with President Carter to avoid any misunderstanding and ensure transparency. Carter wanted to explore the Church's stance regarding the Egyptian-Israeli conflict.

The Pope talked about general principals but left the details to the state. Although Sadat could not fault the Pope, who had invited the Egyptian ambassador to the meeting, he was angry with the fact that the American Administration contacted and met with the Church leader.[53]

Another point of contention was Carter's statement, in a press conference, that the Copts of Egypt numbered seven million: a figure compatible with Church statistics but in disagreement with the Sadat regime's number of about two and a half million.[54] Al-Utayfi's report mentions the official number of churches in Egypt was 1,442.[55] This translates into one church for every five thousand Copts and explains one of the reasons the state underestimated the Coptic population. Thirty five years later, in 2012, the state officially put the number of Copts at 5.1 million.[56]

A few months after Sadat met with the Pope, violence against Copts resumed. It was intense and would mark the rest of Sadat's tenure. In April of 1978, two churches were attacked by radical Islamists on Good Friday in Manufiya. In September of the same year a Coptic priest was killed in Minia. In 1979 the oldest church in Old Cairo was set ablaze.[57] Several churches were burned in Upper Egypt and the Church of Abu Zaabal in Cairo was also burned. In reaction, ninety priests led a protest objecting to the attacks on Copts and churches. Concurrently to this period of turmoil, several officials and writers started calling again for the implementation of the apostasy law.[58]

In a speech on March 26, 1980, Pope Shenouda expressed his fear that *sharia* would be the basis of laws applied to Christians. He also expressed his concern that religion was replacing nationalism. Unhappy with the situation, the Pope annulled the celebration of Easter as a sign of peaceful protest to the indifference of the government to Coptic demands and the lack of protection. The Pope left Cairo and went to his monastery for seclusion to pray for God's intercession in this period of hardship.[59]

Angry at the Pope's unprecedented decision, Sadat went to the Parliament again. He accused the Pope of having political ambitions, trying to be a political leader for the Copts and trying to establish a Coptic state in Upper Egypt with Assiut as its capital. Extremely enraged, Sadat said the Pope had to understand that "I am a Muslim President to an Islamic state."[60] No political leader in Egypt's modern history has bluntly stated Egypt's Islamic identity in the same manner as did Sadat. In the same speech he added, "no politics in religion and no religion in politics," ignoring his own approach.[61] Sadat's accusation of the Pope, although unfounded, reinforced the myth already created by the alleged pamphlet. The reason for such accusation was to defame, silence, and lay the ground for future action against the Pope.

Sadat was already infuriated by the Pope before his decision to cancel the Easter celebration and go to his monastery. The Pope had refused to accompany Sadat on his trip to Israel when he addressed the Israeli Knesset in 1977. There was great public outcry against Sadat's visit and the Pope did not want to oppose the Egyptian public consensus.[62] Moreover, a part of the Egypt-Israel peace treaty in 1979 was the process of normalization where Egyptians and Israelis exchange visits; several thousand Israeli tourists had begun to visit Egypt, but only a few Egyptian tourists had visited Israel. Sadat, unable to make the Muslims visit Israel, wanted Pope Shenouda to encourage the travel of Copts to Jerusalem to visit their holy sites, thus maintaining the image of normalization. Pope Shenouda rejected Sadat's idea, stating that if the Muslims did not want to visit Israel, he did not want the Copts to look like traitors. Sadat, under pressure from the Israelis to carry out his promise of normalization, was furious that the Pope contradicted him. Sadat looked incapable and was isolated from his people as well.[63]

The Pope based his decision to give up visitation of the Holy Sites on sentiments of nationalism to show solidarity with fellow Egyptians even though visiting these sites is a very old tradition and a blessing for the Copts. While the Arabs dishonored Sadat for his visit to Israel and eventually cut off diplomatic relations with Egypt, they revered Pope Shenouda for banning visits to Israel, calling him the "Pope of the Arabs." Still, the Pope's stance didn't make any difference to the radical Islamists, who continued to attack the Copts and their churches.

Sadat not only was furious with the Coptic community, who obeyed their Pope's decision, but he also grew angry with the increasing power of the radical Islamists, which started to jeopardize his regime. They became critical of him for not applying *sharia*. They attacked the military academy in 1974 to obtain weaponry and to be able to forcibly change his regime. The attempt failed and a few people were killed. In 1977, they kidnapped and killed the minister of Islamic religious endowment, Muhammad al-Dahabi, to destabilize Sadat's regime, which they considered un–Islamic. The MB magazine *al-Da'wa*, which Sadat had allowed to return, became the most critical of him and the peace treaty with Israel.[64] The MB became the strongest critics of Sadat's alliances with the U.S. and they regarded Sadat's regime as the reason for all societal ills. They believed its downfall was essential.[65]

Radical Islamists became more critical and violent when Sadat received the Shah of Iran as a refugee after Iran's Islamic revolution in 1979. They refused the idea of hosting the Shah in Egypt and violence erupted, in particular in Upper Egypt. During the violence in Assiut, shops belonging to Copts were looted. Police interference to stop the protests resulted in the death of several protestors. In this tense atmosphere, one of the leaders of the radical Islamists issued a religious decree to confiscate money from the Christians. Financial aid coming to them from Sadat's government had stopped and they needed to find an alternative source of funds.[66] Based on Sheikh Umar Abdel Rahman's decree, they began to attack jewelry shops owned by Christians, resulting in many Coptic casualties. They justified taking the wealth of the *dhimmis* as a form of *jizyah* to finance their jihad; they did not consider it theft.

Radical Islamists' power was also salient in the universities. The radical students dictated that classes start with a prayer and dictated what should and should not be studied. Darwin's theory of evolution was banned because it contradicts Islam. They banned concerts at the university because they see music as incompatible with Islam. They dictated what kind of food should be eaten at restaurants and promoted *halal* (compatible with Islam) food. They assaulted male and female colleagues who were walking together at the university, and they carried knives to threaten people to obey their demands.[67]

These students became future leaders of the Islamic movement and they have posed a threat to Egypt's security in the subsequent years. Some of them are currently in prison under el-Sisi: Khairat al-Shater, the MB's deputy Supreme Guide, and Esam al-Erian, vice chairman of MB's Freedom and Justice Party. Ayman Zawahiri, current al-Qaeda leader, was another leader who rose in power during Sadat's presidency. He once stated, "Once the pressure was released from the Islamic movement the giant was released."[68]

The influence of re-Islamization wasn't only pervasive at universities. It covered the whole society to the extent that people turned the first floor of their buildings into mosques. Sadat's government encouraged this with tax exemptions for these buildings. There are many residences throughout Egypt with mosques on the first floor.[69]

In this atmosphere of social and political change, Sadat's open-door economy failed. Its aim for diversification and foreign investment brought inflation and unequal distribution of wealth. Corruption increased in the society and it became endemic. Luxury European cars moved side by side with buses packed to overflowing with poor people. The failing economy led to great frustration and people rebelled against Sadat in the "Revolution of the Hungry" on January 18–19, 1977. The violence that accompanied it prompted Sadat, who called it *intifadit al-Haramyya* or "uprising of the thieves," to crush it.

In the midst of this great opposition and even though he was becoming isolated and unpopular, Sadat decided to change Article 77 of the constitution which limited the terms of the President in office to two terms. Sadat wanted unlimited periods. Knowing he would not be able to do this without the support of the powerful Islamists, he decided to pair this change with an amendment to Article Two. Article Two was changed to read, "principles of Islamic law are *the* main source of legislation" instead of "…principles of Islamic law are *a* main source of legislation." By changing "*a*" to "*the*" he ruled out any other sources of legislation.[70] A referendum was conducted on May 22, 1980, for these two articles at the same time and it passed by 98.86 percent.[71] If one accepts that the figure of the referendum is correct, then one has to accept that the Copts voted for it, too.

The change to Article Two legalized discrimination against the Copts and it would have serious repercussions on the Coptic community. Copts used to be under the jurisdiction of religious courts which Nasser abolished in 1955 putting them instead under the jurisdiction of national courts.[72] Now, national courts would be guided by Article Two.

Sadat developed Nasser's process of re-Islamization making it wide spread and constitutional. He officially endorsed it, which took Egypt into an era of religious transformation in which the country was on the verge of re-applying *dhimma* status to the Copts. Sadat did not leave any public event without endorsing Egypt's Islamic identity. He made it a habit to go pray every Friday in a different mosque while TV cameras filmed him uttering Quranic verses.[73] When Sadat promised his people prosperity and advancement, he called Egypt "the country of science and religion." While visiting the Pope in St. Mark's Coptic Cathedral, Sadat prayed there and his picture was taken while the Pope and bishops were standing in the background. The next day the picture was published on the front page of all newspapers to illustrate his self-proclaimed title: *al-Ra'is al-Mu'min* (the believer president).[74] While Copts understood that Sadat was adamant to give a big role to religion in the public sphere, it was hard for them to understand the purpose of seeing their leadership in the background standing, watching and listening to Sadat praying.

A year after amending Article Two, one of the worst attacks on Copts occurred in the neighborhood of al-Zawiyah al-Hamra, in June 1981. The issue was again an attempt to build a church. The problem arose in a dispute over a lot of land on which the Copts intended to build a church but that the radical Islamists claimed for themselves. The dispute turned into a street fight that lasted for three days while the regime turned a blind eye.[75] This incident became one of the deadliest attacks on Copts, leaving-eighty one Copts dead according to official accounts and more than one hundred according to Coptic authorities. Twenty Coptic properties were set ablaze.[76]

The Copts were caught between the attacks of the radicals and the lack of protection from the state. Their sense of security had not been that low for decades, and while they were in shock as what would be next, the Coptic diaspora received Sadat's visit to the U.S. in August 1981 with very angry protests. They demonstrated in front of the White House while he was meeting with President Reagan. They paid for half-page advertisements in the *Washington Post* and the *New York Times* expressing their rage at the treatment of the Coptic community in Egypt. They also protested in front of the Metropolitan Museum while Sadat was inaugurating a new section for Egyptian antiquities. When Sadat was in the U.S., a bomb exploded near a church in Masarra, Cairo. killing three people and wounding fifty-nine. It seemed like the radical Islamists also wanted to embarrass Sadat.[77] The Coptic diaspora's protests took place despite the fact that the Pope sent a bishop to the U.S. prior to Sadat's visit in order to calm the angry Copts and to convince them not to provoke Sadat.[78] Yet Sadat's reaction was to blame the Pope. Despite his efforts, Sadat accused and chastised the Pope for playing a political role, when, in fact, Sadat had asked the Pope to do so by requesting that he silence the Coptic diaspora and make Copts visit Israel.

Embarrassed by the Coptic diaspora, challenged by the radicals, unable to rule efficiently and increasingly isolated, the unpopular Sadat was facing serious political turmoil. He did not have political support and his economic policy did not lift the country out of its economic depression. His endeavors to use Islamists to counterbalance the leftists only served to release a trapped demon in the form of radicalism.[79] Sadat's only recourse was to recall the "massacre of the citadel" action. His "corrective revolution" had succeeded in eliminating the Nasserite leaders. Now, it was time to politically assassinate his new opponents if his regime was to survive.

On September 3, 1981, Sadat arrested about 1,500 of his opponents and imprisoned them within 24 hours. Such a mass arrest necessitated the inclusion of key figures from the extreme right to the extreme left, covering the whole political spectrum. Among those who were arrested were Muslims, Copts, men, women, students, professors, reporters, writers, and people from all age groups, from 20 to 80 years old. In one strike, Sadat placed the country's "political class" under arrest.[80] Sadat even arrested his own advisor because he disagreed with him.[81] Among those who were arrested were metropolitans, bishops, priests, and Muslim clergy as well.

For the Coptic community, the biggest shock came when President Sadat included the most important figure for them among those placed under arrest: Pope Shenouda. Sadat put the Pope under house arrest at St. Bishoy Monastery in Wadi al-Natrun. Sadat was hoping to depose the Pope from his See and appoint another patriarch,[82] but he could not. History shows that even though Cyrus was appointed by an Emperor as a patriarch for the Copts, the religious authority lay in the hands of the Coptic Pope Benjamin even while he was on the run. What Sadat was able to do, though, was to withdraw state recognition from the Pope and to form a committee he called the "Papal Committee," consisting of five bishops, to perform papal duties. However, they got instructions from the Pope and prayers were still performed in his name.

But the drama was not yet over. If October 6, 1973, marked the peak of Sadat's political career, the same date, eight years later, was to mark his literal downfall.[83] Although Sadat arrested hundreds of its members as a preemptive measure, the *Jihad* group, an offshoot of the MB, were still strong enough to assassinate him on October 6, 1981.[84] The mere fact that a military officer, a

Jihad group member, was Sadat's assassin and that he killed him in the middle of a military parade demonstrates the extent and level to which radical Islamists had infiltrated society.

Sadat's adoption of Islamic identity alienated the peaceful Coptic community. He publicly attacked the Church in his speeches—using traditional stereotypes—for causing sectarian strife and embracing separatist ambitions. He allowed the Copts to pay the price of violence in return for the support of the Islamists. By creating a myth of Coptic conspiracy, he depicted himself as the defender of Islam.[85]

On the other side of the equation, Pope Shenouda played a distinguished role in reviving the Coptic identity when he revived the Church. He was an active member of the Sunday School Movement led by the reformer Habib Guirguis, of whom the Pope was a student. Habib Guirguis revived and enriched Christian education, and the Pope maintained and developed his teacher's work when he became the Bishop of Education.[86] Through his books and lectures as a Bishop and later as a Pope, he opened up a plethora of Coptic heritage to his audience. Well-educated Copts who chose not to immigrate to North America, Europe or Australia gravitated more and more toward becoming monks and nuns. These middle-class Copts have led a monastic revival. The monasteries of Wadi al-Natrun are full of doctors, engineers, teachers and many other professionals.[87] These monks and nuns are the best preservers of the Coptic identity.

It is true that Sadat achieved great feats in liberating Sinai and making peace with Israel. But as much as Sadat was regarded as a man of peace, for others he was a man of insecurity. Sadat's radical Islamist patron-beneficiaries exposed the Copts to the destruction of homes, burning of churches, plunder of properties, physical attacks and mass killing. Many believe that Sadat planted the seeds of radicalism in Egypt in the 1970s. Then it spread to the world at large; the current Egyptian leader of al-Qaeda was one of Sadat's patron-beneficiaries. Although Sadat promoted Islamic identity, he was considered irreligious. Copts peacefully protested Sadat, they fasted and prayed, but despite this fact, Sadat ignored the pacifists and supported the radicals. When radical Islamists attacked Copts, he did not bring peace but deepened the divide between them. Sadat polarized society, unifying Copts and Islamists only in their disregard for him. When Sadat was assassinated, a lot of Egyptians did not feel grief, but felt sorrow for a man who had gone astray.[88]

Mubarak, 1981–2011

After Sadat's assassination, Vice President Mubarak became Egypt's President, on October 14, 1981; he was another military man but without the record of political activities or affiliations of Nasser or Sadat. Mubarak had to deal with a severed diplomatic relationship with the Arab states and an incomplete Israeli withdrawal from the Sinai. But his most serious challenges were internal: an increasingly deteriorating economy, corruption, jailed political class and a divided nation. Mubarak had to find a way to deal with the powerful Islamists—the demon that Sadat had released and couldn't control.

The assassination of Sadat did not mark an end to radical Islamist violence. Two days after Sadat's assassination, the victorious radicals raided the police headquarters in the southern province of Assiut, killing tens of policemen.[89] With a new President, the Copts were holding their hopes high to regain peace and security. Would Mubarak grant them these basic rights and provide them justice?

Mubarak's policy was reconciliatory as he slowly tried to bring things back to normal. His policy was characterized by gradualism even when expediency was merited.[90] Mubarak started to release Sadat's political detainees shortly after assuming power, but although he released the jailed clergy, he excluded Pope Shenouda. The Coptic community could not find a good reason for this exclusion except to pacify the Islamists. For the Copts, this was not an encouraging start. While criticism for Mubarak was only voiced within the Coptic community in Egypt, the American Copts planned a public protest against Mubarak on his first visit to the U.S. calling for the return of their Pope. Yet the Pope sent a delegation to the American Copts with the message to welcome and pray for the new President.[91] The Pope took the first step towards reconciliation with the state, but the Coptic demands were not among Mubarak's top priorities. Mubarak was preoccupied with finding a way to deal with the threat of the MB and their offshoots.

Mubarak's approach to dealing with the MB was twofold. First, he competed with them in showing favoritism to Islamic ideals and in promoting the Islamic identity of the state; in other words, he tried to outdo them religiously. Mubarak was hoping that the Egyptians would see his regime as devout so he could entrench his position. In this competition between the Mubarak regime and the MB over the intensity and degree of championing Islamic identity and the application of Islamic values in the public sphere, the process of re-Islamization steadily moved forward, and Egypt's Copts got caught between a rock and a hard place. They became Egypt's solitary community, manipulated by both sides for political gain.

Mubarak's second approach was to keep the MB under check but not fully eliminate them from the political scene as Nasser had done, or give them too much freedom, as had Sadat. He enforced an emergency law after Sadat's assassination which gave him a free hand in dealing with the Muslim Brotherhood. Keeping the feared MB reined in allowed him to offer the Copts very little, knowing that they would accept what he offered because the alternative would be worse; hence, he secured their discontented support. On the other hand, offering the Copts very little would guarantee him less antagonism from the MB. Mubarak made it clear that the alternative to his regime was radicalism and chaos, which not only scared the Copts but the international community as well. They accepted Mubarak's rhetoric of compromising democracy to curb the power of the Islamists in order to maintain stability, and they turned a blind eye to his poor human rights record for thirty years.

The MB and the potential danger they could unleash if Mubarak's regime was not there to curb it became the "boogeyman" Mubarak used to strengthen his grip on Egypt and to ensure the support of the West as well as the Copts. Mubarak maintained the MB's status as an outlawed organization in order to keep them under his control, yet he allowed them to run in parliamentary elections—but on his own terms. It was a good deal. For Mubarak, as long as they didn't threaten his regime, the participation of the MB in the political process would tame them and make his regime look democratic, albeit superficially. For their part, the MB accepted conditional freedom and limited political participation for the time being, believing that this stage would be temporary; they were in for the long run.

Throughout the 1980s, the MB became a main player in Egypt's political life. Because it was outlawed, the MB could not form a political party; therefore, they were allowed to join al-Wafd's party electoral lists in 1984 to run for election under its auspices. Al-Wafd was unable to function under Sadat, so it accepted the MB alliance to regain life through the committed Islamists' votes. Their alliance won 58 seats, 8 of which went to the MB. The MB made another attempt in 1987 with another party and was able to secure 36 seats.[92] The alliance with al-Wafd led the Copts to believe that the party was nothing more than a historical symbol of their political power and no longer a viable option for political representation.

On the other hand, Copts were excluded from Mubarak's ruling party based on the assumption that they couldn't win because Egyptian voting behavior was now sectarian. Their social and political issues were also excluded from the agendas of both parties. So, in an attempt to make it look as if they had some political role, Mubarak's regime resorted to appointing Copts to the Parliament, as Nasser and Sadat had done, and the Copts were left with no real representation. With no real change in the political system under Mubarak, the Copts' attachment to the Church was reaffirmed as the only outlet for their social and political concerns. But, it had been four years since Mubarak assumed power and their Pope had still not returned.[93]

On January 3, 1985, after forty months of house arrest, Mubarak issued a presidential decree to return the Pope to his See. The Pope celebrated Christmas in a midnight service at St. Mark's Coptic Cathedral in Cairo with ten thousand worshipers. He asked the people to reconcile with their Egyptian neighbors, be they Muslim or Copt.[94] The Pope, whom the Copts called the 20th century Athanasius, did bring to mind Athanasius, who had also been banished. Whether banished by an emperor or a president, the will of neither of these men was changed by their punishment and both were rapturously welcomed upon their returns.

With the return of the Pope, Mubarak reduced the Coptic community to the character of the Pope. He became the sole representative of the Copts and became the shortest and only route through which the state dealt with its Coptic citizens. Thus, the Pope was positioned to play yet another political role. The state's failure to accommodate its Coptic citizens in a viable political system had not changed.

In general, Mubarak did not change Sadat's policies. He kept Egypt allied with the U.S. and honored the Egypt-Israel peace treaty, completing the return of Sinai. While he kept a no-change policy he managed to resume diplomatic relations with the Arab states and he allowed for the opposition to have more freedom than they experienced under Sadat. The relationship between the state and the Church was no different than under Sadat, except that Mubarak was not as confrontational as his predecessor. On the other side, the Pope's stance concerning normalization did not change, and his visits to his monastery for seclusion to pray and object to the state's policy did not stop. A move that once infuriated Sadat and prompted him to accuse the Pope of establishing a Coptic state seemed not to bother Mubarak.

Up until the return of the Pope, Mubarak faced no real threat of protest or violence. Mubarak had already contained the MB, but early signs of turmoil started to appear in the summer of 1985 with labor protests in factories in Helwan and Alexandria. By the fall there were a series of strikes, protests and student riots. Radical Islamist violence against Copts became more obvious in March 1987 with "burning" as the common denominator. They burned the Church of the Virgin Mary in Sohag, and that was followed by an explosion in the Virgin Mary Church in Minia. In September of 1988, another church was burned in Rode al-Farag, Cairo, and in November, a bomb was thrown at the Virgin Mary Church in Masarra, Cairo, during a wedding celebration. In January 1989, the radicals attacked the Copts in Minia and seized control of the district of Abu Hilal. Sporadic attacks on Copts and their businesses continued in Assiut throughout 1989.[95] In the 1990s, attacks on the Copts intensified and reached record numbers. Most of the incidents happened in the Minia and Assiut area, the same area in which Sadat accused the Pope of establishing a Coptic state. Until today, this part of Egypt gets the lion's share of attacks.

Some of the major incidents include the following: In March 1990, in Abu Qurqas, Minia, the radical Islamists set ablaze 48 Coptic-owned shops and burned the Churches of Virgin Mary and St. Gregory. The following month, they threw a bomb at the Church of Virgin Mary in Ain Shams, Cairo. In February 1991, attacks on Copts moved to Beni Sueif, with the burning of three pharmacies and two shops owned by Copts. By April of the same year attacks ignited again in Minia, with the burning of more Coptic shops and attacks on more Copts. There was a series robberies of Coptic-owned jewelry shops in Ain Shams, Zaitoun and Shoubra in Cairo. Violence didn't cease in 1992; there were 37 incidents throughout Upper Egypt, Cairo and Alexandria, resulting in the destruction of three churches and fourteen shops.[96] In 1994, radicals opened fire on Copts standing in front of al-Muharraq Monastery, killing five Copts, two of whom were monks. Four churches were burned in 1996. In 1997, they opened fire on Coptic worshipers inside Mar Girgis Church in the village of al-Fikrya, Minia, killing nine.[97]

Radical Islamists also attacked political figures. The speaker of the house was assassinated in 1990 and Egypt's prime minister escaped an assassination attempt in 1993. Mubarak himself escaped an assassination attempt in 1995. There were also many attacks on tourists, culminating in the massacre at the Temple of Queen Hatshepsut at Luxor in November 1997, where they killed fifty-eight tourists. When their attacks reached that level, Mubarak's security apparatus cracked down on the MB. They arrested their leaders and raided their offices and businesses.[98] The regime responded quickly after attacks on Egyptian officials and tourists, but their response was insufficient when attacks were on Coptic Christians and their churches. Frequently in these attacks no action was taken. However, by the end of the decade, Mubarak was able to dismantle the infrastructure of the radicals, and he won his war against them.[99]

After this triumph, Mubarak's police became draconian, yet their lack of protection of the Copts continued, as Copts were not Mubarak's concern. The radicals discovered that there was no retribution from the state when they attacked Coptic Christians. Consequently, the new decade began with a bloody attack on the Copts.

On New Year's Eve of 2000 a disagreement between a Coptic merchant and a Muslim client in the village of al-Kosheh in Sohag, Upper Egypt, turned into a religious fight in which radicals destroyed and robbed Coptic-owned shops and properties. More radicals from the surrounding villages gathered to assault the Copts the next day. The attack on the Copts lasted for two days with no intervention from the police: It was a massacre that left twenty Copts dead.[100]

Two years earlier in 1998, Mubarak's police had tortured hundreds of Copts in al-Kosheh, during an investigation into the murder of two Copts by Muslims. The regime was worried about sectarian tension and the police were adamant to find a Copt to blame the crime upon so they could avoid religious tension. While the police were questioning Muslims, they began to arrest Copts. They questioned a number of them and subjected them to torture. Many, including women and children, were tied to doors, beaten, whipped, suspended in the air and subjected to electric shock in different parts of their bodies. In addition to the physical abuse, they were verbally abused; the abusers cursed their crosses, Christianity, their saints and church leaders and called them polytheists. The degree of abuse drew the attention of journalists and human rights organizations inside and outside Egypt. Embarrassed by press reports, the Egyptian ambassador to the U.S. held the bishop of the village of al-Kosheh responsible. He accused him of spreading false information to international organizations outside Egypt and called him a "religious extremist." The bishop was put under investigation and accused of "damaging national unity" and "insulting the government." In the end, the detainees were released and no one has been charged. The regime didn't properly investigate police abuses and all were acquitted. One of the police officers responsible for severe violations of human rights was allegedly even promoted.[101]

Perhaps it was the lack of accountability in the incident of al-Kosheh 1998 that was a major factor leading to the massacre in al-Kosheh 2000. Even the judiciary ruling on the 2000 incident was seen by many as not on par with the crime. Out of ninety-six suspects, only four were found guilty. One of them received ten years in prison for possessing an illegal weapon. The other three received two years in prison for setting a truck trailer alight. None were charged with the murders.[102]

Another factor that led to the events at al-Kosheh was the radicalization of society, which was maintained by Mubarak's policies. Although he periodically arrested MB leaders, Mubarak continued to allow them to freely function on a grassroots level, religiously and socially. All their services and activities are based on and performed in the name of Islamic theology. It was through this provision of social services in poor areas, where the state aid was lacking, that they have become popular on the ground and have successfully radicalized Egyptian society. After the 1992 earthquake south of Cairo, the MB built shelters, schools, and health clinics and provided food, clothing and money for those affected. This was in stark contrast to the state's inability to provide real support to its citizens.[103]

To compete with their growing influence, Mubarak showed favoritism to religion in the public sphere. He allowed al-Azhar to ban books it deemed to be against Islam: *Soqout al-Imam* or *"The Fall of the Imam"* by Nawal el-Saadawi is one example.[104] Some al-Azhar scholars issued *fatwas* against writers, which led to their assassinations, as in the case of the Muslim writer Farag Fouda. He was shot dead in the street after a *fatwa* declaring him an apostate for challenging the application of *sharia*.[105] Islamic scholars had the power to intervene in people's personal lives and dissolve marriages against their will. An Islamic scholar from Cairo University declared fellow Islamic studies professor Nasr Hamid Abu Zeid an apostate because of his writings criticizing certain aspects of Islam. A committee of 20 al-Azhar scholars declared him an apostate and demanded that he repent for his apostasy.[106] Based on Article Two, a law suit was filed against him and a court ruling was issued to dissolve his marriage. Before the ruling, Abu Zeid left for Holland with his wife, who refused to be forcibly divorced from him.

These government-supported Islamic scholars were also very critical of Christians. They publicly called upon them to adopt Islam and much publicity was given to those who had converted.[107] Some Islamic scholars made inflammatory statements publicly about Christianity. Sheikh al-Sha'rawi, one of the most famous al-Azhar scholars and a previous minster of Islamic endowment, referenced the parable of Mathew 25:10: "But while they were on their way to buy the oil, the bridegroom arrived. The virgins who were ready went in with him to the wedding banquet. And the door was shut," in one of his weekly televised Friday sermons. He stated that the parable indicated that Jesus married five wives; it was the only logical conclusion for him if a bridegroom and five virgins enter a place and shut the door. Christians were deeply offended that this could be broadcast on state television.

Mubarak also supported the apolitical, ultra-conservative Salafists, to counter the MB's influence.[108] Mubarak's police apparatus concluded an agreement with the Salafists in which they allowed them to freely preach in return for their political support for Mubarak.[109] While Mubarak imprisoned the MB members when he saw them as a threat, the Salafists were not jailed. The Salafists were not as politically savvy and were less organized than the MB, hence, they posed no threat to Mubarak's regime. But, while they were not threatening to Mubarak, they further radicalized the Egyptian society and were a real threat to the Copts.

The regime's support of the Salafists and the pervasive religiosity in society allowed the Salafists to form the "Coalition for the Support of New Muslims," aimed at setting free new Muslims—people they believed the Christian church was preventing from converting to Islam by holding them captive. Their targets included two priests' wives: Wafaa Costantine and Camelia Shehata, who became causes célèbre when the Salafists targeted them as "new Muslim converts."[110] Despite repeated claims from the Church that no one was being held captive, and a video from Camelia herself declaring her Christian faith, it did not cool the Salafists' zeal.[111] Some believe the police were complacent with the Salafists, holding Wafaa in custody on the pretext that she had converted to Islam. The Pope secluded himself in his monastery to pray in support of the Coptic community's pressure to release Wafaa, and to object to the police's behavior; this prompted Mubarak to intervene and release her.[112]

Salafists protested in front of St. Mark's Coptic Cathedral and, aiming to insult the Pope, hit his picture with their shoes, all the while believing that the Church was hiding the women at the monasteries. The religious fervor even prompted a future Islamist Presidential candidate to declare that monasteries were hiding weapons that they imported from Israel to use against Muslims.[113] Although the claim was dangerous, baseless and an insult to Mubarak's strong police, who had absolute authority and control, the state did not comment.

In this atmosphere of religiosity, some zealots engaged in a plan to forcibly convert Coptic females. This forced conversion was done in systematic and organized ways. Some forced conversions were done by individuals, with the support of their friends, and some were done by well-financed groups.[114] Reports of men kidnapping, forcibly marrying and converting Coptic Christian girls became a phenomenon under Mubarak. These violations seemed to be encouraged and supported by the cultural norms of the radicals' customs that legitimize violence against non–Muslims. Although such violations are on par with the definition of human trafficking used by the United Nations, identifying it as a "crime against humanity," they were met with tacit complicity from the regime. This complicity was evident in their unwillingness to deeply investigate the allegations of rape, kidnapping, and abuse of Coptic women and girls, or to design a policy to protect people from forced conversion. The police repeatedly failed to find and return kidnapped girls; often they wouldn't even search for them. The police's behavior encouraged such crimes, as the perpetrators went unpunished. As early as 1976 Pope Shenouda addressed this issue: "There is pressure being practiced to convert Coptic girls to Islam and marry them under terror to Muslim husbands."[115]

That men are able to force Coptic girls into marriage and, consequently, conversion, is also rooted in the cultural and social norms of society and aided by the political and economic situation. There is a great sense of shame, dishonor and stigma for the victim and her family in crimes of rape and sexual abuse.[116] Because victims are so ashamed, they fear the response of their families if they tell. Victims are also hesitant to report these crimes for the fear of retribution against themselves and their families from the perpetrators. And when they are courageous enough to report them, the authorities are indifferent. Thus, they concede to live with the family and marry their rapists. It became a common occurrence under Mubarak, frequently impacting families of low socio-economic status who did not have the resources, financial or educational, to fight this forced conversion. To complete the marriage the victim has to convert to Islam. After conversion she will be given a Muslim identity card by the authorities and officially becomes Muslim.[117] Once she is a Muslim she faces legal implications based on Article Two for herself and children. She can't go back to Christianity, as she will be charged with apostasy.

Underage Coptic girls are lured into relationships with Muslim men for the purpose of forced marriage, and although some girls agree to a romantic relationship, they don't agree to the loss of identity. Nor do they agree to the isolation or the forced conversion that follows.[118] This is evident in many cases of Coptic girls who wanted, but were unable to get out of, such marriages due to the law and cultural norms that bind them legally and socially.

S. was a 17-year-old Coptic girl still in high school when she disappeared in Sanaboo, Diyrout, Upper Egypt, in July 1, 1998. She was raped in the back of a van on the way to her abductor's home. Her family reported her disappearance to the police. The police didn't do much and gave the regular response that the daughter had probably run away with a young man. She was drugged until her marriage and conversion were finished. Her husband took her to Cairo, away from her village and family who had no news about her for three years. In Cairo she worked as a servant for her husband's first wife and was given very little money to take care of her children. S. and her children slept in a basement with no window, electricity or ventilation. They weren't allowed to eat or interact with the rest of the household. She lived in these conditions for five years before she was able to save enough money from her food allowance and escape with her three sons to her parent's home. Her father, fearing the state security, took her to the Church, which in turn sent her to a crisis home. S. was accepted back into the Church and her three children were baptized. Her father was arrested for hosting his daughter and her children, as they were Muslims and to host them was forbidden, and he was also tortured and humiliated in an attempt to force him to reveal their location. In the end, S.'s father was able to leave Egypt with his sons and live in another country. S. and her children lived in hiding. Her children faced problems joining a school, as their identities would be compromised.[119] She couldn't have a normal life, being in hiding, and she lost her support system after the departure of her family.

If the forced conversion process is not completed, the fate of the victims and their families is serious. In March 6, 1997, Teresa Shakir, a Coptic girl in 8th grade at a government school, was taken by her teacher, a fundamentalist Islamist, to a police station in Wasta, Beni Sueif. With the help of local police he tried to officially declare her a Muslim convert. Her family complained to the police that Teresa was underage and should be returned to her family, but the police who held Teresa at the station didn't concede. Her family complained to human rights organizations, Pope Shenouda, and President Mubarak's office. The higher authorities intervened, leading to Teresa's release. On November 30, 1997, Teresa's brother returned home at 4 a.m. to find his parents and younger brother, Adel, murdered. His sister Nadia was injured with a bullet wound. Teresa was also murdered; her stomach was cut open and she had been disemboweled. This is a common punishment radical Islamists use for those who are accused of apostasy. When the brother went to the police station to report the murders, he was arrested and accused of committing the crime.[120]

Similarly, when the Salafists were unable to force the two priests' wives, Camelia and Wafaa, to convert, ISIS beheaded twenty-one Copts in Libya, in 2015. They justified this act with the claim that these two women were kept in captivity by the Church to ban them from converting to Islam. On the video released by ISIS of the Copts' beheading, a caption declares, "This filthy blood is just some of what awaits you, in revenge for Camelia and her sisters."[121] Also, for the same reason, al-Qaeda in Iraq held Christians hostage at the Church of Saidat al-Nagah, Our Lady of Deliverance, in Baghdad, in 2010. The incident led to the killing of forty-six Iraqi Christians.[122] The radical Islamists justified the murdering, not only of Coptic Christians, but other Christians, regardless of their denomination, as a punishment to the Coptic Church for the alleged ban of these two women from converting to Islam.

In another case, a church leader working with poor Coptic girls who were forced to convert to Islam was a target of radical Islamists. He explained that the girls he helps get raped and become pregnant. He established a center to help these girls, but this brought down the wrath of the radicals. They attempted to murder him and his family. They killed his eleven-year-old daughter and seriously injured his wife when they pushed his car over a cliff.[123]

The phenomenon of forced conversion prompted Pope Shenouda to speak out about one method of abduction of Coptic girls. He said,

> I have received so many letters about what's happening to the Christian girls who go to supermarket stores to shop. At the store, they tell them that they have won (something) and have to go upstairs to receive their reward or prize. After that we don't know what's happening to these girls. There is a lot of talking going on about this matter, and I see that what's happening will create a religious clash in the country. I'm urging the police to take a serious action against what's happening."[124]

The Egyptian Constitution and its legal system offer protection of human rights and the right of freedom of belief. But it retains a loophole clause: Article Two. It makes Egyptian legislation secondary to the principals of the Islamic *sharia* law, which could lead to abuses.[125] If a husband converts to Islam, his Coptic wife not only loses her right to his inheritance, but she also loses custody of her children. The children become Muslims, as they take the religion of their father.[126] Even if the father doesn't push the issue of custody, the children face real challenges.

Fadi's father converted to Islam and left his Christian family when Fadi was five years old. When Fadi became an adult, he was considered a Muslim in the eyes of the government despite the fact that he grew up Christian and had an authentic birth certificate that stipulated his religion as Christian. He applied for an ID, but when they pulled up his name it was listed with his father's new Muslim name and his religion was now wrongfully listed as Muslim. Fadi was charged with trying to forge his ID, birth certificate, diplomas and most importantly with trying to convert from Islam to Christianity. They seized his documents and he was arrested. He was only released after Pope Shenouda intervened with the authorities on his behalf. However, Fadi was unable to get his ID with his actual name and with Christianity as his religion. He said, "In this country, on this issue, life is difficult. Without an ID I have to stay put, I can't take a job in Sharm, I can't go to Alexandria.... I'm walking close to the wall, like a shadow."[127] On the other hand, converts to Islam receive a new birth certificate fast and with no charge. A valid birth certificate is the first step to obtaining an ID.[128]

By law all Egyptians are required to have an ID at the age of 16. Without it no one can apply to a university, transfer property, get a driver's license, cash a check, receive a pension, vote, conduct the most basic financial and administrative transactions, or even get a job. It is illegal for employers to hire anyone without an ID.[129]

Fadi's case is not unique, though, and people like him are a distinct category of Coptic Christians whom the government has labeled as Muslims without their knowledge and against their will. In these cases the fathers were Christians who converted to Islam and the government automatically converted the children without regard to their mothers' or their wishes, and without even informing them. Officially they are Muslims and can face legal issues if they deny it. They are faced with problems getting married and starting a family. In the case of Yusif, he is a Christian who was also mislabeled as Muslim and whose engagement was broken with his fiancé when her family discovered his situation. Their future kids would be listed as Muslim since he is considered Muslim. Even a Muslim woman wouldn't accept him, as he is really Christian.[130]

Legal cases of forced conversion are very complicated and usually hard to solve. Coptic converts to Islam might practice Christianity and may die "Christian" but their descendants are marked "Muslim" and eventually end up becoming Muslim. In this way future generations of Copts lose their identity and religion. Stories exist of government bureaucrats who mistakenly wrote Muslim instead of Christian on a Copt's birth certificate. Whether intentional or not, this typo is extremely difficult to correct.

The Mubarak regime compromised the right of freedom of religion and forced an Islamic religious identity at the expense of human rights.[131] Sometimes Article Two overrules human rights. Putting Islamic qualifications on human rights has the potential to deny these rights, especially the right of religious freedom. The state sees that whenever there is a conflict between the right of the individual and *sharia*, it is the individual who has to give in. The state wants to limit the influence of the individual on the society in fear that such freedom would disturb the moral order of society.[132] In modern political thought, the state is seen as a legal entity and shouldn't assume any religious or moral character. The principals of Islamic *sharia* law are inherently discriminatory against non–Muslims. For a state to adopt any religious character, even if this character is the belief of the majority, indicates that it runs the risk of creating sectarianism and losing its credibility as a neutral entity.[133]

In 2008, radical neighbors kidnapped and tortured three monks from Abu Fana Monastery over a land dispute. They whipped them to force them to deny their faith by saying the Muslim profession of faith: "There is no god but God and Muhammad is the messenger of God." Then they asked them to spit on the cross. Although the motive behind the assault was a land dispute, the attack turned into an attempt to forcibly convert them.[134] Again the Pope intervened and the situation was remedied.

Another form of manipulation the Copts faced under the Mubarak regime was the "contempt of Islam" charge. Hany, a Coptic blogger in Abu Tesht in Upper Egypt, was accused of insulting Islam in his blog. He was arrested in October 2008, but despite a court order to release him in 2010, Mubarak's police rearrested him.[135] Prior to his arrest, Hany was in hiding, so the police arrested two of his brothers, forcing him to surrender. In prison the police tried to pressure Hany to accept Islam in return for his release.[136] While the attempt to force Hany to convert was a byproduct of his arrest, it is indicative of the complicity of Mubarak's police in the forced conversion process and their disrespect for the rule of law.

This negligence of the rule of law during Mubarak's tenure was yet another tool of discrimination used against the Copts. In cases where churches were attacked by radicals, his regime's approach was not to apply the rule of law on the assaulters but rather to apply *galasat urfyyah* or "reconciliation sessions." His police arrested both the aggressors and the victims in preparation for these sessions. In this manner, the Copts are forced to reconcile with the assaulters if they want their fellow Copts released. By reconciling they lose their legal rights in prosecuting the assaulters. The assaulters go with impunity, further perpetuating violence against the Copts, as there is no deterrent. These sessions are arranged mostly by influential Muslims in the area and are under the supervision of the police.

In an incident of forced reconciliation, a Coptic Church facility in Marsa Matruh was attacked on March 13, 2010. The attack lasted for three hours, and although close by, the police took two hours to respond and emergency vehicles took four hours. The attack resulted in the destruction of 9 homes,

3 workshops, a warehouse, and 11 automobiles, all owned by Copts. Thirty assaulters were arrested, but no criminal charges were filed. The state instead organized a reconciliation session where the problem was settled with cash given to the victims whose properties were damaged. The church conceded to the request to knock down the wall that was believed to block an access way to the neighboring mosque—the belief which initiated the attack. Despite the fact that the government-paid imam of that mosque incited the populace to attack the church, all of the perpetrators were set free.[137]

The Copts accept these sessions in fear of retribution from the populace in the form of more violence. A lack of confidence in the regime and in the neutrality of the state are also factors that lead to the acceptance of reconciliation sessions. These sessions reinforce injustice, as they are conducted by and based on the conditions of the more powerful party. The injustice is also evident in the fact that the Copts cannot prosecute the perpetrators to break the cycle of the violence against them, their churches and properties. The fact that the state pushes for and supervises such sessions only confirms its unwillingness to protect Coptic citizens and to address their problems.

The Copts' situation under Mubarak was worse than under Sadat. Whereas Egypt was on the verge of re-applying *dhimma* status on the Copts under Sadat, it was applied under Mubarak in certain parts of Upper Egypt, although not officially by the regime. As recently as the 1990s many Copts near Quisiya, Assiut, were forced to pay *jizyah* and 40 Copts were murdered because they declined to pay. In October of 1994, two brothers who owned a grocery store were paying *jizyah*, but they declined payment of an additional tribute of 50,000 Egyptian pounds. So, radicals broke into their house and murdered them in front of their families.[138] Radical Islamists applied *sharia* law to Copts inside al-Rahman mosque in Ard al-Moled, Minia; after killing the Copts, they hung their heads on telephone poles.[139]

Mubarak's regime maintained an unwritten policy, in force since the time of Nasser, of not allowing Copts to occupy senior state positions, with the exception of a few token Copts in public positions.[140] A Copt cannot be a college dean or a head of a university. Copts' admission to military and police colleges is limited and, while al-Azhar University doesn't accept them, Copts are not allowed to establish a Coptic university either. It is hard to find a Copt as an editor in chief of a major newspaper, a judge, a diplomat, or part of the presidential staff. Copts can't assume high positions of authority over Muslims. They are treated as second-class citizens, the Christian "other," who can be tolerated but are not allowed to have equal rights. It is the old *dhimma* status re-packaged for a modern era.

The discrimination faced by the Copts is brought to light by the media, human rights organizations and members of the Coptic diaspora. Sometimes international media writes about these injustices, but any critical discussions of the situation of the Copts always receives a bad reaction from the state and the fundamentalists alike. They see the West as neocolonialist, thus, any outside talk about the mistreatment of religious minorities makes local Christians suspect of being pawns of western interference.[141] On the other hand, when the Coptic Christians bring their own concerns to the attention of the state they are either ignored or labeled as western agents and, thus, associated with the Christian West and the Coptic diaspora. Egypt's Mubarak did not accept criticism, did not remedy the situation of the Copts and did not want to talk about it either.

With technology, the Coptic diaspora established their own private TV channels, websites and other media outlets from which they talk about their fear for and the concerns of their fellow Copts back home. Just by talking about the Coptic issues, the Coptic diaspora were portrayed by the state-controlled media as traitors whose aim was to divide Egypt and to serve an "external agenda." They were not considered loyal Egyptians, and in tarnishing their image, Mubarak's regime put the Pope and the Coptic community inside Egypt on the defensive.

However, in contrast to Sadat and Nasser, Mubarak implemented some changes. In January 1998, he granted the authority to approve permits for church repairs to the local government. Before 1998, Mubarak had to approve permits to repair churches, even including broken toilets. On April 21, 1991, President Mubarak's office issued the following decree:

> Considering the Constitution and Law no. 15 of 1927 which regulates the religious places, the appointment of religious leaders and the questions related to the religions allowed by the state: Considering Royal Decree no. 30 of 1928 ... Article One: The Coptic Orthodox Church is licensed to renew its toilet which belongs to the Church of Mayiet Bara of the Coptic Orthodox denomination of the Qusan District of Manufiya Province. Article Two: This decree is to be published in the official daily newspaper and is to be effective from the date of its publication. Issued at the President's Office on 6th Shawal 1411, which is April 21, 1991.[142]

While the requirement of this decree was humiliating to the Coptic community, it was not for the President. In an incident in 1995, a church leader took the initiative to repair a broken toilet; he was accused of illegally enlarging the church and was investigated for hours. The officials then ordered the destruction of the toilet because it was fixed without a permit. However, while Mubarak gave the job of granting permits for repairs to the provincial governors, he retained the approval of new church construction for a time. Sometimes securing a permit to build a new church took decades, and even after such a wait, in some cases the request was eventually turned down. A church leader in Upper Egypt had tried for twenty years to get permission to build a church and each time he was denied. In this span of years, before the required permit to construct a church could be obtained, a whole generation passed.¹⁴³ In 2005, Mubarak handed down the approval of permits to build a church to the provincial governors, but this didn't rectify the situation, as the local governments were unwilling to grant church permits.

Under Mubarak, the situation of the Coptic *waqf* lands was better compared to earlier periods. While Nasser confiscated both Muslim and Coptic *waqf* lands, Sadat returned *waqf* lands to the Ministry of Islamic Affairs but rejected the return of Coptic *waqf* lands to the Copts. Mubarak returned some of the Coptic *waqf* lands, but the issue was not fully resolved. Also, while Sadat went back on his promise of granting 50 church permits a year to the Copts, Mubarak granted 10 permits in the first ten years of his authority; that is to say one permit a year.¹⁴⁴

So in a few limited cases, Mubarak paid a little attention to the Copts by restoring certain Church lands and approving the building of a few new churches. In a benevolent gesture, Mubarak made Christmas a national holiday in 2003. However, many believe this was one of several concessions, including the appointment of a woman as a senior judge, made under pressure from the international community, especially the U.S., to enhance human rights. Before this date only Copts had taken off Christmas day. Although it was a positive gesture, it was not related to the suffering of the Copts, except for that of Coptic students, who were often scheduled to take their exams on Christmas day. Still, universities scheduled them for the day before or after the holiday, which in reality was not much different for the students.

The last year of Mubarak's term, 2010, was hard for all Egyptians but was especially traumatic for the Copts. The previous two years had already witnessed at least 53 incidents of sectarian violence—about two incidents a month—in 17 of Egypt's 29 provinces.¹⁴⁵ Not all attacks on Copts were committed by radical Islamists, however. Sometimes regular people were encouraged by the atmosphere of radicalism and the freedom from punishment. The incident of Nag Hammadi is a case in point.

At the beginning of the year 2010, on Coptic Christmas Eve (January 6th), a Muslim man opened fire on Coptic worshippers while they were leaving a church in Nag Hammadi, Upper Egypt. He killed six Copts, mostly young men in their teens, and a Muslim policeman guarding the church. The images of the dead people lying in the street were disturbing and drew widespread internal and external condemnation. Mubarak's regime came under strong criticism because his security apparatus, although powerful, was either unable or unwilling to protect the Coptic worshippers. This is especially clear considering the usually tight security on Coptic religious occasions. So, the beginning of 2010 was a great embarrassment for Mubarak and his police at all levels. The Pope reacted with another trip to his monastery for seclusion to pray and to object to the lack of protection for the Copts.¹⁴⁶

In November of 2010, another incident occurred in al-Omraniya, Giza.

In this case the police were the attackers. The police claimed that the Copts were adding illegal construction to a community center so they could use it as a church. The police surrounded the Copts, who planned to stay inside the building to protect it from police attack. The police attacked the building to force people out, resulting in the death of four Copts and the injury of seventy. Additionally, the police arrested more than one hundred and fifty Copts.[147] Again, the Pope went to his monastery for prayer.[148] The Pope, who was growing very upset, stated that he would do his best to release the arrested Copts and ask for justice for those who killed them, stating that the deceased Copts' blood "is not cheap."[149] In the end, the arrested Copts were released but no retribution was exacted on the killers. The significance of the incident of al-Omraniya was that it was Mubarak's regime, not the radicals, which portrayed itself as the defender of Islam. The state showed its Islamic zeal by surrounding the building with soldiers in a show of force and by imposing a curfew on the surrounding area. The incident happened during the parliamentary elections and the regime wanted to show its religiosity to outdo the MB, its real competitor, and gain the support of the public. Thus, the Copts were scapegoated by the regime.

The very end of 2010 and the beginning of 2011 was the straw that broke the camel's back. While the Copts were celebrating New Year's Eve at The Two Saints Church in Alexandria, a car bomb exploded in front of the church. The explosion left twenty-three Copts dead, a reminder of the incident at al-Kosheh that also started on New Year's Eve ten years earlier. The massacre prompted Mubarak to come on TV for the first time to address the nation in order to show concern and to condemn the action. Two months earlier, al-Qaeda in Iraq had issued a 48-hour ultimatum for the Church to release the "captive women" Wafaa and Camelia.[150] Before the investigation process really started, Mubarak capitalized on the al-Qaeda threat and blamed the massacre on an "external power" to cast off responsibility. Mubarak's concern, however, came too late, and the Copts scoffingly disregarded it. The video clips showing dead Copts, bodies shredded, injured people groaning and blood on the walls of the church was another unforgettable scene and a reminder of the Nag Hammadi incident that had occurred at the beginning of the year. The Copts, who were devastated and had been utterly humiliated for thirty years of Mubarak's tenure, were enraged. Young Copts took to the street to protest in bold defiance of the police apparatus. The latest incident was condemned by presidents, prime ministers and other world leaders including Pope Benedict of Rome. But most importantly, it shocked the consciousness of moderate Egyptian Muslims. It made them aware of the radicalism facing their Coptic neighbors and, in turn, themselves. The image of defiant Coptic protesters encouraged political activists, who were moved by the helplessness of the Copts in the face of the injustice. They joined them in their protests, especially in Shoubra, which has a large number of Copts. The Copts had already protested against the regime's police in front of the Giza government headquarters after the al-Omraniya incident a few weeks earlier. There, for the first time, the desperate Copts called for the downfall of Mubarak and his police state.[151]

There was already a buildup of great frustration among Egyptian political activists, who were infuriated with the perpetual police abuse—most notably the torture and the killing of a young Egyptian, Khaled Said, a few months earlier in Alexandria. These activists had been challenging Mubarak's regime since 2004, and their influence had increased in subsequent years. The *Kefaya* or "Enough" movement was one example of a group of activists who had had enough of Mubarak's regime and were calling for political reforms and freedom. Other activists and university graduates who were fed up with the high rate of unemployment were outraged with the regime's corruption and with Mubarak's police state. The economy was better under Mubarak if compared to the economy under Sadat or Nasser, but its fruits went to the upper echelon and were never enjoyed by the poorer classes. While activists were calling for worker's rights, they were also voicing objection to Mubarak's son Gamal, whom they believed Mubarak was grooming for presidency. The Coptic protests against Mubarak's police was common ground upon which the activists could join the Copts.

The protests worked as a catalyst to set the tone for a larger uprising, three weeks later, against the regime's police, on January 25, 2011. If the Copts, an unorganized group, were able to protest and be vocal against the regime's abuse, the better organized and stronger groups should do better. Not only could the organized activists keep the ball of protest moving, but they could also guarantee the support of a large portion of the Egyptian society, the Copts, towards their mutual cause. Thus, the protests of the Copts in Shoubra gained momentum, which prompted the police to react violently, leading to street fights between protesters and the police. Some police cars were set on fire, shops were closed and the police had to cut off electricity from the area, all of which was repeated in the January 25th Revolution. The Coptic protests were a rehearsal and a spark for the revolution that brought down Mubarak and his regime.

Mubarak did not do justice to the Copts, and his regime remained under strong pressure from the Islamists. The ultimate result of this was maintaining the status quo of the discriminatory policies against the Copts.[152] Although his police state and emergency law lasted for thirty years, it did not protect the Copts but rather empowered the radical Islamists. Those who attacked the Copts received no punishment. He compromised the rule of law for reconciliation sessions and forced the Copts to convert due to his inaction and lack of protection. He did not nominate the Copts in his ruling party, he competed with the MB for religiosity, and his police were compliant in deadly attacks. The number of burned churches and Coptic casualties under Mubarak was its highest yet.

Nasser, Sadat and Mubarak were all military rulers, yet none of them challenged the role of religion in public life. Nasser started the process of re-Islamization, Sadat nourished it and Mubarak maintained it. The Islamic identity championed by Sadat and Mubarak killed one and brought the other down. The difference between these rulers and Islamists is that the latter have been more consistent and successful at using religion to bolster their political agenda.[153] After the January 25th Revolution, Egypt would be governed by a council of military generals, followed by an Islamist president. The Copts would go through rounds of hardship under both rules, but this time the cycle of violence against them would set a new record. The Copts had to navigate their way in this turbulent time before Egypt went through yet another revolution.

Six

Failed Revolution
A Modern Caliph

The January 25th Revolution

Egyptian activists chose Police Day, January 25, 2011, the day police were being officially honored, to protest against them. These were peaceful protests, arranged through social media by educated young Egyptians, with the purpose of speaking out against police abuse. At the beginning, the police seemed indecisive as to how to deal with the peaceful protesters, and whether or not to allow them to protest in the first place. If things got out of control and the police used violence, this might gain the protesters sympathy from the public. Violence could also lead to the mass killing of non-violent protesters which would lead to more criticism of the police, and probably result in more protests. On the other hand, if the police banned the protests, it would seem as if the powerful police were intimidated by peaceful protesters. In the end the police allowed them to proceed on the grounds that peaceful protests should not pose a threat, as long as they were contained. The regime believed the protesters would finish by the end of the day and that allowing them to protest would benefit the regime by making it look democratic. But the protests snowballed very quickly. The police started to hit the protesters with batons, but they cried out, "*Selmia ... Selmia*" or "peaceful ... peaceful," contrasting the violence of the police against the non-violence of the protesters. The word "peaceful" became the magic word that led tens of thousands of young Egyptians to pour into the streets and add their voices. Footage of a desperate yet defiant young Egyptian standing in front of a large police truck to obstruct it from moving forward and attacking his fellow protesters spread through social media. It encouraged more empathetic young Egyptians to participate, giving the protests momentum.

It was not hard to convince them; abuse, humiliation, corruption, oppression, injustice, poverty, and unemployment were just a few issues that made their future so bleak. Angry young Egyptians filled major streets of numerous large cities especially in the Suez and in Alexandria. In Cairo, the police bombarded the protesters with tear gas; nevertheless, they resisted and claimed Tahrir Square as a police-free zone, forming a sit-in right in the middle of downtown Cairo. From there, the ambitious protesters dared to call for the downfall of the regime.

Mubarak's response was to declare that he wouldn't run for a new term; his term was to end in a few months. His compromise came too late, and the activists demanded the end of his regime. They insisted that Mubarak must go, but they did not outline who or what would fill the void, probably because they could not believe that their peaceful protests could remove a well-entrenched autocrat. No one thought that peaceful protests could lead to the collapse of Mubarak's police state, but surprisingly, they did. After 18 days, on February 11, 2011, Mubarak was forced to step down. Egypt would be ruled by the Supreme Council of Armed Forces, the SCAF, during a transitional period in which a new constitution would be drafted, a new Parliament would be elected and a new president would be chosen.

During the early days of the protests, the Copts were split between two camps: those who endorsed Mubarak and those who supported the protests. Despite bloody crimes and police abuse under Mubarak, not all Copts supported the protests at the beginning. It sounds illogical, but the Copts who preferred Mubarak had their own legitimate reasons. The January protests had no clear leaders or organizational body, a fact that concerned the Copts who feared that, if the Mubarak regime fell, the most viable alternative would be the Muslim Brotherhood. Already, the MB were the only real political force that could stand in opposition to Mubarak, made evident by their gaining one-fifth of the Parliament in 2005. The Copts who preferred Mubarak wanted a smooth transfer of power to the future president, especially since Mubarak's term was about to finish, and he stated that he wouldn't run again. They were worried about a political vacuum and the subsequent chaos that would ensue if Mubarak was forced to step down. If security was compromised, they would be the first victims. The Copts who leaned towards Mubarak did not do so out of respect for his regime but rather out of fear of the Islamists and the uncertainty the revolution posed.

The Copts in the second camp supported the protests from the start, believing the time for change was imminent and any leader, as long as he was not an MB member, would be better than Mubarak. At this point they were not so worried about the MB because it had neither initiated nor planned the protests, and when its members joined the protests they kept a low profile. At the beginning, the MB didn't participate in the protests, with the exception of a few of their youth. The MB feared the regime's retribution if the protests failed. When they did join the protests, they declared that they wouldn't have their own separate agenda, and they accepted the general consensus of the activists who called for a liberal, democratic regime based on the rule of law, with no Islamic reference. The protest's motto was secular: bread, freedom, social justice and human dignity. The protesters' concerns were the inability to earn a livelihood and to live in dignity and freedom—all basic human rights which were compromised by the regime's oppression. The Copts who supported the protests did so based on their optimism for a truly secular regime and their lack of respect for Mubarak's regime.

In the early days of the protests, Pope Shenouda and the older generation of Copts formed the first camp, while Coptic youth constituted the second camp. Unlike the active youth, the older Copts were not part of social media. While the situation was dramatically and rapidly changing, the picture was vague for them and they were out of the loop. This split amongst Copts mirrored another split in the larger moderate Muslim population, some of whom preferred Mubarak because they were also apprehensive of the MB themselves.

The split among Copts was a significant development within the Coptic community as, at this stage, the Copts did not have one single voice in the Pope. The Pope's political role, forced upon him by the state, was diminishing, and many Copts went to the street, not the Church, in order to join their moderate Muslim counterparts and voice their mutual concerns. After the January Revolution, Coptic youth took advantage of the newly created atmosphere of freedom to join recently formed political parties. The Free Egyptians Party, founded by the Copt Naguib Sawirus, and the Egyptian Social Democratic Party were the most popular. Some Coptic diaspora returned and participated in the political system from within Egypt, forming a political party for the first time: *al-Haya* or "The Life Party." A Coptic woman founded and headed another party, *al-Haqq* or "The Right Party." Other Copts formed political movements, such as the prominent Maspero Youth Union, which was an organized and influential movement that voiced Coptic concerns and called for civil rights.

Through this new generation, Coptic concerns were directly addressed to the state. For the first time since the liberal era the Copts voiced their demands from outside the walls of the Church. Their concerns were similar to the larger national movement's demands: democracy, freedom, justice and equal opportunities; the Copts and moderate Muslims once again had a shared common ground. Islamism and sectarianism were not promoted in Tahrir. Instead, the activists championed Egyptian identity, which would unify Copts and Muslims in a secular state with secular demands. The January Revolution raised the idea of Egyptian identity, just like the 1919 Revolution. "A Muslim and a Christian are one hand," shouted the protesters in Tahrir Square, declaring unity and common goals. The Copts formed a human shield around the Muslim protesters who were praying in Tahrir in order to protect them from potential attacks from the police and their cronies. "Raise your head up, you are an Egyptian," was another famous slogan in Tahrir, meant to promote Egyptian identity and to lift up the spirits of the Egyptians who were being humiliated by the police. While humiliation of the Copts has been deeply rooted in the Egyptian history, on this rare occasion the Muslim population got a taste of it, though for political not religious reasons. During the 18 days in Tahrir, there were many signs of harmony between the Copts and Muslims, which carried over into the larger population, leading to a general sense of security. Even when violence erupted on Friday, January 28th, known as the "Friday of Anger," Copts were generally as safe as anyone else.

By that day the MB had realized the success of the protests, so right after the Friday prayers they began participating heavily. It was at this point that signs of violence started to emerge, which changed the peaceful nature of the protests. Many police stations were set on fire, others were broken into, looted and the weaponry was stolen. Prisons were attacked and prisoners were set free. According to an official statement over 21,000 prisoners escaped during January and February of 2011.[1] The future President Mohamed Morsi and other prominent leaders of the MB that the regime had jailed were released from prison. They went directly to Tahrir, which was now the political epicenter of Egypt. The police, who were utterly exhausted after living in the streets for four days, vanished for the second half of that day. With no police presence, looting prevailed and chaos reigned, prompting Mubarak to declare a curfew and to call on the military to come out from their barracks to maintain order.

After the police disappeared, security was in the hands of the citizenry. Egyptians had to stand guard in front of their houses; Copts stood side by side with their Muslim neighbors taking shifts to defend their homes and properties. Still, the Copts were as safe as everybody else, except in a few remote areas in the Sinai and Upper Egypt. During this turmoil, the MB was deeply preoccupied with plotting against Mubarak. Keeping the Copts safe was important for them in order to maintain the integrity of Tahrir and to cast out unnecessary divisions at this critical stage. The MB leaders had just joined the protests at Tahrir and any different treatment for the Copts would be associated with their arrival.

However, many believe that the security of the Copts during this period was a sign that the MB was hijacking the peaceful revolution. The MB leaders who went to Tahrir started to guide the protesters, who had no clear vision for the future of Egypt.[2] As the only cohesive political body after Mubarak's downfall, the MB coordinated and allied with the SCAF on the direction of the future of Egypt without regard to the activists' wishes. Although their leaders denied any alliance with the SCAF, reality shows the opposite.

Among the assurances made, the MB assured the SCAF that they wouldn't nominate their members for presidency and would only compete for 25 percent of the Parliamentary seats. They also assured the SCAF that they would not call for the abolishment of the Egypt-Israel peace treaty, a sharp departure from the position the organization had held since the treaty's inception. From its side, when the SCAF formed a committee to write constitutional amendments to the 1971 constitution, three of the eight members of the committee were chosen from the MB. One of them, the judge who headed the committee, had written more than one book outlining the treatment of Copts based on the ideology of political Islam. The other two were active members of the MB, one of whom was a lawmaker during the time of Mubarak. Basically the SCAF allowed the MB to be the only political force represented in the committee.[3]

This committee initially scheduled parliamentary elections at a surprisingly early date, seemingly to allow the MB to secure success. Success in the parliamentary elections would give them the upper hand in choosing the 100 members who would write Egypt's new constitution. The moderate Muslim forces and the Copts requested that the constitution be written first and that the parliamentary elections be postponed to allow the nascent secularist and liberal parties to better prepare for competition with the well-established Muslim Brotherhood. Yet, despite the rationale behind their demands, the SCAF insisted on what many saw as a backwards roadmap: parliamentary elections first followed by the writing of the constitution and then presidential elections. Also, despite the fact that Egyptian law doesn't allow religious-based parties, the SCAF turned a blind eye and allowed the MB to establish one for the first time in their history, the Freedom and Justice Party.[4]

The SCAF called for a referendum regarding the constitutional amendments on March 19, 2011. But the voting turned into a religious fight. The moderate Muslims and the Copts urged a "no" vote to the amendments. The MB and their supporters who would benefit from the amendments urged a "yes" vote. The MB targeted illiterate, poor Muslims. They distributed bags of sugar and bottles of cooking oil in poor areas to encourage a "yes" vote.[5] The official website of the MB accused those voting "no" of fraud and of being paid by the United States to promote its interests.[6] In their process to secure a "yes" vote, the MB harassed Copts, especially in villages with big Coptic populations. They caused a fight in the village of Taieba, in Samalout, which has more than 20,000 Copts, leading the authorities to shut down the polling station, thus impeding the Copts from voting. They banned Copts from voting in the village of Dafsh, in Minia, which has 12,000 Copts.[7]

Their campaign was very successful, and the result of the referendum was a 77 percent "yes" vote. But the result revealed the fact that sectarianism is deeply rooted in Egyptian society. Two months after Mubarak was ousted those who championed Islamic identity had risen up to frustrate the hopes of the Egyptian secularists, the initiators of the revolution, who championed an Egyptian identity. While it is true that the referendum was the first democratic vote in decades, the activists saw the use of religion in the public sphere and the bribing of poor people to direct their vote as against the principals of democracy, not to mention a dangerous practice. Twenty-six percent of Egyptians are illiterate, thus, they are an easily manipulated constituency for the MB. A Salafist sheikh called the Islamist victory "ballot box conquest" referring to Muhammad's conquest of the infidels. He stated that people had said yes to religion and challenged those who didn't like it to leave for the U.S. or Canada.[8]

As things went as they had hoped, the MB became strong backers of the SCAF and turned their backs on the activists. Even though the SCAF was criticized for its slow reforms and authoritarian rule, the MB supported it. The MB criticized the initiators of the revolution, who called for continuing protests, desperately attempting to achieve the secular goals they had sought from the start. The MB were silent when the SCAF forced military trials on civilians, and they refused to participate in protests demanding that the trials cease. These actions on the part of the Muslim Brotherhood led the activists to conclude that the MB had betrayed the secular goals of the January Revolution in their endeavors to advance their Islamic ideology.[9] On its part, the SCAF had been pardoning and releasing quite a few Islamists from prison. Among them were the radicals accused of masterminding the assassination of Sadat, including Nabil al-Maghrabi and Tareq and Abboud al-Zomor. Also among those released was Muhammad Zawahiri, the brother of al-Qaeda leader Ayman Zawahiri. Both Zawahiri and al-Maghrabi were rearrested later for planning attacks on churches and government institutions.[10]

For many, the picture became clear: It was the SCAF and the MB on one side, and moderate Muslims and the Copts on the other. The SCAF and the MB had a common interest in filling the political vacuum that the turmoil had created. The SCAF needed political support that only the MB was willing to provide and, in return, the MB gained certain privileges. Collaboration between the military and the MB has historical precedent. The MB was a part of Nasser's Free Officers Movement. Sadat coordinated with and supported them, while Mubarak opened up the political sphere to their participation. In light of this historical context, it makes sense that the SCAF and the MB formed an alliance. Disagreement and repression erupts, with varying degrees of intensity, when the Muslim Brotherhood seeks what the military generals deem too much power, as had happened with the past three presidents. It is a continually converging or diverging relationship, and at this point in the relationship the two old enemies had to cooperate. The MB were able to achieve political victory because they were better able to control the streets with their Islamic offshoots, which meant the SCAF had to rely upon them, especially after police authority broke down. The broken police system allowed them unchecked power, which they potentially could have used for political gain by destabilizing the situation. Instead, the SCAF relied on the Muslim Brotherhood not only to help in controlling the street, but at times to confront the activists. The combination of unprecedented power for the MB and support from the SCAF turned out to be a serious threat for Copts.

On March 5, 2011, radical Islamists burned down the Church of al-Shahidain (Two Martyrs) St. Mina and St. George in the village of Sul, in Itfeh, south of Cairo. The incident, which was triggered by a relationship between a Christian man and a Muslim woman, ended up being a collective punishment for the Coptic residents of the village. Around 4,000 men attacked Coptic homes and forced many to leave the village. The SCAF troops, which were stationed seven kilometers away, initially did not move into the village.[11] When SCAF troops did arrive, they fired into the air, causing the mobs to disperse—only to reorganize half an hour later to burn down the church, in the presence of the troops. The Copts, who were striving to find a place for themselves in the post–Mubarak era, did not go to the Church to complain, as they had in the past; rather they planned a sit-in in front of Egypt's television building, Maspero. Thus, as a result of the incident at Sul, the Coptic political movement known as the Maspero Youth Union was created. The Copts were joined by many of their moderate Muslim comrades, protesting against the radical Islamists' violence and the SCAF's inaction. They demanded the return of about 7,000 Copts forced to leave their homes, and the rebuilding of the church (which the radicals had already turned into a mosque).[12]

In order to support the sit-in, on March 9, some 500 Copts from the working-class area of Moqattam started to march towards Maspero. On their way they were confronted by mobs. The Copts called upon the military, which sent ten tanks, but the soldiers did not intervene; rather, they shot in the air. Tensions escalated, and the ensuing clashes resulted in the deaths of nine Copts and the injury of 150 more.[13]

Due to public pressure and outrage over the violence that had erupted, the SCAF agreed to rebuild the church in Sul. But instead of applying the rule of law, the SCAF deferred to sheikhs in order to legitimize rebuilding the church. In a live broadcast on the national Egyptian television, a panel of sheiks surrounded the SCAF representative and assured the Muslims of Sul that rebuilding the church they burned was compatible with *sharia*. The panel was led by an ultraconservative sheikh who announced that, based on the religious opinions of some twenty-five scholars, the SCAF had decided to rebuild the church.[14] So, rebuilding a church that was burned down by radicals was not based on the rule of law or a military order, as the Copts thought, but rather it was based on religious opinions of the sheikhs. One SCAF representative even referred to the mob as "tolerant" people: "Based on the tolerant feelings offered by the village youth to rebuild the church, the SCAF appreciated the stance of village youth and decided to rebuild the church ... with the same size and appearance with no decrease or increase."[15]

The televising of the panel of sheiks and the SCAF appreciation of the radical perpetrators' "tolerance" confirmed to the activists not only the alliance of the SCAF and the MB but also that the rule of law, one of the main secular objectives of the January Revolution, was evaporating. The SCAF was unwilling to apply the law in fear of upsetting their new allies, echoing Sadat's approach after al-Khanka.

For the Copts, this was shocking; the incident in Sul was a revival of history from centuries past. Neither an isolated incident nor a new occurrence, what happened in Sul was a page borrowed from history, when churches were burned, razed, pilfered and turned into mosques. As mentioned previously, it was reminiscent of two similar incidents that occurred in the late 10th century. As with the incident during the rule of caliph al-Mu'izz, when a sheikh declared that St. Macarius Church would only be built over his dead body, when burning the church in Sul, the mobs bragged that the church would only be rebuilt over their dead bodies.[16] As happened in the reign of al-Hakim, the radicals in Sul destroyed the church and turned the site into a mosque by initiating the Muslim call to prayer. The statement of the SCAF representative who emphasized that the rebuilding of the church would be identical to the original one is also a repetition of history. During the time of sultan al-Nasser Muhammad ibn Qalawun in 1308, the populace pulled down St. Barbara's church in Harit al-Rum despite the fact that the Sultan had given permission for the Copts to restore it. The reason behind their destruction was that there had been a new addition to the church in the restoration process.[17] Perhaps neither the sheikhs nor the SCAF wanted to give mob an excuse to destroy the church again, which they may have if it looked bigger or different. The Sul incident reinforced Copts' fear of the promoters of Islamic identity and sent them the same old message in a new era: exalting this Islamic identity would come at the expense of churches being burned, as they were identified with non–Muslim infidels. Moreover, by imposing collective punishment and forced migration on the Coptic villagers, a warning was sent to the Coptic community that it would be held collectively responsible for the behavior of its individual members.

Coptic Christians' fears were realized two months later. On May 7th, radical Islamists waged a 14-hour attack, during which they fired upon and threw Molotov cocktails at three churches in Imbaba, Giza; one, St. Mary's, was severely damaged by fire. They also attacked houses and businesses owned by Copts. The alleged reason for the attacks was that a Muslim convert, a Coptic woman who wanted to go back to Christianity, was hiding inside the church. Claiming to be fighting for the rights of women who allegedly converted to Islam, such as cause célèbre Camelia Shehata, is a way to mobilize the populace by playing upon identity politics. The military arrived five hours after attacks started, and the results of the violence were 12 Copts dead and 232 wounded.[18]

The increasingly frustrated Copts protested again. The Maspero Youth Union organized a second sit-in at Maspero to express their anger, demand the application of the rule of law on the assaulters and rebuild their churches. The culture of violence and intolerance of the radicals and the populace was expanding and steadily moving from one spot to the other without anybody able to stop them.

About one thousand kilometers south of Imbaba, in the village of al-Marinab, Aswan, the Church of St. George was torched on October 1, 2011. Because the century-old church was dilapidated, the governor of Aswan had granted a permit to renovate it. With a proper license this time, the radicals could not refuse the renovation, but they refused to allow the church to have a cross, a church bell or a dome—all things that give a building the appearance of a church.[19]

Prior to the attack, the radicals of the village had prevented Christians from leaving their homes or buying food until they removed the dome of the church, which had been reconstructed in its previous location. They threatened that they would destroy the church and turn it into a mosque. In the presence of the security forces, the radicals blocked the roads and did not allow any Christians to leave. When Christians began to starve, security forces accompanied two young Christian men to buy food. One person from the village said, "It was heart-breaking to see the elderly running with the children to get a loaf of bread." Based on a state-supervised "reconciliation session" the Copts were forced to give in to the radicals' demands. "For the sake of peace we agreed to their demands although the approved permit included crosses, bells and domes," the village priest said. The radicals even insisted on the church being called a "hospitality home" and demanded more deconstruction, which would have jeopardized the structure of the church.[20] In the end, one of the mosques' imams instigated people to attack the church after Friday prayers.[21]

With the attack on Aswan, the map of violence against the Copts stretched from far north to far south. Already the radicals had burned the Church of St. George and the Holy Family in Rafah, Northern Sinai, on January 29, 2011.[22] On January 30, 2011, eleven Copts, including children belonging to two families, were murdered inside their homes by their radical Islamist neighbors, in the village of Sharona, in Minia.[23] Neither of these two incidents got sufficient publicity, as they happened during a chaotic period, when communications were severed; Mubarak's regime had cut off the internet and cell phone coverage across Egypt in order to stop the communications of the activists, especially on social media.

With the buildup of attacks, the Coptic community was utterly humiliated and broken. The aftermath of the January Revolution not only made a secular, liberal Egypt a far-fetched dream, but it emphasized radicalism. The older generation of Copts and church leaders were correct in fearing violence after the removal of Mubarak. The Coptic youth were frustrated, seeing the uncontested power of Islamists increasing, while their moderate Muslim activist compatriots were losing control of the revolution and were unable to stop the Islamist influence. The greatest frustration of all was that, in all cases, none of the perpetrators was punished. The assailants were free despite videos of their attacks circulating on social media and revealing their identities. Even those who were arrested by the SCAF were eventually set free. So far the only positive development in response to the attacks on the Copts was that it fueled their ability to organize and protest, but even this would come at a great cost, as the SCAF started to see the Copts not only becoming more defiant and vocal, but also being supported by the activists. The SCAF tolerated no criticism, and they had been arresting and trying activists in military courts.[24]

In despair, Copts planned another peaceful protest at Maspero, on Sunday, October 9, 2011, to object to the burning of the church in Aswan. Although it was a peaceful protest, the military attacked the protesters, resulting in one of the deadliest attacks on Copts in recent times. Twenty-seven Coptic Christians were left dead, and several hundred injured.[25] YouTube videos captured the military's armored cars running over Coptic protesters.[26] "One can only wonder what orders were given that could have led to large military vehicles running down protesters on the streets.... Egypt's Supreme Council of the Armed Forces must urgently explain how a protest against religious discrimination turned into a bloodbath," said Amnesty International. Medical reports stated that deaths were the result of protesters being shot and crushed to death by the military armored vehicles that intentionally ran down the peaceful protesters. The SCAF denied all of the allegations against it, placing blame elsewhere. "The SCAF have been quick to place the blame on foreign 'conspiracies,' sectarian tensions, or with protesters" added Amnesty International.[27]

The SCAF were accused of stirring social instability as a pretext to limit freedom of expression.[28] A key element giving them a free hand in limiting freedom of expression was the continuation of the long-hated emergency law, first enforced during Mubarak's regime and in place since 1981. The activists were calling for its abrogation.[29] An easy way for the SCAF to defend the continuation of emergency law was to scapegoat the Copts. Such a massacre would emphasize a desperate need for emergency law to maintain order and reinforce the SCAF practice of trying civilians in military courts—as Mubarak had done. The easiest group to crack down on is the weakest group, as there is no fear of retribution, and one that has always been the historical scapegoat: the Coptic Christians. The SCAF would have feared terrorist reprisals and suicide attacks by radicals if similar action was directed at the MB and their allies.

The massacre sent a disturbing message to the secular activists about what the SCAF was capable of doing. On the other hand, it strengthened the ties between the SCAF and the MB, who quickly came to their defense. Probably both were thinking that such a massacre would re-alienate the Copts in the post–Mubarak free-for-all era and force them out of participation in the elections. In this manner a solid block of secular voters yearning for democracy would be sidelined. The SCAF did not like the fact that the Copts left the walls of their church and addressed their political and social concerns directly to the state. It was easier when the Copts were represented by one person, the Pope, than by many different political groups.

The incident of Maspero was traumatic, and it showed the unwillingness of the state to offer the Copts an equal place in Egyptian society. Some Copts retreated from the political scene, yet others, emboldened by this tragedy, joined the moderate Muslim activists calling for expediency to finish the transitional period and, thus, end the rule of the SCAF. A renowned Coptic activist, Mina Daniel, was killed at Maspero and became an icon for the revolution. The activists formed a political movement bearing his name that was very critical of the SCAF.

What happened in Maspero was not, however, the first aggression against the Copts by the SCAF. As early as February 23, 2011, seven armored cars, military police vehicles and military men knocked down a security wall built by the monks of St. Bishoy monastery, in Wadi al-Natrun. The monastery is located close to the prison that was attacked to release the MB leaders. During the prison break, the rest of the prisoners were also released. When the police vanished on the "Friday of Anger," the monks were left with no police protection, so they built a wall to protect themselves, as security was the responsibility of the individual Egyptians during the absence of the police. But the SCAF deemed the wall illegal and knocked it down. In the process, they arrested some monks and fired their guns, severely injuring some Copts present on the site, one of whom died a month later.[30] A similar incident had already occurred ten days earlier, on February 13, at the monastery of St. Paul in the Eastern Desert.[31]

The SCAF's behavior towards the Copts encouraged the radical Islamists to take Islamic law into their own hands. On March 20, in Qena, Upper Egypt, they accused a Copt of renting an apartment to a woman they believed had a bad reputation. They cut off one of his ears, mutilated the other and slashed his neck. Emboldened by the SCAF indifference towards the Copts, they informed the security apparatus that they had punished him in accordance with *sharia* law. Instead of arresting them based on their confession, the security apparatus forced a "reconciliation session." In this manner the SCAF continued the Mubarak regime practice in which the Copts were forced to give up their legal rights to prosecute their attackers, thus perpetuating the cycle of violence against the Copts.[32] As the incident was the first of its kind it got widespread media attention, yet the perpetrators were not punished, further emboldening the rest of the radicals in Qena.

Starting on April 15, 2011, more than 10,000 protesters in Qena, mainly Salafists, objected to the appointment of a Coptic governor, Emad Mikhail. Protesters blocked the only railway track connecting Lower Egypt to Upper Egypt for eight days. Protesters shouted, "We will never be ruled by a Christian governor" and "Mikhail is an infidel pig." By April 25, the government conceded to the Salafists' demands and "froze" the appointment of the Coptic governor for three months.[33] In the end, the government appointed a Muslim governor instead. In this case the SCAF took a position that was even a step backward from the policies of Mubarak's regime, as Qena's previous governor under Mubarak was a Copt. There have been no Coptic governors appointed since this incident, keeping the number of the Copts appointed to be governors at two since the time of Ismail Pasha in the 19th century.

Abuse of Copts continued despite a revolution against the abuses of Mubarak's regime. Coptic students in a public secondary school in Beni Mazar, Minia were forced to wear the Muslim hijab. They obeyed under threat from school management that judged them to be flouting Islam by not covering their hair.[34] Abduction of underage Coptic girls for the purpose of forced conversion continued under the SCAF.[35] And, abducting Copts for ransom was also quite common at this time.

Copts who criticized the SCAF management of the transitional period were tried in military courts. Michael Nabil Sanad, a blogger, was tried without the presence of his lawyers and was sentenced to three years in prison. Human Rights Watch described it as "the worst strike against free expression in Egypt since the Mubarak government jailed the first blogger for four years in 2007." "The revolution has so far managed to get rid of the dictator, but not the dictatorship," said Michael in one of his posts.[36]

Copts did not fare any better in civil courts. Based on allegations from Islamist lawyers, a civil court in May 2011 ruled to strip Maurice Sadeq, a Coptic activist in the diaspora, of his Egyptian citizenship when he criticized the state's failure to protect Copts.[37] Withdrawal of Egyptian citizenship from activists was still another backward step compared to Mubarak's regime; it did not happen during his tenure. To the state, Sadeq was more dangerous than al-Qaeda's Ayman Zawahiri, who is still an Egyptian citizen.

In response to the SCAF's practices during the transitional period and the intensity of attacks on Copts, another wave of Coptic exodus occurred. Between March and September of 2011 about one hundred thousand Copts fled Egypt; most immigrated to the United States, Australia, Canada and Europe.[38] This large number reflected the rapid deterioration of civil society after the revolution. Between April 2011 and June 2012, 24 churches were attacked, 124 Coptic families were forced to leave their homes, 62 Copts were killed and 914 were injured in various incidents.[39]

In this environment, with clear indications that the hostility would continue, one can understand why Copts who had the means left their country. Revolutions in Egypt have not treated Copts fairly, as demonstrated by an earlier wave of emigration after the 1952 Revolution. Although the situation of the Copts was not as perilous as that of other Christians in the Middle East who were forced to leave their countries due to the threat of ISIS, the hostility of the radicals was threatening enough for many to leave Egypt.

Leaving their country may not have been the first choice of the Copts, but it was made bearable by Pope Shenouda's aptitude and fortitude in establishing different overseas outposts for the Coptic Church. When Pope Shenouda was ordained, the number of Coptic Churches in the Diaspora was four or five, and there were only three Coptic Bishops outside of Egypt. During his tenure, Pope Shenouda increased the number of Coptic churches to close to four hundred and the number of bishops to twenty-four, on five continents.[40] Hence, those Copts who left usually found a welcoming church community already established in their new locale.

But, the majority of the Copts stayed in Egypt, clinging to their diminishing hopes. The death of Pope Shenouda, on March 17, 2012, at the age of 89, shattered what little hope they had left. He had led them for forty years and he departed at a time of uncertainty and great vulnerability, when the Copts were facing increasing pressure from both the Islamists and the SCAF. Men and women in black mourning clothes packed St. Mark's Coptic Cathedral, raising their hands in prayer, and those who were unable to get inside overflowed into the streets around it. The Pope's funeral drew tens of thousands of Copts, making it the largest funeral after Nasser's. Pope Shenouda did everything he could as a religious leader to bring peace to his Coptic community and to Egypt. When he represented the Copts to the state, he was put under house arrest and his congregation continued to be killed. When his people chose to leave the Church walls and went to the state to represent themselves and to voice their concerns, they were beaten and murdered. Neither the state nor the Islamists have been willing to give the Copts a role in their country. The state offers them second-class citizen status, while the Islamists accept them based on their *dhimma* status. Pope Shenouda, who revived the Coptic identity, departed in the midst of intense fighting centered upon identity politics.

Identity politics dominated the transitional period and were best demonstrated by the Muslim Brotherhood. Many argue that after the MB infiltrated the revolution and steered it towards achieving their own goals, they used the "participation without domination" approach to achieve their Islamic ideology. By at first declaring that they wouldn't have their own separate agenda, they insinuated themselves into Tahrir with the other protesters. Under the pretext of support they began to organize and direct, gradually assuming more and more representation. In the vacuum left by Mubarak's ouster, they allied themselves with those who assumed leadership, the SCAF, to hijack the revolution. Then they used their well-formulated slogan, "participation without domination," to lull people into a sense of security and make them believe that the MB wanted to work with others to re-build the Egyptian political system.

The Rise to Power of the MB's Morsi

In the parliamentary election held at the end of 2011, the MB broke their previous pledge to only compete for 25 percent of the seats; their Freedom and Justice Party won 47 percent of the seats, thus controlling the parliament.[41] By controlling close to half of the seats of the parliament the MB established their control over the choice of the 100 members who would form a constituent assembly to write Egypt's new constitution. Secular and liberal political groups were stunned to see the majority of Egypt's Parliament dominated by the MB and their Salafist counterparts, who had gained around a quarter of the seats. Between the MB and the Salafists, Egypt's Parliament was dominated by Islamists, with secularists rendered irrelevant. The live broadcast of parliament sessions showed imams, sheikhs, and Islamic jurists—people who refused to pledge their allegiance to Egypt when it contradicted *sharia*, people who would not stand to salute the Egyptian flag, and people who launched the Muslim call to prayers while the Parliament was in session. This image reinforced the secularists' argument that no longer was only the revolution hijacked, but Egypt was hijacked as well. The re–Islamization process, which started decades ago, made it possible for the MB to take over Egypt even through democratic means.

The MB also broke their pledge of not running for the presidency by nominating a presidential candidate. As a matter of fact, they nominated two candidates.[42] Their first choice, Khairat al-Shater, who was one of Sadat's student patron beneficiaries and who the SCAF pardoned from prison, was disqualified because of his previous legal issues. So, they nominated Mohamed

Morsi. On June 30, 2012, Morsi became Egypt's first Islamist president, with a narrow majority of 51 percent of the votes over his contender Ahmad Shafiq's 48 percent.

During the presidential elections, not only did the Muslim Brotherhood use religion as a platform, they also banned the Copts from voting at some voting stations. Knowing their voting behavior against the Islamists, they stopped the Copts from voting in some areas in Upper Egypt. In a television interview three years later, a member of the Higher Committee for Presidential Elections confirmed this irregularity. He stated that the majority of the members of the committee voted to move on, without having a revote at these polling stations. He declared that the MB would have burned Egypt if Morsi had not won.[43] If a member of the election committee expresses such a strong statement, one can glean from it that the MB use fear to manipulate public and political will for their gain.

By controlling the legislative and the executive branches, the MB had abandoned their approach of "domination without participation." In the process of reversing their approach, they alienated almost all of their opposition and contenders. Thus, the MB lost its credibility among the January protesters.[44]

Many claim that the MB would not have been able to break their pledges and would not have been able to achieve success in the elections without approval from the SCAF. The situation surrounding the election of Morsi was marred by suspicion and mistrust and suggestions of some kind of bargain between the SCAF and the MB. The presidential election result was scheduled to be released on June 20, 2012, but was postponed until June 24th, with a lack of transparency as to why the vote count was delayed and what happened behind closed doors.[45] It was a period of delay and doubt. Despite leaked information indicating Morsi's competitor, Ahmad Shafiq, was winning, Egyptians woke up to find that the MB had announced Morsi as Egypt's new president and that he had addressed the nation in a press conference at dawn on June 17th.[46] By the time the sun rose, his supporters were in Tahrir Square, celebrating even before any official result was declared.

Already, there had been many abuses and deadly attacks against the activists by the security forces under the SCAF. Tens of activists had been killed on Muhammad Mahmoud Street in downtown Cairo in November 2011, causing a public uproar. Similar violence occurred after the security forces broke up an anti–SCAF sit-in. Soon after, an MB spokesperson declared that the MB would be amenable to a future "safe exit" for military leaders.[47]

After Morsi took over, none of the senior military officers were tried for wrongdoing. The Prime Minister praised the role the SCAF played during the transitional period. Field Marshal Tantawi, the head of the SCAF and the de facto president of Egypt, and General Anan, the chief of staff, were given

Egypt's highest medal of honor after Morsi retired them.[48] Moreover, they were offered presidential advisory appointments, and when a judge in October 2012 ordered an investigation regarding accusations that Tantawi was involved in the deaths of protesters in the transitional period, there was complete silence about the findings.[49]

After the MB sidelined the military generals from politics and controlled both the executive and the legislative branches, the judiciary was left alone to play a one-sided role in the checks and balances. The first test came on June 14, 2012, two weeks before Morsi was sworn into office. Egypt's Supreme Constitutional Court ordered the dissolution of the Parliament on the grounds that one third of its members were illegally elected. In July, in an unprecedented break with the rule of law, President Morsi ordered the return of the MB-dominated Parliament. But, in September, the Supreme Administrative Court upheld the dissolution of the Parliament.[50] The activists saw that the democratically elected president did not show respect for the rule of law, which set off further alarm bells.

Already, in March 2012, the MB-controlled Parliament had chosen 100 members to form a constituent assembly to draft Egypt's constitution, but they unlawfully chose 50 of those members from the Parliament. On April 10th, the Administrative Court dissolved the assembly, prompting the Parliament to form a new one. By December 1st the assembly had presented the draft to Morsi to call for a national referendum. To protect the draft, a week earlier on November 22nd, Morsi had issued a constitutional declaration making his decrees and the constituent assembly immune from judicial review until a new Parliament was elected. Furthermore, he retired the prosecutor general and appointed his own.[51] Such moves were not only unprecedented, but unlawful as well. Even the powerful Nasser did not have such control, and neither did Mubarak's thirty-year tenure witness such a monopoly. In simple terms, Morsi put himself and the MB above the law in order to concentrate power into their hands and to make themselves the sole planners of Egypt's future and to implement their Islamic ideology.

The liberal, secularist Muslims and the Copts had already withdrawn from the MB-dominated constituent assembly because of the Islamist monopoly and the committee's lack of focus on protecting freedom of expression and belief.[52] Their withdrawal posed a judicial threat to the legitimacy of the constituent assembly, thus, Morsi issued his constitutional declaration to protect Egypt's new Islamist constitution. The newly born democracy produced a president who utilized measures to force his MB vision on the citizenry and to fully ignore the rule of law.[53] The activists could not allow Morsi to have such a free hand.

Other than Islamists, all segments of Egyptian society arranged a series of protests to reject Morsi's draconian power, and tens of thousands of demonstrators marched to the presidential palace. Yet, only the Copts and the Church were accused of being behind the protests. The MB pointed to their withdrawal from the constituent assembly to back their claims that the Copts were undermining Morsi.[54] The MB declared that 60 percent of the protesters in front of the Presidential palace were Copts. "A message to the Egyptian Church from an Egyptian Muslim: I tell the Church, I swear to Allah, and again, I swear to Allah, if you conspire and unite with the *felool* [remnants of Mubarak's regime] to bring Morsi down, we will have another matter ... there are red lines, our red line is the legitimacy of Dr. Muhammad Morsi. Whoever splashes it with water, we will splash him with blood," said a prominent MB leader to tens of thousands of Islamists, who enthusiastically shouted, "*Allah Akbar*."[55]

Accusing the Church was the MB's way to lobby their supporters to protest in favor of Morsi's moves. The street was divided between Islamists and others, and while the peaceful protesters were staging a sit-in in front of the palace to call for the annulment of the constitutional declaration, they were attacked by the MB protesters. The area turned into a street fight between Morsi's supporters and the rest of the Egyptians. The violence resulted in many injuries and seven casualties. One of the people killed was a Copt and a member of the Maspero Youth Union: Karam Sergius.[56] Another Copt, Mina Philip, became the face of the tactics used by the MB. He was caught on camera in front of the presidential palace, half-naked and bleeding as a result of a severe beating.[57]

Fearing the spread of violence, the military warned of "disastrous consequences" if the constitutional crisis was not resolved. This was an early sign of the rift forming between the MB's Morsi and the military.[58] But the rift between Morsi and the judiciary was growing wider. The Judge's Club, the Cassation Court, Supreme Constitutional Court and The Supreme Council of the Judiciary criticized Morsi's constitutional declaration, calling it "unprecedented aggression" on the independence of the judiciary.[59]

The pressure on Morsi also came from inside his office. Morsi neither consulted nor informed his aides before taking his position, and some of them resigned in reaction to his constitutional declaration.[60] His assistant for democratic transition, Samir Morcos, a Copt, learned of it from the television, prompting him to resign three months after his appointment. Having a Copt as the president's assistant was evidently cosmetic for Morsi, and Morcos refused to be "part of his decoration."[61] Due to mounting pressure, Morsi annulled the constitutional declaration, but he ignored the turmoil in the street and called for a vote on a national referendum for the new constitution on December 15th.[62]

His December 1st decision to call for a referendum came only an hour after he received the draft. The constituent assembly had just stayed overnight to finish the draft. The reason for this hasty process was the fear that the Constitutional Court might order the dissolution of the constituent assembly. Therefore, on that same day, the MB sent their supporters to besiege the court, in order to prevent the judges, who were scheduled to meet on the next day, December 2nd, from getting into the courthouse. Unable to enter, the judges suspended the Court session until they felt safe, and declared it "a dark day in the history of the Egyptian judiciary."[63]

Amid a call from the opposition to boycott voting, the constitution passed by 64 percent, with a voter turnout of only 33 percent.[64] Morsi relied on his well-organized MB, Salafists and other Islamist groups to lobby and vote "yes" for the referendum. In order to lobby their constituencies and achieve a good turnout, the MB accused the Church of mobilizing the nuns and monks to vote against the constitution.[65]

This constitution was more Islamic than any constitution in Egypt's history, and many saw it as setting the groundwork for the establishment of a theocracy. The constitution emphasized the supremacy of Egypt's Islamic identity, not the nation's joint Egyptian identity. It provided for a much stricter implementation of the principals of Islamic *sharia* law than before, raising fears among opponents that it would limit civil liberties and the rights of women and Copts.[66] In addition to keeping Article Two, other articles were created to promote the role of Islam in the public sphere. Article 219 was created to interpret Article Two; it states, "The principles of Islamic *Sharia* include general evidence, foundational rules, rules of jurisprudence, and credible sources accepted in Sunni doctrines and by the larger community." Previously, the interpretation of Article Two was left for the court. But, based on this article, many believed that *sharia* would penetrate social and personal life, allowing for a literal and archaic interpretation of the Islamic law, which in turn would have a great impact on the forms of punishment for crimes.[67] Article Four gave a new consultative role to a religious body, al-Azhar, stating, "Al-Azhar Senior Scholars are to be consulted in matters pertaining to Islamic law.... The State shall ensure sufficient funds for Al-Azhar to achieve its objectives." Article Ten outlines the role of religion in the family: "The family is the basis of the society and is founded on religion, morality and patriotism...." Article Eleven states, "The State shall safeguard ethics, public morality and public order, and foster a high level of education and of religious and patriotic values, scientific thinking, Arab culture, and the historical and cultural heritage of the people...."[68] For the Copts a fundamental component of the "cultural heritage" referred to in Article Eleven is their historical *dhimma* status, which has accounted not only for their past plight, but is also a threat to their future.

After the passing of the constitution, Morsi's MB escalated their confrontation with the judiciary, which they saw as a real threat to their full domination. They pushed to adopt a law to reduce the age of retirement for judges from seventy to sixty years old. The law would guarantee the retirement of 3,000 senior judges.[69] It would also ensure the MB appointment of its own judges. Such a move would empty Egypt's courts of the senior judges who were obstructing the MB's political ambitions in what the national movement called "Brotherhoodization." It is a term created to mean the appointing of MB members to influential positions in Egypt's various institutions in order to ensure their domination and to expedite the process of establishing an Islamic state or "caliphate" in Egypt.

Within eight months, Morsi appointed 8 ministers, 5 governors and 8 staffers at the presidential office. Five governors' deputies, 13 governors' advisors, and 12 district heads also were hired from the MB. Muslim Brotherhood members were able to move into 20 different ministries as minister advisors, spokesmen and office mangers.[70] Within the judiciary, MB judges were organized and attracted sympathizers through the "Judges for Egypt Movement."[71] Morsi's unlawful appointment of a new prosecutor general was a blatant example of "Brotherhoodization" that drew great resentment. The Coptic Church objected to the appointment of the prosecutor general and to the attempts to dismiss the senior judges. The Church objection was voiced by its new leader, Pope Tawadros.

Pope Tawadros succeeded Pope Shenouda as the 118th Pope of the Coptic Church in November 2012, five months after Morsi assumed office. "The judiciary is one of the pillars of the Egyptian society and must not be touched," the Pope said.[72] Such a statement not only was meant to support the national movement's objection to the Brotherhoodization, but also indicated that the new Pope was adopting a critical tone towards the MB. Perhaps the Pope had his own reasons to be critical of Morsi.

In an unprecedented move, on April 7, 2013, St. Mark's Coptic Cathedral came under attack during a funeral held for victims of radical Islamist violence. The attack lasted for several hours and aired live on numerous TV channels. During Friday prayers two days earlier, on April 5, an imam in the area of al-Khusus near Cairo instigated the people to violence against the Copts. Two hours later rampaging radicals attacked and destroyed two churches, a Coptic pre–school, and Coptic-owned homes and businesses. In the violence, four Copts were shot dead and a Muslim was found dead.[73] No one knows the real reason for the incident, but some said unidentified children were drawing on the wall of an Islamic institute; their drawing looked like a swastika or a cross, which reportedly upset the locals.[74]

On April 7, the four victims of al-Khusus were taken to St. Mark's Coptic Cathedral for a mass funeral, which was attended by a few thousand Copts and some moderate Muslims. While the coffins were departing the Cathedral, a mob outside started to pelt the mourners with stones. Violence erupted and moved to a sweeping attack involving firearms, fire bombs, and cars being set aflame. The police arrived, but they stood by watching while radicals scaled the walls of the Cathedral compound, throwing projectiles and firing at the people trapped inside. Then police joined the fray by firing tear gas at the Copts inside the compound. At least one Copt died from a gunshot wound and more than thirty Copts were injured. The Cathedral looked like it was under siege.[75]

The attack on the Cathedral was nerve-wracking for the Copts and it inflicted a much deeper humiliation than the list of churches that had been attacked before. St. Mark's Coptic Cathedral is the headquarters of the Church, the residence of the Pope and an important symbol for the Copts; St. Mark the Evangelist and Athanasius's relics are interred inside. In this incident the radical Islamists struck at the heart of the Church, reaching the Pope's doorstep, as if to say no place or person, regardless of their position, is safe from their reach. For the first time in the history of Egypt, the police attacked the Cathedral with tear gas.

Morsi stated, "Any attack against the Cathedral is like an attack against me personally." But, on the other hand, Morsi's top aide and a member of the MB blamed the Copts for the violence.[76] Conflicting messages cast doubt on Morsi's sincerity. By now the credibility of the MB was at its lowest point and Pope Tawadros openly questioned it. "The authorities led by the MB provide assurances, but they did not take measures to protect them [the Copts] from violence," he said. The Pope stated that the Copts felt marginalized, ignored and neglected by the authorities led by the Muslim Brotherhood.[77]

In response to Morsi's top aide blaming the Copts for the violence, the Pope bluntly labeled it "pure fabrication."[78] On the other hand, Morsi's statement was only an empty gesture, as he had refused an invitation by the Holy Synod to attend the seating ceremony of Pope Tawadros at the same cathedral. If his convictions did not allow him to visit a church, his statement could not carry much weight for Copts.[79] Morsi spoke extensively during his campaign about tolerance and freedom, but this was another pledge he had broken just as he had broken his pledge of appointing two vice presidents: a woman and a Copt. So, Pope Tawadros's adoption of a critical tone toward Morsi and the MB in their conflict with the judiciary was not only based on his objection to the Brotherhoodization, but was also influenced by his experience with them. The Pope also described the MB constitution as discriminatory, saying that some of its clauses were "distorted by a religious slant." He argued that "the constitution is supposed to unite and not divide."[80]

The new blood that came with the change of leadership of the Church combined with the fact that the Egyptians broke the barrier of fear after the January Revolution made it easier for the new Pope to criticize Morsi and the MB. The fact that the Copts were also supported by moderate Muslims who share the same goals for Egypt's future provided him with a buffer zone of sorts against Morsi and the MB. Yet, his words still demonstrated bravery, as his predecessor, Pope Shenouda, was put under house arrest when he spoke out against Sadat. Attacking the Cathedral was a major impetus for the Pope and his congregation to be critical of Morsi and the MB, but it was not the only attack that roused their discontent.

The "contempt of Islam" charge that was used against the Copts under Mubarak become more popular with the rise of the MB after the January Revolution. With their Salafist allies, they provided a long list of Islamist lawyers to pursue these cases. In October 2011, Ayman Yousef Mansour was sentenced to three years in prison for insulting Islam and Muhammad on Facebook. In January 2012, Gamal Abdou Masoud, a 17-year-old, was also sentenced to three years in prison on a similar charge. In September 2012, the court upheld the three-year prison sentence of teacher Bishoy Kameel for posting a cartoon deemed insulting to Muhammad on Facebook.[81] The Islamist lawyers also used the contempt of Islam charge to terrify and silence secular Muslim journalists and public figures. Since the rise of the MB after the January Revolution, Copts constituted 40 percent of the defendants in these cases, and most were based on flawed charges.[82] There was a surge in these cases, reflecting the increasing power of the Islamists. During Mubarak's time in office, there was a case or two a year, but under Morsi there were about 10 cases in one year.[83]

The case of the female Copt, teacher Dimyana Abdel-Nour in Luxor, is an instructive example of a flawed trial, as her accusers were children. Three ten-year-old students accused her of showing disgust when she talked about Islam in her class while teaching the history of religions. The head of the parent's council at the school, a Muslim, accused fundamentalists of being the engineers behind the accusations. His daughter, among many other Muslim students, denied any wrongdoing on the part of Dimyana. But because of the increasing power of the Islamists, any baseless rumor could spread in rural areas, and once it reaches the attention of the Islamists, it turns into a battle in which they need to exalt Islam. Dimyana's lawyer said hers is his 18th case of a person—many of them school teachers—imprisoned over insulting Islam. He added that his other 17 clients received three to six years in prison.[84]

Penalties in blasphemy cases can go as far as the death penalty. In a famous case, seven Coptic Christians living in the United States were sentenced to death in absentia. They were convicted of insulting Islam based on a YouTube video they produced, which started waves of protests in September 2012. Dimyana's case was a much weaker one, as the main basis against her was the testimony of the children. Yet, she was detained for a week, then released on bail after paying quite a large sum: approximately $3,000.[85] In

June 2014 an Egyptian appeals court upheld the earlier conviction of blasphemy against Dimyana, and they also imposed an additional sentence of 6 months imprisonment on top of an approximately $14,000 fine.[86] Her fine is much larger than had ever been levied before, and it would take many years to pay it off, as a typical teacher does not make much money.

Contempt of Islam was not the only challenge facing the Copts; forced migration was also on the rise. In July 2012, 120 Coptic families had to flee their village in Dahshur, Giza, in fear of angry mobs when a fight broke out after a Coptic ironing man accidentally burned the shirt of one of his Muslim customers. In the fray a Muslim man was killed.[87] In September of 2012, Copts were forced to leave their homes in the town of Rafah, in Northern Sinai. Radical Islamists, who were gaining power in this remote area on the border with Gaza, were calling for the establishment of an Islamic state in the Sinai. In order to change the demography of the area, they issued an ultimatum for the Copts there to leave the town within 48 hours, otherwise, they threatened, the Copts would be killed. Instead of protecting the Copts, the governor of North Sinai helped families to relocate in the neighboring city of al-Arish. This situation prompted the Coptic Church to issue a statement criticizing the state and demanding protection.[88] A similar incident happened in February 2017. Seventy-five Coptic families were forced to leave their homes in al-Arish due to the increase in attacks, which left seven Copts dead in just a few weeks, and the fear engendered by a video aired by ISIS vowing to escalate attacks on them.[89] The Governor of North Sinai, who helped to relocate the Copts in the province of Ismailia, stated that the Coptic families were not forced to migrate, but rather they willingly left because they were afraid of the escalation of violence.[90] The activists criticized the government for its lack of protection of Copts.

In addition to forced migration, the abduction of underage Coptic girls for the purpose of forced conversion has also been increasing since the rise of the MB after the January Revolution. More than 500 Coptic girls were kidnapped between 2011 and 2013.[91] A 14-year-old Sarah Ishaq Abdelmalek vanished on her way to middle school in al-Dabaa, Marsa Matruh. In October 2012, during Morsi's visit to Marsa Matruh, the Church tried to petition and inform him of her abduction. The priest said the police knew where she is but were unwilling to return her to her family. The Salafi Front issued a statement saying that Sarah had converted to Islam, married a Muslim and that she had full freedom to do so as she had reached puberty.[92] Kidnapping was not restricted to underage Coptic girls; adults and children were kidnapped as well in order for the kidnappers to ask for ransom.

In Minia alone there have been more than 150 cases of kidnaping of Copts since the revolution; 37 of these case happened under Morsi. In January 2013, a Coptic doctor was kidnapped by masked gunmen, he was beaten and insulted while blindfolded, his mouth was sealed with a bandage and his ears were stuffed with cotton balls. He was released the next day after his family paid the equivalent of $40,000 in ransom money. As they are the most vulnerable when there is no protection, extortion of Copts became an easy way to make money.[93] In another case of abduction in May 2013, even though the family of Kyrillos Yousef, a six-year-old Coptic boy in Delga, Minia, paid the equivalent of $4,000 in ransom, the kidnapper killed the boy.[94] Wealthy Muslims were also targeted for kidnapping, but the Copts suffered the brunt of it, especially in Upper Egypt.

The lack of protection in Morsi's government was widespread. During his one-year term, a total of 24 churches were attacked with 17 Copts killed.[95] These attacks were threatening and were mirrored in another wave of Coptic exodus. In March 2013, an independent Egyptian newspaper reported 83,000 Copts had immigrated to the country of Georgia within a fourteen-month period; most of them were businessmen and professionals. Such a large mass immigration in a very short time prompted the Coptic Church to send Coptic priests to serve the newly founded community in a different country. Georgia isn't economically robust; rather, the choice was based on the simple fact that about 88 percent of its population is Christian, and it would serve as a safe haven for Coptic immigrants.[96]

However, most Copts did not immigrate, and many joined their moderate Muslim fellow activists to form a strong opposition to Morsi's regime and the Brotherhoodization process, which was not abating and moving from one institution to the other. After decades of deprivation, it was impossible for the Muslim Brotherhood to rise above its own desire for power and fuel the religious divide, to its own benefit.

Morsi tried to control the media in Egypt in order not only to promote the MB Islamic agenda but, more importantly, to silence his critics. He appointed a MB member as Information Minister. The MB assigned new editors to the state-owned newspapers who were either MB members or sympathizers. *Akhbar al-Youm*, the second largest newspaper, would be managed by a descendant of the MB's founder. At the bottom level, hundreds of MB supporters, especially the Salafists, besieged Egypt's main media complex, the media production facilities in 6th of October City, in an attempt to intimidate the secular media. Some journalists and anchors were physically assaulted and humiliated, and impeded from performing their work. The authorities shut down *al-Faraeen* TV because its owner was critical of Morsi. They pulled copies of the Christian-owned newspaper *al-Dustour* from news shops on the pretext that it was "harming the president through phrases and wording punishable by law." The newspaper had written an editorial expressing fear that the MB was taking over Egypt.[97]

Egypt's Ministry of Culture has always been the custodian of Egyptian identity. In many cases its intellectuals have criticized al-Azhar when it has banned novels and issued *fatwas* that accuse writers of blasphemy, some of which have led to their assassinations. It was only logical that the Ministry of Culture was the next ministry for Morsi to attempt to control by appointing a Muslim Brotherhood member as its head. All too quickly, the new minister sacked the heads of the General Egyptian Book Organization, the Fine Arts Sector and the National Library and Archives. It was the sacking of the Cairo Opera House head, a female musician, that generated the most outrage. The Brotherhoodization of the Ministry of Culture is based on their old belief that Egypt's identity has been stolen by a few westernized intellectuals and that it was the time for Egypt to restore its Islamic identity.[98]

The intellectuals' apprehension and suspicion of Morsi and the MB were already established when Morsi pardoned 18 radicals, including Aboul Ela Muhammad, who was convicted in the assassination of the renowned intellectual Farag Fouda during Mubarak's presidency.[99] Morsi also appointed as governor of Luxor a member of the radical group that massacred fifty-eight tourists at the Temple of Queen Hatshepsut in November 1997.[100] Luxor is famous for cultural tourism and the intellectuals criticized Morsi's decision as an attempt to kill tourism and stifle Egyptian culture.

In fear of the Brotherhoodization of the Ministry of Culture, writers, movie directors, producers, stars and other liberal artists planned a sit-in beginning on June 5, 2013, in front of the Ministry, to demand the resignation of the MB-appointed minister. The intellectuals protested every evening with artistic performances including music, singing and poetry. Despite the relaxed nature of the sit-in, the Muslim Brotherhood's followers attempted to dismantle it. There were some skirmishes but no serious injuries.[101] The MB was quite careful in dealing with such a famous and influential class of people, as news about them generally hit the headlines fast. The MB was also careful as their sit-in was organized only three weeks before a well-planned massive anti–Morsi protest on June 30th. By now most Egyptians had concluded that their elected president was acting like a Muslim caliph.

Seven

Long Live Egypt
A Return to Military Rule

The June 30th Revolution

In late April 2013, activists formed the grassroots opposition movement *Tamarod*, or "Rebel," to protest Morsi's and the Muslim Brotherhood's domination of the political scene. With no power sharing on the part of the MB, it became obvious to the activists and many other Egyptians that Egypt was moving in the direction of an Islamic state. The activists' objectives of a secular state, democracy and the rule of law were compromised by Morsi. With no legitimate channels to express their political and social concerns, *Tamarod* activists took to the street to bring public attention to the real objectives of the new regime. Their idea was to gather people's signatures on a petition in the hope that the signatures would outnumber the 13 million votes Morsi obtained in the presidential election. This would allow them to organize massive protests to demand early presidential elections. Just as they chose Police Day to protest against police abuse, they chose Morsi's first anniversary in office, June 30, 2013, to protest against his abuse of power and to delegitimize him.

The *Tamarod* activists printed copies of the petition which, among other things, highlighted the absence of security, the economic deterioration, the absence of social justice and the laxness of Morsi's regime to bring to justice those responsible for killing protesters. They distributed the petitions for the public to sign all over the country. *Tamarod*'s idea quickly took hold as a way to escape Morsi's grip on power. It snowballed like the January Revolution, gaining *Tamarod* legitimacy to lobby opposition parties, various political and social movements and, above all, the large moderate Muslim society. In a press conference they declared that they had accumulated 22 million signatures; the atmosphere of the January Revolution was brought back to life. With the exception of the Islamists, Egyptian society was ready to protest and to rescind legitimacy from Morsi and the MB.¹ The *Tamarod* Movement had the support of Copts since its inception. Moheb Doss, one of the five cofounders of *Tamarod* was a Copt.² "Egypt needs every Egyptian today! We must think, discuss, and express our desire for our nation together without violence, enmity or bloodshed," Pope Tawadros wrote on social media to support the protests.³

The MB regime had already tried to pressure the Pope to discourage the Coptic community from participating in the protests, but it was hard to convince him, especially since *Tamarod* was formed in April—the same month St. Mark's Coptic Cathedral was attacked, with no one held accountable. The Pope also rejected the advice of the U.S. Ambassador to Egypt, who suggested that he discourage participation by the Copts. He stated that the right to protest is a personal choice. When the MB leaders threatened the Copts in different provinces, neither the Pope nor the Copts changed their oppositional stance.⁴

"If you are going out on June 30 ... be aware that a liter of benzene [gas] can burn your [shops], houses and churches ... if you are not afraid of this, be afraid for your children," said a letter distributed in Minia, to intimidate the Copts against participating in the protests. On the other hand, a banner by moderate Muslims in Cairo tried to encourage the Copts to participate; it read, "You, Copt don't be afraid—we will carry you on our shoulders."⁵ The sheer number of the Copts would make a difference, whether they joined the protests or refrained from joining.

Anti-Morsi protesters camped out at Tahrir Square and in front of the presidential palace. The MB and their sympathizers camped out at the nearby Rabaa al-Adawia Square. Egyptian society was polarized, the atmosphere became tense and Egypt seemed to be on the brink of a civil war, with both groups headed towards a confrontation. By June 29th, in various provinces, eight Egyptians had been killed and 606 had been injured in clashes between Morsi supporters and opponents.⁶

On June 30th, millions of Egyptians poured into the streets of Egypt, including those in Upper Egypt, where people had been absent from the scene during the January Revolution. The number of protesters far exceeded the January Revolution, marking it the largest protest in the history of Egypt, and many argue in the world as well. The Copts participated heavily, and unlike the January Revolution, the Coptic community formed an undivided camp. Both the older and younger generations of Copts had one stance, which was also shared by an undivided moderate Muslim bloc. The Copts were very conspicuous, eliciting the praise of the moderate Muslims but also the wrath of the MB.

It was not difficult for *Tamarod* to organize millions of Egyptians against the MB regime, as the people had reached such a level of despair. Many Egyptians agreed that Mubarak was an autocrat, but they argued that Morsi was even more so. Morsi did not learn from Mubarak's missteps and he, too, was accused of killing protesters. While Mubarak suspended the Parliament during his tenure following the Constitutional Court decision that some of its members were illegally elected, Morsi refused the court ruling and called upon the Parliament to reconvene. Mubarak did not fire a prosecutor general, but Morsi did. Mubarak gave the appearance that he respected the law although the regime was corrupt. Morsi defiantly put himself above the law, setting a precedent for others to follow, thus, his regime presented a clearer case of corruption. Morsi monopolized power far more than Mubarak ever did. Perhaps this is why it took Egyptians only a year to rebel against Morsi, while it took them thirty years to rebel against Mubarak. Morsi shocked the Egyptians by acting like a Muslim caliph, putting himself and the MB above all.

During the protests the Egyptians shouted in the streets: *"Enzil ya Sisi! Morsi mish ra'isi!"* or "Come out Sisi! Morsi is not my president!" The desperate Egyptians wanted the military to force Morsi out. Opposition leaders expressed the same desire. This can be understood against the historical backdrop that the only two real political powers and historical rivals in Egypt are the military and the Muslim Brotherhood.

On July 1, 2013, General el-Sisi issued a 48-hour ultimatum for all political forces to reach a compromise; otherwise, the military would impose a "road map for the future" that "will not exclude anyone." This was not the first ultimatum; a week earlier el-Sisi had urged the Egyptians to reach a compromise, stating that the military would not allow an "attack on the will of the people."[7] The rift between the military and the MB was growing wider.

Morsi, insisting he was the legitimate president, ignored the ultimatum, and he refused to listen to the demands of the millions still in the streets. Although the MB is organized and powerful, it still doesn't represent the majority of Egyptians, a fact the masses of demonstrators made clear. While Mubarak accepted the will of his people whether he liked it or not, Morsi refused. Perhaps Morsi's keen desire to maintain power caused him to overlook what Nasser had done to the MB. The fact that he fired and hired defense ministers didn't guarantee him power over the generals, nor did it allow him to secure any of their loyalties.

On July 3rd, el-Sisi appeared on TV to declare Morsi's removal. In front of a panel representing the different political forces across the spectrum, el-Sisi announced a road map for a post–Morsi government which included temporary suspension of the constitution, the appointment of the head of the Constitutional Court as interim president, the formation of a committee to amend the constitution and a plan for new presidential and parliamentary elections. While el-Sisi was speaking, Morsi was in military custody involuntarily following Mubarak as Egypt's second deposed president.

Among the people who appeared behind el-Sisi were religious leaders including the sheikh of al-Azhar and a representative from the Salafi Call who, ironically, endorsed Morsi's removal, as they felt excluded themselves by the MB's political domination. Pope Tawadros was included in the panel in recognition of the extensive support the Coptic community gave to the anti–Morsi protests. Given a turn to address the nation, he declared his endorsement of the road map that he and the rest of the participants had formulated.

But his appearance on the panel confirmed for the Muslim Brotherhood its own allegations that the Copts were the real power behind Morsi's removal. The MB and their supporters, driven by extreme anger, started sporadic attacks on Copts in various parts of the country. The next day on July 4th, MB supporters in the coastal city of Marsa Matruh broke the windows of the Virgin Mary Coptic Orthodox Church and burned the security room. In Delga, Minia, a building belonging to the Church of St. George was burned to the ground. On July 5th, four Copts were murdered, and two dozen Coptic homes were burned by a mob, compelling some to seek shelter at the local Church of St. John, in the village of Nagaa Hassan, in Luxor. The same day, MB supporters tried to storm Coptic Orthodox churches in Qena and Luxor. The security forces used teargas to disband them, leaving 13 wounded. On July 6th, a Coptic priest was shot dead while walking in a public market in al-Arish, Sinai. The same day a Coptic businessman was abducted in Sheikh Zuwayed, Sinai, only to be found beheaded five days later.[8]

In this period of hostility, many churches decided it was no longer safe to hold regular worship services or Sunday school. In some parts of Upper Egypt, the service finished by 7 a.m., and then the churches were shut and put under guard. Death threats forced Pope Tawadros to leave his residence at St. Mark's Coptic Cathedral in Cairo for a secret place.[9]

It is undeniable that the tremendous Coptic presence in the protests helped greatly in tilting the scale away from the MB, but they didn't constitute the majority. The moderate Muslim protesters were the larger number. The MB's allegation that the Copts were the real power behind ousting Morsi was reinforced in their minds when the Copts wholeheartedly participated in another massive June 30th-like protest called for by el-Sisi on July 26th, to give him a mandate to confront terrorism in the streets. The Pope tweeted: "The national responsibility of the Coptic Church of Egypt demands us all to support the measures that protect our country and achieve our freedom without violence or recklessness. Long live Egypt, safe and secure."[10]

In asking for a mandate, el-Sisi wanted to prove that the support for the military move against Morsi was based on unfailing popular will and in no way was instigated by the military. Although the MB, as well as many in the international community, presented Morsi's removal as a military coup, millions of Egyptians refused the idea. They proved it was their will through a massive turnout in the street to support el-Sisi's mandate. Unlike Nasser and the Free Officers, who did not warn Egypt's king Farouk when they toppled him, the military issued Morsi two ultimatums asking him to listen to the demands of his people. Morsi could have avoided such an end had he accepted early elections. Morsi lost the legitimacy that was given to him by the public and, in the absence of a parliament that can represent the people and impeach the president, the public took the issue into its own hands and went to the street to impeach the illegitimate president themselves. El-Sisi also asked for the mandate because he expected violence from the Muslim Brotherhood in retaliation for Morsi's removal and wanted to have the needed political support. Their first well-planned violent action was directed at the Copts.

When the interim government moved to break up the MB sit-in calling for the return of Morsi at Rabaa al-Adawia Square in August 14, the MB and their followers launched the largest wave of mass church burnings as has occurred in any country in recent history. In the midst of the attacks on churches throughout Egypt, a statement on an MB's Freedom and Justice Party Facebook page read, "The church's pope is involved in deposing the first elected, Islamic president.... And for the church to declare war against Islam and Muslims is the worst offense. For every action there is a reaction."[11] As mentioned in the introduction, the violence resulted in the burning and destruction of 73 churches throughout Egypt, the deaths of 15 people, and the displacement of more than a 1,000 Copts, in addition to the looting, destruction and burning of numerous Coptic homes and businesses.[12]

The Copts paid a high price to practice their right of political participation, and the attacks on them continued for the next few months, although they became more sporadic. A major attack occurred in October 2013 in al-Warraq, Giza. Radical Islamists indiscriminately opened fire on Copts leaving the Church of the Virgin Mary, killing four people. Among the victims was a 12-year-old girl who died from 13 bullet wounds to different parts of her body.[13]

Despite the violence, the June protests, popularly called the June 30th Revolution, marked a success for the moderate Muslims, and even more so for Copts. Not only did this revolution bring down the MB regime, but it also proved Coptic patriotism. The MB believes that the Coptic *dhimmis* could not be true citizens, as they could serve Egypt's enemy or a "foreign agenda." As mentioned in previous chapters, the Copts were attacked during the Crusaders' campaigns in fear that they might collaborate with their co-religionists against Muslims. This concept carried on into the French and British occupation of Egypt. When Egypt got its full independence, the Copts were still suspected of being pawns, tools of Western Christian interference in Egypt. Despite the fact that history has never proven such claims against the Copts, it bears repeating that al-Hidibi, the MB's General Guide and their highest authority, said the Copts should be expelled from the military and any posts attached to national defense because they could be the agents of the enemy.[14] And, yet another MB General Guide, Muhammad Mahdi Akef, went as far as to support any non–Egyptian Muslim even if he was "from Malaysia" over an Egyptian Copt for Egypt's presidency. When he was criticized for his stance, he made his infamous statement, "Tuz fi Masr" roughly, "To hell with Egypt," stating that "nationality is Islam."[15] Hence, one is a national of an Islamic nation, or caliphate and not a single country. But, political developments since Morsi became president highlighted to moderate Muslims that the MB blamed the Copts for what they, themselves, are guilty of: allying with a foreign power.

The Muslim Brotherhood has received a lot of support from Qatar in order to bolster its political position. This has resulted in a tense diplomatic relationship between Egypt and Qatar post–Morsi, leading the two countries to mutually withdraw their ambassadors.[16] During the mayhem leading up to the June protests, the U.S. had been in contact with senior leaders of the MB. The U.S. Ambassador to Egypt defended Washington's relationship with the MB and called upon the military not to interfere in politics. The activists put a video on social media showing the Ambassador leaving the house of the MB General Guide's Deputy, Khairat al-Shater.[17] After Morsi's removal, many of the MB leaders traveled to Turkey and Qatar to use them as host countries from which to try to organize their constituencies to protest and undermine the government inside Egypt. According to a top aide to Sudan's President, Morsi was willing to give parts of Egypt's southern borders, Halayeb and Shalatin, to the Islamic regime in Sudan.[18] The head of the Palestinian Authority, Mahmoud Abbas, stated that Morsi had offered to give parts of Egypt's Eastern border in the Sinai to Islamic Hamas to enlarge Gaza. Morsi's Islamic ideology was compromising to Egypt's sovereignty, prompting el-Sisi, then defense minister, to issue a statement declaring that Sinai land is a national security issue.[19] In a televised appeal during the MB sit-in in Rabaa al-Adawia Square, a prominent leader of the MB bluntly demanded that the international community interfere on their behalf to save them from what they called the "bloody criminal coup regime."[20] For moderate Muslims each of these events demonstrates that it is the Muslim Brotherhood and not the Copts who seek out, cooperate and ally with foreign powers to serve their own agenda.

Moderate Muslims realized that the MB couldn't get support, meet secretly with foreign representatives, use host countries as political platforms and attempt to give part of Egypt to neighboring Islamic regimes without being part of a "foreign agenda" one way or another. Therefore, they charged the MB with being agents of foreign powers, the same charge that the fundamentalists have been falsely accusing the Copts of through the ages. They argued that the MB is devoid of Egyptian identity and they charged that the MB was working to establish a nation of Islam with Egypt as a province. This was clear in the willingness to cede parts of Egyptian land to foreign countries and entities just because they were Islamic regimes. It became apparent that Morsi's promotion of Islamic identity didn't uphold the sovereignty of Egypt. Morsi's Islamic ideology was clearly revealed a few days before his removal when he publically encouraged Egyptians to go to Syria for *jihad*.[21]

After Morsi's removal, the government took the MB leaders to court, and in June 2015, Morsi and senior MB members were found guilty of espionage on behalf of Iran and two Islamist groups: the Lebanese Hezbollah and the Palestinian Hamas. Morsi was sentenced to life in prison. A year later, in June 2016, the court handed Morsi a second life sentence in another espionage case involving Qatar.[22] Morsi became the first Egyptian president to be charged with espionage. Among the many accusations against Mubarak, he has never been accused of espionage. Despite their lack of respect for Mubarak's regime, Egyptians acknowledge his patriotism, as he led Egypt's Air Force in the October War to regain Egypt's sovereignty over its land. There are other cases filed against Morsi and MB members, and all cases against him are either pending, appealed, upheld or being retried.

At this stage of Egypt's history, the Copts are seen as more patriotic than the Muslim Brotherhood. The Copts have not called for foreign protection, they have not cooperated with a foreign power nor have they received support from abroad, despite the fact that they have regularly been killed and their homes and churches burned. El-Sisi acknowledged the patriotism of the Copts, stating that the Copts' reaction to the mass church burning would be recorded in history both domestically and internationally. No one was able to manipulate or take advantage of their issue: "It was a clear, conscious, patriotic stance," el-Sisi said in a television interview.[23]

Still, the MB and their followers did not change their perception of the Copts as collaborators and the principal actors behind Morsi's removal. Although supporting the June protests did not involve collaboration with a foreign enemy or co-religionists, the MB saw the Copts as collaborators with a local enemy to depose Morsi. They also accused them of supporting an irreligious government that defamed Islam by removing the MB president. Since its inception in 1928, the Muslim Brotherhood's objective was to reach power in order to implement *sharia* and re-establish an Islamic state. When Morsi was sworn into office, there was Egyptian consensus that the MB rule would last for centuries, like previous Islamic dynasties had. But, it was the very process of Brotherhoodization, undertaken to pave the way towards an

Islamic state, that led to their downfall, rather than Coptic interference in Egyptian affairs.

One can surmise that the new leadership of the military was very wary of the Brotherhoodization process, as it could eventually reach the military, which is a secular institution. This concern would be especially strong for el-Sisi, as he was the head of military intelligence, which made him more aware than others of the MB and their goals. Although a previous member of the SCAF, el-Sisi revised the SCAF's policy of cooperation with the MB and ushered in a new stage of the relationship between the military and the MB. In the power struggle between them, the June Revolution provided the military with the needed legitimacy to curb the power of the MB. The MB had acquired far too much power for the comfort of the military. In the long line of convergence and divergence between the military and the Muslim Brotherhood, this most recent stage definitely has not been a Sadat-like alliance, but rather a Nasser-like division.

On the cultural level, the MB directly attacked Egypt's cultural elites, charging them with blasphemy in an attempt to scare them in the same manner they had the Copts. Not only were members of the cultural elite astounded by the swift progression toward Islamism, but so were most other Egyptians, who are not fanatic and who are moderate by nature. Despite the re–Islamization process going on in Egypt for decades, the class of the cultural elite has kept its secular orientation, and it was very difficult for the MB to contain them. They strongly resisted Brotherhoodization and were the last nail in its coffin.

Economically, Morsi and the MB failed to provide a vision for Egypt's future, beyond offering a utopian religious ideology that could not feed the people, decrease fuel prices, lower unemployment, stop routine power outages or raise Egypt's foreign reserves. They had neither plans nor enthusiasm for bringing more tourists to Egypt, a main source of income that would bolster the moribund economy. Foreign direct investments were not heading toward Egypt either, due to the rapid societal changes and political unrest aggravated by the MB regime.

Morsi proved to many Egyptians that his Islamic ideology not only was unable to feed people but was also incompatible with the principals of democracy. Although he was democratically elected, they did not think he governed in a democratic fashion, but instead excluded the interests of all Egyptians, beyond the Muslim Brotherhood. Many claimed that he used democracy as a ladder to reach power, and he then pushed the ladder down so no one else could use it. The MB shocked the awareness of the moderate Egyptians who were yearning for freedom and democracy. This is why they launched two revolutions in under three years, one to get rid of an autocrat and the other to oust an Islamist.

But, the MB could only see Morsi's ouster as the result of a coup. Whether Morsi's ouster was caused by a revolution or a coup was not the underlying question; the real issue was the struggle between secularists and Islamists over the nature of Egypt's identity. While the secularists emphasized Egyptian nationalism, the Muslim Brotherhood and its followers stressed Islamism and succeeded, for a while, in presenting Egypt as an Islamic-looking state. On the social scene there were increasing numbers of bearded men and fully covered women seen in everyday activities, and more Islamic talk shows criticizing everything not Islamic were broadcast. Sheiks became like movie stars, cinema production came to a halt, and music and concerts were nonexistent. Christians continued to be killed, more churches were burned, and even Muslims were massacred and their bodies paraded in the street just because they were Shiites.[24] There was an overdose and saturation of religiosity in society. Referring to Egyptian official reports, Egypt's Minister of Culture stated in 2015 that some two million Egyptians had adopted atheism in response to MB religiosity.[25]

After removing the MB from power, the main task of interim President Adly Mansour's government was to re-write the constitution. A committee of 50 members, including representatives from the Church and al-Azhar, was formed to undertake the task. In the absence of MB members and other Islamists, the Salafi al-Nour party represented political Islam, but the committee was dominated by secularists with the goal of writing a more secular-leaning constitution. Perhaps this explains why the new constitution gave more rights to women and enhanced the position of Copts. Still, it was not what many Coptic Christians and secularists were hoping for.

The new constitution acknowledges the Church in the preamble: "On its land, Egyptians welcomed Virgin Mary and her baby and offered up thousands of martyrs in defense of the Church of Jesus." Article 244 guarantees appropriate representation of Copts at the first Parliament and Article 53 criminalizes all forms of discrimination. There are other articles, like other constitutions, that establish basic rights, equal opportunities, citizenship and freedom, but most importantly, the constitution addresses, for the first time, the most troubling issue of church building and renovation in Article 235: "In its first legislative term after this constitution comes into effect, the House of Representatives shall issue a law to organize building and renovating churches, guaranteeing Christians the freedom to practice their religious rituals." However, religious references made their way into the new constitution. Article 24 kept religious education as a core subject and Article 2 was kept intact. While Article 2 protects the Islamic identity of Egypt, Article 47 protects the Egyptian identity. It states that "the state is committed to protecting Egyptian cultural identity with its diverse civilizational origins." Yet, the preamble stresses the Arab identity of Egypt: "the Arab nation of Egypt is the heart of the whole world." So, the new constitution falls short in addressing the core issue facing Egyptians: the lack of a well-defined national identity.

These identities are intertwined yet contradictory, and led to a revolution to bring down the Muslim Brotherhood and their constitution. Keeping Article Two revealed that Islamic *sharia* principles would continue to play an essential political and legal role in Egypt's society. The Salafi al-Nour party was the strongest supporter of Article Two and al-Azhar representatives also would not tolerate its removal or any changes to it. The Salafi al-Nour party threatened to withdraw from the 50 member committee when they thought that its members were jeopardizing *sharia* and undermining the Islamic identity of the state.[26]

The government appeased the Salafists of the al-Nour party to uphold the legitimacy of the committee and, apparently, to keep the Islamist front divided. Certainly, the government did not want the ultra-conservative Salafists to jump on the bandwagon with the Muslim Brotherhood. Violence was mounting internally and Egypt was facing external challenges from other radicals infiltrating its borders, especially from chaotic Libya and the Gaza Strip. In December 2013, a few weeks before a national referendum on the new constitution, a car bomb blast at a police headquarters in Mansoura, Delta, killed at least 14 people, mostly police personnel, and injured more than a hundred. It was only then that the government declared the MB a terrorist organization.[27] Although Muslim Brotherhood violence had been continuously perpetuated on the Copts, the state only reacted when the violence reached its doorstep.

The majority of the 50-member committee writing the constitution, although secularists, were not overtly concerned about Article Two, especially as they had eliminated other controversial Islamic articles and because Article Two would please the Salafists of al-Nour and the members from al-Azhar. The Copts wouldn't stand alone to challenge it; they would not be able to change it without support. The situation was similar to Egypt's first constitution of the liberal era, when the popular and liberal al-Wafd did not risk opposing an article which stipulated that "Islam is the state religion." As this article provided a precedent, and it has been a part of Egypt's constitution thereafter, Article Two, which includes this phrase, followed suit.

Article Two guarantees that Egypt will not become a fully secular state and that its Coptic citizens will retain their second class citizen status. The Copts went through a tough journey in their fight for equality. But the MB in the post–Mubarak era brought society down to such a level that after two revolutions, the Copts were only able to rise to the same previous legal status they held under Mubarak—back to square one. The question is not whether Islamic ideology will have an impact on society, it is how intense the impact will be. It all depends on the will of the ruler, as has been the case since the time of the Islamic caliphate. It can and will vary, depending on who is in office.

A small gesture of acknowledgment came to the Copts from interim President Adly Mansour, who visited the Pope's residence at St. Mark's Coptic Cathedral on January 5, 2014, to wish him Merry Christmas. Despite renewed statements from the Salafists that wishing Copts "Merry Christmas" is against Islam, Mansour became the first Egyptian president to visit the Cathedral compound for that purpose. Nasser visited it twice and Sadat visited it once, but both did so for political reasons. Mubarak visited it twice to offer condolences for lost Coptic dignitaries, and Morsi's followers would not have allowed him to visit even if he had wanted to.[28]

On January 13th, the Pope wrote an article to explicitly call for a "yes" vote for the constitution, stating that it was "suitable and balanced to a large extent."[29] Most Egyptians also supported the constitution and, on January 15, 2014, it passed by 98 percent, with a turnout of 38 percent, higher than the 33 percent of the previous Islamists' constitution. The vote was boycotted by the MB but endorsed by the Salafi al-Nour Party.[30] Yet, despite the Coptic community's support for the new constitution and the government, the police continued to fall short in protecting them. In addition to mass church burnings, kidnapping Copts for ransom and forced conversion skyrocketed during the interim government, with more than five hundred cases, mainly in Minia, Assiut, Sohag and Qena.[31] The Copts held onto their hopes for a better situation with the coming of a newly elected president.

El-Sisi, the People's Choice

One of the outcomes of the January Revolution was the end of military rule in Egypt, yet many believed that the civilian rule that replaced it had been leading to a theocracy. Egypt had been ruled by caliphs for centuries until the rule of Muhammad Ali and his family, which led to the liberal era. Nasser ended the liberal democracy experiment in 1952, and with him military rule was instated. History reveals that Egypt has been fluctuating between military or religious rule; therefore, el-Sisi became a logical contender not only because he ended the MB regime, but also because he was a military man.

The pro-democracy activists were hoping that el-Sisi would remove Morsi but would not run for presidency nor would any member of the military for that matter, thus, allowing secular contenders to compete for the presidency. But secular parties have been weakened and unable to organize since the 1952 Revolution. The secular activists who initiated the January Revolution have been themselves unorganized, thus, unable to guard their revolution which allowed the better organized MB to assume power. On the other hand, the military has been the strongest player in the political equation since Nasser and most Egyptians, who are naturally moderate, prefer the military rule to a theocracy. So, it was only natural that they called for el-Sisi to nominate himself even before he decided to.

On the personal level, el-Sisi is charismatic and many compared his popularity and charisma to Nasser's. Like Nasser he sidelined the MB, but unlike Nasser el-Sisi is reviving the Egyptian identity not Arab nationalism. Egyptian nationalism, not Arabism, would be the unifying ground for Copts and moderate Muslims to confront the promoters of the Islamic identity. So when el-Sisi ran in the presidential election, it was not surprising that he won over Sabahi, a Nasserite, with 96 percent of the votes excluding the MB vote and that of their supporters. Moderate Muslims and the Copts enthusiastically voted for el-Sisi. Pope Tawadros had already called his nomination for presidency "a patriotic act" and called him a "hero." On Sunday June 8, 2014, el-Sisi became Egypt's president and with him the military regime was reinstated.[32]

The support the Copts gave to el-Sisi did not fall on deaf ears. On Coptic Christmas Eve, January 6, 2015, el-Sisi visited St. Mark's Coptic Cathedral while Copts were celebrating Christmas. "It was necessary for me to come and wish you a Merry Christmas.... I want to tell you that, God willing, we will build our country together, we will accommodate each other and love each other, love each other for real so the people may see," el-Sisi said in a five minute speech that was frequently interrupted by thousands of Coptic congregants enthusiastically cheering for him. He became the first Egyptian leader ever to attend while the holy liturgy was being celebrated. The service stopped and the Pope came down from his See to receive him. "I only say the word Egyptians, it is not right to call each other anything but Egyptians, we are Egyptians, no one should ask, what kind of Egyptian are you?" el-Sisi said. His Egyptian nationalism speech confronted Morsi's divisive Islamic ideology and aimed to restore Egyptian identity, which had been undermined since the 1919 Revolution.

For fear of upsetting the MB and other Islamists, all previous presidents were unwilling to pay such a visit, despite the fact that they attended all major Islamic celebrations. This historical practice of exclusion has led Copts to believe that Egypt's president stands not for all Egyptians but, rather, as Sadat bluntly put it, is "a Muslim President to an Islamic state." Not treating Copts with the same respect as Muslims revealed the state's discriminatory attitude and reinforced the second-class citizen status of the Copts, not only in their minds but in the minds of the radicals as well. The great price that Copts paid to help remove Morsi and bring el-Sisi to power was acknowledged by this historic visit.

El-Sisi introduced himself both externally and internally as a moderate Muslim, and is even popular among Egypt's Coptic Christians. The international community has always used Egypt's poor record of human rights violations against the Copts to press previous Egyptian leaders to make political concessions. By demonstrating his popularity among the Copts, el-Sisi was limiting the international community's ability to pressure the state, at least on the issue of the treatment of minorities. Domestically, he portrayed himself as neither Sadat-like nor Morsi-like, leaders who relied on the Islamists for support, but rather as someone whose base is made up primarily of moderate Muslims and of Copts. His popularity among Copts stands in stark contrast to that of previous leaders and highlights the polarizing policies of the Muslim Brotherhood, which, during Morsi's rule, had allowed the very same cathedral el-Sisi visited on Christmas Eve to come under attack.

El-Sisi's visit to St. Mark's Coptic Cathedral was repeated about a month later, on February 16, 2015. This time the occasion was to pay condolences after ISIS beheaded 21 Coptic hostages in Libya. Once again, it was a first visit of its kind, a president offering condolences for Coptic murder victims. In the past, Copts have been murdered by radical Islamists and no president has paid such a visit, but this time the Coptic community felt the president could feel their agony. El-Sisi had already addressed the nation shortly after ISIS aired the video recording the decapitation of the Copts, and he declared a week of national mourning. A few hours after his speech, he ordered the Egyptian air force to raid ISIS military camps and ammunition depots inside Libyan borders. In another televised address to the nation, el-Sisi declared the Coptic victims martyrs:

> I pay condolences to our martyrs who fell in Libya. Those martyrs are innocent and were slaughtered while working, they simply went there to work for the livelihood for their families. It was a great gruesome action against Egypt and its children. I would have not been able to pay condolences unless your military force avenged you so decisively and powerfully.... Your military force did what should be done in response, I say in response, we don't assault, we don't attack, we don't invade rather we protect our country and our people ... long live Egypt, long live Egypt, long live Egypt.[33]

El-Sisi's statements that the slain Copts are martyrs stood in sharp contrast to the Islamist belief that infidels cannot be martyrs. In his attempt to promote Egyptian nationalism, el-Sisi did not base his statement on theological grounds; rather, he wanted to identify the Coptic victims as Egyptians, on the same level with Muslim Egyptian victims. Declaring them martyrs gave the sense of inclusion with Muslims who also have fallen victim to radical Islamist attacks. By taking swift and strong action against ISIS, el-Sisi won the hearts and minds of not only Copts, but moderate Muslims, who are proud of being Egyptian. They, too, were angry and embarrassed to see the mass slaughter of their fellow Egyptians in such an inhuman fashion, with the murders committed in the name of Islam.

El-Sisi has tried to make a difference and the Copts have placed a lot of hope in him, but the fundamentalists have challenged him at each step. In the first few months of his term, he undoubtedly did more than his predecessors to include the Copts. But fanaticism has well-established historical roots in Egyptian society, and attacking ISIS in Libya might be easier than attacking radicals at home. A month after el-Sisi raided ISIS in Libya, in March 2015, the radical Islamists attacked the Virgin Mary Church in the village of al-Or in Minia. El-Sisi had promised to build a church in this village in honor of the Copts who were beheaded in Libya because it is the hometown of most of the victims. Angry at the president's decree to build a new church, after Friday prayers, radicals marched toward the church where the Copts were commemorating the victims and tried to set it on fire. They also opened fire on the church, leaving 18 people injured.[34]

While attacks on churches have been a common occurrence, one would think that this particular village should be exempt. The tragedy the families of the decapitated Copts went through was extremely traumatic; for a church to bear the names of the victims is only a small token of consolation in healing the families' wounds. But, the radical Islamists are too fanatical to be sympathetic and even went as far as to attack the house of one of the decapitated Copts.[35] The fact that the President would not cancel his decree, if only out of deep embarrassment, did not stop the radicals from voicing their objection in the strongest manner. This in itself is revealing of their power and fanaticism, even without the MB regime in place.

The local police arrested some of the attackers but released them after a "reconciliation session" in order for the Copts to be able to build their church in peace.[36] Thus, the police once again established a culture of impunity under the new president. This was an opportunity for el-Sisi to set a precedent by instructing the police to arrest the attackers and thereby demonstrate that there must be respect for the rule of law. It would have been a much-needed message to the police as to what was expected of them, and a deterrent against further attacks by radicals.

Disrespect for the rule of law by both the local police and radicals was brought to light a few weeks before the issue in al-Or village. When radical Islamists in the village of al-Galaa, in Minia, stopped Copts from replacing an old church to accommodate a growing congregation, the police arranged a "reconciliation session." Although the Copts had obtained the proper permit, the radicals rejected it. Under police patronage, they put a set of conditions on the building based on *sharia*: the projected church should not show a cross or a steeple, Copts would not be allowed to restore the church in the future and, in case of collapse, the Copts would not be allowed to rebuild it.

They wanted the Copts to sign off on these conditions and stamp them at the government notary public, in order that it would be a legally binding document.[37] As signing these conditions meant a return to *dhimma* status, the Copts refused, and the issue reached the secular media. In the end the police pressured the radicals into compromising and allowing the Copts to build the church. However, as in the incident of the church of al-Marinab during the era of SCAF, the radicals did not concede to allowing the church to have a steeple, cross or bell—no symbol of Christianity.[38] Perhaps the behavior of the radicals and the response of the police in al-Galaa village encouraged the radicals' attack in al-Or. The police set them free in both incidents.

In a television interview in May 2015, a bishop from Minia province lamented the fact that he repeatedly has failed to get a permit from security to build bathrooms in the Church of the Virgin Mary, in the village of Safanyyah. During a meeting at police headquarters with security officials, the Bishop asked to build a church in the village of Mayyanah, but the police requested that he sit with the village's Muslims to see if they would allow him to do so. If they agreed the police would, too. Before the Bishop had even left the meeting, security officials had contrived to notify the fundamentalist Islamists in the village to object to the building of the church. In this case, the local authorities coordinated with local people to use the pretext of violence to deny the building of a church for the Copts. The Bishop stated, "Copts are caught between the nation's anvil and the aggressors' hammer."[39]

The defiance of radicals continued, and resurfaced a few months later, in July 2015, when they attacked the Church of the Fathers in Alexandria with Molotov cocktails.[40] Yet another, much worse, incident occurred ten months later, in May 2016. An armed mob looted and burned seven Coptic homes, fueled by rumors of a romantic relationship between a Coptic man and a Muslim woman. Burning and collective punishment have been practiced against the Coptic community before, but the striking element to this recent attack was stripping the clothes off the 70-year-old mother of the Coptic man, who had fled the village earlier. They paraded her naked through the streets of the village of Karm in Minia.[41] "They burned the house and went in and dragged me out, threw me in front of the house and ripped my clothes. I was just as my mother gave birth to me and was screaming and crying," the elderly woman said.[42] This incident echoes that of the Coptic nuns who were disrobed and taken as slaves in 1320 and that of the Coptic nuns paraded through the streets like war prisoners after Morsi's removal in 2013; the radical behavior has not changed throughout history. El-Sisi responded by promising to repair the destroyed properties and calling for the attackers to be held accountable.[43]

Trials of Copts for the crime of insulting Islam have continued. In a thirty-second cell phone video, four Christian high school students criticized ISIS's beheading of the Copts. Their Coptic teacher had the video on his cell phone, but when he lost the memory card from his phone and the villagers of al-Naseriah, Minia, saw the video, they accused them of insulting Islam. The court sent the teacher to prison for three years. Even harsher sentences of five years were issued to the students.[44]

Abduction of Copts has not ceased. In the same television interview mentioned above, the bishop from Minia stated that he had documented and reported to the police 25 cases of the kidnapping and disappearance of Copts, including women and underage girls in his diocese.[45] In December 2015, masked gunmen abducted a 10-year-old Coptic child on his way to school in al-Rahmanyya village in Qena. These crimes target young and old, but still the main victims are Copts.[46]

Forced migration persists despite Article 63 of the new constitution, which states: "All forms of arbitrary forced migration of citizens are forbidden. Violations of such are a crime without a statute of limitation." A Copt working and residing in Jordan posted an image on his Facebook page that the radicals of his village, Kafr Darwish, in Beni Sueif, found offensive to Muhammad. Angry, they indiscriminately hurled stones and Molotov cocktails at the homes of local Copts, destroying more than ten houses. The local police conducted the usual "reconciliation session" and the decision reached was to force the wife and children of the Copt to leave the village. In May 2015, the mayor of the village concluded another "reconciliation session" and the decision was expanded to force the extended family of the Copt to leave the village, including his 75- and 80-year-old parents and three brothers with their wives and children. The Copt was also accused of contempt of Islam.[47]

While the Copts were forced to leave their home village, the Grand Sheikh of al-Azhar condemned forced migration of the Muslims in Myanmar. He asked the free people of the world to take immediate action to save the Muslims of Myanmar from persecution and forced migration. He stated that what is happening to the Muslims there is a shame on the forehead of humanity.[48] Many remarked that the Grand Sheikh should have addressed the forced migration of his fellow Egyptians as well.

Al-Azhar was also criticized by many moderate Muslims for considering ISIS believers despite their questionable practices. Al-Azhar issued a statement on December 11, 2014, refusing to declare ISIS apostates.[49] A senior sheikh at Egypt's Ministry of Religious Endowment said that as long as ISIS and their followers say the Islamic *shahada* or testimony declaring belief in the oneness of God and the acceptance of Muhammad as His prophet and pray, no one can consider them apostates.[50] Aware of radicalism in Egypt and worldwide, el-Sisi addressed al-Azhar scholars on January 1, 2015, and called for a "religious revolution." He said that it is not conceivable that the thinking that we hold sacred should cause the Islamic world to be a source of anxiety, danger, killing and destruction for the rest of the world. He stated that this thinking is inimical to the entire world and that it has become very difficult to get rid of it. He added that it is impossible that 1.6 billion Muslims would want to kill the rest of the world's people so that they themselves may live.[51] Six months later, in June 2015, *Al-Azhar Magazine* distributed a booklet as part of a free publication program entitled, "Why am I a Muslim?" which explains why Christianity is a "failed religion."[52]

When el-Sisi addressed the *ulama* he vocalized concerns that intellectuals share, but are hesitant to voice publicly, in part due to fear of the "contempt of Islam" charge. In May 2015 Islam al-Bihiri, a researcher in Islamic affairs and a famous religious television host, was sentenced to five years in prison for contempt of Islam. In his attempt to renew the religious discourse, he challenged some ideas in Islamic heritage books. Forty-five lawsuits were filed against him, but al-Azhar's suit was the most salient.[53] In December 2015 the court lowered his sentence to one year in prison. "I thank very much President el-Sisi and I thank his religious revolution," said al-Bihiri, dejectedly, after the verdict.[54]

The activists acknowledged el-Sisi's attempt to renew the religious discourse, but al-Bihiri's case shows how little the effect has been. Although the court outlawed the MB political party, el-Sisi's government continued to allow the Salafi al-Nour party to be part of the political process. As the SCAF turned a blind eye towards the MB and allowed them to form a political party after the January Revolution, the government continued to turn a blind eye to the Salafi al-Nour party, despite the fact that the constitution does not allow religious-based parties. The activists cited the contradiction in the constitution that bans political parties based on religion while it retains a religious reference in Article Two. By allowing the Salafi al-Nour party, the government seemingly wants to keep the Islamist front divided, and while effective to a certain extent, the harm could outweigh the benefit. Although the Salafists are politically less sophisticated and less organized, they are more conservative than the MB and they constitute more than one faction. One of their factions, *Hazemoon*, consists of jihadists, and some have traveled to Syria to join ISIS and al-Qaeda.[55]

The Salafists also pose a challenge to the moribund economy as they are against tourism and a modern banking system, which they equate with usury, believing it is against Islamic *sharia* and Islamic identity. They brazenly called for the destruction of the pyramids and the Sphinx as symbols of idolatry, and described the Egyptian Pharaonic history as a "rotten culture." During an election in Alexandria, they covered a statue of mermaids, and they destroyed a statue of Nasser's head in Sohag. Their point of view is similar to the Afghan Taliban, which destroyed the Banyam Buddhas in 2001, and to ISIS, which destroyed priceless Assyrian statues in Iraq, in February 2015.[56]

While the government has reconciled with the Salafists, it used a new protest law issued under the interim President Adly Mansour to continue cracking down on secular activists who see el-Sisi's ascendency to the presidency as a hindrance to the democratic process towards a secular state. They perceive him as a military man who reinstated the military regime that they once thought ended when they pushed Mubarak out. They believe that el-Sisi's government is limiting their political participation by sending many of them to prison. These activists are against Islamic ideology and strongly object to the MB as well as the Salafists; they are the same organizers of the June protests that allowed el-Sisi to remove Morsi. Although they supported el-Sisi, they have a different vision for Egypt's future. The military does not share the same view as the secular activists, or the MB, which totally disagrees with both.

Within a year of el-Sisi's assumption of power, reports of police misconduct started to appear again. Violations of personal rights were committed, leading the victim's families and their sympathizers to protest against the police. Although the policemen involved in these incidents go under investigation and are taken to court, the fact that police violations have still not diminished is chilling to many people across the political spectrum.[57] In May 2016 the police raided the Journalists' Syndicate to arrest two reporters who were critical of the government, causing a strong reaction from the community of journalists.[58] A few months earlier the Doctors' Syndicate issued a statement complaining of physical abuse at the hands of the police, causing doctors to partially shut down one hospital.[59] The Lawyers' Syndicate already expressed similar complaints in June 2015.[60] For the activists, the fear is that it is the same old game but with different players.

The activists acknowledged that el-Sisi is promoting an Egyptian identity, but on the other hand they claim that he is ignoring one of its strongest backers—them. They argue that while the court outlawed the MB political party based on its ideology, the government did not translate separation of religion from politics into policy. El-Sisi called for a religious revolution, but he did not set forth a plan for how religious reform would proceed. He is showing real support for the Copts yet letting the local police infringe on their rights. He acknowledged their patriotism yet has not allowed them full citizenship. He determinedly and swiftly targeted militants in Libya, but he fell short in targeting radicals at home. There is no change in government policy regarding the reconciliation secessions, the forced migration and the collective punishment that follow them, or the "contempt of Islam" charge. Copts are still discriminated against and still denied top positions. These points were put forth by the activists to highlight that el-Sisi's government is not showing enough progress in moving towards a secular, democratic state. The effectiveness with which the government deals with the concerns facing the Copts is a barometer of how fast it is moving towards a secular, democratic state and whether or not it has the will to do so.

Perhaps such a gap between intention and reality could be bridged if translated into laws by the new Parliament. After the Egyptians wrote their constitution and elected their President, they conducted Parliamentary elections in two stages, held between October and December of 2015. The Parliament was the last stage of the road map set forth after Morsi's removal.

The result of the elections was significant for the Copts as, for the first time in the history of Egypt's Parliament, Copts obtained 39 seats out of 596, or 6.5 percent of the seats. Out of the 39 seats, 24 were secured through a one-time deal of affirmative action for marginalized groups and 12 seats were secured through direct elections. An additional 3 seats went to the Copts through direct appointment by el-Sisi. This tradition of appointing members to the Parliament made its way into the new constitution and election law and el-Sisi is required to appoint 5 percent of the total number of representatives, a total of 28 members. As the Copts secured a large number of seats, el-Sisi did not appoint as many as had previous presidents.

Away from the quota and the appointments, although the success of winning 12 seats through direct elections was significant for the Copts, it did not match what they achieved in the liberal era. In the first Parliamentary election in 1924 the Copts won 16 seats out of 214, or around 7.5 percent. The number fluctuated up and down in the following years but they were able to secure the highest number of seats in 1942 with 27 seats out of 264, or more than 10 percent.[61] The Copts won 27 seats when their population was roughly 2 million in 1942.[62] But they won only 12 seats when their population is between 9 and 13 million in 2015. This is not only an indicator of underrepresentation for their population but also a clear indication of the strong tide of radicalism Egypt has gone through.

During the liberal era the MB was being formed and had not yet established its strong roots in society, which is reflected in the Copts winning a large number of seats. The absence of the MB from the political scene after the June Revolution greatly aided Copts, who nominated themselves in large numbers without fear of abuse from the Muslim Brotherhood and its supporters. The absence of MB propaganda and *fatwas* against the Copts broadcast over religious channels or from mosques greatly decreased sectarian discourse and division. In their history, Copts only secured significant numbers of seats in Parliament during the liberal era, before the Muslim Brotherhood gained power, and after it was forced out of the political scene, on June 30, 2013.

The lack of religious discourse that helped the Copts to win was also the reason that the Salafists, remarkably, lost. The Salafists did not openly use religion to lobby their followers, as secular parties and the media were vigilant in rooting out such discourse. The Salafists also have been under severe criticism from the MB not only for participating in "illegitimate" elections, but for supporting the removal of Morsi. Relying only on their supporters, without the rest of the Islamists, who boycotted the elections, the Salafi al-Nour party only won a total of 12 seats, or 2 percent. This was a surprise, as it had secured 111 seats of the post–January, Islamist-dominated Parliament.[63]

The absence of the MB and most other Islamists, along with their religious discourse, created a general atmosphere of anti-extremism and opened the door for many Muslims to vote for qualified Copts. The 12 seats the Copts secured through direct elections had to come through the support of moderate Muslims. The Copts could not have made it if they had relied only on Coptic votes, as the Copts don't constitute a majority in any given electoral district. Samir Ghattas, a Coptic Christian, won 53,770 out of 95,000 votes in the first round of elections in Nasr City, a majority Muslim district.[64]

Copts achieved the highest representation in both the liberal era and in el-Sisi's term because an Egyptian national identity was promoted over Islamic identity. In between, there was very low Coptic representation, prompting Nasser, followed by Sadat, Mubarak and then the SCAF, to appoint some Copts to the Parliament in order to address the deficit. In the previous Islamist-dominated Parliament there were only 11 Copts out of 508 representatives, or 2 percent. Five were appointed and 6 were elected. This percentage was similar under Mubarak. During Sadat their number was closer to 3 percent, although in 1976 no Copts won in the elections. During Nasser's tenure their percentage fluctuated between zero and 3 percent, although, again, in 1957 no Copts won by election.[65]

Through the championing of Egyptian national identity, the largest three parties in the new Parliament were secular. The liberal Free Egyptians Party, founded by the Copt Naguib Sawirus, won 65 seats, allowing it to be the largest party in the Parliament. The Nation's Future Party won 50 seats while the historically liberal al-Wafd came in third, with 45 seats.[66] Only through the promotion of Egyptian identity were secular parties able to come first, and the Salafi al-Nour party was relegated to last place. The focus on national identity over religious identity not only garnered the Copts a large number of seats, it also allowed women to gain a record number of seats. For the first time in Egypt's Parliamentary history, women secured 99 seats.[67]

Most Egyptians believe that the new secular-leaning Parliament would not have become reality if el-Sisi had not responded to the demands of the millions of June 30th protesters, who demanded an end to the Muslim

Brotherhood regime. El-Sisi also gets the credit for reviving the Egyptian identity, which is the only identity that has room for Copts to unite with their Muslim compatriots. Nasser's Arab nationalism plunged Egypt into unnecessary wars, and its economy has never recovered. Sadat's flirtation with the Islamic identity got him assassinated by radical Islamists. Mubarak's inaction and deals with the Muslim Brotherhood got him toppled and, ironically, replaced by Islamic identity revivalists in Morsi, and yet again a commitment to Islamic identity over national identity eventually led to his removal. While the promoters of Islamic identity tore apart communities in Libya, Yemen, Syria and Iraq, el-Sisi kept Egypt from collapsing by clinging to its Egyptian identity. By reviving this identity he pulled Egypt back the brink of civil war, which is where the country stood towards the end of Morsi's term—a major reason for el-Sisi's popularity.

His popularity among the Copts soared when he visited St. Mark's Coptic Cathedral again during Christmas liturgy on January 6, 2016, not only to wish them Merry Christmas but to also give them an unprecedented public apology for the mass church destruction caused by the radicals and the mobs after Morsi's removal. El-Sisi promised them to finish the rebuilding of the burned churches by the end of 2016. El-Sisi said, "We were late in restoring and repairing what had been burned, we were late; God willing this year all the delay, your Holiness, will be fixed. Please let me tell you [congregants] I hope you accept our apology for what happened ... we won't forget your or his Holiness's great honorable patriotic stance that was taken at this period, I thank you your Holiness and thank you all ... long live Egypt, long live Egypt, long live Egypt, Merry Christmas!"[68]

Before the year had ended and before el-Sisi had fully delivered on his promise, a suicide bomber struck inside al-Boutrossyia Church, on December 11, 2016, killing 29 Copts, mainly women and children. Al-Boutrossyia Church is located within the walls of St. Mark's Coptic Cathedral compound, across from the Pope's residence. For the first time in Egypt's history, a suicide bomber detonated his explosives inside a church. The attacker blew himself up among worshippers in the middle of the Sunday liturgy, targeting the section of the church where the women and children sit. To acknowledge the tragedy of the incident and revere the victims, el-Sisi granted them an official funeral. The coffins, wrapped in Egyptian flags, were carried by soldiers in a procession that was joined by el-Sisi, Pope Tawadros, state officials and the mourning families. El-Sisi also declared three days of national mourning.

Not only did the radicals strike deeper than ever at the symbol of Coptic identity, but they conveyed the message that they could penetrate the heart of the Church despite heavy security. The Coptic victims, now known as al-Boutrossyia martyrs, became the most recent addition to the Calendar of

Martyrs. From the Umayyads to the Ottomans, from Sadat to Mubarak, and after two revolutions, the Copts have witnessed violence that has targeted them physically and mentally. The Copts continue their quest for equal citizenship in their own country, and unfortunately, the cycle of violence against them continues as well.

Conclusion
Egypt's Future Identity?

Since the time of the Islamic caliphate in Egypt, religion has played an uninterrupted role in politics. In conjunction, the history of the Copts has been an unbroken cycle of aggression with occasional periods of respite. Once the granary of the world, Egypt has gone through a steady decline in agricultural production and now imports many staples, including wheat, the most strategic commodity. During the January Revolution, the Egyptians, sadly, cried out for "bread" while they were calling for "freedom." So, could it be that religion in the political sphere has led to these realities? Is separation between religion and state possible?

According to the fundamentalists, religion and state are inseparable. They believe that Islam is *deen wa dawla*, or "a religion and a state." Because its system of governance is based on *sharia*, which is dictated by Allah, it is perfect and eternal. If someone disagrees with it, he actually disagrees with God and will be considered an infidel or an apostate, both of which are punishable by death. For them, democracy is erroneous not only because it is a man made, but also because it is a Western creation.

The state, on the other hand, claims that it is secular, yet it constitutionalizes the principals of Islamic *sharia* law. With the state partly secular and partly religious, its identity is confused. This keeps the door open for and incubates an environment ripe for political Islam to re-assume power. With the state's unclear national identity, it is only a matter of time before the Muslim Brotherhood comes back onto the political scene. At this stage in history, the state has forced them out of the political process, but by no means will they vanish. The MB has historically been an underground organization, yet their network made it possible for them to assume the presidency. If Morsi was not the right man this time, another member will be next time. They will keep trying; the Islamic caliphate and the application of *sharia* are the ultimate expressions of their beliefs. In a free environment, the state's undefined identity can allow an organization with such an ideology to assume power. So, does the state have the political will to de-constitutionalize religious references and clearly define a national identity and change the rules of the game?

The state's crackdown on the MB and their offshoots will not solve Egypt's ills. Nasser tried, but repression only empowered them and allowed them to reach office. The state is fighting the Muslim Brotherhood, yet the issue facing Egypt is not the MB per se, but rather the ideology they represent. The MB has been killing Copts and burning their churches since the Islamic caliphates. They might not have had the exact same name back then, but it is not the name that really matters; rather, it is the ideology, which does not allow for peaceful co-existence alongside those with different beliefs.

To combat such ideology, the state is petitioning al-Azhar to undertake religious reform. However, quite a few Muslims see al-Azhar as either incapable or unwilling to undertake such a task. Other Muslims feel that al-Azhar itself needs to be reformed and they think it has been infiltrated. Some of its scholars are very conservative and anti-reform. Although it has moderate scholars, others have been spiritual leaders of radical groups; some are Salafists, and others are MB members.

Mukhtar Noah, a previously prominent MB member, said that the Muslim Brotherhood is a "creation of al-Azhar." He added that no matter what el-Sisi says regarding reform, al-Azhar will not change. He stated that Egypt is an "exporter" not a "resister" of terrorism, claiming that the military and police fight terrorists, but they encourage terrorist thinking because they don't confront those who spread this thinking among the people.[1] Some argue that the state is fighting terrorists, but not fighting terrorism.

Al-Azhar teaches Islamic texts that ISIS and al-Qaeda use to justify their jihad and other actions. Its curriculums teach that jihad against the infidels "is a must for every sensible, free and capable man." During the jihad, the Muslims can "vandalize their [the infidels] plants and trees and burn them...."[2] Al-Azhar refused to declare ISIS apostate, even though they burned a Jordanian pilot alive and beheaded twenty-one Copts. Yet, some of al-Azhar *ulama* declared the liberal Muslim intellectual Taha Hussein an apostate because they perceived his writings as being against Islam. They also declared the Muslim scholar Nasr Hamid Abu Zeid an apostate for the same reason. Al-Azhar's Scholar Front declared the Muslim writer Farag Fouda an apostate, which led to his assassination, because he challenged the application of *sharia*. The Scholar Front includes *ulama* who were among President Morsi's supporters. The head of the Scholar Front was the dean of two colleges at al-Azhar and helped in writing al-Azhar University curriculum. A Muslim intellectual and an MB defector, Tharwat al-Kherbawi, said that the reason for al-Azhar's rejection of ISIS as apostates is because ISIS's actions don't depart from al-Azhar teachings.[3]

Al-Azhar has an independent education system consisting of a vast network of more than 9,000 schools encompassing more than 2 million students who abide by its curriculum. There are about 450,000 students attending al-Azhar University and its research centers. Some of these students are also a challenge to reform or change. Al-Azhar's university campuses witnessed numerous violent protests in support of the MB after el-Sisi deposed Morsi, and some students went to Syria for jihad.[4] In March 2016, the authorities charged some al-Azhar students with premeditated murder for the assassination of the prosecutor general, who oversaw cases against MB leaders.[5] Thousands of international students have studied at al-Azhar; in the year 2014–2015, it educated 39,694 students from different parts of the world.[6] Some students who studied at al-Azhar have become radicals, such as Abd Allah Azzam, a Palestinian graduate, the father of global *jihad*, co-founder of al-Qaeda with Osama Ben Laden and his spiritual leader.

Article 7 of the Constitution guarantees the independence of al-Azhar and outlines its role: "Al-Azhar is an independent scientific Islamic institution, with exclusive competence over its own affairs. It is the main authority for religious sciences, and Islamic affairs. It is responsible for preaching Islam and disseminating the religious sciences and the Arabic language in Egypt and the world. The state shall provide enough financial allocations to achieve its purposes...." Al-Azhar also reviews and censors publications and media productions to make sure they are not insulting to Islam and it bans any materials it deems against the teaching of Islam.[7] Al-Azhar shapes the collective consciousness of Egyptians by deciding what materials it deems appropriate for reading or watching.

In light of the opinions of Muslim intellectuals like Noah, al-Kherbawi and others with similar positions, al-Azhar should not be the only place to implement religious reform or fight radical ideology. Noah stated that "we are still afraid to clash with al-Azhar and get imprisoned...."[8] The state will not be able to combat radicalism by deferring to al-Azhar only, or by fighting the radicals, but rather through other measures, most importantly supporting civil society, reforming education and applying the rule of law.

Institutions of civil society, including human rights organizations, are not endorsed by the state. Cultural productions, frowned upon as non–Islamic, and the intellectual class behind them suffer from an unfriendly environment. The "contempt of Islam" charge is just one example of the restriction of cultural activity. Intellectuals, with their diverse backgrounds and interests, have been the guardians of the secular Egyptian identity, and in an environment free of hostility they can challenge the power of the fundamentalists. In this way society will be given the chance to balance itself.

Before Nasser, when Egypt was open to different cultures, the society was described as diverse, resilient and tolerant. This atmosphere produced classic icons and led to a plethora of cultural enrichment. When Egyptians began to develop a uniform way of thinking shaped by a specific religious discourse, they lost their creativity and, consequently, their influence, as evident in the deterioration of the cultural productions that once made Egypt the leading power and cultural capital of the Arab World. The religious discourse segregated and, therefore, weakened the society, creating divisions between men and women, veiled and unveiled, Sunni and Shiites, Islamists and non–Islamists, and Copts and Muslims.

Education reform is pivotal in order to combat radical ideology and in order to progress. It is hard for Egypt to find a place for itself or compete with other nations of the world if over a quarter of its population is illiterate (around 24 million people). The illiterate are dependent on others to interpret religion for them. Illiterate men are potential terrorist recruits or suicide bombers, to be used to attack the government. The educated issue the *fatwa*, but, usually, they don't execute its ruling; they let the uneducated masses do the hard work. These illiterate men also form the easily mobilized mobs used by hardliners to attack Copts. The mobs are made up of the disadvantaged, so attacking the Copts allows them to alleviate their sense of inferiority. They make up the Islamists' constituency, and due to their sheer numbers allow them to have an edge in any given election.

Egyptian women constitute the portion of society with the highest illiteracy rate. They cannot educate their children or obtain a job with a living wage; thus, they have little economic power. They often have many children, believing this will increase their status as mothers and ensure they have care in their old age. Hence, these children became a source of income; instead of sending them to school or even allowing them to finish their education, they force many of them to work to support the family. Women's lack of education and inability to make their own choices sentences them and their families to a lifetime of poverty and ignorance, fertile ground for radicalism to take root and grow. Ignorance breeds radicalism and radicalism feeds ignorance, and both are aggravated by poverty. This cycle of ignorance and radicalism in the family spreads to society, and is a prescription for social, political and economic stagnation and unrest.

Egyptian students are required to take religious education in public schools, and it is not comparative world religion. Instead of creating an environment conducive to cooperation, the students get classified and segregated at a young age based on religion. When it contradicts religion, science is ridiculed and put down, especially in small towns and villages. Instead of concentrating on the teaching of science and technology, the system focuses on ensuring that the Coptic students memorize sections of the Quran, as part of Arabic language classes, in order to pass for the next year, forcing them to learn Islamic teachings that contradict their Christian faith. Most of the

Arabic language teachers are graduates of al-Azhar, who in their discussion of *dhimmis* put down the Christian students. Instead of supporting a segment of the society that historically appreciates education, the system is creating an unfriendly learning environment for Coptic students and creating a general anti-science environment for all students. In 2016 Egypt ranked 136 out of 138 countries for quality of education at the secondary and tertiary levels by the World Economic Forum—only ahead of Mauritania and Yemen.[9] Egypt will progress when it starts to consider education a national security issue.

Those who are able to get an education are not taught to be critical thinkers. The educational system of rote memorization neutralizes independent thinking, long considered a threat to various authoritarian regimes. Different regimes tried to rewrite history. After Nasser assumed power, the history curriculum erroneously taught the Egyptian students that Nasser was their first president. And, after the death of Sadat, it made Mubarak the hero of the October War, crediting him with the crossing of the Suez Canal. In its attempt to emphasize Egypt's Islamic identity, the state dropped the Coptic era out of the education system so that the history of Egypt starts at the 7th century, with the Arab conquest. There is no single department at any Egyptian university dedicated to Coptic studies. The pharaonic period does not get much attention either. The world is amazed by the very history the Egyptians are overlooking. Yet, this rewritten history did not convince radicals that Sadat was the "believer president," as it did not convince moderates of Morsi's patriotism.

Respect for the rule of law is vital to combat radicalism. Reconciliation sessions are only one example that shows that the rule of law is ignored by both the state and by radicals. Law enforcement officials have been the first to break the law, and their violations were a main reason behind the January Revolution. The absence of deterrence led the state to lose its prestige and led the radicals to be more violent against the Copts. The state has not played its intrinsic role of competently maintaining law and order in order to create a safe and secure environment.

The state also has its own loopholes concerning the rule of law. While Egypt's constitution and its legal system offer protection of human rights and the right of freedom of belief, this is misleading, as Article Two forms a significant escape clause. It forces Egyptian legislation to subordinate its law to the principals of *sharia*, thus discriminating against the Copts and other non–Muslims and their basic rights.[10] Between the state and the fundamentalists, Coptic rights are threatened by the legal system, discriminatory government policies, unfair treatment of local security forces, the extremists' ideology and the radicals' attacks.

It has become very hard for Copts to overcome feelings of alienation. In the early days of Arab rule, Copts left their villages to escape the burden of the *kharaj*. To escape the *jizyah*, other Copts left their religion and converted to Islam. In recent years thousands of Copts left Egypt after the fundamentalists attempted to return the country to the time of the early Islamic caliphate, rejecting modernity and equality.[11]

The Islamic caliphate is charged with placing many hardships on Egypt and the Copts. But the Copts have developed a deep sense of identity that has allowed them to survive and stay committed to their faith, despite the economic, social, political and legal benefits of abandoning their religion and converting to Islam. The Copts cultivated professional expertise that was indispensable to their Muslim governors, and they developed a distinct ability to function within the Islamic state while still maintaining their identity.[12] They resisted passively and leaned upon their heritage in their endeavors through the centuries, giving them a strong Christian spiritual identity enhanced by their culture, their history and, for some time, their own Coptic language.[13] Yet despite their pacifism, Copts suffered great violence. They have learned that keeping their beliefs comes at the expense of their human rights. Many bowed to pressure and converted to Islam, but many did not. Those who remain committed to their faith should not, in today's world, continue to pay a price for their beliefs.

The Coptic identity is a religious as well as a cultural identity, similar to the Islamic identity. The difference is that the Islamic identity is intrinsically political and is based on the doctrine of jihad and *dhimma*. And, as the radicals stay in a permanent state of struggle in jihad, the Copts stay in a permanent state of insecurity. Among Muslims, the difference between fundamentalists and moderates is that the latter are not religiously politicized, yet they are not fully politically secular either. Copts live in between the two camps; whoever is stronger determines their status. During the liberal era and under el-Sisi, the second camp was stronger and it raised a national, secular Egyptian identity, thus allowing the Copts room for political participation. But because neither of the two periods has been truly secular, in both the constitutions of 1923 and 2014, the role of religion in politics in each was enshrined in law. So, the role of religion in politics since the Islamic caliphate continues. El-Sisi is promoting a secular Egyptian identity, but can secularism be fully adopted in Egypt? Will Egypt define its political identity outside of religion? If it can, many argue that this will solve a lot of Egypt's problems. If not, others argue that any reforms, although vital, will not bear the expected fruit. The status of the Copts will continue to fluctuate, depending on the benevolent will of the ruler and the challenge posed by the fundamentalists, and the cycle of violence will continue, preventing Copts from enjoying political or social stability—something that none in Egypt will enjoy, for that matter. The hope for a better life for the Coptic Christians and the moderate Muslims will forever be a challenge.

Epilogue

Two suicide attacks occurred on Palm Sunday April 9, 2017. The twin attacks rocked the Coptic community and panicked the nation. In the first, a suicide bomber blew himself up at St. George Church in Tanta during the service, killing 28 Copts. Within hours another suicide bomber detonated his explosives at the entrance of the St. Mark's Coptic Cathedral in Alexandria, the historic See of the Coptic Pope, killing ten Copts and seven police officers who were guarding the Cathedral. ISIS declared responsibility for the two incidents, which were carried out by its Egyptian affiliates. Beyond those killed, the bombings left more than 120 people injured.

No longer was the al-Boutrossyia incident in December of 2016, which left 29 Copts dead, the most devastating attack on Copts and their churches, nor were the al-Boutrossyia martyrs the most recent addition to the Calendar of Martyrs. The attacks turned Palm Sunday celebrations, which mark the beginning of the Holy Week and lead up to Easter, into a bloodbath full of grief and pain for the Copts. The Coptic Church restricted the celebration of Easter, usually a festive occasion, to only religious rituals in mourning for the Coptic victims. Copts attended Easter service under unusually heavy security, with checkpoints and 400-meter security cordons around churches to prevent vehicles from approaching. Security agents surrounded Pope Tawadros as he entered the Cathedral to lead Easter service. At least eight security agents walked next to him in his procession, which consisted of bishops, priests and deacons. It was an unprecedented scene reflecting an unparalleled threat, adding to the uncertainty already felt by the Coptic community.

In February 2017, ISIS aired a video of the al-Boutrossyia suicide bomber encouraging other ISIS followers to take action, and the group stated that the attack was "only the beginning." In the video, ISIS described the Copts as the group's "favorite prey." They claimed that the Copts revoked the *Covenant of Umar*; therefore, they are no longer protected *dhimmis*. For them, *dhimma* status is a privilege that, by now, the Copts do not qualify to enjoy. The video showed Pope Tawadros as one figure of the "favorite prey."

It seems that by attacking St. Mark's Coptic Cathedral in Alexandria, the radicals were not only targeting a symbolic cathedral, but also a symbolic figure; Pope Tawadros was inside the Cathedral leading the Palm Sunday service. Stopped by the Coptic security guard and unable to get inside, the suicide bomber detonated his explosives at the gate of the Cathedral.

Within a span of four months in late 2016 and early 2017, ISIS had launched vicious attacks on Copts in Egypt's three largest cities. The severity of the incidents and the fact that two of them happened in one day not only indicates thorough planning, but conveys ISIS's message of what lies ahead. In response, el-Sisi declared a three-month state of emergency. A state of emergency has been enforced in North Sinai since October 2014, yet it did not stop the radicals from killing army and police men. Nor did it stop them from forcing 75 Coptic families to leave their homes in al-Arish in February 2017 due to the increase in attacks that left 7 Copts dead in just a few weeks. A state of emergency was in place during Mubarak's thirty-year tenure, yet it did not protect the Copts celebrating New Year's Eve at the Two Saints Church in Alexandria in 2010 when a car bomb killed 23 Copts. Nor did it reveal the perpetrators. Neither did the state of emergency secure the lives of the 20 Copts who were killed by radicals on New Year's Eve of 2000 in al-Kosheh, Sohag. And, it did not protect the dozens of Copts who were killed by radicals during their insurgency in the 1990s.

Four days after the state of emergency was declared and as the Copts were still mourning their dead, fundamentalist villagers of Kom al-Lufi, Minia attacked the Copts, setting some of their houses on fire. The Copts had used a house for prayers which raised suspicions among the fundamentalists that the Copts were turning it into a church. Declaring a state of emergency may be one solution, but probably not a principal one. Understanding why some people still believe in treating Christians as *dhimmis* is more essential, and understanding why someone willingly sacrifices his own life in order to kill innocents is crucial.

Chapter Notes

Introduction

1. David Zeidan, "The Copts—Equal, Protected or Persecuted? The Impact of Islamization on Muslim-Christian Relations in Modern Egypt," *Islam and Christian-Muslim Relations* 10, no. 1 (1999): 60.
2. B.L. Carter, *The Copts in Egyptian Politics* (London: Croom Helm, 1986), 98–99.
3. Zeidan, "The Copts—Equal, Protected or Persecuted?," 60.
4. Saad Eddin Ibrahim, *Egypt, Islam and Democracy: Twelve Critical Essays* (Cairo: American University Press, 1996), 187–188.
5. Zeidan, "The Copts—Equal, Protected or Persecuted?," 61.
6. Ibrahim, *Egypt, Islam and Democracy*, 187–188.
7. "Mahdi Akef Murshed al-Ikhwan al-Sabiq," (Mahdi Akef the Previous Muslim Brotherhood Guide) *Sada al-Balad*, May 27, 2012, accessed June 15, 2013, http://www.elbalad.news/174785/mhmd-mhdy-aakf-mrshd-ale.aspx.
8. Zeidan, "The Copts—Equal, Protected or Persecuted?," 60–62.
9. Ann Elizabeth Mayer, *Islam and Human Rights: Tradition and Politics* (Boulder, Colorado: Westview Press, 1999), 132–136.
10. Zeidan, "The Copts—Equal, Protected or Persecuted?," 61–62.
11. Ibrahim, *Egypt, Islam and Democracy*, 188.
12. Aziz S. Atiya, *A History of Eastern Christianity* (London: Methuen, 1968), 16.
13. Ragnhild Bjerre Finnestad, "Images as Messengers of Coptic Identity: An Example from Contemporary Egypt," *Open Journal System* 16 (1996): 107, accessed December 12, 2014, https://ojs.abo.fi/index.php/scripta/article/viewFile/491/1038.
14. "Mahdi Akef Murshed al-Ikhwan al-Sabiq."
15. Zeidan, "The Copts—Equal, Protected or Persecuted?," 53.
16. Ibrahim, *Egypt, Islam and Democracy*, 189–190.
17. Zeidan, "The Copts—Equal, Protected or Persecuted?," 53.
18. Shaaban Hedia and Michael Faris, "al-Aqbat Yadfaaun Fatorat Tafaggor Mogat al-Irhab Baad azl Morsi" (The Copts pay the price of the explosion of terrorism wave after Morsi's removal) *al-Youm al-Sabia*, October 21, 2013, accessed October 22, 2013, http://www.youm7.com/story/0000/0/0/-/1306241#.Vkti-PmrTIU.
19. Mustafa Rahouma, "al-Watan Tarsod 64 Halat Itidaa ala Alknais Walaqbat Khilal 12 Saa" (al-Watan Registers 64 Cases of Aggression on Churches and the Copts Within 12 Hours), *al-Watan*, August 15, 2013, accessed August 17, 2013, http://www.elwatannews.com/news/details/260930.
20. Remoun Nagi, "Fudd Rabaa" (Break Up of "Rabaa"), *Veto*, August 13, 2014, accessed September 17, 2014, http://www.vetogate.com/1165936.
21. Hedia and Faris, "al-Aqbat Yadfaaun Fatorat Tafaggor Mogat al-Irhab Baad azl Morsi."
22. Kirsten Powers, "The Muslims Brotherhood's War on Coptic Christians," *The Daily Beast*, August 22, 2013, accessed August 25, 2013, http://www.thedailybeast.com/articles/2013/08/22/the-muslim-brotherhood-s-war-on-coptic-christians.html.
23. Antonious al-Antony, *Wataniet al-Kanisah al-Qibtia Watarikhaha* (The Patriotism of the Coptic Church and Its History) (Cairo: al-Tibaa al-Masryyah, 2004), 263–266.
24. Mounir Megally, *Claremont Coptic Encyclopedia*, s.v. "Waq'at AL-kana'is" (The incident of the Churches), in the Claremont Colleges Digital Library (Claremont Graduate University, School of Religion, 1991), accessed November 10, 2013, http://ccdl.libraries.claremont.edu/cdm/singleitem/collection/cce/id/1921/rec/1.
25. *Ibid*.

Chapter One

1. Atiya, *A History of Eastern Christianity*, 16.
2. Janet A. Timbie, "Coptic Christianity," in *The Blackwell Companion to Eastern Christianity*, ed. Ken Parry (Malden, MA: Blackwell, 2007) 94.
3. Atiya, *A History of Eastern Christianity*, 25.
4. Pope Shenouda III, *Morcos al-Rasool* (Mark the Disciple) (Cairo: Anba Ruies, 1968), 56–57.
5. Fr. Tadros Y. Malaty, *Introduction to the Coptic Orthodox Church* (Alexandria: St. George's Church, 1993), 9–10.
6. Aziz S. Atiya, "The Copts and Christian Civilization," Copt-Net Repository, accessed May 18, 2013, http://www.coptic.net/articles/CoptsAndChristendom.txt.
7. Aziz S. Atiya, "The Copts and the Bible," Neal A. Maxwell Institute For Religious Scholarship, accessed July 11, 2013, http://publications.mi.byu.edu/fullscreen/?pub=1128&index=6.
8. John H. Watson, *Among The Copts* (Brighton: Sussex Academic Press, 2000), 2, accessed August 23, 2013, https://books.google.com.eg/books?id=jP5RDWywAx8C&printsec=frontcover&dq=coptic+christian&hl=en&sa=X&ei=tEeiUJadKs-4hAeL9YCgBg&sqi=2&redir_esc=y#v=onepage&q=coptic%20christian&f=false.
9. Pope Shenouda III, *Morcos al-Rasool*, 60–64.
10. Timbie, "Coptic Christianity," 96.
11. Iris Habib el Masri, *The Story of the Copts: The True Story of Christianity in Egypt*, 4th ed. book one (Johannesburg: Coptic Bishopric for African Affairs, 1987), 74.
12. Pope Shenouda III, "Tarikh al-Kanisah Liqadasat al-Baba Shenouda al-Thalith 18" (Church History by His Holiness Pope Shenouda III Lecture 18) (youtube audio, published August 19, 2014), accessed October 21, 2014, https://www.youtube.com/watch?v=V0y7bPYI_O8.
13. el Masri, *The Story of the Copts*, 74.
14. Howard Middleton-Jones, "An Introduction to the Coptic Period in Egypt. The Early Christian era 1st Century AD-7th Century AD," *Egyptological*, accessed November 12, 2013, http://egyptological.com/2011/12/07/an-introduction-to-the-coptic-period-in-egypt-the-early-christian-era-1st-century-ad-7th-century-ad-6210.
15. B.C.,"Pope Francis and the Copts: Blood and ecumenism" *The Economist*, February 17, 2015, accessed February 20, 2015, http://www.economist.com/blogs/erasmus/2015/02/pope-francis-and-copts.
16. Staff, "Coptic Church recognizes martyrdom of 21 Christians killed by ISIS," *Catholic Herald*, February 23, 2015, accessed February 23, 2015, http://www.catholicherald.co.uk/news/2015/02/23/coptic-church-recognises-martyrdom-of-21-egyptians-killed-by-isis/.
17. el Masri, *The Story of the Copts*, 13–14.
18. Malaty, *Introduction to the Coptic Orthodox Church*, 9–10.
19. Atiya, "The Copts and Christian Civilization."
20. "The Writings of St. Clement," Coptic Orthodox Church Network, accessed October 19, 2013, http://www.copticchurch.net/topics/patrology/schoolofalex/IV-StClement/chapter2.html.
21. el Masri, *The Story of the Copts*, 15–16.
22. *Ibid.*, 18–19.
23. Atiya, *A History of Eastern Christianity*, 35.
24. el Masri, *The Story of the Copts*, 27–29.
25. "Origen's Writings," Coptic Orthodox Church Network, accessed October 19, 2013, http://www.copticchurch.net/topics/patrology/schoolofalex2/chapter02.html.
26. Atiya, *A History of Eastern Christianity*, 35–36.
27. el Masri, *The Story of the Copts*, 30–33.
28. Atiya, "The Copts and Christian Civilization."
29. Atiya, *A History of Eastern Christianity*, 33–34.
30. *Ibid.*, 40–41.
31. *Ibid.*, 40–41.
32. *Ibid.*, 42.
33. Malaty, *Introduction to the Coptic Orthodox Church*, 46.
34. Atiya, "The Copts and Christian Civilization."
35. Atiya, *A History of Eastern Christianity*, 43–44.
36. *Ibid.*, 43.
37. el Masri, *The Story of the Copts*, 116–117.
38. *Ibid.*, 102–106.
39. Pope Shenouda III, *Qanoun al-Iman* (The Creed) (Cairo: Coptic Seminary, 1997), 8.
40. Malaty, *Introduction to the Coptic Orthodox Church*, 46–47.
41. el Masri, *The Story of the Copts*, 135–144.
42. Atiya, *A History of Eastern Christianity*, 45.
43. El Masri, *The Story of the Copts*, 153–155.
44. *Ibid.*, 106.
45. Atiya, *A History of Eastern Christianity*, 45.
46. *New World Encyclopedia*, s.v. "First Council of Constantinople," accessed November 11, 2013, http://www.newworldencyclopedia.org/entry/First_Council_of_Constantinople.
47. Malaty, *Introduction to the Coptic Orthodox Church*, 47.

48. el Masri, *The Story of the Copts*, 188–189.
49. Pope Shenouda III, "Tarikh al-Kanisah Liqadasat al-Baba Shenouda al-Thalith 11" (Church History by His Holiness Pope Shenouda III Lecture 11) (youtube audio, published July 26, 2014), accessed October 21, 2014, https://www.youtube.com/watch?v=JxFa_VxYYo8.
50. *Ibid.*
51. Atiya, *A History of Eastern Christianity*, 45–46.
52. el Masri, *The Story of the Copts*, 203–207.
53. Atiya, *A History of Eastern Christianity*, 47–48.
54. el Masri, *The Story of the Copts*, 205–219.
55. Pope Shenouda III, *Tabiat al-Maseeh*, 12th ed. (The Nature of Christ) (Cairo: Coptic Seminary, 2007), 11.
56. *Ibid.*, 11–12.
57. el Masri, *The Story of the Copts*, 237–243.
58. Atiya, *A History of Eastern Christianity*, 58.
59. Pope Shenouda, *Tabiat al-Maseeh*, 8.
60. Atiya, *A History of Eastern Christianity*, 58–59.
61. Pope Shenouda, *Tabiat al-Maseeh*, 8.
62. Timbie, "Coptic Christianity," 94.
63. Atiya, *A History of Eastern Christianity*, 58.
64. Atiya, "The Copts and Christian Civilization."
65. Pope Shenouda III, "Tarikh al-Kanisah Liqadasat al-Baba Shenouda al-Thalith 12" (Church History by His Holiness Pope Shenouda III Lecture 12) (youtube audio, published July 26, 2014), accessed October 21, 2014, https://www.youtube.com/watch?v=VpVE_KSRFnY.
66. *Ibid.*
67. Atiya, "The Copts and Christian Civilization."
68. *Ibid.*
69. Barbara Watterson, *Coptic Egypt* (Edinburgh: Scottish Academic Press, 1988), 54–56.
70. Pope Shenouda III, "Tarikh al-Kanisah Liqadasat al-Baba Shenouda al-Thalith 3" (Church History by His Holiness Pope Shenouda III Lecture 3) (youtube audio, published July 6, 2014), accessed October 30, 2014, https://www.youtube.com/watch?v=pBlMt8cdq_k.
71. Watterson, *Coptic Egypt*, 56–59.
72. Atiya, "The Copts and Christian Civilization."
73. Watson, *Among The Copts*, 19.
74. Watterson, *Coptic Egypt*, 56–61.
75. Atiya, "The Copts and Christian Civilization."
76. Watson, *Among The Copts*, 19.
77. Watterson, *Coptic Egypt*, 61–63.
78. Alastair Hamilton, *The Copts and the West 1439–1822: The European Discovery of the Egyptian Church* (Oxford: Oxford University Press, 2006), 12.
79. Watterson, *Coptic Egypt*, 61–63.
80. Atiya, "The Copts and Christian Civilization."
81. *Ibid.*
82. Pope Shenouda III, "Tarikh al-Kanisah Liqadasat al-Baba Shenouda al-Thalith 3" (Church History by His Holiness Pope Shenouda III Lecture 3).
83. Timbie, "Coptic Christianity," 109.
84. Atiya, *A History of Eastern Christianity*, 66–67.
85. Watterson, *Coptic Egypt*, 70.
86. Timbie, "Coptic Christianity," 109–110.
87. Atiya, "The Copts and Christian Civilization."
88. *Ibid.*
89. *Ibid.*
90. *Ibid.*
91. "Saint Maurice and the Theban Legion," Coptic Orthodox Church Network, accessed November 23, 2013, http://www.copticchurch.net/topics/synexarion/maurice.html.
92. Atiya, "The Copts and Christian Civilization."
93. Ezzat Indrawis, "Alqedisa Verina" (Saint Verina), *Coptic History*, last updated March 15, 2010, accessed November 23, 2013, http://www.coptichistory.org/untitled_1544.htm.
94. Atiya, "The Copts and Christian Civilization."
95. AFP, "Egyptian papyrus found in ancient Irish bog," *Daily News Egypt*, September 7, 2010, accessed August 11, 2013, http://www.dailynewsegypt.com/2010/09/07/egyptian-papyrus-found-in-ancient-irish-bog/.
96. Ragheb Moftah, "Coptic Music from Mothers Chanting to Mlm. Mikhail Al-Batanony Hymns," Coptic.org, January 7, 1995, accessed July 27, 2013, http://www.coptic.org/music/xmas95.htm.
97. Atiya, "The Copts and Christian Civilization."
98. Moftah, "Coptic Music from Mothers Chanting to Mlm. Mikhail Al-Batanony Hymns."
99. *Ibid.*
100. Ragheb Moftah, "Coptic Music: Value and Origins," Coptic.org, accessed July 27, 2013, http://www.coptic.org/music/valnorig.htm.
101. Atiya, "The Copts and Christian Civilization."
102. Raymond Stock, "Preserving Pharos Psalms For Christ," Coptic.org, April, 1997, accessed July 27, 2013, http://www.coptic.org/music/today.htm.

103. Atiya, "The Copts and Christian Civilization."
104. "An Introduction to the Coptic Art of Egypt," Copt-Net Repository, accessed August 11, 2013, http://www.coptic.net/articles/CopticArtOfEgypt.txt.
105. Atiya, "The Copts and Christian Civilization."
106. "St. Menas Pilgrim-Flasks or Ampullae," St. Mina Monastery, last modified October 16, 2003, accessed August 11, 2013, http://www.stmina-monastery.org/ampullae.htm.
107. Atiya, "The Copts and Christian Civilization."
108. *Ibid.*
109. *Ibid.*
110. Middleton-Jones, "An Introduction to the Coptic Period in Egypt."
111. Atiya, "The Copts and Christian Civilization."
112. *Ibid.*
113. Atiya, *A History of Eastern Christianity*, 69–70.
114. Atiya, "The Copts and Christian Civilization."

Chapter Two

1. Atiya, *A History of Eastern Christianity*, 79–80.
2. Theodore Hall Patrick, *Traditional Egyptian Christianity: A History of the Coptic Orthodox Church* (Greensboro, NC: Fischer Park Press, 1996), 52.
3. Saieda Ismail al-Kashif, *Masr fi Fagr al-Islam: Min al-Fatih al-Arabi ela Qiyam al-Dawla al-Tolonia* (Egypt in the Dawn of Islam: From the Arab Conquest to the Establishment of the Tulunid Dynasty) (Cairo: Dar al-Fikr al-Arabi, 1947), 51.
4. Atiya, *A History of Eastern Christianity*, 80.
5. Alfred J. Butler, *The Arab Conquest of Egypt: and The Last Thirty Years of the Roman Dominion*, ed. P.M. Fraser (Oxford: Oxford University Press, 1978), 256–261.
6. Atiya, *A History of Eastern Christianity*, 80–81.
7. Patrick, *Traditional Egyptian Christianity*, 53.
8. Butler, *The Arab Conquest of Egypt*, 263.
9. *Ibid.*, 183–190.
10. *Ibid.*, 273–274.
11. Muhammad al-Arifi "Essayida Mariyyah al-Qibtiyyah" (Lady Mary the Copt) (youtube video, February 13, 2009), accessed January 14, 2014, https://www.youtube.com/watch?v=TPpG8ETYcMQ.
12. Atiya, "The Copts and Christian Civilization."
13. Atiya, *A History of Eastern Christianity*, 82.
14. Butler, *The Arab Conquest of Egypt*, 450.
15. Jack Tajir, *Aqbat wa Moslimoon mintho al-Fatih al-Arabi ela Aam 1922* (Copts and Muslims since the Arab Conquest until the Year 1922) (Cairo: Karasat al-Tarikh al-Masry, 1951), 105.
16. Albair Mansour, *Qadar al-Masihien al-Arab wa Khiarhom* (The Fate of Arab Christians and Their Choices) (Beirut: Dar al-Gadid, 1995), 25–26.
17. Bat Ye'or, *The Dhimmi: Jews and Christians Under Islam* (New Jersey: Associated University Press, 1985), 132.
18. Patrick, *Traditional Egyptian Christianity*, 54.
19. Tajir, *Aqbat wa Moslimoon mintho al-Fatih al-Arabi ela Aam 1922*, 130–131.
20. Ye'or, *The Dhimmi: Jews and Christians Under Islam*, 48–49.
21. *Ibid.*, 45.
22. Bat Ye'or, *The Decline of Eastern Christianity Under Islam: From Jihad to Dhimmitude, Seventh-Twentieth Century* (London: Associated University Press, 1996), 40.
23. *Ibid.*, 40–41.
24. Ye'or, *The Dhimmi: Jews and Christians Under Islam*, 62–63.
25. *Ibid.*, 203.
26. *Ibid.*
27. *Ibid.*, 197–198.
28. *Ibid.*, 196.
29. *Ibid.*, 156.
30. *Ibid.*, 145–146.
31. Samuel Shahid, "Rights of Non-Muslims in an Islamic State," Answering Islam, accessed May 14, 2014, http://www.answering-islam.org/NonMuslims/rights.htm.
32. Ye'or, *The Dhimmi: Jews and Christians Under Islam*, 188.
33. *Ibid.*, 53–54.
34. *Ibid.*, 192.
35. *Ibid.*, 201.
36. Laurent Chabry and Anni Chabry, *Siasa wa Aqaliat fi al-Sharq al-Adna: al-Asbab al-mo'adia lilinfigar* trans. Dhoqan Qarqoot (Politics and Minorities in the Near East: The Reasons Leading to the Explosion) (Cairo: Madboli Press, 1991), 26–33.
37. Watterson, *Coptic Egypt*, 150–151.
38. Ye'or, *The Dhimmi: Jews and Christians Under Islam*, 51.
39. Ye'or, *The Decline of Eastern Christianity*, 263–265.
40. Asmaa Badawi, "Umar Abdel Rahman..." *al-Watan*, June 29, 2012, accessed August 30, 2013, http://www.elwatannews.com/news/details/22001.

41. Shahid, "Rights of Non-Muslims in an Islamic State."
42. James White, "Breaking the Cross, Killing the Swine: Truly Thinking About ISIS and the Murder of 21 Copts" *Alpha &Omega*, February 16, 2015, accessed February 20, 2015, http://www.aomin.org/aoblog/index.php/2015/02/16/breaking-the-cross-killing-the-swine-truly-thinking-about-isis-and-the-murder-of-21-copts/.
43. Sophia Jones, "ISIS Boasted Of These Christians' Deaths. Here Are The Lives They Lived," *The World Post*, February 18, 2015, accessed February 19, 2015, http://www.huffingtonpost.com/2015/02/18/isis-christians-killed-_n_6703278.html.
44. *Ibid.*
45. *Ibid.*
46. Butler, *The Arab Conquest of Egypt*, 263–264.
47. Atiya, *A History of Eastern Christianity*, 83–85.
48. Al-Kashif, *Masr fi Fagr al-Islam*, 216–217.
49. Ye'or, *The Dhimmi: Jews and Christians Under Islam*, 143–144.
50. Al-Kashif, *Masr fi Fagr el-Islam*, 55–58.
51. M. Wassermann, "The Process of Islamization in Egypt: possible causes and the extent thereof up to the 14th century A.D.," Answering Islam, accessed December 1, 2013, http://www.answering-islam.org/history/islamization_egypt.html.
52. Hugh Goddard, *A History of Christian-Muslim Relations* (Chicago: New Amsterdam Books, 2000), 71.
53. Al-Kashif, *Masr fi Fagr al-Islam*, 206.
54. A.S. Tritton, *Caliphs and their non-Muslim Subjects: A Critical Study of the Covenant of Umar* (London: Cass, 1930), 5–6.
55. Al-Kashif, *Masr fi Fagr al-Islam*, 208.
56. Andrew Bostom, "Quenching Sharia Thirst on the Nile," *American Thinker*, December 23, 2012, accessed January 10, 2013, http://www.americanthinker.com/blog/2012/12/quenching_sharia_thirst_on_the_nile.html.
57. Ye'or, *The Dhimmi: Jews and Christians Under Islam*, 52.
58. *Ibid.*, 143–144.

Chapter Three

1. Watterson, *Coptic Egypt*, 148–150.
2. *Ibid.*, 148–150.
3. Yaqub Nakhla Rofila, *Tarikh al-Umma al-Qibtia*, 2nd ed. (The History of the Coptic Nation) (Cairo: Metropol Press, 2000), 60–61.
4. Hamilton, *The Copts and the West 1439–1822*, 26.
5. Butler, *The Arab Conquest of Egypt*, 460–461.
6. Al-Kashif, *Masr fi Fagr al-Islam*, 222–223.
7. Wassermann, "The Process of Islamization in Egypt."
8. Patrick, *Traditional Egyptian Christianity*, 56.
9. Al-Antony, *Wataniet al-Kanisah al-Qibtia Watarikhaha*, 91–94.
10. Rofila, *Tarikh al-Umma al-Qibtia*, 70.
11. Al-Kashif, *Masr fi Fagr al-Islam*, 199.
12. Al-Antony, *Wataniet al-Kanisah al-Qibtia Watarikhaha*, 90.
13. Tajir, *Aqbat wa Moslimoon mintho al-Fatih al-Arabi ela Aam 1922*, 93.
14. al-Kashif, *Masr fi Fagr al-Islam*, 199–210.
15. Isabel Coles, "With sledgehammer, Islamic State smashes Iraqi history," *Reuters*, February 26, 2015, accessed February 28, 2015, http://www.reuters.com/article/us-mideast-crisis-iraq-museum-idUSKBN0LU1CW20150226.
16. Yaser Abdel Aziz, "Aada' al-Hadarah," (The Enemy of Civilization) *al-Masry al-Youm*, August 3, 2014, accessed August 4, 2014, http://today.almasryalyoum.com/article2.aspx?ArticleID=433099.
17. al-Antony, *Wataniet al-Kanisah al-Qibtia Watarikhaha*, 94.
18. Rofila, *Tarikh al-Umma al-Qibtia*, 68–73.
19. al-Antony, *Wataniet al-Kanisah al-Qibtia Watarikhaha*, 93.
20. Rofila, *Tarikh al-Umma al-Qibtia*, 71.
21. al-Antony, *Wataniet al-Kanisah al-Qibtia Watarikhaha*, 94.
22. Rofila, *Tarikh al-Umma al-Qibtia*, 72–74.
23. al-Kashif, *Masr fi Fagr al-Islam*, 198.
24. Watterson, *Coptic Egypt*, 151.
25. Rofila, *Tarikh al-Umma al-Qibtia*, 78.
26. Watterson, *Coptic Egypt*, 151.
27. al-Antony, *Wataniet al-Kanisah al-Qibtia Watarikhaha*, 98–100.
28. Watterson, *Coptic Egypt*, 151–152.
29. al-Antony, *Wataniet al-Kanisah al-Qibtia Watarikhaha*, 113–115.
30. Manassa Yohanna, *Tarikh al-Kanisah al-Qibtia* (The History of the Coptic Church) (Cairo: Maktabit al-Mahabba, 1924), 337–338.
31. al-Antony, *Wataniet al-Kanisah al-Qibtia Watarikhaha*, 122–123.
32. Patrick, *Traditional Egyptian Christianity*, 61.
33. Tajir, *Aqbat wa Moslimoon mintho al-Fatih al-Arabi ela Aam 1922*, 101–102.
34. Patrick, *Traditional Egyptian Christianity*, 61.
35. Tajir, *Aqbat wa Moslimoon mintho al-Fatih al-Arabi ela Aam 1922*, 101–102.
36. al-Antony, *Wataniet al-Kanisah al-Qibtia Watarikhaha*, 122–123.

37. Tajir, *Aqbat wa Moslimoon mintho al-Fatih al-Arabi ela Aam 1922*, 104.
38. al-Kashif, *Masr fi Fagr al-Islam*, 238–240.
39. Patrick, *Traditional Egyptian Christianity*, 61.
40. Yohanna, *Tarikh al-Kanisah al-Qibtia*, 365.
41. Patrick, *Traditional Egyptian Christianity*, 61.
42. Goddard, *A History of Christian-Muslim Relations*, 66–67.
43. Ye'or, *The Dhimmi: Jews and Christians Under Islam*, 58–60.
44. Yohanna, *Tarikh al-Kanisah al-Qibtia*, 366–367.
45. al-Antony, *Wataniet al-Kanisah al-Qibtia Watarikhaha*, 116.
46. Yohanna, *Tarikh al-Kanisah al-Qibtia*, 367.
47. Rofila, *Tarikh al-Umma al-Qibtia*, 93–96.
48. al-Antony, *Wataniet al-Kanisah al-Qibtia Watarikhaha*, 125.
49. Watterson, *Coptic Egypt*, 152–153.
50. Ibid., 152.
51. Patrick, *Traditional Egyptian Christianity*, 63.
52. Tajir, *Aqbat wa Moslimoon mintho al-Fatih al-Arabi ela Aam 1922*, 112.
53. al-Antony, *Wataniet al-Kanisah al-Qibtia Watarikhaha*, 141.
54. Rofila, *Tarikh al-Umma al-Qibtia*, 107.
55. al-Antony, *Wataniet al-Kanisah al-Qibtia Watarikhaha*, 143–144.
56. Atiya, *A History of Eastern Christianity*, 86.
57. Tajir, *Aqbat wa Moslimoon mintho al-Fatih al-Arabi ela Aam 1922*, 114–115.
58. Atiya, *A History of Eastern Christianity*, 86.
59. Tajir, *Aqbat wa Moslimoon mintho al-Fatih al-Arabi ela Aam 1922*, 113–114.
60. Watterson, *Coptic Egypt*, 155.
61. Tajir, *Aqbat wa Moslimoon mintho al-Fatih al-Arabi ela Aam 1922*, 114–115.
62. al-Antony, *Wataniet al-Kanisah al-Qibtia Watarikhaha*, 145.
63. Ibid., 144–146.
64. Watterson, *Coptic Egypt*, 155.
65. Tajir, *Aqbat wa Moslimoon mintho al-Fatih al-Arabi ela Aam 1922*, 116.
66. Ibid., 116–117.
67. al-Antony, *Wataniet al-Kanisah al-Qibtia Watarikhaha*, 147–148.
68. Yohanna, *Tarikh al-Kanisah al-Qibtia*, 381.
69. al-Antony, *Wataniet al-Kanisah al-Qibtia Watarikhaha*, 157–158.
70. Watterson, *Coptic Egypt*, 156.
71. Patrick, *Traditional Egyptian Christianity*, 74.
72. Yohanna, *Tarikh al-Kanisah al-Qibtia*, 381.
73. Tajir, *Aqbat wa Moslimoon mintho al-Fatih al-Arabi ela Aam 1922*, 118–119.
74. Patrick, *Traditional Egyptian Christianity*, 75.
75. Tajir, *Aqbat wa Moslimoon mintho al-Fatih al-Arabi ela Aam 1922*, 120.
76. Atiya, *A History of Eastern Christianity*, 87.
77. Sawirus ibn al-Muqaffa Bishop of al-Ashmunin, *History of the Patriarchs of the Egyptian Church, Known as the History of the Holy Church*, vol. 2, part 2 (Cairo, 1948) 94–96.
78. Ibid., 96–97.
79. Atiya, *A History of Eastern Christianity*, 88.
80. Tajir, *Aqbat wa Moslimoon mintho al-Fatih al-Arabi ela Aam 1922*, 122.
81. Patrick, *Traditional Egyptian Christianity*, 76.
82. Tajir, *Aqbat wa Moslimoon mintho al-Fatih al-Arabi ela Aam 1922*, 122–125.
83. Ibn al-Muqaffa, *History of the Patriarchs of the Egyptian Church*, 121.
84. Andre Ferre, *Claremont Coptic Encyclopedia*, s.v. "Hakim Bi-Amr-Illah Abu 'Ali Mansur, Al-," in the Claremont Colleges Digital Library (Claremont Graduate University, School of Religion, 1991), accessed November 10, 2013, http://ccdl.libraries.claremont.edu/cdm/singleitem/collection/cce/id/935/rec/15.
85. Ibn al-Muqaffa, *History of the Patriarchs of the Egyptian Church*, 122–123.
86. Ibid., 124–125.
87. Ibid., 127–132.
88. Patrick, *Traditional Egyptian Christianity*, 76–77.
89. Tajir, *Aqbat wa Moslimoon mintho al-Fatih al-Arabi ela Aam 1922*, 129.
90. Ibid., 130.
91. "Daaish yahdem wayanbish mohtawayat 2000 qabr..." (ISIS destroys and unearths contents of 2000 graves...) *al-Watan Newspaper*, January 24, 2016, accessed January 25, 2016, http://alwatan.kuwait.tt/articledetails.aspx?id=464899.
92. al-Antony, *Wataniet al-Kanisah al-Qibtia Watarikhaha*, 169–170.
93. Wayne King, "Islamic Mob Burns Down Church in Egypt," *World Watch Monitor*, March 8, 2011, accessed March 9, 2011, https://www.worldwatchmonitor.org/2011/03-March/69546/.
94. Girgis Bushra and Theresa Samir, "Al-Halaa Yositer ala Aqbat Sul...," (Fear Controls the Copts of Sul...), Copts United, March 7, 2011, accessed March 8, 2011, http://www.copts-united.com/Article.php?I=735&A=32325.
95. Atiya, *A History of Eastern Christianity*, 89.

96. al-Antony, *Wataniet al-Kanisah al-Qibtia Watarikhaha*, 172.
97. A.H. Hourani, *Minorities in the Middle East* (London: Oxford University Press, 1947), 45.
98. Tajir, *Aqbat wa Moslimoon mintho al-Fatih al-Arabi ela Aam 1922*, 130–131.
99. Al-Antony, *Wataniet al-Kanisah al-Qibtia Watarikhaha*, 170.
100. Tajir, *Aqbat wa Moslimoon mintho al-Fatih al-Arabi ela Aam 1922*, 130–131.
101. Ibn al-Muqaffa, *History of the Patriarchs of the Egyptian Church*, 137.
102. Rofila, *Tarikh al-Umma al-Qibtia*, 128–129.
103. Atiya, *A History of Eastern Christianity*, 90.
104. Yohanna, *Tarikh al-Kanisah al-Qibtia*, 399.
105. Ibn al-Muqaffa, *History of the Patriarchs of the Egyptian Church*, 187–188.
106. al-Antony, *Wataniet al-Kanisah al-Qibtia Watarikhaha*, 173.
107. Patrick, *Traditional Egyptian Christianity*, 79.
108. Gary Leiser, "The Madrasas and the Islamization of the Middle East the Case of Egypt," *Journal of the American Research Center in Egypt* 22 (1985): 30.
109. *Ibid.*, 31.
110. Wassermann, "The Process of Islamization in Egypt."
111. Leiser, "The Madrasas and the Islamization of the Middle East the Case of Egypt," 31–32.
112. *Ibid.*, 33.
113. *Ibid.*, 33–34.
114. *Ibid.*, 34–35.
115. Atiya, *A History of Eastern Christianity*, 94–95.
116. *Ibid.*, 92–93.
117. Patrick, *Traditional Egyptian Christianity*, 83.
118. *Ibid.*, 83–84.
119. Leiser, "The Madrasas and the Islamization of the Middle East the Case of Egypt," 35–37.
120. *Ibid.*, 45–46.
121. *Ibid.*, 38–43.
122. Atiya, *A History of Eastern Christianity*, 92–93.
123. al-Antony, *Wataniet al-Kanisah al-Qibtia Watarikhaha*, 225–228.
124. Patrick, *Traditional Egyptian Christianity*, 84.
125. Atiya, *A History of Eastern Christianity*, 92–93.
126. Timbie, "Coptic Christianity," 107.
127. Yohanna, *Tarikh al-Kanisah al-Qibtia*, 417.
128. Rofila, *Tarikh al-Umma al-Qibtia*, 170.
129. Al-Antony, *Wataniet al-Kanisah al-Qibtia Watarikhaha*, 229–230.
130. Rofila, *Tarikh al-Umma al-Qibtia*, 181.
131. Patrick, *Traditional Egyptian Christianity*, 85.
132. Rofila, *Tarikh al-Umma al-Qibtia*, 202–203.
133. Watterson, *Coptic Egypt*, 157.
134. Rofila, *Tarikh al-Umma al-Qibtia*, 220–222.
135. Leiser, "The Madrasas and the Islamization of the Middle East the Case of Egypt," 46.
136. Tajir, *Aqbat wa Moslimoon mintho al-Fatih al-Arabi ela Aam 1922*, 172.
137. al-Antony, *Wataniet al-Kanisah al-Qibtia Watarikhaha*, 249–250.
138. Donald P. Little, "Coptic Converts to Islam during the Bahri Mamluk period," in *Conversion and Continuity: Indigenous Christian Communities in Islamic Lands Eighth to Eighteenth Centuries*, ed. Michael Gervers and Ramzi Jibran Bikhazi (Toronto: Pontifical Institute of Medieval Studies, 1990), 263.
139. Patrick, *Traditional Egyptian Christianity*, 100.
140. Atiya, *A History of Eastern Christianity*, 97.
141. Tajir, *Aqbat wa Moslimoon mintho al-Fatih al-Arabi ela Aam 1922*, 174.
142. Al-Antony, *Wataniet al-Kanisah al-Qibtia Watarikhaha*, 254–256.
143. Tajir, *Aqbat wa Moslimoon mintho al-Fatih al-Arabi ela Aam 1922*, 178–179.
144. Patrick, *Traditional Egyptian Christianity*, 97.
145. Ye'or, *The Dhimmi: Jews and Christians Under Islam*, 198.
146. Tajir, *Aqbat wa Moslimoon mintho al-Fatih al-Arabi ela Aam 1922*, 192.
147. Ibrahim Isa, "Ibrahim Isa Yasdom Algameea…," (Ibrahim Isa Shocks Everyone…) (youtube video, February 3, 2015), accessed February 10, 2015, https://www.youtube.com/watch?v=238H7myxGQ8.
148. Little, "Coptic Converts to Islam during the Bahri Mamluk period," 264–265.
149. *Ibid.*, 264–265.
150. *Ibid.*, 278–280.
151. al-Antony, *Wataniet al-Kanisah al-Qibtia Watarikhaha*, 274–275.
152. Leiser, "The Madrasas and the Islamization of the Middle East the Case of Egypt," 46.
153. Wassermann, "The Process of Islamization in Egypt."
154. Tajir, *Aqbat wa Moslimoon mintho al-Fatih al-Arabi ela Aam 1922*, 192–194.
155. Rofila, *Tarikh al-Umma al-Qibtia*, 244.
156. Patrick, *Traditional Egyptian Christianity*, 97–99.

157. Wassermann, "The Process of Islamization in Egypt."
158. Hamilton, *The Copts and the West 1439–1822*, 29–30.
159. Watterson, *Coptic Egypt*, 153.
160. al-Antony, *Wataniet al-Kanisah al-Qibtia Watarikhaha*, 101–102.
161. Butler, *The Arab Conquest of Egypt*, 461.
162. al-Kashif, *Masr fi Fagr al-Islam*, 249–252.
163. Georges C. Anawati, "The Christian Communities in Egypt in the Middle Ages," in *Conversion and Continuity: Indigenous Christian Communities in Islamic Lands Eighth to Eighteenth Centuries*, ed. Michael Gervers and Ramzi Jibran Bikhazi (Toronto: Pontifical Institute of Medieval Studies, 1990), 242.
164. *Ibid.*, 241–242.
165. *Ibid.*, 242.
166. *Ibid.*, 241–242.
167. al-Kashif, *Masr fi Fagr al-Islam*, 249.
168. Tritton, *Caliphs and their non-Muslim Subjects*, 5–6.
169. al-Antony, *Wataniet al-Kanisah al-Qibtia Watarikhaha*, 236–237.
170. Tajir, *Aqbat wa Moslimoon mintho al-Fatih al-Arabi ela Aam 1922*, 300–302.
171. Anawati, "The Christian Communities in Egypt in the Middle Ages," 243–244.
172. Tajir, *Aqbat wa Moslimoon mintho al-Fatih al-Arabi ela Aam 1922*, 303.
173. al-Antony, *Wataniet al-Kanisah al-Qibtia Watarikhaha*, 238.
174. *Ibid.*, 237–238.
175. Tajir, *Aqbat wa Moslimoon mintho al-Fatih al-Arabi ela Aam 1922*, 302–303.
176. al-Antony, *Wataniet al-Kanisah al-Qibtia Watarikhaha*, 322–323.
177. Watterson, *Coptic Egypt*, 157–158.

Chapter Four

1. Hamilton, *The Copts and the West 1439–1822*, 30.
2. Carter, *The Copts in Egyptian Politics*, 3.
3. Atiya, *A History of Eastern Christianity*, 99–100.
4. Aziz S. Atiya, *Claremont Coptic Encyclopedia*, s.v."Ottomans, Copts Under The," in the Claremont Colleges Digital Library (Claremont Graduate University, School of Religion, 1991), accessed November 10, 2013, http://ccdl.libraries.claremont.edu/cdm/singleitem/collection/cce/id/1495/rec/6.
5. Atiya, *A History of Eastern Christianity*, 99–100.
6. Hamilton, *The Copts and the West 1439–1822*, 31.
7. al-Antony, *Wataniet al-Qibtia Watarikhaha*, 321.
8. Heba Habib, "Ramadan edict against eating in public infuriates some Muslims in Egypt," *The Washington Post*, June 17, 2016, accessed June 20, 2016, https://www.washingtonpost.com/news/worldviews/wp/2016/06/17/ramadan-edict-against-eating-in-public-infuriates-some-muslims-in-egypt/.
9. Ye'or, *The Dhimmi: Jews and Christians Under Islam*, 212–216.
10. al-Antony, *Wataniet al-Kanisah al-Qibtia Watarikhaha*, 325.
11. Hamilton, *The Copts and the West 1439–1822*, 179.
12. al-Antony, *Wataniet al-Kanisah al-Qibtia Watarikhaha*, 320.
13. Hamilton, *The Copts and the West 1439–1822*, 32.
14. *Ibid.*, 32–33.
15. *Ibid.*, 32–33.
16. Patrick, *Traditional Egyptian Christianity*, 107.
17. Hamilton, *The Copts and the West 1439–1822*, 34–35.
18. *Ibid.*, 36–37.
19. Patrick, *Traditional Egyptian Christianity*, 112.
20. Atiya, *A History of Eastern Christianity*, 100.
21. Atiya, *Claremont Coptic Encyclopedia*, s.v. "Ottomans, Copts Under The."
22. Atiya, *A History of Eastern Christianity*, 101.
23. Tajir, *Aqbat wa Moslimoon mintho al-Fatih al-Arabi ela Aam 1922*, 207–210.
24. Patrick, *Traditional Egyptian Christianity*, 118–121.
25. Iris Habib el Masri, *Qisat al-Kanisah al-Qibtia: wahia Tarikh al-Kanisah al-Orthozoksia al-Masria allati Assasha Mar Morcos al-Bashir*, book 4 (The Story of the Coptic Church: The History of the Egyptian Orthodox Church Established by St. Mark the Evangelist) (Sporting, Alexandria: Maktabit Kanisat Mar Girgis, 1992), 194–199.
26. Atiya, *A History of Eastern Christianity*, 101.
27. Tajir, *Aqbat wa Moslimoon mintho al-Fatih al-Arabi ela Aam 1922*, 211–212.
28. Atiya, *A History of Eastern Christianity*, 101.
29. Tajir, *Aqbat wa Moslimoon mintho al-Fatih al-Arabi ela Aam 1922*, 213–214.
30. al-Antony, *Wataniet al-Kanisah al-Qibtia Watarikhaha*, 352.
31. *Ibid.*, 355.
32. Patrick, *Traditional Egyptian Christianity*, 118–121.
33. el Masri, *Qisat al-Kanisah al-Qibtia*, 199.

34. Anwar Louca, *Claremont Coptic Encyclopedia*, s.v. "Ya'qub, General," in the Claremont Colleges Digital Library (Claremont Graduate University, School of Religion, 1991), accessed January 14, 2014, http://ccdl.libraries.claremont.edu/cdm/ref/collection/cce/id/1927.
35. al-Antony, *Wataniet al-Kanisah al-Qibtia Watarikhaha*, 358–360.
36. Dioscorus Boles, "The Face Of Mu'allem Ya'qub Hanna, The Great Coptic Hero, By The French Artist Vivant Denon," *On Coptic Nationalism*, May 31, 2012, accessed February 23, 2014, https://copticliterature.wordpress.com/2012/05/31/the-face-of-muallem-yaqub-hanna-the-great-coptic-hero-by-the-french-artist-vivant-denon/.
37. Louca, *Claremont Coptic Encyclopedia*, s.v."Ya'qub, General."
38. Patrick, *Traditional Egyptian Christianity*, 121–122.
39. al-Antony, *Wataniet al-Kanisah al-Qibtia Watarikhaha*, 365–366.
40. Patrick, *Traditional Egyptian Christianity*, 118–121.
41. Helen Chapin Metz, ed., "Muhammad Ali, 1805–48," in *Egypt: A Country Study*, Country Studies, accessed February 23, 2014, http://countrystudies.us/egypt/21.htm.
42. Watterson, *Coptic Egypt*, 158–159.
43. el Masri, *Qisat al-Kanisah al-Qibtia*, 262–263.
44. al-Antony, *Wataniet al-Kanisah al-Qibtia Watarikhaha*, 372–377.
45. *Ibid.*, 372.
46. el Masri, *Qisat al-Kanisah al-Qibtia*, 274–276.
47. Ibrahim, *Egypt, Islam and Democracy*, 94.
48. Patrick, *Traditional Egyptian Christianity*, 123.
49. Metz, ed., "Muhammad Ali, 1805–48."
50. Ibrahim, *Egypt, Islam and Democracy*, 109–111.
51. Patrick, *Traditional Egyptian Christianity*, 123.
52. al-Antony, *Wataniet al-Kanisah al-Qibtia Watarikhaha*, 373.
53. *Ibid.*, 371–376.
54. Saad Eddin Ibrahim, et al., *The Copts of Egypt* (London: Minority Rights Group International, 1996), 11.
55. el Masri, *Qisat al-Kanisah al-Qibtia*, 259.
56. al-Antony, *Wataniet al-Kanisah al-Qibtia Watarikhaha*, 378.
57. *Ibid.*, 378.
58. *Ibid.*, 379.
59. Patrick, *Traditional Egyptian Christianity*, 124–126.
60. *Ibid.*, 122.
61. *Ibid.*, 129.
62. al-Antony, *Wataniet al-Kanisah al-Qibtia Watarikhaha*, 380.
63. *Ibid.*, 385–386.
64. Ye'or, *The Dhimmi: Jews and Christians Under Islam*, 98–101.
65. *Ibid.*, 99.
66. Mansour, *Qadar al-Masihien al-Arab wa Khiarhom*, 31–32.
67. Ibrahim, et al., *The Copts of Egypt*, 11.
68. *Ibid.*, 11–12.
69. Paul Marshall, *Egypt's Endangered Christians* (A Report by the Center for Religious Freedom of Freedom House, 1999), 41.
70. *Ibid.*, 39.
71. al-Antony, *Wataniet al-Kanisah al-Qibtia Watarikhaha*, 385–386.
72. *Ibid.*, 385–386.
73. Patrick, *Traditional Egyptian Christianity*, 128–129.
74. al-Antony, *Wataniet al-Kanisah al-Qibtia Watarikhaha*, 387–392.
75. el Masri, *Qisat al-Kanisah al-Qibtia*, 392–393.
76. Ibrahim, *Egypt, Islam and Democracy*, 95.
77. Patrick, *Traditional Egyptian Christianity*, 133.
78. al-Antony, *Wataniet al-Kanisah al-Qibtia Watarikhaha*, 388–392.
79. Hourani, *Minorities in The Middle East*, 46.
80. el Masri, *Qisat al-Kanisah al-Qibtia*, 345–346.
81. Zakharias al-Antony, *al-Baba Kyrillos al-rabia Abu al-Islah* (Pope Kyrillos the 4th Father of Reform) (Cairo: Dar al-Tibaa al-Qawmya, 1994), 242, accessed March 12, 2014, http://www.calloflove.net/copticlibrary/history/popekyrlos4th/241.htm.
82. Patrick, *Traditional Egyptian Christianity*, 129–133.
83. Ibrahim, *Egypt, Islam and Democracy*, 95.
84. Watterson, *Coptic Egypt*, 159.
85. Carter, *The Copts in Egyptian Politics*, 58–59.
86. Doris Behrens-Abouseif, *Claremont Coptic Encyclopedia*, s.v."British Occupation of Egypt," in the Claremont Colleges Digital Library (Claremont Graduate University, School of Religion, 1991), accessed January 14, 2014, http://ccdl.libraries.claremont.edu/cdm/ref/collection/cce/id/382.
87. Patrick, *Traditional Egyptian Christianity*, 143–144.
88. Carter, *The Copts in Egyptian Politics*, 58–59.
89. Watterson, *Coptic Egypt*, 174–175.
90. Patrick, *Traditional Egyptian Christianity*, 144.
91. *Ibid.*, 142.

92. *Encyclopedia Britannica*, s.v. "Dinshaway Incident," accessed March 12, 2014, http://www.britannica.com/topic/Dinshaway-Incident.
93. Patrick, *Traditional Egyptian Christianity*, 145.
94. Carter, *The Copts in Egyptian Politics*, 12–13.
95. Kenneth Cragg, *The Arab Christian: A History in the Middle East* (Louisville: Westminster/John Knox Press, 1991), 171.
96. Muhammad Hassanien Hikel, *Kharif al-Ghadab* (Autumn of Fury) (Cairo: al-Ahram Center for Translation and Publication, 1988), 272–273.
97. Cragg, *The Arab Christian*, 171.
98. Ibrahim, et al., *The Copts of Egypt*, 12.
99. Abouseif, *Claremont Coptic Encyclopedia*, s.v. "British Occupation of Egypt."
100. Ibrahim, et al., *The Copts of Egypt*, 12.
101. Cragg, *The Arab Christian*, 170.
102. *Encyclopedia Britannica*, s.v. "Dinshaway Incident."
103. Patrick, *Traditional Egyptian Christianity*, 139–140.
104. Abouseif, *Claremont Coptic Encyclopedia*, s.v. "British Occupation of Egypt."
105. Hikel, *Kharif al-Ghadab*, 273.
106. Patrick, *Traditional Egyptian Christianity*, 149.
107. Abouseif, *Claremont Coptic Encyclopedia*, s.v. "British Occupation of Egypt."
108. Carter, *The Copts in Egyptian Politics*, 290–291.
109. *Ibid.*, 60–63.
110. Gaber Asfour,"Thawrat 19 baad Tesaeen Aman..." (Revolution 19 After Ninety Years...) *al-Shorouq*, June 18, 2009, accessed August 4, 2014, http://www.shorouknews.com/columns/view.aspx?cdate=18062009&id=c212ef85-8dc3-42ed-801f-053bd09e16f2.
111. Abouseif, *Claremont Coptic Encyclopedia*, s.v. "British Occupation of Egypt."
112. Carter, *The Copts in Egyptian Politics*, 71–72.
113. *Ibid.*, 79.
114. Carter, *The Copts in Egyptian Politics*. 161–164.
115. Abouseif, *Claremont Coptic Encyclopedia*, s.v. "British Occupation of Egypt."
116. Patrick, *Traditional Egyptian Christianity*, 153.
117. Yunan Labib Rizq, "Egyptian Women Make Their Mark," *al-Ahram Weekly Online*, May 11–17, 2000, accessed August 4, 2014, http://weekly.ahram.org.eg/Archive/2000/481/chrncls.htm.
118. Colin Schultz, "In Egypt, 99 Percent of Women Have Been Sexually Harassed," *Smithsonian*, June 13, 2014, accessed August 20, 2014, http://www.smithsonianmag.com/smart-news/egypt-99-women-have-been-sexually-harassed-180951726/?no-ist.
119. Asfour,"Thawrat 19 baad Tesaeen Aman."
120. Carter, *The Copts in Egyptian Politics*, 130–133.
121. Hourani, *Minorities in The Middle East*, 42–43.
122. Carter, *The Copts in Egyptian Politics*, 211–217.
123. *Ibid.*, 223–225.
124. "Al-Qeddes Habib Guirguis 1876–1951, part 2," (St. Habib Guirguis 1876–1951), The Monastery of St. Macarius the Great, accessed April 2, 2014, http://www.stmacariusmonastery.org/st_mark/sm101303.htm.
125. Rodolph Yanney, "Light in the Darkness: Life of Archdeacon Habib Guirguis," *Coptic Church Review* 5, no. 2 (1984):47.
126. "Al-Qeddes Habib Guirguis 1876–1951" (St. Habib Guirguis 1876–1951), The Monastery of St. Macarius the Great, accessed April 2, 2014, http://www.stmacariusmonastery.org/st_mark/sm091303.htm.
127. Hikel, *Kharif al-Ghadab*, 273.
128. Y. Masriya, "A Christian Minority: The Copts in Egypt," reprinted from *Case Studies on Human Rights And Fundamental Freedoms: A World Survey, Volume Four* (The Hague: Martinus Nijhoff, 1976), 86, accessed May 11, 2014, http://www.*dhimmitude*.org/archive/by_copts_1976.pdf.
129. Mark Curtis, "Britian and the Muslim Brotherhood: Collaboration during the 1940s and 1950s," *Mark Curtis*, December 18, 2010, https://markcurtis.wordpress.com/2010/12/18/britain-and-the-muslim-brotherhood-collaboration-during-the-1940s-and-1950s/.
130. Masriya, "A Christian Minority: The Copts in Egypt," 86–87.
131. Carter, *The Copts in Egyptian Politics*, 274–277.
132. Ibrahim et al., *The Copts of Egypt*, 14.
133. Masriya, "A Christian Minority: The Copts in Egypt," 87.
134. Carter, *The Copts in Egyptian Politics*, 274–277.
135. Hourani, *Minorities in The Middle East*, 43–44.
136. Mirrit Boutros Ghali, *Claremont Coptic Encyclopedia*, s.v."Egyptian National Identity," in the Claremont Colleges Digital Library (Claremont Graduate University, School of Religion, 1991), accessed February 21, 2014,. http://ccdl.libraries.claremont.edu/cdm/ref/collection/cce/id/776.
137. Curtis, "Britian and the Muslim Brotherhood."
138. Ghali, *Claremont Coptic Encyclopedia*, s.v."Egyptian National Identity."

139. *Encyclopedia Britannica*, s.v. "Muslim Brotherhood," accessed August 3, 2014, http://www.britannica.com/topic/Muslim-Brotherhood.
140. Masriya, "A Christian Minority: The Copts in Egypt," 87.

Chapter Five

1. Robert St. John, *Encyclopedia Britannica*, s.v. "Gamal Abdel Nasser," accessed September 1, 2014, https://www.britannica.com/biography/Gamal-Abdel-Nasser.
2. Ghali, *Claremont Coptic Encyclopedia*, s.v. "Egyptian National Identity."
3. St. John, *Encyclopedia Britannica*, s.v. "Gamal Abdel Nasser."
4. Ghali, *Claremont Coptic Encyclopedia*, s.v. "Egyptian National Identity."
5. Ibrahim, *Egypt, Islam and Democracy*, 97.
6. "Abdel Nasser wa al-Gama'a min al-Wifaq ela al-Shiqaq…," (Abdel Nasser and the Group from Accord to Discord…) *al-Masry al-Youm*, October 3, 2010, accessed December 15, 2014, http://www.almasryalyoum.com/news/details/89847.
7. Magdi Abdelhadi, "Egypt: from Nasser's ideological hotchpotch to an Islamist landslide," *The Guardian*, January 2, 2012, accessed January 4, 2012, http://www.theguardian.com/commentisfree/2012/jan/02/egypt-nasser-islamist.
8. Ibrahim et al., *The Copts of Egypt*, 16.
9. Abdelhadi, "Egypt: from Nasser's ideological hotchpotch to an Islamist landslide."
10. Ibrahim Isa, "Gamal Abdel Nasser Awal man Gama' al-Quran Baad Abi Bakr…" (Gamal Abdel Nasser the First to Collect the Quran After Abu Bakr…) (youtube video, March 25, 2015), accessed March 25, 2015, https://www.youtube.com/watch?v=Ub1c0fTMHQw.
11. Abdelhadi, "Egypt: from Nasser's ideological hotchpotch to an Islamist landslide."
12. Yvonne Yazbeck Haddad, *Contemporary Islam and the Challenge of History* (Albany: State University of New York Press, 1982), 213, accessed March 20, 2015, https://books.google.com/books?id=qJGkzwljG-IC&pg=PA213&lpg=PA213&dq=Nasser+said+Islam+is+a+socialist+religion&source=bl&ots=_L0kEyknDV&sig=T9fELlE1qBxU58ClTj0Lvy40-S8&hl=en&sa=X&ved=0CB4Q6AEwAGoVChMIrLLM18L-xgIVDD4-Ch3VUwfp#v=onepage&q=Nasser%20said%20Islam%20is%20a%20socialist%20religion&f=false.
13. Patrick, *Traditional Egyptian Christianity*, 155.
14. *Ibid.*, 155.

15. Ibrahim et al., *The Copts of Egypt*, 16.
16. Dioscorus Boles, "Nasser's Damage to the Copts is Enormous," *On Coptic Nationalism*, July 23, 2012, accessed October 30, 2014, https://copticliterature.wordpress.com/2012/07/23/nassers-damage-to-the-copts-is-enormous-but-his-greatest-damage-is-the-forced-arabisation-of-copts-through-the-state-education-system/.
17. Ibrahim, *Egypt, Islam and Democracy*, 119–121.
18. Hikel, *Kharif al-Ghadab*, 279–281.
19. Said Shehata, "al-Aqbat fi Maglis al-Shaab," (Copts in the People's Assembly) *BBC Arabic*, March 19, 2012, accessed March 20, 2012, http://www.bbc.com/arabic/middleeast/2012/03/120319_christians_egypy_parliament_number_.shtml.
20. Zeidan, "The Copts—Equal, Protected or Persecuted?," 57.
21. Hikel, *Kharif al-Ghadab*, 283–284.
22. *Ibid.*, 286–287.
23. *Ibid.*, 284–287.
24. Zeidan, "The Copts—Equal, Protected or Persecuted?," 57.
25. "Report by Dr. Jamal al-'Utayfi on the al-Khankah sectarian events," Arab West Report, April 1, 2009, accessed June 11, 2011, http://www.arabwestreport.info/en/year-2009/week-13/2-report-dr-jamal-al-utayfi-al-khankah-sectarian-events.
26. Patrick, *Traditional Egyptian Christianity*, 155.
27. Ibrahim, *Egypt, Islam and Democracy*, 202.
28. "Anwar Sadat," Global Security, accessed November 11, 2014, http://www.globalsecurity.org/military/world/egypt/sadat.htm.
29. Ibrahim, *Egypt, Islam and Democracy*, 203.
30. Mikhail E. Mikhail, "His Holiness Pope Shenouda III-Biography," Coptic Orthodox Church Network, accessed November 14, 2015, http://www.copticchurch.net/topics/pope/#Biography.
31. *Ibid.*
32. "Report by Dr. Jamal al-'Utayfi on the al-Khankah sectarian events," Arab West Report.
33. Ezzat Indrawis, "al-Badeel Tarsod Mozakirat al-Baba Shenouda…" (al-Badeel Records the Journals of Pope Shenouda…) Coptic History, February 9, 2009, accessed May 23, 2015, http://www.coptichistory.org/new_page_6880.htm.
34. "Report by Dr. Jamal al-'Utayfi on the al-Khankah sectarian events," Arab West Report.
35. Special Report, "Al-Sadat wa al-Baba" (Sadat and the Pope), *al-Masry al-Youm*, No-

vember 14, 2009, accessed May 23, 2015, http://today.almasryalyoum.com/article2.aspx?ArticleID=233190.
36. "Report by Dr. Jamal al-'Utayfi on the al-Khankah sectarian events," Arab West Report.
37. Ibid.
38. Hassanien Karrom, "Gezor al-Azma..." (The Roots of the Crisis...), al-Masry al-Youm, September 10, 2008, accessed May 23, 2015, http://today.almasryalyoum.com/article2.aspx?ArticleID=177981.
39. "Liqa Amr Adeeb maa Qadasat al-Baba..." (Meeting Between Amr Adeeb and Pope Shenouda...) (youtube video), accessed February 23, 2015, https://www.youtube.com/watch?v=yKuPyBTqZgo.
40. Ibrahim, Egypt, Islam and Democracy, 203.
41. Farrag Ismail, "Baad Hewar maa Jihan al-Sadat..." (After a Dialogue with Jihan Sadat...), Al Arabiya, March 4, 2007, accessed April 13, 2015, http://www.alarabiya.net/articles/2007/03/04/32270.html.
42. Abdel Reheem Ali, "al-Sadat wa al-Ikhwan..." (Sadat and the Brotherhood), Al Bawaba, July 26, 2015, accessed July 30, 2015, http://www.albawabhnews.com/1414306.
43. Hikel, Kharif al-Ghadab, 295–296.
44. "Anwar Sadat," Global Security.
45. Hikel, Kharif al-Ghadab, 372–373.
46. Ibrahim et al., The Copts of Egypt, 18.
47. Hikel, Kharif al-Ghadab, 374–375.
48. Ibid., 376.
49. Ibrahim, et al., The Copts of Egypt, 18.
50. Ezzat Indrawis, "al-Baba Shenouda wa al-Aqbat wa Qanon al-Ridda" (Pope Shenouda, the Copts and the Apostasy Law),Coptic History, last updated March 11, 2016, accessed March 15, 2016, http://www.coptichistory.org/new_page_709.htm.
51. "Liqa Amr Adeeb maa Qadasat al-Baba...," (youtube video).
52. "Al-Nasara Todafa ann Aqbat al-Mahgir..." (Christians Defend Coptic Immigrants...) (youtube video) accessed February 23, 2015, https://www.youtube.com/watch?v=9I8KxTFOUIE.
53. Remoun Nagi, "al-Baba Shenouda bain Sedam al-Sadat wa afw Mubarak..."(Pope Shenouda Between Sadat's Confrontation and Mubarak's Amnesty...), Veto, November 14, 2014, accessed November 15, 2014, http://www.vetogate.com/1326380.
54. Ibid.
55. "Report by Dr. Jamal al-'Utayfi on the al-Khankah sectarian events," Arab West Report.
56. "Awel Ihsa' Rasmi..."(The First Official Census...), Al Arabiya, September 25, 2012, accessed August 12, 2015, http://www.alarabiya.net/articles/2012/09/25/240149.html.
57. E.J. Chitham, The Coptic Community in Egypt: Spatial and Social Change (Durham: University of Durham, 1986), 105–106.
58. Ibrahim, et al., The Copts of Egypt, 19.
59. Hikel, Kharif al-Ghadab, 375–377.
60. Ibid., 377–378.
61. Ibid., 377.
62. Francois Basili, "al-Baba Shenouda: Arbaon Aman Yaqoud al-Kanisah wa Yahtadin al-Watan" (Pope Shenouda: Forty Years Leading the Church and Upholding the Homeland), Alquds, March 28, 2012, accessed April 1, 2013, http://www.alquds.co.uk/pdfarchives/2012/03/03-27/qmd.pdf.
63. Hikel, Kharif al-Ghadab, 378–379.
64. Ibid., 249–251.
65. Ibrahim, Egypt, Islam and Democracy, 39–43.
66. Hikel, Kharif al-Ghadab, 380–381.
67. Ibid., 253.
68. Ali, "al-Sadat wa al-Ikhwan...."
69. Hikel, Kharif al-Ghadab, 251–254.
70. Sonia Farid, "Tracking Egypt's Islamic identity in the constitution," Al Arabiya, October 7, 2013, December 11, 2013, http://english.alarabiya.net/en/perspective/analysis/2013/10/07/Tracking-Islamic-identity-in-Egypt-s-constitution.html.
71. Salah Montasir, "Hikayat al-Sharia al-Islamiya wa Taadeel al-Dostor" (The Story of the Islamic Sharia and Amending the Constitution), al-Masry al-Youm, June 23, 2015, accessed June 30, 2015, http://today.almasryalyoum.com/printerfriendly.aspx?ArticleID=468688.
72. Bat Ye'or, Islam and Dhimmitude: Where Civilizations Collide, trans. Miriam Kochan and David Littman (Lancaster, UK: Gazelle Book Service Ltd., 2002), 180, accessed September 12, 2013, https://books.google.com/books?id=n4kTdYgwQPkC&pg=PA180&dq=The+abolition+of+the+ecclesiastical+courts+in+1955&hl=en&sa=X&ved=0ahUKEwir96Hr3ubMAhVJNT4KHV3_DjcQ6AEIHTAA#v=onepage&q=The%20abolition%20of%20the%20ecclesiastical%20courts%20in%201955&f=false.
73. Hikel, Kharif al-Ghadab, 248.
74. Ibid., 297.
75. Ezzat Indrawis, "Hadithat Hayy al-Zawiyah al-Hamra Bilqahira..."(The Incident of the Neighborhood of al-Zawiyah al-Hamra in Cairo...), Coptic History, last updated May 20, 2011, accessed June 3, 2012, http://www.coptichistory.org/new_page_1009.htm.
76. Muhammad Ebied, "al-Fitna al-Ta'ifiya fi Masr..." (Sectarian Strife in Egypt...), Al Arabiya, January 3, 2011, accessed January 4,

2011, http://www.alarabiya.net/articles/2011/01/03/132018.html.
77. Ibrahim, et al., *The Copts of Egypt*, 19.
78. Hikel, *Kharif al-Ghadab*, 393.
79. Patrick, *Traditional Egyptian Christianity*, 172.
80. Ibrahim, *Egypt, Islam and Democracy*, 212.
81. Hikel, *Kharif al-Ghadab*, 396.
82. Watterson, *Coptic Egypt*, 174–176.
83. Ibrahim, *Egypt, Islam and Democracy*, 202.
84. *Ibid.*, 61–62.
85. Zeidan, "The Copts—Equal, Protected or Persecuted?," 57.
86. Ezzat Indrawis, "Nemw Anshitit wa Tatawor Khidmit Madaris al-Ahad Bilkanisa al-Qibtia" (The Growth of Activities and the Development of Sunday School Service in the Coptic Church), Coptic History, last updated July 28, 2016, accessed July 30, 2016, http://www.coptichistory.org/untitled_1845.htm.
87. Patrick, *Traditional Egyptian Christianity*, 173.
88. Ibrahim, *Egypt, Islam and Democracy*, 202.
89. Muhammad Ashour, "Aasim Abel Magid: Qatl Dobbat al-Shorta fi Hadthat Assiut 1981 Sharf lee" (Aasim Abel Magid: Killing Police Officers in Assuit Incident in 1981 is an Honor to Me), *al-Watan*, May 14, 2013, accessed August 11, 2015, http://www.elwatannews.com/news/details/181884.
90. Patrick, *Traditional Egyptian Christianity*, 173.
91. Ibrahim et al., *The Copts of Egypt*, 20–21.
92. "Politics and the Brotherhood in the Mubarak Era," Islamopedia, accessed September 1, 2015, http://www.islamopediaonline.org/country-profile/egypt/politics-and-muslim-brotherhood/politics-and-brotherhood-mubarak-era.
93. Ibrahim, et al., *The Copts of Egypt*, 20–21.
94. Watterson, *Coptic Egypt*, 176.
95. Ibrahim, et al., *The Copts of Egypt*, 21.
96. *Ibid.*, 21.
97. "Awalan: Harqq Wahadm al-Kana'is Waliatida' ala al-Musalien Waqaflaha" (First: Burning, Destroying and Closing Churches and Attacking Worshippers), *Alkalema*, accessed January 12, 2014, http://www.alkalema.net/persecuate/persecuate29.htm.
98. "Politics and the Brotherhood in the Mubarak Era," Islamopedia.
99. Zeidan, "The Copts—Equal, Protected or Persecuted?," 57.
100. Saad Eddin Ibrahim, "The Road of Thorns from al-Khanka 1972 to al-Kosheh 2000," Arab West Report, February 13, 2000, accessed June 11, 2011, http://www.arabwestreport.info/en/year-2000/week-7/21-road-thorns-al-khanka-1972-al-kosheh-2000.
101. Marshall, *Egypt's Endangered Christians*, 19–21.
102. Yustina Saleh, "Law, the Rule of Law, and Religious Minorities in Egypt," Rubin Center, December 7, 2004, accessed May 2, 2014, http://www.rubincenter.org/2004/12/saleh-2004-12-07/.
103. "Politics and the Brotherhood in the Mubarak Era," Islamopedia.
104. Ala Abd al-Rihim, "Nawal al-Saadawi…," *Veto*, December 16, 2014, accessed February 10, 2015, http://www.vetogate.com/1381698.
105. Hoda Zakaria and Loai Adly, "Fi Zekra Taasisu…" (On the Anniversary of its Establishment…), *al-Youm al-Sabia*, July 23, 2015, accessed July 30, 2015, http://www.youm7.com/2275165.
106. Ahmed Fouad, "Al-Azhar refuses to consider the Islamic State an apostate," *al-Monitor*, February 12, 2015, accessed February 19, 2015, http://www.al-monitor.com/pulse/originals/2015/02/azhar-egypt-radicals-islamic-state-apostates.html#.
107. Zeidan, "The Copts—Equal, Protected or Persecuted?," 57–58.
108. Abdelhadi, "Egypt: from Nasser's ideological hotchpotch to an Islamist landslide."
109. Mukhtar Shoeeb, "al-Tiar al-Salafi…," (The Salafi Current…) *Elaph*, January 12, 2012, accessed February 3, 2012, http://elaph.com/Web/NewsPapers/2012/1/708744.html.
110. Mary Abdelmassih, "Muslims in Egypt Demand Release of Alleged Convert to Islam," *AINA*, March 30, 2011, accessed April 2, 2011, http://www.aina.org/news/20110329221230.htm.
111. Camelia Shehata, "Camelia Shehata confirms her Christian faith," (youtube video, February 17, 2011) accessed February 20, 2011, https://www.youtube.com/watch?v=pglZwQekZfE.
112. Naiem Yousef, "al-Baba Shenouda wa al-Sadat wa Mubarak…" (Pope Shenouda, Sadat and Mubarak…), Copts United, March 17, 2015, accessed April 20, 2015, http://www.copts-united.com/Article.php?I=2206&A=194078.
113. Muhammad Himida, "Balagh ela al-Naib al-Aam Yattahem Muhammad Selim al-awa Be'itharat al-Fitna al-Ta'ifya" (A Report to the Prosecutor General Accusing Muhammad Selim al-awa of Stirring Sectarian Strife), *Elaph*, September 20, 2010, accessed April 10, 2014, http://elaph.com/Web/news/2010/9/597880.html.
114. Robert Spencer, "Persecution, Kidnapping and Forced Conversions of Christians in

Egypt," *Human Events*, December 9, 2004, accessed March 12, 2015, http://humanevents.com/2004/12/09/persecution-kidnapping-and-forced-conversions-of-christians-in-egypt/.

115. *The Disappearance, Forced Conversions, and Forced Marriages of Coptic Christian Women in Egypt*, a Report commissioned by Christian Solidarity International (Westlake Village, California) and Coptic Foundation for Human Rights (Zurich, Switzerland), November, 2009, 1.

116. *Ibid.*, 6.
117. *Ibid.*, 12.
118. *Ibid.*, 10–11.
119. *Ibid.*, 39–40.
120. Marshall, *Egypt's Endangered Christians*, 52–53.
121. Leonard Blair, "Heartbreaking: Egyptian Christians Were Calling for Jesus During Execution by ISIS in Libya," *The Christian Post*, February 18, 2015, accessed February 19, 2015, http://www.christianpost.com/news/heartbreaking-egyptian-christians-were-calling-for-jesus-during-execution-by-isis-in-libya-134340/.
122. "Tanzeem Dawlat al-Iraq al-Islamiya Yatawaad al-Masihien" (Islamic State of Iraq Threatens Christians), *BBC Arabic*, November 3, 2010, accessed April 15, 2014, http://www.bbc.com/arabic/middleeast/2010/11/101102_coptic_egypt_qaeda_iraq.shtml.
123. Marshall, *Egypt's Endangered Christians*, 32.
124. Spencer, "Persecution, Kidnapping and Forced Conversions of Christians in Egypt."
125. Saleh, "Law, the Rule of Law, and Religious Minorities in Egypt."
126. Watterson, *Coptic Egypt*, 175.
127. *Egypt Prohibited Identities: State Interference with Religious Freedom* (Human Rights Watch and EIPR, November 2007) 19, no. 7(E), 76, accessed June 2, 2015, http://eipr.org/en/publications/prohibited-identities (pdf).
128. *Ibid.*, 56.
129. *Ibid.*, 1–2.
130. *Ibid.*, 76–78.
131. Mayer, *Islam and Human Rights*, 10–13.
132. *Ibid.*, 81–82.
133. Saleh, "Law, the Rule of Law, and Religious Minorities in Egypt."
134. Ezzat Indrawis, "Hegom Mosalah Bilmadafea al-Rashasha Ala Rohban Dier Abu Fana..." (Armed attack with Machine Guns on the Monks of Abu Fana Monsastery...), Coptic History, last updated August 11, 2010, accessed December 15, 2013, http://www.coptichistory.org/new_page_5373.htm.
135. *Egypt: Keep Promise to Free Detainees by End of June...* (EIPR, June 29, 2010), accessed February 21, 2012, http://www.eipr.org/en/press/2010/06/egypt-keep-promise-free-detainees-end-june-may-11-emergency-law-revisions-mean-no.

136. Emad Khalil, "al-Shabaka 'al-'Arabya Tatahim Segn Borg al-Arab Bimusawamat Nazer..." (The Arab Net Accuses Borg al-Arab Prison of Negotiating with Nazer...), Copts United, June 8, 2009, accessed March 11, 2011, http://www.copts-united.com/article.php?I=163&A=5936.

137. U.S. Department of State. Bureau of Democracy, Human Rights, and Labor. *International Religious Freedom Report 2010*, November 17, 2010, accessed April 10, 2012, http://www.state.gov/j/drl/rls/irf/2010/148817.htm.

138. Marshall, *Egypt's Endangered Christians*, 36.

139. Hany Nasirah, "al-Ta'ifya Qabl Wabaad al-Thawra al-Masryah" (Sectarianism Before and After the Egyptian Revolution), *Aljazeera*, July 23, 2011, accessed April 10, 2012, http://studies.aljazeera.net/ar/issues/2011/07/201172374514916553.html.

140. Zeidan, "The Copts—Equal, Protected or Persecuted?," 58.

141. Mayer, *Islam and Human Rights*, 132–133.

142. Marshall, *Egypt's Endangered Christians*, 39–40.

143. *Ibid.*, 40–42.

144. Zeidan, "The Copts—Equal, Protected or Persecuted?," 57–58.

145. *Two years of sectarian violence: What happened? Where do we begin?* (Freedom of Religion and Belief Program, EIPR, April 2010), 5, accessed August 1, 2013, http://eipr.org/sites/default/files/reports/pdf/Sectarian_Violence_inTwoYears_EN.pdf.

146. Yousef, "al-Baba Shenouda wa al-Sadat wa Mubarak."

147. Rania Nabil, "Min Hadithat al-Khanka 1972 Hata Hadithat al-Omraniya 2010," (From the Incident of al-Khanka 1972 Until the Incident of al-Omraniya 2010) Copts United, December 20, 2010, accessed August 2, 2013, http://www.copts-united.com/Article.php?I=971&A=27454.

148. "Hawl al-Eitikaf al-Gadid Lilbaba Shenouda" (About the New Seclusion of Pope Shenouda), Copts United, December 18, 2010, accessed August 2, 2013, http://www.copts-united.com/article.php?I=660&A=27379.

149. Pope Shenouda, "Rad al-Baba Hawl Ahdath Kanisah al-Omraniya" (Pope Shenouda's Answer Regarding the Incident of the al-Omraniya Church) (youtube video, December 12, 2010), accessed August 3, 2013, https://www.youtube.com/watch?v=PNH7VhqcmBM.

150. Abdel Reheem Ali, "Hadithat al-Qideseen Waltareeq ela 25 Yanaier..." (The Incident of al-Qideseen and the Road to January

25...), *Al Bawaba*, December 31, 2014, accessed August 6, 2013, http://www.albawabhnews.com/1013258.

151. *Rose al-Yousif*, Robeer al-Faris, "al-Aqbat ... Shararat al-Thawarat," (The Copts ... The Spark of the Revolutions) Masress, January 25, 2014, accessed February 1, 2014, http://www.masress.com/rosaweekly/1005816.

152. Zeidan, "The Copts—Equal, Protected or Persecuted?,"57.

153. Abdelhadi, "Egypt: from Nasser's ideological hotchpotch to an Islamist landslide."

Chapter Six

1. Hosam Bahgat, "Who Let the Jihadists Out?," *Mada*, February 16, 2014, accessed February 20, 2014, http://www.madamasr.com/en/2014/02/16/feature/politics/who-let-the-jihadis-out/.

2. Mourad Wahba, interview by Muhammad Nasr, "Mourad Wahba fi Hewar lelbawaba..." (Mourad Wahba in His Interview with Al Bawaba...), *Al Bawaba*, October 6, 2015, accessed October 7, 2015, https://www.albawabhnews.com/1533608.

3. Sherif Tarek, "Egypt's Muslim Brotherhood and Ruling Military: Deal or no deal?," *Ahramonline*, September 28, 2011, accessed September 30, 2011, http://english.ahram.org.eg/NewsContent/1/64/22042/Egypt/Politics-/Egypts-Muslim-Brotherhood-and-ruling-military-Deal.aspx.

4. Ibid.

5. Noora Fakhry, Muhammad al-Bedewy and Ramy Nawar, "Sekhonat al-Istefta' Tasil Zorwataha..." (The Heat Surrounding the Referendum Reaches its Peak...), *al-Youm al-Sabia*, March 19, 2011, accessed March 20, 2011, http://www.youm7.com/story/0000/0/0/-/372929.

6. Ahmad Mahgob, "al-Ikhwan Tattahem Rafedi Ta'dil al-Dostor..." (The Brotherhood Accuses Refusers of the Constitution Amendment...), *al-Masry al-Youm*, March 17, 2011, accessed March 17, 2011, http://www.almasryalyoum.com/news/details/119714.

7. Remoun Yousef, "Ighlaq Amakin al-Iqtira..." (Closing the Polling Stations...), Copts United, March 19, 2011, accessed March 20, 2011, http://www.copts-united.com/Article.php?I=2214&A=33109.

8. Muhammad Hussein Yaqub, "Ghazwat al-Sanadiq" (The Ballot Box Foray) (youtube video, March 22, 2011), accessed March 23, 2011, https://www.youtube.com/watch?v=tnOxAQGFSHU.

9. Tarek, "Egypt's Muslim Brotherhood and Ruling Military: Deal or no deal?"

10. Bahgat, "Who Let the Jihadists Out?"

11. Mary Abdelmassih, "Nearly 4000 Muslims Attack Christian Homes in Egypt, Torch Church," *AINA*, March 5, 2011, accessed March 6, 2011, http://www.aina.org/news/2011030422016.htm.

12. Mary Abdelmassih, "Christian Copts in Egypt Protest Muslim Attacks," *AINA*, March 8, 2011, accessed March 8, 2011, http://www.aina.org/news/20110307205517.htm.

13. Mary Abdelmassih, "9 Christians Killed, 150 Injured in Attack By 15,000 Muslims and Egyptian Army," *AINA*, March 9, 2011, accessed March 9, 2011, http://www.aina.org/news/20110308211907.htm.

14. "Kalimat al-Sheikh Muhammad Hassan fi Sul, Itfeh" (The Speech of al-Sheikh Muhammad Hassan in Sul, Itfeh) (youtube video, March 14, 2011), accessed March 15, 2011, https://www.youtube.com/watch?v=iFrdRE2lz9o.

15. "'Ala Nafaqatiha al-Khasa..." (At Its Own Expense...) (youtube video, March 13, 2011), accessed March 14, 2011, https://www.youtube.com/watch?v=HqVz2_PJcE0.

16. Girgis Bushra and Theresa Samir, "al-Hala' Yositer 'ala Aqbat Sul..." (Fear Dominates the Copts of Sul...), Copts United, March 7, 2011, March 7, 2011, http://www.copts-united.com/Article.php?I=735&A=32325.

17. Megally, *Claremont Coptic Encyclopedia*, s.v. "Waq'at AL-kana'is."

18. Mary Abdelmassih, "Muslims Attack Christians in Egypt, 12 Killed, 232 Injured," *AINA*, May 8, 2011, accessed May 10, 2011, http://www.aina.org/news/20110508144114.htm.

19. Mary Abdelmassih, "Muslim Mob Torches Coptic Church in Egypt," *AINA*, October 1, 2011, accessed October 2, 2011, http://www.aina.org/news/20110930204413.htm.

20. Mary Abdelmassih, "Muslims Blockade Christian Village in Egypt, Demand Demolition of Church," *AINA*, September 8, 2011, accessed September 8, 2011, http://www.aina.org/news/20110908193725.htm.

21. Abdelmassih, "Muslim Mob Torches Coptic Church in Egypt."

22. *Al-Tahgir al-Qasry liaqbat Rafah...* (Forced Migration of the Cops of Rafah...) (EIPR, September 30, 2012), accessed October 2, 2012, http://eipr.org/pressrelease/2012/09/30/1505.

23. Mary Abdelmassih, "Muslims Attack Two Christian Families in Egypt, 11 Killed," *AINA*, February 3, 2011, accessed February 3, 2011, http://www.aina.org/news/20110202205758.htm.

24. *Egypt: New Law Keeps Military Trials of Civilians* (Human Rights Watch, May 7, 2012), accessed May 10, 2012, https://www.hrw.org/news/2012/05/07/egypt-new-law-keeps-military-trials-civilians.

25. "Masirah Bimasr Tohamil al-Maglis al-Askry Mas'oliat Qatl 27 Nashitan Masihian," (A Cairo Protest Blames the SCAF for the Death of 27 Christian Activists) *Reuters*, November 12, 2011, accessed November 12, 2011, http://ara.reuters.com/article/topNews/idARACAE7AB00K20111112.

26. "Chars de l'armée égyptienne écrasé les manifestants égyptiens" (Egyptian Army Tanks Crushed Egyptian Protesters, October 15, 2011), accessed October 16, 2011, https://www.youtube.com/watch?v=ooKcRlRytrY&feature=player_embedded.

27. *Egyptian army must answer for deadly toll at Coptic protest* (Amnesty International, October 11, 2011), accessed October 12, 2011, https://www.amnesty.org/en/latest/news/2011/10/deadly-clashes-coptic-protest-egypt-show-urgent-need-reform/.

28. Jack Shenker and Barry Neild, "Cairo clashes leave at least 24 dead," *The Guardian*, October 9, 2011, accessed October 11, 2011, http://www.theguardian.com/world/2011/oct/09/egypt-protests-cairo-clashes.

29. Tony Karon, "As Violence Roils Cairo's Streets, What Does Egypt's Junta Want?," *Time*, October 9, 2011, accessed October 11, 2011, http://world.time.com/2011/10/09/as-violence-roils-cairos-streets-what-does-egypts-junta-want/.

30. Ezzat Indrawis, "Hegom al-Gish al-Masry Bilmodraat ala Dier al-Anba Bishoy," (Egyptian Army Tank Attack on St. Bishoy Monastery) Coptic History, last updated March 28, 2015, accessed May 30, 2015, http://www.coptichistory.org/untitled_1512.htm.

31. "Tafaseel Aeteda' al-Gish ala Dier al-Anba Boula Belbahr al-Ahmar-Part One and Two," (The Details of the Army Aggression on St. Paul Monastery in the Red Sea) (youtube video, February 27, 2011), accessed March 3, 2011 (part one) https://www.youtube.com/watch?v=E8dE-L3jSf8 and (part two) https://www.youtube.com/watch?v=jis8jnOsUv4.

32. Paul Marshall, "Egypt's Other Extremists: While the Muslim Brotherhood get all the ink, the Salafists go on a rampage," *The Weekly Standard*, May 16, 2011, accessed May 17, 2011, http://www.weeklystandard.com/egypts-other-extremists/article/559363.

33. *Ibid*.

34. Mary Abdelmassih "Egyptian Christian Girl Banned from School for Not Wearing a Veil," *AINA*, September 28, 2011, accessed September 28, 2011, http://www.aina.org/news/20110928112952.htm.

35. Ashraf Sadeq, "Modir Amn al-Minia: Christin wa Nancy Qaseratan…," (Minia Chief of Police: Christin and Nancy are Underage…) *al-Ahram*, accessed July 20, 2011, http://www.ahram.org.eg/archive/The-First/News/84291.aspx.

36. Saki Knafo, "The Story Of Maikel Nabil Sanad: The Egyptian Blogger Jailed For Taking On The Military," *The World Post*, April 15, 2011, accessed April 20, 2011, http://www.huffingtonpost.com/2011/04/15/maikal-nabil-sanad_n_849603.html.

37. "Mahkama Masriya Tolzem al-Hokomah Be'isqat al-ginsiyah 'an Nashit Qibti," (An Egyptian Court Orders the Government to Rescind a Coptic Activist's Citizenship) *Reuters*, May 22, 2011, accessed May 22, 2011, http://ara.reuters.com/article/topNews/idARACAE74L0GY20110522?pageNumber=1&virtualBrandChannel=0.

38. Mary Abdelmassih, "100,000 Christians Have Left Egypt Since March: Report," *AINA*, September 26, 2011, accessed September 26, 2011, http://www.aina.org/news/20110926194822.htm.

39. Soliman Shafiq, "al-Nokhab al-Qibtia al-Gadida min al-Ta'ifya Lilwatanya" (The New Coptic Elite from Sectarianism to Patriotism), *al-Watan*, September 7, 2013, accessed September 10, 2013, http://www.elwatannews.com/news/details/307635.

40. Pope Tawadros, "Leqa' al-Baba Tawadros…" (Interview with Pope Tawadros…) (youtube video, March 20, 2014), accessed April 11, 2014, https://www.youtube.com/watch?v=wrXQM2UyGG4.

41. Farida Alim, "The Politics of the Brotherhood Democracy: How the Muslim Brotherhood Burned Their Bridges," *Jadaliyya*, July 19, 2013, accessed September 30, 2013, http://www.jadaliyya.com/pages/index/13062/the-politics-of-the-brotherhood-democracy_how-the-.

42. *Ibid*.

43. "Ibrahim Yo'kid: Tam mana al-Aqbat min al-Taswet Bilintikhabat al-Ri'asya Limorsi" (Ibrahim Confirms: The Copts were Banned from Voting in Morsi's Presidential Elections), Copts United, March 10, 2015, accessed May 2, 2015, http://www.copts-united.com/Article.php?I=2199&A=192988.

44. Alim, "The Politics of the Brotherhood Democracy: How the Muslim Brotherhood Burned Their Bridges."

45. Wael Eskandar, "Brothers and Officers: A History of Pacts," *Jadaliyya*, January 25, 2013, accessed March 1, 2013, http://www.jadaliyya.com/pages/index/9765/brothers-and-officers_a-history-of-pacts.

46. "Muhammad Morsi Ya'lin Fawzoh Bir-i'asat Masr Qabl Aelan al-Natiga Rasmyan" (Muhammad Morsi Declares his Presidential Victory Before the Official Results Announcement) (youtube video, June 17, 2012), accessed

June 17, 2012, https://www.youtube.com/watch?v=BC54Y5JS_uE.
47. Eskandar, "Brothers and Officers: A History of Pacts."
48. Ibid.
49. Alim, "The Politics of the Brotherhood Democracy: How the Muslim Brotherhood Burned Their Bridges."
50. Mustafa Rizq, "Morsi wa al-Qadaa...," (Morsi and the Judiciary...) *Aljazeera*, last updated June 30, 2013, accessed July 28, 2013, http://www.aljazeera.net/news/reportsandinterviews/2013/6/30/%D9%85%D8%B1%D8%B3%D9%8A-%D9%88%D8%A7%D9%84%D9%82%D8%B6%D8%A7%D8%A1-%D8%B5%D8%B1%D8%A7%D8%B9-%D8%A7%D9%84%D8%A5%D8%B1%D8%A7%D8%AF%D8%A7%D8%AA.
51. Ibid.
52. "Nabza Aan al-Ikhwan al-Muslmeen fi Masr," (A Brief about the Muslim Brotherhood in Egypt) *BBC Arabic*, July 7, 2013, accessed September 9, 2013, http://www.bbc.com/arabic/middleeast/2013/07/130706_ikhwan_profile.
53. Alim, "The Politics of the Brotherhood Democracy: How the Muslim Brotherhood Burned Their Bridges."
54. "Al-Aqbat fi Aahd Morsi" (The Copt in Morsi's Era), *Islamists Movements*, February 2, 2014, accessed March 20, 2014, http://www.islamist-movements.com/2290.
55. Safwat Higazy, "Safwat Higazy ya'tarif...," (Safwat Higazy Confesses...) (youtube video, August 21, 2013), accessed August 22, 2013, https://www.youtube.com/watch?v=Az7L8BGZndA.
56. "Magzarat al-Itihadya..." (The Slaughter at al-Itihaya Palace...), *Al Bawaba*, December 5, 2013, accessed December 20, 2013, http://www.albawabhnews.com/249460.
57. "Darb Wasahl Waihana Muhandis Mina Philip" (Beating, Dragging and Insulting Engineer Mina Philip) (youtube video, December 9, 2012), accessed December 15, 2012, https://www.youtube.com/watch?v=HpEJUDTeRD4.
58. Alim, "The Politics of the Brotherhood Democracy: How the Muslim Brotherhood Burned Their Bridges."
59. Rizq, "Morsi wa al-Qadaa."
60. Amr Khan, "Azmaat al-Magalis al-Istesharia fi Masr Baad Thawrat Yanaier..." (The Crisis of Advisory Boards After the January Revolution...), *Veto*, September 7, 2014, accessed September 20, 2014, http://www.vetogate.com/1211261.
61. "Samir Morcos: Qararat Morsi Mu'awiqa Lildemocratya" (Samir Morcos: Morsi's Decisions are Hindering Democracy), *Al Arabiya*, November 24, 2012, accessed December 1, 2012, http://www.alarabiya.net/articles/2012/11/24/251455.html.
62. "Morsi Yolghi al-Aelan al-Destori..." (Morsi Annuls the Constitutional Declaration...), *Al Arabiya*, December 9, 2012, accessed December 9, 2012, http://www.alarabiya.net/articles/2012/12/09/254060.html.
63. Flex 10, "Egypt: Huge crowds of Brotherhood besieging the Supreme Constitutional Court in Egypt," *CNN iReport*, December 1, 2012, accessed December 3, 2012, http://ireport.cnn.com/docs/DOC-889221.
64. Nicolas Weid, "Masr: Maza Takshif Nata'ig al-Intikhabat..." (Egypt: What Do the Results of the Elections Reveal...), *BBC Arabic*, August 30, 2013, accessed September 13, 2013, http://www.bbc.com/arabic/middleeast/2013/08/130830_egypt_ikhwan_politics.
65. Muhammad Khial, "Ghorfit 'Amaliat al-Ikhwan Tatahim al-Kanisah bihashd al-Rahibat" (The Brotherhood Operation Room Accuses the Church of Mobilizing the Nuns), *al-Shorouk*, December 15, 2012, December 23, 2012, http://www.shorouknews.com/news/view.aspx?cdate=15122012&id=170e4633-a89d-4517-b076-3ce963a1da07.
66. Robert Spencer, "Egypt: Coptic Pope criticizes Sharia constitution," Jihad Watch, February 6, 2013, accessed March 1, 2013, https://www.jihadwatch.org/2013/02/egypt-coptic-pope-criticizes-sharia-constitution.
67. Markus Tozman, "Old Wine, New Skin? An Analysis of Egypt's New Constitution," *Charisma News*, January 16, 2014, accessed January 20, 2014, http://www.charismanews.com/opinion/42439-old-wine-new-skin-an-analysis-of-egypt-s-new-constitution.
68. Nariman Youssef, "Egypt's draft constitution translated," *Egypt Independent*, December 2, 2012, accessed December 3, 2012, http://www.egyptindependent.com/news/egypt-s-draft-constitution-translated.
69. Rizq, "Morsi wa al-Qadaa."
70. Mustafa al-Marsafawy, Aiat al-Habbal and Umar Abdel Aziz, "Al-Masry al-Youm Tarsod Amaliet Akhwanat al-Dawla..." (Al-Masry al-Youm Records the Country's Brotherhoodization Process...), *al-Masry al-Youm*, February 14, 2013, accessed March 1, 2013, http://www.almasryalyoum.com/news/details/286656.
71. Reham Mokbel, "Egypt forces Brotherhood judges to retire," *Al-Monitor*, January 7, 2015, accessed January 9, 2015, http://www.al-monitor.com/pulse/ar/originals/2015/01/egypt-president-decision-muslim-brotherhood-judges-retire.html.
72. "Moqabala-Baba al-Aqbat al-Orthozox..." (Interview with the Coptic Orthodox Pope...), *Reuters*, April 26, 2013, accessed April 30, 2013, http://ara.reuters.com/article/topNews/idARA

CAE9B2A1I20130426?pageNumber=1&virtualBrandChannel=0.
	73. "Christian Killed in Attack on Coptic Mourners in Egypt," *Morning Star News,* April 7, 2013, accessed April 10, 2013, http://morningstarnews.org/2013/04/christian-killed-in-brazen-attack-on-coptic-mourners-in-egypt/.
	74. "Al-Sabab Wara' Magzarat al-Aqbat wa al-Muslmeen fi al-Khusus" (The Reason Behind the Slaughter of Copts and Muslims in al-Khusus) (youtube video, April 6, 2013), accessed April 11, 2013, https://www.youtube.com/watch?v=TLKqmD8ImHU.
	75. "Christian Killed in Attack on Coptic Mourners in Egypt."
	76. Mustafa Rahouma, "Tafasil Inqlab al-Kanisa ala Morsi…" (The Details of the Church's Dissatisfaction with Morsi…), *al-Watan,* April 11, 2013, accessed April 13, 2013, http://www.elwatannews.com/news/details/162696.
	77. "Moqabala-Baba al-Aqbat al-Orthozox."
	78. *Ibid.*
	79. "Ghomod Hawl Hedor Morsi Marasim Tansib al-Baba" (Mystery Surrounding Morsi's Attendance at the Pope's Installation), *Al Arabiya,* November 10, 2012, accessed November 15, 2012, http://www.alarabiya.net/articles/2012/11/10/248708.html.
	80. Associated Press, "Coptic Pope Tawadros II criticizes Egypt's Islamist leadership, new constitution," *Ahram Online,* February 5, 2013, accessed February 7, 2013, http://english.ahram.org.eg/NewsContent/1/64/64135/Egypt/Politics-/Coptic-Pope-Tawadros-II-criticises-Egypts-Islamist.aspx.
	81. *Egypt 2013 Annual Report,* United States Commission on International Religious Freedom, 6–7, accessed March 11, 2015, http://www.uscirf.gov/sites/default/files/resources/Egypt%202013.pdf.
	82. *Egypt 2014 Annual Report,* United States Commission on International Religious Freedom, 52, accessed March 11, 2015, http://www.uscirf.gov/sites/default/files/Egypt%202014.pdf.
	83. Associated Press, "Coptic Christian latest target of blasphemy frenzy under Islamist-ruled Egypt," *Fox News,* May 18, 2013, accessed May 30, 2013, http://www.foxnews.com/world/2013/05/18/coptic-christian-latest-target-blasphemy-frenzy-under-islamist-ruled-egypt.html.
	84. *Ibid.*
	85. *Ibid.*
	86. Associated Press, "Egyptian Christian teacher sentenced for blasphemy," *Al Arabiya,* June 16, 2014, accessed June 20, 2014, http://english.alarabiya.net/en/News/2014/06/16/Egyptian-Christian-teacher-sentenced-for-blasphemy.html.
	87. Mary Abdelmassih, "120 Christian Families Flee Egyptian Village Following Death of a Muslim," *AINA,* July 31, 2012, accessed August 2, 2012, http://www.aina.org/news/201207 31192433.htm.
	88. Mary Abdelmassih, "Muslims Order Christians Out of Their Village in Egypt," *AINA,* September 28, 2012, accessed September 30, 2012, http://www.aina.org/news/2012092819 2826.htm.
	89. Ashraf Sweilam and Maggie Michael, "Christians flee Egypt's Sinai after militant killings," *The Washington Post* (Associated Press), February 24, 2017, accessed February 24, 2017, https://www.washingtonpost.com/world/middle_east/egypt-officials-christian-killed-in-sinai-sixth-in-a-month/2017/02/24/4dc95816-fa65-11e6-aa1e-5f735ee31334_story.html?utm_term=.dbeba19f587f.
	90. Mustafa Mahmoud, "Video Muhafiz Shamal Sina: al-Ailat al-Qibtya Lam Tohagar min al-Arish" (Video the Governor of North Sinai: The Coptic Families Were not Forced to Migrate from al-Arish), *al-Wafd,* February 25, 2017, accessed February 26, 2017, http://alwafd.org/article/1465319.
	91. Cam McGrath, "Missing Christian Girls Leave Trail of Tears," *Inter Press Service,* April 16, 2013, accessed May 30, 2013, http://www.ipsnews.net/2013/04/missing-christian-girls-leave-trail-of-tears/.
	92. Mary Abdelmassih, "Coptic Christian Girl, 14, Abducted By Muslim in Egypt," *AINA,* November 2, 2012, accessed November 3, 2012, http://www.aina.org/news/20121101201755.htm.
	93. Hamza Hendawi, "Kidnappers target Christians in Egyptian province," *Associated Press,* April 4, 2013, accessed April 15, 2013, http://bigstory.ap.org/article/kidnappers-target-christians-egyptian-province.
	94. Abul Ezz Tawfiq, "Niabit Deir Mowas Toqarir Habs al-Motahim…" (Deir Mowas Prosecutor Decided to Imprison the Accused…), Copts United, May 29, 2013, accessed June 11, 2013, http://www.copts-united.com/Article.php?I=1973&A=96636.
	95. Shafiq, "al-Nokhab al-Qibtia al-Gadida min al-Ta'ifya Lilwatanya."
	96. Gamal Girgis al-Mizahim, "Bilswar… Akbar Higra Gamaiya Lilaqbaat ela Georgia…" (With Pictures… The Largest Coptic Group Immigration to Georgia…), *al-Youm al-Sabia,* March 21, 2013, accessed April 11, 2013, http://www.youm7.com/988386.
	97. Joel Hilliker, "The Shockingly Rapid Radicalization of Egypt," *The Trumpet,* August 22, 2012, accessed February 11, 2013, https://www.thetrumpet.com/article/9774.7.0.0/religion/islam/the-shockingly-rapid-radicalization-of-egypt.

98. Zenobia Azeem, "Is Egypt Culture Ministry Sit-In a Warm Up for June 30 Protests?," *al-Monitor*, June 12, 2013, accessed July 30, 2013, http://www.al-monitor.com/pulse/originals/2013/06/sit-in-warm-up-june-30-protests-in-egypt.html#.
99. Bahgat, "Who Let the Jihadists Out?"
100. "Muhafiz al-Oxor Yastaqeel min Mansibu..." (The Governor of Luxor Resigns...), Radio Sawa, June 23, 2013, accessed June 25, 2013, http://www.radiosawa.com/content/luxor-governor-resigns-debate-gamaa-islamiya/226086.html.
101. Azeem, "Is Egypt Culture Ministry Sit-In a Warm Up for June 30 Protests?"

Chapter Seven

1. "Harakit Tamarod," (Tamarod Movement) *Aljazeera*, June 29, 2013, accessed July 17, 2013, http://www.aljazeera.net/news/reportsandinterviews/2013/6/29/%D8%AD%D8%B1%D9%83%D8%A9-%D8%AA%D9%85%D8%B1%D8%AF.
2. Sheera Frenkel, "How Egypt's Rebel Movement Helped Pave The War For A Sisi Presidency," *Buzzfeed News*, April 15, 2014, accessed April 16, 2014, https://www.buzzfeed.com/sheerafrenkel/how-egypts-rebel-movement-helped-pave-the-way-for-a-sisi-pre?utm_term=.theMjQ8Dk#.dpev4G8mO.
3. Asma Ajroudi, "Four years on from Egypt's uprising, are Copts better off?" *Al Arabiya*, January 24, 2015, accessed January 24, 2015, http://english.alarabiya.net/en/perspective/analysis/2015/01/24/Four-years-on-from-Egypt-s-uprising-are-Copts-better-off-.html.
4. Khalid Zaki, "Baba al-Aqbat al-Batriark Yoalen al-Ghadab" (The Coptic Pope the Patriarch Declares Anger), *Veto*, July 3, 2015, accessed July 12, 2015, http://www.vetogate.com/1708112.
5. "Al-Irhabion Yohadidon Aqbat Masr..." (The Terrorists Threaten Egypt's Copts...), *Almogaz*, June 29, 2013, accessed July 12, 2015, http://almogaz.com/news/politics/2013/06/29/982481.
6. Samir Umar and Aya Radi, "Masr Tata'hhab Lisaat al-Sifr" (Egypt Gets Ready for Zero Hour), *Sky News Arabia*, June 29, 2013, accessed July 13, 2013, http://www.skynewsarabia.com/web/article/314342/%D9%85%D8%B5%D8%B1-%D8%AA%D8%AA%D8%A7%D9%87%D8%A8-%D9%84%D8%B3%D8%A7%D8%B9%D8%A9-%D8%A7%D9%84%D8%B5%D9%81%D8%B1.
7. "Egyptian army issues all parties 48-hours ultimatum to reach resolution," *Al Arabiya*, July 1, 2013, accessed July 13, 2013, http://english.alarabiya.net/en/News/middle-east/2013/07/01/Egyptian-army-issues-all-parties-48-hour-ultimatum-to-reach-resolution.html.
8. Naiem Girgis, "Scapegoating the Copts," *National Review Online*, July 31, 2013, accessed August 30, 2013, http://www.nationalreview.com/article/354793/scapegoating-copts-girgis-naiem.
9. Ibid.
10. Ajroudi, "Four years on from Egypt's uprising, are Copts better off?."
11. *All According to Plan* (Human Rights Watch, August 12, 2014), accessed August 30, 2014, https://www.hrw.org/report/2014/08/12/all-according-plan/raba-massacre-and-mass-killings-protesters-egypt.
12. Shaaban Hedia and Michael Faris, "al-Aqbat Yadfaaun Fatorat Tafaggor Mogat al-Irhab Baad azl Morsi,."
13. Mustafa Muhammad, "Tahqiqat al-Niaba fi *Hadith* Kanisat al-Warraq" (Prosecution Investigation into the Incident of al-Warraq Church), *al-Shorouk*, October 21, 2013, accessed October 21, 2013, http://www.shorouknews.com/news/view.aspx?cdate=21102013&id=40f6641e-1a6e-4eb5-9ba0-e5b415920a0f.
14. Mayer, *Islam and Human Rights*, 136.
15. "Mahdi Akef Murshed al-Ikhwan al-Sabiq."
16. Muhammad Sobhi, "al-Watan Tarsod Abraz al-Mawaqif al-Qatariya al-Daima Lilikhwan" (al-Watan Records the Most Salient Situation of Qatari Support to the Brotherhood), *al-Watan*, July 5, 2015, accessed July 30, 2015, http://www.elwatannews.com/news/details/763997.
17. "Safirat America Totheer Ghadab al-Muaarada wa al-Askar Bimasr" (U.S. Ambassador Elicits Anger of the Opposition and the Military in Egypt), *CNN Arabic*, June 21, 2013, accessed June 22, 2013, http://archive.arabic.cnn.com/2013/middle_east/6/21/egypt.UAambassador/.
18. "Bea Masr..." (Selling Egypt...), *al-Watan*, April 7, 2013, accessed June 9, 2013, http://www.elwatannews.com/news/details/160188.
19. Ashraf Abdel Hamid, "Abbas: Rafadt Istlam 1000 km fi Sina Ayam Morsi"(Abbas: Refused to Receive 1000 km in Sinai During Morsi), *Al Arabiya*, November 9, 2015, accessed December 30, 2015, http://ara.tv/2m355.
20. "Al-Biltagy Yotalib Biltadakhol al-Dawli Lihmaiet Motazahiri Rabaa..."(Al-Biltagy Demands International Intervention to Protect the Demonstrators of Rabaa...) (youtube video, July 14, 2014), accessed July 15, 2014, https://www.youtube.com/watch?v=FvwMoYIgW_s.
21. "Kalimat al-Ra'is Muhammad Morsi fi Mo'tamar Daem al-Thawra al-Soriya Bilistad"

(President Muhammad Morsi's Speech in a Stadium Rally to Support the Syrian Revolution) (youtube video, June 15, 2013) accessed June 16, 2013, https://www.youtube.com/watch?v=uAqVca4LCgs.

22. "al-Ahkam wa al-Mutabaat al-Qadaiya fe Haq Morsi"(Morsi's Verdicts and Results), *Aljazeera*, November 18, 2016, accessed November 18, 2016, http://www.aljazeera.net/encyclopedia/events/2016/11/17/%D8%A7%D9%84%D8%A3%D8%AD%D9%83%D8%A7%D9%85-%D9%88%D8%A7%D9%84%D9%85%D8%AA%D8%A7%D8%A8%D8%B9%D8%A7%D8%AA-%D8%A7%D9%84%D9%82%D8%B6%D8%A7%D8%A6%D9%8A%D8%A9-%D9%81%D9%8A-%D8%AD%D9%82%D9%82%D9%82%D9%82%D9%82%D9%85%D8%B1%D8%B3%D9%8A.

23. "El-Sisi: al-Aqbat Leabu dawran Watanian Aqib Harq al-Kana'is Baad 30 Yonio"(El-Sisi: The Copts Played a Patriotic Role When Churches Burned After June 30) (youtube video, May 19, 2014) accessed May 20, 2014, https://www.youtube.com/watch?v=k01QuZxjWWg.

24. "Itihad al-Muhamin al-Arab Yodin Qatl 4 Shiite Masrieen..." (Arab Lawyers Union condemns the Killing of 4 Shiite Egyptians...), *al-Watan*, June 24, 2013, accessed June 25, 2013, http://www.elwatannews.com/news/details/209112.

25. "Wazeer al-Thaqafa Masr Dawla 'ilmaniya," (The Minister of Culture: Egypt is a Secular State) (youtube video, November 29, 2015), accessed December 1, 2015, https://www.youtube.com/watch?v=KWbtRBsEYCQ.

26. Ahmad Dawd, "Lagnat al-Khamseen Tonaqish Moswadat al-Dostor..." (The 50 Member Committee Discusses the Draft Constitution...), *al-Akhbar*, October 27, 2013, accessed October 28, 2013, http://akhbar.akhbarelyom.com/newdetails.aspx?sec=dd&g=6&id=160166.

27. "Egypt Labels Brotherhood 'terrorist' Group," *Al Arabiya*, December 24, 2013, accessed December 24, 2013, http://english.alarabiya.net/en/News/middle-east/2013/12/24/Egypt-s-PM-labels-Brotherhood-terrorist-group-html.

28. Safa' Salih, "al-Ra'is fi al-Katedra'ya..." (The President at the Cathedral...), *al-Masry al-Youm*, January 7, 2014, accessed June 2, 2015, http://today.almasryalyoum.com/article2.aspx?ArticleID=409419.

29. Al-Baba Tawadros al-Thani, "Qawl Naam Yazid al-Niaam" (Saying Yes Increases Grace), *al-Ahram*, January 13, 2014, accessed January 15, 2014, http://www.ahram.org.eg/NewsQ/253064.aspx.

30. Patrick Kingsley, "Egypt's new constitution gets 98% 'yes' vote," *The Guardian*, January 18, 2014, accessed January 20, 2014, http://www.theguardian.com/world/2014/jan/18/egypt-constitution-yes-vote-mohamed-morsi.

31. Zakaria Ramzy, "Al-Minia fi al-Markaz al-Awal bi 64 Hala..." (Minia in First Place with 64 Cases...), *al-Sabah*, July 19, 2014, accessed July 30, 2014, http://www.elsaba7.com/NewsDtl.aspx?Id=132179.

32. Ajroudi, "Four years on from Egypt's uprising, are Copts better off?."

33. "Kilmat al-Ra'is el-Sisi Lilshaab..." (The Speech of President el-Sisi to the Public...) (youtube video, February 22, 2015), accessed March 12, 2015, https://www.youtube.com/watch?v=XyPCBo82TXM.

34. "Mosallahoun Yaatadoun Ala Kanisat al-Saieda al-Azra' Beloor" (Armed People Attack the Virgin Mary Church in al-Or), *MCN*, March 27, 2015, accessed March 30, 2015, http://www.mcndirect.com/showsubject_ar.aspx?id=60306#.V0a7E5ErLIU.

35. *Ibid.*

36. "Galsa Urfiya Taqdi Binaql Makan Kanisat al-Or min Makanaha" (A Reconciliation Session Judges to Move the al-Or Church from its Place), *MCN*, March 29, 2015, accessed March 30, 2015, http://www.mcndirect.com/showsubject_ar.aspx?id=60331#.V0a9OZErLIU.

37. Nader Shoukry, "Fi Qariat al-Galaa Bilminia..." (In the Village of al-Galaa in Minia...), *Watani*, March 1, 2015, accessed March 3, 2015, http://www.wataninet.com.

38. "Al-Motashadidoun Yafredoun Shorotahom Beadam Benaa Manara aw Agras" (The Fundamentalists Impose Their Conditions of No Steeple or Bells), *MCN*, April 9, 2015, accessed April 13, 2015, http://www.mcndirect.com/showsubject_ar.aspx?id=60505#.V0a_NZErLIV.

39. "Al-Anba Aghathon: Risala Shadidat Allahga..." (Bishop Aghathon: A Strong Message...) (youtube video, May 1, 2015), accessed May 30, 2015, https://www.youtube.com/watch?t=23&v=KiWUcYxrnm8.

40. Haitham al-Sheikh and Hazem al-Wakil, "al-Irhab Yastaqbil al-Sief Behegoum...," (Terrorism Receives Summer with an Attack...) *al-Watan*, July 21, 2015, accessed July 22, 2015, http://www.elwatannews.com/news/details/772936.

41. Hamza Hendawi, "Muslim mob attacks Christians, parade naked woman," *The Associated Press*, May26, 2016, accessed May 27, 2016, http://bigstory.ap.org/article/0df5295f1c6849db98eb1e7ffe7c0338/muslim-mob-attacks-christian-homes-egyptian-province.

42. Mohamed Abdellah and Ahmed Aboulenein, "Egypt Muslims attack Christian woman, houses after affair rumor," *Reuters*,

May 26, 2016, accessed May 27, 2016, http://www.reuters.com/article/us-egypt-violence-id USKCN0YH1UP.
43. Hendawi, "Muslim mob attacks Christians, parade naked woman."
44. "Labod min Ilgha' Qanon Izdera' al-Adian" (It is a Must to Cancel the Contempt of Religion Law), *MCN*, February 25, 2016, accessed February 27, 2016, http://www.mcndirect.com/showsubject_ar.aspx?id=66007#.V0bC75ErLIV.
45. "Al-Anba Aghathon: Risala Shadidat Al-lahga..."
46. "Ikhtitafa Tefl Qibti Benaga Hammadi Ala Aidy Molathameen" (The Disappearance of a Coptic Child in Nag Hammadi at the Hands of Masked Men), *MCN*, December 8, 2015, accessed December 12, 2015, http://www.mcndirect.com/showsubject_ar.aspx?id=65223#.V0bDrZErLIV.
47. Girgis Wahib, "Galsa Urfiya Taqdi Bitahgeer Walid wa Asheqa' al-Motaham..." (Reconciliation Session Judges Forced Migration for the Father and the Brothers of the Accused...), Copts United, May 27, 2015, accessed May 28, 2015, http://www.copts-united.com/Article.php?I=1982&A=205711.
48. Loa Ali, "Sheikh al-Azhar: Ma Yahdoth Bihaq al-Muslimeen..." (Sheikh al-Azhar: What Happens to the Muslims...), *al-Youm al-Sabia*, June 2, 2015, accessed June 4, 2015, http://www.youm7.com/2207681.
49. Fouad, "Al-Azhar refuses to consider the Islamic State an apostate."
50. Isra' Salaheddin, "Al-Awqaaf: Irtikab Daeish Ligara'im Deid al-Insaniyah la Yokaferaha" (The Religious Endowment: ISIS Committing Crimes Against Humanity Does not Make Them Apostates), *al-Wafd*, December 10, 2015, accessed December 12, 2015, http://alwafd.org/article/982154.
51. "Kalimat al-Raies Abdel Fattah el-Sisi khilal Ihtifal Wizarat al-Awqaf..." (The Speech of President Abdel Fattah el-Sisi During the Celebration of the Ministry of Endowment...) (youtube video, January 1, 2015), accessed January 2, 2015, https://www.youtube.com/watch?v=B_L9zuLdaWc.
52. Rober al-Faris, "Imara fi Magalat al-Azhar: al-Masihiya Deana Fashila" (Imara in *al-Azhar Magazine*: Christianity is a Failed Religion), *Al Bawaba*, June 6, 2015, accessed June 7, 2015, http://www.albawabhnews.com/1332427.
53. "Masr: Hokm Bisegn Islam Bihiri 5 sanawat...," (Egypt: Verdit of 5 Years in Prison for Islam al-Bihiri...) *BBC Arabic*, May 31, 2015, accessed June 1, 2015, http://www.bbc.com/arabic/middleeast/2015/05/150531_egypt_buheiri_sentence.
54. Bahi Hasan, "Islam Bihir Baad Habsu Aaman..." (Islam al-Bihiri After His Year Sentencing...), *al-Masry al-Youm*, December 29, 2015, accessed December 29, 2015, http://www.almasryalyoum.com/news/details/864557.
55. Lutfi Salman, "Jihadi: Aghlab al-Masrieen fi Soria min..." (Jihadi: Most Egyptians in Syria are from...), *al-Watan*, October 20, 2014, accessed October 21, 2014, http://www.elwatannews.com/news/details/579950.
56. Yaser Abel Aziz, "Aada' al-Hadara" (Enemy of Civilization), *al-Masry al-Youm*, August 3, 2014, accessed August 10, 2014, http://today.almasryalyoum.com/article2.aspx?ArticleID=433099.
57. "Habs 4 Dobat Shorta...," (4 Police Officers Imprisoned...) *Reuters*, December 4, 2015, accessed December 15, 2015, http://ara.reuters.com/article/topNews/idARAKBN0TN14P20151204.
58. "al-Amn al-Masry Yaqtahim Niqabat al-Sahafien ..." (Egyptian Security Storms the Journalist Syndicate...), *CNN Arabic*, May 2, 2016, accessed May 5, 2016, http://arabic.cnn.com/middleeast/2016/05/02/egypt-journalists-syndicate-interior-ministry.
59. Bahi Hasan, "Atibaa Mostashfa al-Mataryah Yaghliqoon al-Istiqbal..." (al-Mataryah Hospital's Doctors Close the Reception...), *al-Masry al-Youm*, January 28, 2016, accessed May 5, 2016, http://www.almasryalyoum.com/news/details/882606.
60. "Idraab Aam Lilmuhamin...," (General Strike for the Lawyers...) *Mohamah News*, June 3, 2015, accessed May 5, 2016, http://www.mohamahnews.com/?PUrl=News&ID=1556.
61. Ahmed Fouad, "Can Women, Copts make it to parliament without the quota?," *al-Monitor*, November 20, 2015, accessed November 21, 2015, http://www.al-monitor.com/pulse/originals/2015/11/egypt-parliament-elections-quota-women-copts.html.
62. Muhammad Shanh, "Min Muhammad Ali ela el-Sisi..." (From Muhammad Ali to el-Sisi...), *al-Watan*, February 11, 2015, accessed February 19, 2015, http://www.elwatannews.com/news/details/660792.
63. Hany Ramadan, "Maglis al-Shaab al-Masry 2012..." (The Egyptian People's Assembly 2012...), *BBC Arabic*, January 23, 2012, accessed March 30, 2012 http://www.bbc.com/arabic/middleeast/2012/01/120123_egypt_palt_hani.
64. Muhammad Shanah, "Hamlit Samir Ghattas..." (Samir Ghattas' Campaign...), *al-Watan*, November 24, 2015, accessed November 26, 2015, http://www.elwatannews.com/news/details/844362.
65. Shehata, "al-Aqbat fi Maglis al-Shaab."
66. Moustafa Abdel Tawab, Islam Said, Ramy Said and Ahmad Arafa "Bilarqaam...Kharitat

al-Ahzab Taht al-Qoba…," (By Number… the Map of the Parties Under the Dome of the Parliament…) *al-Youm al-Sabia,* December 3, 2015, accessed December 4, 2015,. http://www.youm7.com/2473711.

67. 14 Saida wa 3 Aqbat wa 9 min al-Shabab…," (14 Women, 3 Copts, 9 Young People …) *al-Youm al-Sabia,* December 31, 2015, accessed December 31, 2015, http://www.youm7.com/2517402.

68. "Kilmat al-Ra'is el-Sisi Liltahni'a fi Aid al-Milad…," (President el-Sisi's Speech of Greeting on Christmas…) (youtube video, January 6, 2016), accessed January 9, 2016, https://www.youtube.com/watch?v=r4EqWJBpyek.

Conslusion

1. "Mukhtar Noah Yohagim al-Azhar…," (Mukhtar Noah Criticizes al-Azhar…) (youtube video, December 17, 2015), accessed December 20, 2015, https://www.youtube.com/watch?v=kHpvr0Mpc60.

2. Iman al-Warraqi, "Manahig al-Azhar…," (al-Azhar Curriculum…) *al-Youm al-Sabia,* November 26, 2014, accessed November 29, 2014, http://www.youm7.com/1966773.

3. Fouad, "Al-Azhar refuses to consider the Islamic State an apostate."

4. Mahmoud Mourad and Yara Bayoumy, "Special Report—Egypt deploys scholars to teach moderate Islam, but scepticism abounds," *Reuters,* May 31, 2015, accessed June 15, 2015, http://af.reuters.com/article/worldNews/idAFKBN0OG07R20150531.

5. Mahmoud Abd al-Rady, "Bilvideo wasowar…Aeterafat al-Mutahamin Beghtial Hisham Barakat…" (In Video and Pictures… Confessions of the Suspects in the Assassination of Hisham Barakat…), *al-Youm al-Sabia,* March 6, 2016, accessed March 10, 2016, http://www.youm7.com/2616981.

6. "Taqnin Awdaa al-Wafidien Bi al-Azhar" (Regulating the Status of Incoming Student to al-Azhar), *al-Ahram,* October 18, 2015, accessed December 11, 2015, http://www.ahram.org.eg/NewsQ/444390.aspx.

7. Magnus Bredstrup, "Religious Censorship in the Azhar," Arab West Report, Paper 12, January 12, 2009, accessed December 11, 2015, 6, http://www.arabwestreport.info/sites/default/files/paper11.pdf.

8. "Mukhtar Noah Yohagim al-Azhar."

9. "The Global Competitiveness Report 2016–2017," World Economic Forum, accessed February 15, 2017, http://reports.weforum.org/global-competitiveness-index/competitiveness-rankings/#series=GCI.B.05.02.

10. Saleh, "Law, the Rule of Law, and Religious Minorities in Egypt."

11. Mansour, *Qadar al-Masihien al-Arab wa Khiarhom,* 150.

12. Atiya, *A History of Eastern Christianity,* 84.

13. Ye'or, *The Dhimmi: Jews and Christians Under Islam,* 154.

Bibliography

al-Antony, Antonious. *Wataniet Al-Kanisah Al-Qibtia Watarikhaha* (The Patriotism of the Coptic Church and Its History). Cairo: al-Tibaa al-Masryyah, 2004.
Atiya, Aziz S. *A History of Eastern Christianity.* London: Methuen, 1968.
_____. "The Copts and Christian Civilization." Copt-Net Repository. Accessed May 18, 2013. http://www.coptic.net/articles/CoptsAndChristendom.txt.
Butler, Alfred J. *The Arab Conquest of Egypt and the Last Thirty Years of the Roman Dominion.* Edited by P. M. Fraser. Oxford: Oxford University Press, 1978.
Carter, B. L. *The Copts in Egyptian Politics.* London: Croom Helm, 1986.
Chabry, Laurent, and Annie Chabry. *Siasa Wa Aqaliat Fi Al-Sharq Al-Adna: Al-Asbab Al-Mo'adia Lilinfigar* (Politics and Minorities in the Near East: The Reasons Leading to the Explosion). Translated by Dhoqan Qarqoot. Cairo: Madboli Press, 1991.
Chitham, E.J. *The Coptic Community in Egypt: Spatial and Social Change.* Durham: University of Durham, 1986.
Cragg, Kenneth. *The Arab Christian: A History in the Middle East.* Louisville: Westminster/John Knox Press, 1991.
The Disappearance, Forced Conversions, and Forced Marriages of Coptic Christian Women in Egypt. A Report commissioned by Christian Solidarity International, Westlake Village, California and Coptic Foundation for Human Rights, Zurich, Switzerland. November, 2009.
Gervers, Michael, and Ramzi Jibran Bikhazi, ed. *Conversion and Continuity: Indigenous Christian Communities in Islamic Lands Eighth to Eighteenth Centuries.* Toronto: Pontifical Institute of Medieval Studies, 1990.
Goddard, Hugh. *A History of Christian-Muslim Relations.* Chicago: New Amsterdam Books, 2002.
Hamilton, Alastair. *The Copts and the West 1439–1822: The European Discovery of the Egyptian Church.* Oxford: Oxford University Press, 2006.
Hikel, Muhammad Hassanien. *Kharif Al-Ghadab* (Autumn of Fury). Cairo: al-Ahram Center for Translation and Publication, 1988.
Hourani, A.H. *Minorities in the Middle East.* London: Oxford University Press, 1947.
Ibn al-Muqaffa, Sawirus (Bishop of al-Ashmunin). *History of the Patriarchs of the Egyptian Church, Known as the History of the Holy Church.* Vol. 2, part 2. Cairo, 1948.
Ibrahim, Saad Eddin. *Egypt, Islam and Democracy: Twelve Critical Essays.* Cairo: American University Press, 1996.
_____. "The Road of Thorns from Al-Khanka 1972 to Al-Kosheh 2000." Arab West Report. February 13, 2000. Accessed June 11, 2011. http://www.arabwestreport.info/en/year-2000/week-7/21-road-thorns-al-khanka-1972-al-kosheh-2000.
_____, et al. *The Copts of Egypt.* London: Minority Rights Group International, 1996.
al-Kashif, Saieda Ismail. *Masr Fi Fagr Al-Islam: Min Al-Fatih Al-Arabi Ela Qiyam Al-Dawla*

Al-Tolonia (Egypt in the Dawn of Islam: From the Arab Conquest to the Establishment of the Tulunid Dynasty). Cairo: Dar al-Fikr al-Arabi, 1947.

Leiser, Gary. "The Madrasas and the Islamization of the Middle East the Case of Egypt." *Journal of the American Research Center in Egypt* 22 (1985): 29–47.

Malaty, Fr. Tadros Y. *Introduction to the Coptic Orthodox Church.* Alexandria: St. George's Church, 1993.

Mansour, Albair. *Qadar Al-Masihien Al-Arab Wa Khiarhom* (The Fate of Arab Christians and Their Choices). Beirut: Dar al-Gadid, 1995.

Marshall, Paul. *Egypt's Endangered Christians.* A Report by the Center for Religious Freedom of Freedom House, 1999.

Marshall, Paul, and Nina Shea. *Silenced: How Apostasy and Blasphemy Codes Are Choking Freedom Worldwide.* Oxford: Oxford University Press, 2011.

el Masri, Iris Habib. *The Story of the Copts: The True Story of Christianity in Egypt.* 4th ed. book one. Johannesburg: Coptic Bishopric for African Affairs, 1987.

———. *Qisat Al-Kanisah Al-Qibtia: Wahia Tarikh Al-Kanisah Al-Orthozoksia Al-Masria Allati Assasha Mar Morcos Al-Bashir*, Book 4 (The Story of the Coptic Church: The History of the Egyptian Orthodox Church Established by St. Mark the Evangelist). Sporting, Alexandria: Maktabit Kanisat Mar Girgis, 1992.

Mayer, Ann Elizabeth. *Islam and Human Rights: Tradition and Politics.* Boulder, CO: Westview Press, 1999.

Parry, Ken, ed. *The Blackwell Companion to Eastern Christianity.* Malden, MA: Blackwell, 2007.

Patrick, Theodore Hall. *Traditional Egyptian Christianity: A History of the Coptic Orthodox Church.* Greensboro, NC: Fischer Park Press, 1996.

"Report by Dr. Jamal Al-'Utayfi on the Al-Khankah Sectarian Events." Arab West Report. April 1, 2009. Accessed June 11, 2011. http://www.arabwestreport.info/en/year-2009/week-13/2-report-dr-jamal-al-utayfi-al-khankah-sectarian-events.

Rofila, Yaqub Nakhla. *Tarikh Al-Umma Al-Qibtia*, 2nd ed. (The History of the Coptic Nation). Cairo: Metropol Press, 2000.

Saleh, Yustina. "Law, the Rule of Law, and Religious Minorities in Egypt." Rubin Center. December 7, 2004. Accessed May 2, 2014. http://www.rubincenter.org/2004/12/saleh-2004-12-07/.

Shenouda III, Pope. *Morcos Al-Rasool* (Mark the Disciple). Cairo: Anba Ruies, 1968.

———. *Qanoun Al-Iman* (The Creed). Cairo: Coptic Seminary, 1997.

———. *Tabiat Al-Maseeh*, 12th ed. (The Nature of Christ). Cairo: Coptic Seminary, 2007.

Tajir, Jack. *Aqbat Wa Moslimoon Mintho Al-Fatih Al-Arabi Ela Aam 1922.* (Copts and Muslims since the Arab Conquest until the Year 1922) Cairo: Karasat al-Tarikh al-Masry, 1951.

Tritton, A.S. *The Caliphs and Their Non-Muslim Subjects: A Critical Study of the Covenant of Umar.* London: Cass, 1930.

Watson, John H. *Among the Copts.* Brighton Portland: Sussex Academic Press, 2000.

Watterson, Barbara. *Coptic Egypt.* Edinburgh: Scottish Academic Press, 1988.

Ye'or, Bat. *The Decline of Eastern Christianity Under Islam: From Jihad to Dhimmitude, Seventh-Twentieth Century.* New Jersey: Associated University Press, 1996.

———. *The Dhimmi: Jews and Christians Under Islam.* London: Associated University Press, 1985.

Yohanna, Manassa. *Tarikh Al-Kanisah Al-Qibtia* (The History of the Coptic Church). Cairo: Maktabit al-Mahabba, 1924.

Zeidan, David. "The Copts—Equal, Protected or Persecuted? The Impact of Islamization on Muslim-Christian Relations in Modern Egypt." *Islam and Christian-Muslim Relations* 10, no. 1 (1999): 53–67.

Index

Abba Salama (Frumentius), Bishop 27
Abbas, Caliph 50
Abbasid 43, 50–56, 80
Abdel Rahman, Umar 39, 116
abduction/kidnapping 52, 67, 116, 127, 129, 131, 149, 159–160, 172, 177
Abraham, Patriarch 57–58
Abu Bakr, Caliph 47, 68
Abu Fana Monastery incident 131
Abu Nasr, Malik Mu'ayyad (Sultan) 67–68
Abu Zeid, Nasr Hamid 126, 185
Abyssinia 27, 61
activists 101, 135–136, 138–141, 143–145, 147–149, 152–153, 159–160, 162, 167, 172, 178–179
Age of Persecution 13
agrarian/agricultural/land reform 82, 84, 102–103, 105
Akef, Muhammad Mahdi 4 5, 167
al-Adid, Caliph 62–63
al-Azhar 2, 39–40, 43, 45, 56, 63, 76, 78–79, 84, 92, 95, 97, 102, 110, 113, 125–126, 132, 155, 161, 165, 170–171, 177–178, 185–186, 188
al-Aziz, Caliph 57–58
al-Boutrossyia Church bombing 182, 190
al-Emir, Caliph 61
al-Erian, Esam 117
Alexandria 8–9, 11–16, 18–19, 21–24, 27–31, 33–34, 54–55, 58, 64, 71, 82, 92, 108, 112, 114, 123–124, 130, 135–136, 139, 176, 178, 190–191
al-Ezabi, Pasha 85–86, 109, 114
al-Fa'iz, Caliph 62
al-Fikrya village shooting 124
al-Galaa incident 175–176
al-Gauhari, Girgis 77, 78, 82
al-Gauhari, Ibrahim 77
al-Hafiz, Caliph 61–62
al-Hakim, Caliph 8, 41, 58–62, 72, 145
al-Hidibi, 4, 167
Ali, Caliph 46–47
Ali, Muhammad 35, 77, 80–84, 87–88, 100–101, 107, 172

al-Ikhshidi, Muhammad 55
al-Jamali, Badr 61
al-Kamil, al–Malik 65
al-Khanka incident 108–111, 145
al-Khusus incident 156
al-Kosheh incidents 124–125, 135, 191
al-Marinab incident 146, 176
al-Mu'izz, Caliph 56–57, 59, 145
al-Muharraq Monastery shooting 124
al-Musta'in, Caliph 53
al-Mustansir, Caliph 61
al-Mutawakkil, Caliph 52–53
al-Omraniya incident 134–136
al-Or incident 175–176
al-Salih, al–Malik 69
al-Sayyid, Lutfi 91
al-Shahidain (Two Martyrs) Church incident in Sul 59, 144
al Shater, Khairat 117, 151, 167
al-Utayfi, Gamal (report) 108–111, 114–115
al-Wafd Party 91–95, 97–98, 104, 111–112, 122, 171, 181
al-Walakhshi, Ridwan b. 62, 64
al-Wardani 90
al-Warraq shooting 166
al-Zafir, Caliph 62
al-Zahir, Caliph 61
al-Zawiyah al–Hamra incident 118
Antioch 11, 19, 22, 51
Apollinaris 19
apostasy law 112–113, 115
Arab Socialist Union 104, 107
Arabic 2–3, 5, 11, 37, 41, 44, 48, 60, 71–73, 88, 103, 186–188
arabism/arab nationalism 2, 5, 100–101, 106, 173, 182
arabization 1, 35, 49, 70–72, 103
Arius, Arian(ism) 17–19, 21, 32
Armenian 11, 22, 61–62, 89
Article Two 112, 117–118, 126–127, 129–130, 133, 155, 171, 178, 188
Athanasius, Pope 17–20, 24–25, 27–29, 32, 108, 123, 157

217

Index

August 2013 mass church attack (Black Wednesday) 2, 7–8, 67
Awlad al-Assal 72
Aybak, Sultan 66
Ayyubid 63–65

Bahram 61–62
Barakat, Mu'allem 75
Barquq, Sultan 69
Barsoum al-Erian Monastery 60
ben Abd al-Aziz, Umar (Caliph) 43, 49
ben Abd al-Malik, Abd Allah (ruler) 48–49, 71
ben Abd al-Malik, Hisham (Caliph) 48, 70
ben Abd al-Malik, Yazid (Caliph) 49
Benjamin, Patriarch 23, 34, 119
ben Marwan, Abd al-Aziz (ruler) 47–48
Bishay, Sedhom 83
British 5–6, 28, 79–81, 83, 88–93, 98, 166
Brotherhoodization 156–157, 160–161, 168–169
Byzantine 22–23, 26, 29, 32–35, 55, 60

Catechetical School of Alexandria (School of Alexandria) 9, 14–16, 18, 24, 27–28, 31, 96–97, 108
Catholicism 11, 18, 22, 31–32, 75, 81–82
Church of Alexandria 16, 21
Clement 15–16, 29
collective punishment 144–145, 176, 179
conquest 1, 23, 32–36, 53, 77–79, 101, 143, 188
Constantinople 20–22, 28, 33, 72
constituent assembly 151, 153–155
constitution 5–6, 92, 95, 109, 112, 117, 129, 133, 139, 142, 151, 153–155, 157, 164, 170–172, 177–178, 180, 186, 188–189
constitutional amendments 95, 142
constitutional declaration 153–154
contempt of Islam 131, 158–159, 176–179, 186
Coptic architecture 28–31, 39, 54
Coptic art 29–30, 32, 101
Coptic Calendar (Calendar of Martyrs) 13–14, 182, 190
Coptic/Christian conference 90–91, 112–113
Coptic diaspora 113–114, 118–119, 132–133, 140, 149–150
Coptic exodus/immigration 60, 104–105, 150, 160
Coptic language 12, 15, 32, 49, 59–60, 70–73, 101, 189
Coptic legion 79
Coptic literature 26, 31–32
Coptic missions/missionaries 27–29
Coptic music 29–30, 101
Coptic press 89, 104
Coptic revolts 44, 51–52, 70
Coptic schools 87–88, 96, 103
Costantine, Wafaa 126, 129, 135
Council of Chalcedon 1, 19–23, 26–27, 31–32, 34
Council of Constantinople 19–20

Council of Ephesus 20
Council of Nicaea 17–18, 27
Covenant of Umar 44, 49, 66–67, 71, 190
Crommer, Lord 89
Crusades 4, 41, 59, 62–66, 84, 89, 166
Cyril, Pope 20, 26, 29, 32
Cyrus, Chalcedonian Patriarch-Prefect 32–34, 44, 119

Dair al-Quaseer Monastery 55
Daniel, Mina 148
Demetrius, Pope 19
Desaix, General 79
Descrioption de l'Egypte 80
dhimmi/dhimma 3–4, 35–39, 43–45, 52, 55–57, 61, 68, 74, 77–78, 82, 84–86, 91, 101, 103, 112, 117–118, 132, 150, 155, 166, 176, 188–191
Dier al-Sultan (Monastery of the Sultan) 65
Diocletian 13–14
Dionysius, Patriarch 19
Dioscorus, Pope 20–23
Docetism 17
dyophysite 21–22, 34

Easter 18–19, 34, 59, 115, 190
Ebeid, Makram 93, 98
ecumenical councils 16, 21, 24
Egyptian nationalism 6, 91, 170, 173–174
election 93, 104, 122, 135, 142, 148, 151–152, 162, 165–166, 173, 178, 180–181, 187
el-Saadawi, Nawal 125
el-Sisi, President 6, 58, 117, 164–169, 172–182, 185–186, 189, 191
emergency law 121, 136, 147–148
Eritrean 11, 22
Ethiopia 11, 22, 26–27, 96, 105
Eutyches/Eutychianism 20–22

Farouk, King 97, 100, 166
Fatimid 8, 41, 56, 62–63, 71–72, 80
forced conversion 49, 57, 60, 66, 69, 85, 127–131, 136, 149, 159, 172
forced migration 145, 159, 177, 179
foreign missions/missionaries 24, 31, 81–82, 87–89, 96
Fouad, King 97
Fouda, Farag 125, 161, 185
14th century mass church attack 7–8, 67
Free Officers 99–101, 106, 143, 166
Freedom and Justice Party (MB political party) 117, 142, 151, 166, 178–179
French 72, 74, 76–82, 88–89, 92, 103, 166
Friday of Anger 141, 148

Gabriel ibn Turaik, Patriarch 72
Ghali, Boutros 90
Gnosticism 12, 17
Greek 11–12, 14–17, 19, 22, 26, 30, 32, 34
Guirguis, Habib 96–97, 120

Index

Hamayoni Decree 85–86, 109
Hasan, Pasha 74
Helmy, Abbas 84
heresy/heretic 15–22, 35, 64, 75, 89
Hussein, Taha 3, 185

ibn al-As, Amr 33–34, 43–44, 46–47, 53, 60, 68, 71
Ibn al-Makin 72
ibn al-Muqaffa, Sawiris (Severus), Bishop 57, 72
ibn Qalawun, al-Nasser Muhammad (Sultan) 7, 67, 145
Ibn Tulun, Ahmad 53–55
Ikhshidid 55–56
the Ikhshidid, Cafour 55–56
Imbaba incident 145–146
interim government 166, 172
Islamic conference 91, 113
Islamic State in Iraq and Syria (ISIS) 14, 41, 49, 59, 68, 129, 150, 159, 174–175, 177–179, 185, 190–191
Islamism/Islamic nationalism 2, 5, 92, 97–98, 112, 140, 169–170
Islamization 1, 33, 35, 42, 44–45, 49, 63, 97, 100, 102, 106, 117–118, 121, 137, 151, 169
Ismail, Pasha 87–88, 149

January 25, 2011 Revolution 6, 59, 104, 136–138, 140, 143, 145, 147, 157–159, 162–163, 172, 178, 184, 188
Jerusalem 11, 15, 30, 58–59, 61, 62, 64–65, 75–76, 83, 106, 116
jizyah 3, 36–38, 40–44, 47–51, 53, 82, 85, 117, 132, 188
John, Patriarch 48
June 30, 2013 Revolution 6–7, 161–163, 165–166, 169, 180–181

Kamil, Mustafa 90, 97
Karm (village) 176
Khalil, al-Ashraf (Sultan) 67
Kha'il, Patriarch (under the Tulunid) 54–55
Kha'il, Patriarch (under the Umayyad/Abbasid) 50
kharaj 36, 44, 48, 50, 54, 188
Khumarawayh 55
Kleber, General 78–79
Kyrillos the 4th, Pope 86–88, 110
Kyrillos the 6th, Pope 105, 107, 110

Leo, Pope of Rome 21

Ma'mun, Caliph 51
Macarius II, Pope 62
Macedonius 19, 21
madrasa 63–64, 81, 84
Mahfouz, Naguib 94–95
Mamluk 7, 65–67, 69–70, 72–74, 77–81

Mansour, Adly (interim president) 164, 170, 172, 179
manuscript 12, 17, 27–28, 54
Mark, Pope 65
martyr(dom) 12–16, 23, 28, 30, 32, 41, 59, 83, 144, 170, 174, 182–183, 190
Marwan, Caliph 50, 71
Maspero killing 147–148
Maspero Youth Union 140, 144, 146, 154
the massacre of the citadel 81, 107, 119
Melkite 22–23, 34, 54–55
Menou, General 79
Michael, Patriarch 71
Mikhail, Emad 149
Mina, Patriarch 51
Moftah, Ragheb 29
monasticism 18, 24–28, 120
monophysite 21–22, 32, 34, 64
Moqattam incident 144
Moqattam Mountain 57, 61
Morsi, Mohamed (president) 6–7, 45, 67, 141, 151–170, 172–174, 176, 179–182, 184–186, 188
Moussa, Nabawiya 93
Mu'awiya, Caliph 46–47, 50, 71
Mu'tasim, Caliph 53
Mu'taz, Caliph 53
Mubarak, Hosni (president) 6, 75, 120–128, 130–137, 139–144, 147–149, 151, 153–154, 158, 161, 164–165, 168, 171–172, 179, 181–183, 188, 191
Mukhtar, Mahmoud 94
Muslim Brotherhood (MB) 4, 6–8, 40, 97–99, 101–102, 105–106, 110–111, 116–117, 119, 121–126, 135, 137, 139–145, 148, 151–175, 178–182, 184–186

Nabarawi, Ceza 93
Nag Hammadi shooting 134–135
Naguib, Muhammad (president) 100
Nahas, Pasha 98
Napoleon 72, 77–79
Nasif, Pasha 78
Nasser, Gamal Abdel (president) 5, 99–107, 110–111, 118, 121–122, 132–134, 136–137, 143, 150, 153, 164, 166, 169, 172–173, 178, 181–182, 185–186, 188
Nasserite 107, 110, 119, 173
nationalization 102–104
Nestorius, Nestorianism 20–21, 32
Nicene Creed 18–20
Nile 27, 49, 54–56, 61, 83, 86, 100
1919 Revolution 79, 88, 91–93, 95, 140, 173
Nubia 26–27, 61, 65

Obeidallah, Caliph 56
October War 111, 114, 119, 168, 188
Origen 15–16, 27
Othman, Caliph 46–47
Ottoman 5, 72–81, 85–86, 91, 97, 113, 183

Index

Pantaenus 15, 28
parliament 86–87, 93, 104, 108, 111, 113, 115, 122, 135, 139, 142, 151, 153, 164, 166, 170, 180–181
Peter, Patriarch (under Muhammad Ali) 83, 87
Peter, the 27th Coptic Pope 23
Pharaoh 2, 5, 12, 15, 29–32, 49, 94, 178, 188
Protestant(ism) 11, 22, 31–32, 81–82

Rabaa al-Adawia 7, 163, 166–167
reconciliation session 131–132, 136, 146, 149, 175, 177, 179, 188
Red Monastery 31
referendum 117–118, 142–143, 153–155, 171
Revolution of the Hungry 117
Rizq, Mu'allem 77
road map 164–165, 180
Rome 11, 18–19, 21–22, 25, 28, 93, 135
Russia 11, 83, 87

Sabillius 19
Sadat, Anwar (president) 106–123, 132–134, 136–137, 142, 145, 151, 158, 169, 172–174, 181–183, 188
Said, Pasha 84, 86–88, 110
St. Anthony 18, 24–26, 70
St. Anthony Monastery 70
St. Bishoy monastery incident 148
St. George Church bombing in Tanta 190
St. Macarius Monastery 65
St. Macarius the Great 26
St. Mark 12, 14, 23, 27, 29, 157
St. Mark's Coptic Cathedral bombing in Alexandria 190–191
St. Mark's Coptic Orthodox Cathedral 105, 118, 122, 127, 150, 165, 172–174, 182; incident in Cairo 45, 156–158, 163, 174
St. Maurice 28
St. Mena 30–31
St. Pachom 25–26
St. Paul 24
St. Paul Monastery 70, 148
St. Samuel 23
St. Shenoute of Atrip 26, 31
St. Simon Monastery 65
St. Verena 28
St. Victor 28
Saladin (Salah al-Din) 63–65
Salafi 49, 126–127, 129, 143, 149, 151, 155, 158–160, 165, 170–172, 178–179, 181, 185
Sawirus, Naguib 140, 181
sectarianism 34, 120, 122, 124, 131, 134, 140, 142, 147, 180
Selassie, Haile (emperor) 105
Selim I, Sultan 73, 75
Sergius, priest 92
Shafiq, Ahmad 152

Sha'rawi, Hoda 93
sharia 3–6, 35–37, 41, 46, 53, 83, 94–95, 97, 102, 106, 112–116, 125, 129, 131–132, 144, 149, 151, 155, 168, 171, 175, 178, 184–185, 188
Sharona murder 146–147
Shawar 62–64
Shehata, Camelia 126, 129, 135, 146
Shenouda, Pope 107–110, 113–116, 119–121, 127–130, 140, 150, 156, 158
Shiite 38, 47, 56, 63, 170, 187
Suez Canal 84, 87–88, 111, 188
Suez War 102, 106
Sunday School Movement 96, 120
Sunni 2, 38, 56, 63, 155, 187
Supreme Constitutional Court 153–155, 164
Supreme Council of Armed Forces (SCAF) 139, 141–145, 147–152, 169, 176, 178, 181
Syria 11, 14, 22, 26–28, 44, 55, 62, 89, 106, 168, 178, 182, 186

Tahrir Square 139–141, 151–152, 163
Tamarod Movement 162–163
Tantawi, Mohamed Hussein (field marshal) 152–153
Tawadros, Pope 14, 156–157, 163, 165, 173, 182, 190–191
Temple of Queen Hatshepsut massacre 124, 161
Theban Legion 28
theocracy 95, 97, 155, 172–173
Theodosius, Pope 23
Timothy, Pope 19–20
Timothy, the 26th Coptic Pope 23
transitional period 139, 148–153
Tulunid 53–54
Tumanbay, Sultan 73, 75
Two Saints Church bombing in Alexandria 135, 191

ulama 64, 78, 80–81, 85, 178, 185
Umar, Caliph 33, 44–47, 70
Umayyad 43, 46–47, 50–51, 53, 71, 183
Umm Kulthum (singer) 94

Wahba, Yousef 92
War of 1967 (*naksa*) 106, 110, 111
Wassef, Wissa 93
White Monastery 31

Ya'qub, Mu'allem 79–80
Yazid, Caliph 47
Yousab, Patriarch 51

Zacharias, Patriarch 58
Zaghlul, Saad 91–94
Zaghlul, Safia 94
Zawahiri, Ayman 117, 143, 149